DIMENSIONS

OF THE SIGN IN ART

Vincent van Gogh, *The Night Café*. Courtesy of the Yale University Art Gallery. Bequest of Stephen Carleton Clark, B.A. 1903.

DIMENSIONS
OF THE SIGN IN ART

Albert Cook

 PUBLISHED FOR BROWN UNIVERSITY PRESS BY
UNIVERSITY PRESS OF NEW ENGLAND
HANOVER AND LONDON

UNIVERSITY PRESS OF NEW ENGLAND

BRANDEIS UNIVERSITY

BROWN UNIVERSITY

CLARK UNIVERSITY

UNIVERSITY OF CONNECTICUT

DARTMOUTH COLLEGE

UNIVERSITY OF NEW HAMPSHIRE

UNIVERSITY OF RHODE ISLAND

TUFTS UNIVERSITY

UNIVERSITY OF VERMONT

Printed in the United States of America

LIBRARY OF CONGRESS CATALOGING-IN-PUBLICATION DATA

Cook, Albert Spaulding.
　Dimensions of the sign in art.
　Bibliography: p.
　Includes index.
　1. Signs and symbols in art.　I. Title.
N7565.C64　1989　　701　　88–5564
ISBN 0–87451–448–7

5　4　3　2　1

To Rene and Ted Silverman
fellow art lovers

CONTENTS

Part Two. MODERN INSTANCES

FIGURES

PREFACE

This book is the third in a series about the use of images for signification. It extends more generally my book on the iconology of fifteenth-century painting, *Changing the Signs: The Fifteenth-Century Breakthrough*. And in its second part it looks more intensively, and exclusively at the visual arts, in the modern work that is the prevailing concern of *Figural Choice in Poetry and Art*.

It has been my intention to address theoretical questions in such a way that their application to individual works is facilitated; and, conversely, to address individual works in ways that extend and enrich theoretical questions. In that sense my first part title, "Extensions of Visual Realization," could apply to the whole book. The artists discussed in the second part, "Modern Instances," are adduced both for that purpose and for an examination of the signification that resides in their particular works. As always in such an enterprise, one risks a certain disproportion in trying to carry out these two tasks concurrently. But one also separates them at one's peril.

Indeed, this very general subject, signification, stands variously at the center of all my critical-theoretical writing. These books dealing with utterances that are not mainly verbal can be seen as complementary to the superficially very different book I have just completed, *History/Writ-*

ing (Cambridge, 1988), in which the utterance shapes itself on a complex referent that is posited as emphatically there. One could construct various theoretical bridges connecting these enterprises, but my plans are to go on, instead, with extending questions about signification in other kinds of utterances, poetry and classical philosophy among them. I do so in the conviction, assumed but not unexamined, that the connections among the domains of inquiries emerge in the inquiries themselves.

ACKNOWLEDGMENTS

My debts over time have been to the many astute and well-disposed readers who have helped me with parts of this manuscript: Edward Snow, Aaron Rosen, Irving Massey, Marshall Brown, John Dixon Hunt, Claudette Columbus, Alan Trueblood, James Bunn, Thomas MacCary, and an anonymous reader for the University Press of New England, whose perceptive structural suggestions have helped me to improve the overall manuscript.

My research assistant, Dr. Blossom S. Kirschenbaum, has once again proved her cheerful resourcefulness and discrimination by helping with every aspect of the manuscript from stylistic suggestions and negotiation for actual and potential plates to preparation of the index.

I am grateful to the journals, and their editorial staffs, where parts of this book have appeared in somewhat earlier versions: *Word and Image, The Kenyon Review, The Stanford Literary Review, The Journal of Aesthetics and Art Criticism,* and *Hebrew University Studies in Art and Literature.*

A number of institutions have been of great help to me: Brown University (which gave a subvention to help defray the cost of plates) and its Department of Comparative Literature; the Rockefeller Library at Brown; the librarians at the Philadelphia Museum of Art, who gen-

erously assembled all their bibliographical materials on Marcel Duchamp for my use on one of my visits there, very considerably
facilitating that part of my work; the libraries of the Fondazione Giorgio Cini and I Tatti; and Clare Hall, Cambridge, where as a fellow in
the winter and spring of 1982 I first undertook to put together some
notes that were the beginnings of this book.

Most of all I am indebted to my wife, Carol, faithful and resonant
companion in everything, including the joys of lingering together for
decades in the museums of the world.

EXTENSIONS OF
VISUAL REALIZATION

Part One

RHETORIC AND RAPTURE

The Interdependence of Signification

and Depth-Communication in the Arts

Chapter 1

I

The world is full of signs, some of them structured into languages, of which perhaps the most structured are the languages we speak and write. Yet one cannot live without turning even the barest recurrences in nature into signs: the drop of a cliff indicates the necessity of walking carefully; the green of a leaf shows that the weather, in conjunction with other signs, may be warm enough so we can walk in light garments, and the green leaf also shows that people who have come, after millennia of interpreting such signs, to tending the crops, are closer to harvest time than they are when the branches are bare. But the recurrences in visible nature (there are of course signs attached to other senses) are less structured as signs than are the sentences of a language.[1]

The necessarily culture-bound signs built into works of visual art share some of the direct and arguably univocal indications of signs in visible nature, which they may appropriate. Green leaves and bare branches, and also cliffs, are to be found in paintings. And the signs in paintings also share some of the structural properties of language. This intermediate status for art, between natural signs for the eye and conventionally structured linguistic signs, produces complexities and richnesses of possibility for the visual artist, and recent philosophical discussion has addressed the preconditions of such possibilities from various angles. The mechanics of signification, as it rests upon the interchange of natural and artificial signs and also on the distinctions and expansibilities of signifier, signified, and referent, has engaged the attention of many theoreticians from Chrysippus through Charles Sanders Peirce. It has been taken up by many recent writers on art, for the mechanics of communicative significations offers a completely absorbing repertoire of questions and problems.[2]

While there is much peripheral yield from asking how convention radically conditions the production of art, the description of conventions remains preliminary to how the signs actually work: one can no more approach a painting adequately just by discussing puzzles about mimesis than one can adequately discuss large segments of discourse like plays or novels, or even speech acts, by establishing what has by now become a truism, their dependence on convention. Nor can one reach an adequate approach to paintings by clarifying their referential presuppositions. Correspondingly, the philosophical puzzles about resemblance, representation (or Nelson Goodman's "representation as"), copy, depiction, description, denotation, and the like have been felt since Plato to be connected to the preconditions of art. But solving the epistemological puzzles involved in these terms, while an acutely engaging philosophical occupation, is neither a necessary nor a sufficient condition for discussing art.[3] It is not necessary, because a great deal can be said validly about even representation, as Leonardo and Piero, or Ruskin and Adrian Stokes, have done, without much engaging these questions. Nor would a satisfactory account of mimesis be sufficient; once such discriminations have been made, they no more constitute "the languages of art" than phonetics, morphemics, and semantics, or the physiology of hearing, or the conventions surrounding the transmission of language are sufficient for discussing poems, though poems obviously incorporate all these.

The situation is made more difficult because the perceptual conditions and attributes of visual coding are indeed intricated into paintings. By contrast, for the figures of geometry, from the time of Pythagoras, or at least from the time of Plato, there has been a clear distinction between a square drawn on a tablet and the theoretical square of the mathematician, what Plato calls "the square itself."[4] We can deal with the drawn square and the conceptual square separately, even if the relation between the two does lead to the perceptual puzzles that Plato and Aristotle, among many others, have addressed. In a painting, however, what is painted on the canvas is inseparable from "the painting itself" conceived by the artist and perceived by the viewer. One cannot, as the mathematician does, hold off one as a mere reminder while discussing the other. For that reason the logical approach to the perceptual conditions and cultural constraints on the painting, while intimately indissociable from it, does not bring one up to an adequate discussion of "the painting itself." And indeed, by analogy with the square, it is all the more difficult to discuss the painting itself since what immediately presents itself to the viewer of the painting seems to be what is physically present, like the square drawn on a tablet.

Painters write about perspective, from Piero to Klee, just as modern theoreticians do. Klee's puzzles, however, are aimed not just at distinctions, Plato's "method of division," as is the discussion of one puzzle from Klee by Nelson Goodman.[5] Klee's own writings show them to be aimed, rather, at Plato's "method of construction."[6] Since the visible painting and its signification are indissociable, the ascertainment of the conditions under which various matching operations take place provides nothing equivalent to a syntax for painting. Rather, it establishes some of the constraints under which (to continue the linguistic analogy) the diction of the painting may operate. But one may bracket these discussions (since they are not necessary, however engaging they may be). And, having done so, one may proceed directly to the discussion of how the signification comes about in a painting.

Even constructive discussions, like those of Kant and Charles Sanders Peirce, tend to be merely preliminary: they help to account for a syntax. Peirce in particular offers not just categories and distinctions but principles that allow for the combinatory interaction of the categories and distinctions, even though his own brief combinatory indications—given under such forbidding rubrics as "rhematic indexical sinsign" and the like—have been followed less often than have some of his simple categories.

The question of mimesis, as Goodman has elaborately discussed it, involves careful attention to puzzles about the differences between resemblance and representation. And, as Gombrich complexly reminds us, we are caught in sets of conventional cues if we are viewers, of conventional techniques if we are painters, in handling the color green and certain strokes of the brush, or black ink and certain lines of the engraver's tools, so as somewhat arbitrarily to "represent" grass in ways that may or may not make the artifact convincingly or plausibly resemble blades growing in the field. Further, to represent grass at all in an art work is a fairly advanced choice, and one not made in most early societies. That choice carries with it sets of mental constructs, what Peirce would call symbols or ideas. Still, these are wordless, and they involve at least some convergence between the "sense" of the visible artifact and its "reference," in Lyotard's view.[7] As for words, in single lexical items, there is a distinction to be made, as Frege has shown, between the "sense" of the individual terms "evening star," "morning star," and "Venus" and their common "reference" to a distant body twinkling in the sky (to which we give the same name of reference, "Venus"). In an imaginable painting of a dim sky with that star distinctly discernible in it, we could not choose among these lexical terms to indicate that body; and so, for the items of the painting, the sense and the reference would be in partial convergence—except that the painting would have to include more than the single lexical item for us, in the absence of a verbal label, to distinguish it as that particular star. Consequently, within the painting the star would be included in a larger statement, which in turn would have a sense, as opposed to the reference of its particular items. These global references would themselves converge in the single painting to produce a work that would bear certain resemblances to a work of literature in its "phonemic, morphemic, syntactic, semantic, and pragmatic relations."[8]

Moreover, as Gombrich reminds us in a somewhat different though related connection, giving a rich profusion of historical examples, "We cannot tackle this kind of question at all unless we are ready to abandon the assumptions about the function of the image we usually take for granted. We are used to making a clear distinction between two of these functions—that of representation and that of 'symbolization.'"[9]

Even something so simple as grass is natural before it is a sign; it grows before any sign-making creatures arrive to see it. And it is seen before it is included in periodicities to become a natural sign of the time for growing; it arguably requires the neolithic revolution for the periodicities to be perceived and connected with grass. Much, then, goes into a natural sign even before it is included in the conventions inseparable from naming. (It is possible to conceive of recognizing the periodicities of nature without having a language to name or discuss them.)

When we go to even something so simple as grass in a painting, the discussions of iconologists have produced a number of interlocking categories and sets of categories to account for how the significations, both natural and artificial, might work, after the initial step has been taken for the viewer to know that he is looking at a painting and to recognize that such-and-such strokes or marks represent the green growths underfoot.

Representation in painting, so to speak, for all its problems of definition and constructive skills requisite for its felicitous transposition, is logically prior to signification—though inseparable from it. Closeness of representation entails signification. Turner, Ruskin is at pains to point out, gets a lot of (the actual effect of) light into his paintings, and this means something. A constructive "mimesis" may generate delight that the (conventional) resemblance has been carried off so well; that Philip IV or Góngora seems alive on the canvas of Velázquez. But if it gets too close, Naomi Schor skillfully reminds us, as in the sculpture of Duane Hanson or other photorealists (who in fact are actually more "constructive" than a photograph would be in some respects), the representation produces a sense of uncanniness, which in turn calls for the analysis of how uncanniness can lead to aesthetic satisfaction.[10]

The pair *representation* and *object* are inescapably before us, though in the case of grass, it would be hard for the uncanny to be present in itself, unless juxtaposed against other objects, as in the *Étant donnés* of Marcel Duchamp. All the questions to be raised about *mimesis* bear on such a pairing of representation and object, as do those around the *signifier* and the (in this case wordless) *signified*. "Primary" signification in Erwin Panofsky's terms cannot be divorced from "secondary," even with something so simple as grass. And when it appears in a painting, it would be inescapably caught in a wordless *discourse* and so involve a *figure*.[11] Thereby it would draw on conventions that would intricate it variously to such *motifs* of luxuriant nature, tying in with (and supporting) the *theme* of the beautiful landscape. Further terms like *emblem* and *expression*, or even *meaning* and *being*, may be brought to bear. Even grass can serve as an emblem, aid expression, encapsulate meaning, and stand for sheer being.

The luxuriant grasses in the paintings of Renoir enlist all these methods of signification, and the grasses of Cézanne enlist them in still further ways. The schematic grass in certain of Klee's paintings would constitute a metacommentary on them all, and on these impressionist and post-impressionist uses. Klee's paintings in turn enlist conventional uses, or absorb them and comment on them by giving grass a color not seen in nature, as Matisse and others do. Van Gogh's predilection for yellows, which I shall discuss below, predisposes him often to ground cover other than grasses, to wheat fields, and to country scenes where roads are dominant. It can be said, in this light, that the assertions-in-nature that Turner mounts are involved in a sort of transcendent anti-grass; grass is present by its very absence as a convention not often adopted, a convention linked to "the picturesque" and also to "the beautiful," where Turner aimed for "the sublime." His choice of Alpine subjects heavily disposed him to the rocks and roughnesses associated with the sublime; mountain scenes in snow, or of locations with steep ravines and gorges, make the absence of grass all but inevitable. Even such exceptions as his *Mortlake Terrace* modify the grass. In that work the foliage on the trees is not strikingly luxuriant, the grasses on the foreground lawn are sunlit, and water and sky are still predominant. In Turner's repertoire of model landscapes for students, the *Liber Studiorum,* the "sublime" subjects preponderate somewhat over those where grass and foliage are appropriate. Here Turner's practice differs deeply, in this as in other ways, from that of landscapists contemporary with him such as Constable and Corot, those notable depicters of grassy extents, as well as from the impressionists with whom he is often compared. Venice, Turner's suasive icon, is notable for being a city where virtually no blade of grass appears. Water does duty for it. And in a painting like *Rain, Steam and Speed,* Turner has contrived to show his onrushing train as it is crossing a trestle over water, in one of the rare moments when there would not be grasses beyond the railroad bed.

There is a gain in approach to a constructive use of these preliminaries, without any effective loss of philosophical adequacy, in Rudolf Arnheim's organization of these questions under the categories of balance, shape, form, growth, space, light, color, movement, dynamics, and expression.[12]

In a different constructive focus, one "trichotomy" in Peirce's elaborate semiology has proved especially fertile in the semiotic discussions of our time, his categories of "icon," "index," and "symbol."[13] For Peirce a sign is "iconic" in a number of instances, which would include photographs, diagrams, and—through an argument not needing reproduction here—even algebraic formulas. Diagrams are "dyadic" and involve relations; but this makes them, taken by themselves, defective for not being "triadic," as any full Peircean set must be. It is germane to our discussion that maps are occasionally classed as art works in our time, though not conceived as such by their producers, who were unaware of the implicit postulates of space built into them.[14] The kind of icon most attended to by modern semioticians, however, is that which in some way resembles the object, as a painting of cliff or grass or star in some way resembles cliff or grass or star. With some qualifications (under the term "hypoicon"), Peirce asserts that "any material image, as a painting, is largely conventional in its mode of representation . . . [and so] may represent its object mainly by its similarity . . . [and with other qualifications] every picture is essentially a representation of that kind"—by which Peirce means not only that it resembles its object (without undertaking to discuss the puzzles about representation) but that it constitutes "an assertion."

Peirce's second class, "the index," "refers to its object not so much because of any similarity or analogy with it, nor because it is associated with general characters which that object happens to possess, as because it is in dynamical (including spatial) connection both with the individual object, on the one hand, and with the senses or memory of the person for whom it serves as a sign on the other hand." Thus an arrow pointing to an open door or a street sign or a barometer reading or a lightning flash is an index, but only to those whose conventions include arrows and houses and a written language and weather instruments, or at least the rudimentary social experience of a possible storm.

A "symbol" in Peirce's minimal but useful sense is "a Representamen whose Representative character consists precisely in its being a rule that will determine the interpretant." The symbol is, in another character-ization, an idea. All paintings are symbols in this minimal sense; with-out some sort of idea they could not exist as paintings, even if the idea were arguably no more than the conviction that "exact" representation of a landscape is pleasing to a viewer as distinct from the pleasure of looking at the landscape itself. And if all paintings are also icons, they carry through the characteristic Peircean act of combining his catego-ries. Few paintings are indicial as a whole; if they were, they would be indicating ideas, and that would also assimilate them to the Peircean symbolic. But paintings do contain indices, both natural and artificial signs for and/or of something. Grass and cliffs and stars, and even barometers, may be found in a painting, to say nothing of lightning flashes; it is a tiny, unobtrusive representation of a lightning flash that gives its name to Giorgione's *La Tempesta*—a name given not by Gior-gione but by an early commentator who connected it to whatever the painting may signify.[15] And within even so conventional a system as Russian icon painting, signs may refer to other signs in a given work, as Boris Uspensky has shown, in "a supplementary re-coding of mean-ings on a higher level, which is analogous to the re-coding that takes place in natural languages in the formation of phraseological units. Precisely this complication of the connection between signifier and sig-nified, which increases the distance between them, may be considered characteristic of symbolic representation . . . where the degree of con-ventionality is determined according to the number of connecting links between signifier and signified, i.e. according to the number of com-ponents in the sequence: 'the sign of a sign of a sign . . .' etc."[16] As though to enrich and complicate these categories, Klee adds mysterious arrows, often pointing nowhere, to his paintings. They adduce, and at the same time deflect, the indicial, and thereby they "bracket" the iconic in Peirce's sense,[17] all in favor of the "symbolic," and thereby in favor of a sort of implied querying of the symbolic. This would be the case for Peirce's minimal, constructive sense of the word "symbolic," and also of the poweful set of rich senses that the word has accrued in its heavy honorific use from romantic times to now.

The image, taken by itself, poses many questions. And it is never taken by itself; it exists in an inescapably pragmatic context—one form of which may be the "isolation" from context that itself constitutes a metacontext. I am, again, not mainly discussing abstract painting in this book, but it may be said that all abstract painting undertakes an isolation of the image in such a way as to provide a metacontext, all the more when even such schemas as Miró's diagram stars or Klee's diagram squares are left behind for various pure combinations of color, as happens in the works of Rothko or Kandinsky or Pollock or Morris Louis or Frank Stella, with sets of metacontexts that can themselves be distinguished from one another, beginning with (but not confined just to) significative properties of color that I broach in my chapter on color.

In verbal contexts the image cannot really be adequately discussed separately from the whole verbal construction, poem or philosophical discourse, of which it is a part.[18] In painting and in other nonverbal contexts, the image, as I have been saying, involves complex relations among not only signifier, signified, and referent, but also *being* and *seeming, emblem* and *expression, theme* and *motif* and their combinations into *discourse* and *figure,* especially as, in some kinds of paintings (but not the kind I will largely be discussing here), a story formulated in a book or carried by tradition is "represented" in the painting.[19] In Umberto Eco's analysis the very openness of metaphor, visual or other, prohibits our providing an algorithm for it (as many analysts have effectually tried to do). That openness provides the possibility, however, for extending associations, and also in painting, an "unlimited semiosis," in which a metaphoric connection can be reinvented, as (the example is Eco's) Modigliani reinvents the visual metaphor that compares the neck of a woman to the neck of a swan.[20] Questions of resemblance and representation, complex iconographic connections and substitutions, and the artist's metacommentary upon them, are all included, for example, in Klee's *Irma Rossa the Animal Tamer* (*Irma Rossa die Bändigerin,* 1918). The work shows a number of people and upside-down birds, but oddly no animals, while the animal tamer herself has an upside-down heart colored red on her *right* side. Among the social conventions referred to and skewed here are all those surrounding the circus and its people, and their framing in literature and art by Huysmans, Andreyev, Seurat, and Picasso, among others. The conventions within art itself are here reaching out to embrace the creativity inherent in children's drawing, which the sophisticated Klee imitates, making the "mistake" of allowing the heart to be transparent and also to be placed, as a child might do it, on the wrong side of the body. The inversions criticize the perspective to which at the same time the sophistication of the deliberate errors does homage. Any interpretation of such a work would have to account for the tonal archness inherent in such procedures, and for the connections as well as the presence of so much signification.

2

Without more exhaustively examining the theory of signs, one can move on not just to the range of combinatory possibilities bound into the complex communications made by paintings—the area in which most of my discourse will be centered here—but also to questions about the result or effect of such communications. Indeed, one has finally to do so, if one is to broach what is ultimately signified in a painting or paintings with any approach to adequate fullness. Though results or effects depend on the mechanics of communication—and may themselves be referred to one or another psychoanalytic or philosophical account of "emotion"—it is possible, once again, to address the question of effect also without fully accounting for it. And indeed, it is necessary to forego a full account in this domain as in others, since such preliminary questions demand full attention in themselves if they are to be addressed. One can boldly but not too precariously bypass puzzles about these "emotional" effects of painting too, as well as about perceptual and logical preconditions. Occupying still another "more advanced" angle, one can address, however tentatively and partially, final questions about the depth-communications that are carried through by works of visual art.

Communicative strategies, insofar as they structure signification, belong to rhetoric, the theory of persuasion. Much of this book addresses the significative constituents in art works. I occupy a middle ground between preliminary justifications and final meanings. In other words, I discuss rhetorical combinations, but with as much of a view as I can manage to what lies beyond rhetoric. At another time, when schools of rhetoric dominated the Western world, one rhetorician set himself to expound the ways in which the central feature of the verbal arts was their mastery at getting beyond the persuasion of rhetoric. Persuasion is the goal of rhetoric, however complexly the message may be of which the auditor (or by extension, the viewer) is to be persuaded. But rapture is another goal. In that light the auditor is not (just) to be won over by a set of communicated ideas but rather to be put in an altered state. The existence of this altered state, not its definition, is indicated by terms like "ineffable" and "sublime." "Not to persuasion but to rapture [ecstasy] does the sublime lead its hearers," says Longinus, and his title term, "the sublime," has been variously taken as an ideal for verbal art, getting its rise in the seventeenth century from Boileau and carrying through Pope and the later eighteenth century.[21] The sublime, thereupon, was applied to visual art, and to visual experience, by Edmund Burke, and then protractedly by Kant, as a profound center for what happens in the creation or apprehension of an art work, verbal or visual. Without at first unreservedly adopting the term, we may look at it as a reminder that there is something in the experience of art more unitary, more "uplifting" in Longinus's metaphor, than just Kant's rhythmic apprehension of experience or even that with which Kant begins and ends, the pleasurable apprehension of a formally purpose-free teleology. And one can take this sublimity as (the name for) a fact in our experience of paintings, a fact that can therefore be approached and discussed in the way that we discuss other facts. We can approach sublimity hermeneutically, in the confidence of its centrality to the experience of art, as well as of its existence, the existence of something that it named and names.

Longinus changes the term in the quotation given, from the "sublime" ("*hypsos,*" "lofty") of his title to the "super-natural" ("*ta hyper-phua*"). Indeed, "the super-real" would not mistranslate it. The super-"ordinary" and super-"given" and super-"existent" are all justifiable renderings of "*ta hyper-phua,*" which could serve as a root rendering of "surrealism," and so could be brought to bear on most of the modern artists I discuss here, as well as on those from a time when the term itself was more current. Surrealism, that large umbrella term, almost always entails both a technical reshuffling of significative properties in the work, visual or verbal, and a rapturous, a dreamlike reaction in the viewer.[22]

The intense discussion of verbal and visual art in modern times, and particularly in this century, has tended, in ways this book presses, to modify Longinus's distinction between "persuasion" and "ecstasy" ("*ek-stasin*"), since it has become increasingly clear that the two are intimately intertwined. Persuasion and ecstasy are so intertwined that there is a party willing to surrender the artistic effect, however intricately, just to persuasion—to rhetoric in literature and to iconography or to elementary visual mechanisms in art. Another party impatiently insists just on ecstasy. I want with some deliberation to locate a discussion of ways in which "persuasion" and "ecstasy," or "rhetoric" and "rapture," are best understood in interrelation.

Longinus's "ec-stasy" is ambiguous. Etymologically it refers to a state that takes one outside oneself. One "stands apart." Yet in some of its implication, as well as in its developed use, it suggests access to a rapture that accords with a higher union and integration of the self, just as the art work is at once apart from "things as they are" ("*phu*") and their highest expression. "*Ta hyperphua*" is ideal reality, along the semi-Platonic lines of Longinus's treatise, and it is also something above reality.

The plural, "*hyperphua*"—"super-natural things"—which is, however, a common grammatical form for abstractions in Greek—helps to enforce this expansion of its implication.

Because aesthetic experiences and creations cannot be detached from our perceptions, our desires, and their relation to the total economy of all our extra-aesthetic activities, discussion about art must necessarily, and at once, lead to such more general questions. Those questions cannot be bracketed, but neither can they be addressed satisfactorily, unless they are allowed to take over the discussion. Even Kant is forced by the logic of his demand for adequacy to expand "judgment" somewhat beyond the aesthetic. And even he is found to slight both art objects and the principles of creating them in favor of questions about perception.

It is impossible to address such questions of adequate philosophical definition proportionally. It is also impossible to ignore them. Hence a tactic of keeping them in view without surrendering to them must govern any viable discussion about first principles in art. Such discussion must content itself with remaining less than rigorous as a protection against involving itself in other issues that cannot be solved, or perhaps even advanced, on the ground of aesthetics.

3

From a constructive point of view, there are several levels of correspondence between the coordinated signs in a work of art, taken as coherent networks of signifiers, and their coded references to the "signifieds" that are themselves coherent networks at different levels of generality. Even for the wordless and at first seemingly cueless structures of music, a range of correspondences to coding can be enlisted by the composer for a range of expressive congruences. As Lyotard can discuss the "metaphoric" properties of painting by classifying them through the four mechanisms of Freud's dream theory—in effect relating rapture to the unconscious—so Claude Lévi-Strauss can classify music according to the constituents of code, message, and (surprisingly) myth, assigning predominances of each to classical, to modernist, and to later composers.[23] So, in his hearing, Bach, Stravinsky, and Webern emphasize the *code*; Beethoven, Ravel, and Schoenberg have a narrative component that emphasizes the *message*; while Wagner, Debussy, and Berg incorporate a prior legendary narrative and may be said to emphasize the *myth*.

This set, indeed, can be seen to obtain at only one level of the correspondence between a musical work and the signification that the auditor is enraptured to be entering. At a simpler and lower level, to begin with, there can be a discernible correspondence between musical sound and the real sound prior to it, as when in certain Renaissance music the screeching of cats or the singing of birds is mimicked. Such *mimicry* itself poses questions about the overall, and the final, musical effect to be gained by such excerpting—questions raised when actual tapes of whales sounding in the deep are scored together with other musical passages in Alan Hovhanness's *Song of the Humpbacked Whale,* or indeed when random street noises, voices, and even the sounds of musical instruments are scored together by such post-atonalist composers as Karlheinz Stockhausen and George Crumb. Such mimicry, however scored, can be distinguished from general "program music" (a second level) in which, as in Beethoven's Sixth Symphony, a coming storm is not reproduced but somewhat more abstractly indicated. Still more in Debussy's *La Mer* is the impression of the sea abstracted, though with a correspondence that would retain it roughly on this level of mimicry. At another level up (and not to be separated off as "myth" from "code" and "message") is a third kind of correspondence, the patterned evocation with Wagner's *leitmotifs* of a particular point in narrative or a particular character. "Siegfried," "Wotan," "Forest Noises," "Rainbow," "Rheingold," and the like permute, but these motifs are always discretely indicated. Wagner's recourse to chromatics itself may be heard as an effort to modify these demarcations by permitting unusual fusions in the key signatures. The particular emotional associations of individual *key signatures* themselves constitute still another level, a fourth one, of patterning for music.

A fifth level, distinct from all four of these, is the assignment of emotional or intellectual sequences to such simple movements as rising and falling on the scale. This "abstractive correlative"—for example, where rising notes signified hope, falling notes, despair—was a predominant practice and also a dominant theory in the sixteenth and seventeenth centuries.[24]

If music be taken, with romantics like Beethoven and Mendelssohn, as the tonal sequencing of precise emotional perceptions for which there is no other language, such integral correspondences would transcend the point-for-point matching of an "abstractive correlative." They would constitute still another level, a sixth one, more abstract from one point of view, though really uncharacterizable as to degree of abstraction.

Lévi-Strauss's musical *myth, code,* and *message* would be a seventh level, comprising all the levels to this point.

Distinct from all of these—abstract but not "more" or "less" abstract than such emotional geometries—would be, at an eighth level, the sort of Hegelian or Foucauvian congruence that Jacques Attali finds between the music of an era and its economic and social organization as these correspond to the predominance of main structural emphases for the music.[25] In Attali's analysis the earliest music, accompanying "sacrifice," is produced to "make one forget." The "representations" in a succeeding music are set to "make one believe." Then come the "repetitions" of Renaissance counterpoint, designed to "make one be silent." And finally the "compositions" of the modern era in the last two centuries amount to what he calls a "self-communication." Without criticizing Attali's divisions and correlations, we can see that they constitute still another level of signification for music.

4

All these levels could be paralleled and used as organizing principles for painting, and also for literature, or for that matter for an architecture which since Kant, Hegel, and Ruskin has been interpreted as encoding the expressive voice of a culture. Music and literature, in a characterization common since Lessing, are temporal arts. We apprehend them for the most part in time. The visual arts are apprehended for the most part in space, and their wordlessness at first sight seems to distinguish them from literature, though the heavy coding of the signs they enlist brings them into further rapprochement, "word and image" in a variety of conjunctions. Music is more resistant than literature or painting to local coding within a work, if not to the overall codings discussed above. Literature has, in Roman Jakobson's terms, a "poetic" emphasis on the message. But music, since it cannot have separate lexical entries, has to be totally identified with whatever its message might be. It either emphasizes the message totally (at one vantage) or is totally constrained from doing so (at another).

The same is true of the *code* and even of the *myth*. As for *mimicry*, onomatopoeia in literature corresponds to the lowest mimicry in music, and further sound patterns to a higher mimicry, as in the striking case where a writer catches not only a person's specific phrases but his specific intonation patterns. Patterned *repetitions* and *leitmotifs* abound in literature, as do the *abstractive correlatives* of rising and falling movement, both locally in phrases and in such large constituents as plot structure.

Poetry and literature generally define emotional and intellectual sequences by embodying them. Literature has been shown, more often than music, to exemplify in Hegelian fashion the whole psychological-spiritual state of an epoch, so that Attali's conjunctions of an era's music with its other activities could be extended to its literature, and also to its art.

The visual arts lie between music and literature, sharing the word-lessness of the former with the latter's recourse to given icons and preexistent narratives, while differing from both in the predominant spatiality of its presentation to a viewer.

Mimesis as a strategy, and as a problem, embraces more in the visual arts than in music or literature. A painting's confinement to space re-inforces an arrested gathering of the beholder's perception. In painting the codes involve techniques for mimesis.[26] The message of a painting, too, is often, and characteristically, rooted in mimesis. Mimesis often shapes itself around the figures in myth. Hence a procedure in some ways equivalent to the mimicry that is marginal to literature and music tends to be central to painting and sculpture, and also more inclusive.

Furthermore, painting combines music's directness with literature's access to coded signifiers, and these two features admit of many per-mutations in definition. For the visual arts the particular mix of di-rectness and indirectness in signifiers and signifieds allows a range of mimetic correspondences. Even the single life-size model of a bird, for example, may enlist a range of signs (where isolated from a natural setting) and so add to the model the signification of framing. The decoys taken as art objects have a different sign function from that of the Egyptian hawk or the thunderbird of the Pacific Northwest. Mi-metic representations may embody all sorts of distortions, combina-tions, settings, and progressively inclusive abstractions, as the discus-sions of Gombrich and Goodman help us to see (if not to explain).

Attention in our time to the constructive aspect of artistic apprehen-sion has tended to obscure the desire of the apprehending consciousness to immerse itself in the object. In reading or hearing literature—and reading is a form of suspended hearing—the reader or listener enters the paradox of suspending dialogic interchange, while participating in it ideally. In live music the sound at its ideal surrounds the auditor stereophonically. His ears are filled, and he is ideally immobilized to attend to the paradox of this pure motion, "as a Chinese jar still Moves perpetually in its stillness."

This immersion of a beholder is especially apparent in landscape gardening, where he stands in the midst of a scene that has been con-structed round him on all sides. Architecture, too, invites to an im-mersion, either actually, when the beholder is inside home or temple, or prospectively, when he approaches it. His desire to enter is part of his perception. The arch, the colonnade, the window, the recess, the bay, not only organize design and interrupt the view by imposing values of light and dark upon it; they also play upon the beholder's expectation that this will be so. Architecture, insofar as it creates the illusion of immersion even in the absence of the beholder's body from the site, is evoked by the other visual arts; and paintings in both ancient and modern times have often represented buildings. Indeed, sometimes in the sculptures on Gothic cathedrals, and sometimes in their panels of stained glass, buildings or parts of buildings are represented on the cathedral building.

The immersive attitude is urged by the painting or sculpture, which would have the beholder arrest himself and not move imperceptibly past it. Not only this general condition but the specific context of the painting in Western tradition reinforces immersion, before some idealized other in the portrait, before an object to be adored in the painting of Virgin or saint, in the immersive area of a landscape, in the open and surrounding panorama of a history painting, or in the pointed group of objects, the still life, which is usually imagined as in some interior that includes the beholder, with the rest of the world left "outside." The abstract painting, in a sense, presupposes that the trained beholder has learned this immersive attitude when it arrests him before pure design and color.

5

To state this idea somewhat differently, the art work sets up communication between the observer and an absent other. Many psychological and epistemological questions about human interaction and many philosophical questions about the phenomenology of intersubjectivity can be brought to bear upon this dialogic situation. But, again, such endless questions do not have to be solved, nor need one offer a depth-psychological explanation for artistic production and experience,[27] in order to observe some features of this arrested and exalted dialogue. It enlists, to begin with, a presence, the object, that in the absence of the creator paradoxically sets up an intimate intersubjectivity with the beholder and seals off the dialogue in a virtuality that preserves it from the quick fading of normal live dialogue. In his absence the creator through the dialogue sets up a supreme presence. This happens even when the constituents of the work are (seen or imagined as) live actors in a theater piece, across the barrier that forbids actual dialogic response. Then the beholder transcends the paradox by abiding with it in a pure form, through a formed experience (Dewey) or the attainment of a goal not diverted to practical purposefulness (Kant).

This merging into an otherness also mirrors the self. The absence of the other totalizes the intersubjectivity, which would remain stubbornly partial, and inescapably evanescent, in the actual live presence of the other. The other who is an artist has found the communicative strategy that totalizes this dialogue at the cost of his withdrawing from it totally.

The withdrawal, the "death," is a condition of its plenitude. In the act of bringing the work before its beholder, the creator has mixed his dominance with his self-sacrifice, silence with full speaking, concealment with revelation.

The other is thus most actualized when his presence assumes a character of virtuality, as Lacan has extensively shown for his own concerns. Further, the message coded into an art work draws on, reinforces, and to some extent transcends that virtuality through the intensifications without which it would not draw the attention. Virtuality, of course, is not virtuosity. The skill at manipulating conventions to produce, within them, the impression of accurate representation does not of itself attain to intensification. The illusionist effect of Zeuxis or Apelles is a curiosity. The "faithful" rendering of this stag by Landseer, or that time-specific set of behaviors by Sinclair Lewis, has lost the intensification of closeness in time, where across long stretches of time Praxiteles and Sophocles do not significantly lose their intensification. They remain impressive and imposing virtual others. Nor is it just the Oedipus complex that "grips" the spectator, to follow Freud's language. Other plays of Sophocles have a force comparable to that of *Oedipus Rex,* and many ephemeral plays lacking that force still do faithfully evoke the situation of an Oedipus complex. (Indeed, on Freudian principles they could not refrain from doing so.)

The operation of manifold rhetorical and contextual constituents in no way mitigates the "rapture" of the beholder, to which they saliently contribute. If it did, the "rapture" would be an illusion, and the intricate organization would be at worst a waste of time. At best it would be an adept communicative act, to which "rapture" would be an incidental aftereffect or a mere registering signal.

With his term *"plaisir"* ("pleasure") Roland Barthes names the rapture and gives a sensitive account of some of its effects, while reducing it to a sort of frisson, a simple delectation like those of all other successfully assimilated communicative acts, and of such pleasurable gestures as eating ice cream or scratching a bite.[28] Kant, by contrast, sees the cultural function of artistic experience as something close to a Freudian sublimation, a liberation from desire. And in an easy solution to his intricate preliminaries, he sees the beauty in art as a symbol of the moral good.[29] Yet Kant arrives at this definition only by further organizing his already complex acts of judgment, as they mediate between the "freedom" of practical reason and the given condition ("Natur") of understanding. He provides a redefinition of symbol or "hypotyposis" that does not just connect the tenor and the vehicle in a metaphoric process but, once again, enlists either the theoretical concepts of understanding or the practical ones of reason. When he approaches a resolution of his antinomy between the possibility and the impossibility of grounding aesthetic concepts, he has recourse to something like rapture in a reference to the supernatural—which he qualifies by a "perhaps," in keeping with the virtuality of the experience.[30] And yet with all this, Kant somewhat slights the communicative, the rhetorical, constituents of art; and so he slights the other, when he brings together the perception of beauties in nature with those in human artistic productions.[31] Setting Barthes's "pleasure" against Kant's "liberation from desire," into a sort of antinomy, underscores the lack of finality in either term of this opposition. Art suggests Kant's good but neither embodies it nor represents it. Art does evoke Barthes's pleasure and yet also mysteriously arrests it by transforming it. Here, too, in the affective or ideal dimension of the beholder's relation to the other who has produced the coded statement of the art work, a virtuality obtains that cannot be translated, withdrawn, or even relativized (though interpretation, it can easily be demonstrated, is endlessly subject to relativization).

There are many ways of approaching an awareness of the other's virtuality as it is achieved in the work of art. Such an awareness in modern times is approached, often, by features within the work itself. But even so, the "silence" that governs this virtuality forbids our defining it in any way besides a circular one. Hence the appositeness of Heidegger's "hermeneutic" approach, which with "circular" reasoning describes a situation instead of trying to prove a position. The stresses and condensations possible in this area of aesthetic discourse are highlighted in his dialogue, "From a Talk about Talking" ("Aus einem Gespräch von der Sprache"), where he sets the cultural relativity of aesthetic terminology against the cross-cultural identity posed by such virtuality. He does so by posing a dialogue between himself and a Japanese who had been a student of a student of his, rounding the cross-cultural circle. The term "*Iki*" covers much of the same aesthetic ground as a term like "the ineffable" or even "the sublime," and it overlaps with Kant's insistence on the presence of both the natural and the supernatural.[32]

In "The Origin of the Work of Art" ("Der Ursprung des Kunstwerkes") Heidegger presses toward the communication of an unconcealing ("*Unverborgenheit*") in art, linking it to his originary derivation of the Greek term for truth, "*a-letheia*": "Beauty is a means for truth to exist as un-concealment."[33] The canny purchase of Heidegger's terminology gives it a grip on aspects of both "rhetoric" and "rapture," since the communication turns out to be a revelation, and vice versa. He stresses as well the notions of "instrument" ("*Zeug*") and "thing" ("*Ding*"), bringing the "work" into the perspective of his metaphysics, in its relation to "*Techne*" and hence to human otherness, to reciprocity.

("Für-und Miteinandersein"), through a number of other terms that either graze the sublime or imply it.

Lacan's categories of the real, the imaginary, and the symbolic define and dialectically structure the discourse between self and other in ways that painting and the other arts may intensely reproduce—and also transcend. In his terms the symbolic function is itself transcendental, and he formulates it in a way that easily fits and describes such discourse between the beholder and the work of art: "It is presence in absence and absence in presence."[34] Yet the symbolic is deduced so intricately as a total order that Lacan does not really provide a Kant-like dialectic for its incorporation or rejection of the imaginary, and when asked how graphic design bridges this gap, or obscures it, he fudges an answer.[35] And his various elaborations of kinds of discourse, as in the four proposed in his seminar on "*jouissance*,"[36] never broach—though of course he would want to include—the particular intensities of artistic discourse, even though he reproduces works of art here as especially apposite. The fruitional joy of sexual satisfaction, his "*jouissance*," when it is symbolized, would have to extend to the discourse in art, which indeed would offer the opportunity for the sort of supplementary account to Lacan's system that Kant's *Critique of Judgment* offers to his other critiques.

Lyotard speaks of "the presence of the distancing in seeing in the experience of discourse" ("la présence de la distanciation du voir dans l'expérience du discours").[37] His distancing allows at once for all the possible dialectic of interaction between seeing and discourse, and also for its transcendence in the "rapture" of the beholder. In modern painting the artist variously presses these conditions. And such modern forms as the photograph and the film press them in the very preconditions of their art. The photograph arrives at its effect by forcing a transcendence through what is presented as the record of a moment. The visual document, through structuring and framing, asks to engage a discourse. Film moves this moment along as a process by first fixing an object as such a resonant sight and then either dwelling on it in variously angled structures or moving to another—sea or woman, mountain or labyrinthine street, open plain or empty room plumbing the loneliness that the film overwhelms by doubling it back into discourse.

In any art the structured significations lead to depth-communications. In one way this point is obvious and even incontravertible. But attention to significations, to rhetoric, can lead to slighting, or losing sight of, the depth-communication that resides in, and alone justifies, human attention in the first place to significations that are not tied to immediate effectuations. The rhetoric leads to rapture.

6

For a long time in the West, as well as at all times in some other cultures, painting and sculpture tended to illustrate a preexisting text or known legend. Such evocation itself is a rhetorical gesture. It communicates, and it can lead to the force of rapture. I have discussed elsewhere the communicative force that may reside in various attempts to disengage painting from this broad assumption.[38] I will not here repeat that discussion, nor will I continue it, though the partial disengagement of the visual work from a preexisting text in the fifteenth century, with a resultant rhetorical force, is also to be found in many richly significative paintings of the sixteenth and seventeenth centuries—in the somewhat arbitrary collocations of Giovanni Bellini's *The Feast of the Gods* and Titian's *Allegory of Music*; in the pressing of allegory by Poussin's *A Dance to the Music of Time* and Bronzino's *Cupid and Venus*; in the archness of certain paintings by Veronese; and also in the entire tradition of Dutch seventeenth-century painting, where the elaboration of both landscape and still life, as well as the deep and complex collocations carried through by Rembrandt and Vermeer (among others), mingle preexisting iconographic associations, some of them allegorical, in frames of direct observation, radical qualification, or integral redefinition.[39]

My purpose in this book is to address some interrelated problems where the "dimensions" of the sign in art are at their most ramified or their most enigmatic. It is no accident that such questions bear especially on modern art, and of course there are many modern artists other than those discussed here whom I might have considered in this connection. The second part of this book addresses the work of four especially problematic modern artists. In the first part of the book I have considered some general questions, with illustrations largely from Renaissance painters. And I have examined the work of two nineteenth-century painters who are strongly innovative. Turner presses representation and Goya presses signification in ways that lead to modern art and modern viewing. The four twentieth-century artists whom I have chosen have all at one time or another, and sometimes consistently, been called surrealists, a useful term that has had the unfortunate side effect of obscuring the actual communicative properties of certain painters—and poets. What Marcel Duchamp called the "meta-irony" of his work necessitates even more exposition than it has received, as does the relation between the strangely unitary effect of the paintings of Klee and the elaborate system of visual effects discussed in Klee's *Das Bildnerische Denken*. Magritte's works, and his extensive comments on them, imply and incorporate an intricate network of definitions that press the dream beyond assertion of its validity as an instrument of perception. The collage novels of Max Ernst, too, only begin with their reshuffling of the already complex icons drawn from the nineteenth-century graphics that the artist clipped and reassembled, arranging them in a spatial collocation to which he then gave an immediately discontinuous but ultimately continuous temporal sequence. The absence of color in these works itself indicates their restriction from the representational continuum that Ernst, a notable colorist, used in his other works. And the absence of color in these visual novels may also be read as a correlative to their construction of a dream life, since dreams notably lack color, and since it is the unconscious that their abstractions schematize.

Color, like painting itself, intersects the purely visual (where it is a puzzle for the philosopher) and the significative. Color, alone or in combination, functions as a sign. And as Matisse insisted, it has the especial force of leading to immediate rapture, to "*la joie*." In a painting the visual and the significative always come together, in ways that are especially rich for some painters. In my general chapter on color, I have tried to extend from the focus of color the "readings" of certain paintings of Titian and Van Gogh, among others.

The mirror, which seems a blank, is also coded, and elaborately. Mirrors, as it was felt particularly in the early Renaissance, have an especial relevance to the perspectival means of the painter; that is why they are commented on in the notebooks of Leonardo. But again, just as the function of mirrors is intricate in other cultures, so there is more to their use in Renaissance painting than just the visual-perspectival. They invoke, extend, and interpret the uncanny. Mirrors, too, intricately mingle the visual and the significative. Seeing them this way allows us, as I try to show, not only to make some general inferences but also to interpret certain paintings of van Eyck and Titian, among others, by attending to other features of the mirrors in their paintings than the use of the visual-perspectival.

The act of painting in itself carries signification, and it also has a locus in a culture. Turner's confrontation of Venice, and others' confrontation of that confrontation, cross the problem of the relation between representation and vision with the problem of how prior cultural definitions are met in landscape. Goya presses those significations, and he makes them perform the sort of all-embracing commentary that is usually assigned to words. He transmutes the satiric element in painting and graphic representation as much as Blake does satiric poetry, in ways that have consequences for his powerful visual resources. The rich problems and solutions that all these artists pose may serve for a rich lexicon of the complexities that the combination of the visual and the verbal may offer.

As in all my books, I have tried here to make a number of interrelated discussions bear upon some central questions, rather than to offer a sequenced argument. Indeed, I cannot imagine how these questions could be arranged in a sequenced argument without impoverishment—and ultimately without a corollary loss of genuine coherence.

MIND, EYE, AND BRUSH
Turner's Venice

Chapter 2

       The term "the sublime," or some equivalent for it, is indispensable, I have been arguing, for discussing the effect of art on the viewer, and initially on the artist. Such a term, of course, involves "the mind," and it does not involve it simply. The presuppositions behind such a term, even before it gets applied to painting, rest on interconnected ideas. The existence of these ideas in a tradition entails their use by other minds. Thereby, for adequate theoretical justification, a host of problems presses for attention, even before the relation between the mind of the painter and the "other mind" of the viewer is addressed. When the painter does carry off successfully a sublime painting, he creates an effect that evokes a mood: it "elevates." And that mood is not to be disconnected from congeries of ideas.

    Modern commentators who wish implicitly to bracket all these questions and who hold, also implicitly, that to use a term like "the sublime" is to refuse to bracket them, have recourse to two strategies, sometimes combining them. First, they may refer only in passing to the effect of art, talking simply about the artistic effect or the mystery of connoisseurship or some such.[1] Second, they may historicize the question more or less explicitly, asking what might have been taken for the sublime in the late eighteenth and early nineteenth centuries, coming up with conclusions, however subtle, that tend to avoid the question of what the validity of the term, or of some equivalent, might be.

It is clear that painting such as Turner's involves not only the mind, but also the eye. This situation brings up another whole set of questions that must be bracketed if they are not to take over the discussion entirely, the set of questions bearing on the relationship between the mind and the eye. There is also the set of questions about the relationship between the (mind and the) eye and an object, and then between the eye and an art object. All of this presupposes the prior social demarcation, and its corresponding coding. They set off an object with the label "art object," a process of signification given attention by both artists and theoreticians in our time. Then further, for these questions, taken together or separately, there is the set of questions about the relationship between seeing and drawing, between eye and brush, and all the puzzles about the copy, the resemblance, the correspondences, the patterns, and so forth. Lawrence Gowing, effectively and simply, condenses all these questions into the terms "imagination" and "reality," coming down, again somewhat simply, on the side of "imagination" for Turner, on the grounds that so much more is involved in the painting of this pre- or early impressionist than just the bald copying of reality.[2]

Turner's sublime, though, involves all three—the mind, the eye, and the brush—in a probably inextricable relationship that requires the capacity of a Ruskin or an Adrian Stokes to hold in balance. Ruskin set the tone for such discussions by expatiating on the sublime in Turner, but also by carefully arguing for the triumphs of his draftsmanship seen both from the angle of what the eye could register and from that of what the brush could render.

The choices that an artist makes of a subject, both in the large (landscape, cityscape) and in the small (a particular mountain location like the Alps, a particular city like Venice), are ipso facto endowed with signification in the choice. And they are themselves full of prior signification before the choice has been made, both generally in social implication and specifically in the iconography of art. That the majesty of mountains was coded for the complex notion of the sublime before Edmund Burke wrote *On the Sublime and Beautiful* was a necessary precondition for his being able to single them out. And much dingier landscapes than mountains, painted in our own time, refer to that coding by resolutely being anti-sublime. Cityscapes can partake of the sublime (or the anti-sublime), especially in certain light, such as that of early morning, when they may look like landscapes. So Wordsworth's sonnet "Composed upon Westminster Bridge" declares, "Earth has not anything to show more fair." Here, to be sure, "fair" suggests Burke's "beautiful," a term counterbalancing the sublime, and "beautifully" is a word used in the poem; but other words in it like "majesty," "splendour," and "mighty" are more in the domain of the sublime, and the list of "Ships, towers, domes, theatres and temples" assimilates the view to objects often seen as sublime, and certainly given a sublime cast in the cityscapes of Turner, a painter whom Ruskin saw as Wordsworthian. Wordsworth's susceptibility to prior coding here undergoes modification, almost consciously on Turner's part. Of course usually he preferred mountains to cities, an already conventional choice to which he had given his strong personal stamp, as visual artists also preeminently do. Corot came to the Roman Campagna, and Turner to Venice, in the wake of a long iconographic tradition, to which these painters added their personal stamp.

All of this is well known, and yet it bears restating as we assess how regular, coded significations of complex scenes in the world get expressed and somewhat modified by individual painters in ways that involve so much of convention that they do not immediately lend themselves to the sort of direct, general approach that may apply to more easily abstractable constituents of paintings like color, design, and technique, or subjects like mirrors and virgins. Specifically what Venice meant to Turner, and comes to mean to us through Turner, may be distinguished from the related question about visual representation that also has been posed about Turner's work from Ruskin's time to our own, namely, the particular mix, and proportion, of his representation of an actual scene on the one hand and his attention to pure creation with paint on the other. As with other "impressionists," but perhaps in more extreme form, the mix of "reality" and "imagination" bears upon significations, and we need at every point to resist settling, with this or that critic, simply for one or the other, "reality" or "imagination." The coding of the mind interacts with the fresh activity of the eye as mind and eye guide the constructions of the brush.

A painter may be completely immersed in the significations of what he has been given as aesthetic and still make these constituents yield a sort of self-revelation. This is the normal case, reaching heights of realization in a painter as commanding as Turner. Turner's pressure on representation deliberately sets enigmas for the relation between such a traditional physical scene as the city of Venice, with all the significations coded into its presence, and the act of painting; between mimetic accuracy and overall painterly vision; and between the mimetic and the visionary. These relations become further engaged, if we come at Turner, the way we must, through the relations between the long-given attitudes of the picturesque and the sublime in his work, as these may flow into each other, and as they may both overshadow and draw

on the mimetic powers that Ruskin explicitly and Stokes implicitly
linked to the sublime—especially as it was suggested by Venice, and
the Venetian painters, for Turner. In these traditional circumstances he
triumphantly heightened his significations while facing roughnesses,
indeterminacies, and contradictions.

The familiar connections will retain, as perhaps they would have to,
a stubborn tinge of possibility as opposed to actuality if we try to assess
the various conventional streams of seeing and representing Venice that
find their confluence in Turner. For the connection between Turner
and Venice, indeed, Titian remains an imposing, a cloudy and chromatic, presence. Ruskin, when he expatiates on Turner's "teachers,"
emphasizes the Venetians to the extent that he must downplay inter-
mediary figures like Claude, whom he scantly allows any influence because he disdains Claude's mimetic powers. Nor does he give much to
Rubens, though he esteems him somewhat more generously. Still less
does he allow force to Canaletto, whose landscapes he calls merely
"picturesque" rather than sublimely "contemplative" in the grand manner of Turner's,[3] even though the Palladian Venice of Canaletto looked
in fact more like the Venice of Ruskin's imagination, and his experience,
than did the Venice of Giorgione and Titian. Turner, we may say oversimply, saw Venice with Titian's eyes, though the Venice he saw was
not Titian's. Titian's effects, applied to Canaletto's Venice by a Turner
who sketched views of the city while visiting it, may be said to give a
particular Venetian aura, a pervasive suggestiveness, to all of Turner's
painting.

For us the visual qualities in Turner that Ruskin was virtually the
first to establish most resemble the visual qualities of Titian and of
Tintoretto, if less emphatically of Giorgione to our post-impressionist
eyes. In these resemblances Turner resurrects, deflects, and glosses their
significations. The qualities of Turner's handling of color and light are
present in Giorgione, but more muted, at least to my eye, though
Ruskin praises these qualities more pronouncedly in Giorgione than in
Titian.[4] Ruskin, interestingly, when he contrasted Turner's gloomy
childhood ambience with the sunlit ambience of a Venetian painter,
matched him not to Titian but to Giorgione:[5]

what a world [Giorgione's] eyes opened on . . . A city of marble . . . a golden
city, paved with emerald . . . no foulness, nor tumult, in those tremulous
streets . . . but rippled music of majestic change, or thrilling silence. No weak
walls could rise above them; no low-roofed cottage, nor straw-built shed.
Only the strength as of rock . . . Such was Giorgione's school, such Titian's
home . . .
  Turner saw the exact reverse of this. In the present work of men, meanness,

aimlessness, unsightliness: thin-walled, lath-divided, narrow-garreted houses
of clay; booths of a darksome Vanity Fair, busily base.

Near the south-west corner of Covent Garden, a square brick pit or well
is formed by a close-set block of houses, the back windows of which admit
a few rays of light . . . None of these things very glorious . . . Consequently,
he attaches himself with the faithfullest love to everything that bears an image
of the place he was born in. No matter how ugly it is,—has it anything
about it like Maiden Lane, or like Thames' shore . . . Dead brick walls, blank
square windows, old clothes . . . anything fishy and muddy . . . had great
attraction for him; black barges, patched sails, and every possible condition
of fog . . . No Venetian ever draws anything foul; but Turner devoted picture
after picture to the illustration of effects of dinginess, smoke, soot, dust, and
dusty texture; old sides of boats, weedy roadside vegetation, dung hills, straw
yards, and all the soilings and stains of every common labour.[6]

This Turner of oppression and grime is not exactly the Turner we
most saliently know, though it is one drawn by a man who knew
Turner's work more intimately perhaps than anyone has since. The
Venetians, in this light, turned his eyes away from the strong element
of the subjects of his that Ruskin describes to a kind of opposite, or
Yeatsian anti-self, as a ground for signification. Yet Ruskin, who characteristically mastered his own contradictions, is carried away here, for
all the presence of such subjects in Turner's work. He has also forgotten
his own derivation of Turner's boyhood from Yorkshire in the much
earlier first volume of this series. Nor is the Venice that Ruskin depicts
here the one Titian and Giorgione knew. They grew up in a crowded,
wooden Venice, as Stokes strikingly reminds us.[7] The Palladian Venice
of marble, the stones of Venice, rose later. Even the splendid San Marco
of Gentile Bellini's great painting is partially muted by this wooden
Venice that Ruskin has conveniently forgotten, because it did also not
persist in representation widely enough to confront Turner either. In
a sense for different reasons he has also forgotten the very Venice of
Turner.

What Titian may be said to stand for is pervasive in Turner's work
generally, and was so well before he had a chance to see Venice. Indeed
a very early work, *Moonlight: A Study at Millbank* (1797), already manages a Venetian effect that is quite unlikely for that particular setting.
A few small sails in the foreground ride on an expanse of water, with
a low, punctuated skyline in the distance, very much like some of Turner's late Venetian paintings and watercolors, which are structured pretty
much on this pattern. Venice, in the somewhat hyperbolic words of
Max F. Schulz, moved Turner to represent "an Atlantean world in
which sea and sky, the city and its waters, reflecting life and death,
unite in a seamless continuum."[8] But this description also applies to
work painted before he saw Venice. Furthermore, Ruskin's contrast

holds less forcefully for the fact that Turner infrequently painted London, and when he did so, he tended to choose monumental buildings and the like. There is, in fact, a Palladian aspect of the monumental London, an aspect that Stokes derives ultimately from Venice.[9]

In tracing Turner's early impressions through his paintings, whether to London or to Yorkshire, Ruskin adduces the principle that "all great painters . . . have been great only in their rendering of what they had seen and felt from early childhood."[10] Indeed, so far as open spaces are concerned, it is not Yorkshire villages or moors but rather the sea, a presence both Venetian and English, that pervades Turner's imagination and provides a bridge between what he had seen and what he willed to see, along with the mountains that were even less a visual backdrop for his boyhood.[11] Turner calls Italy "the land of all bliss."[12] And if bliss in painting is derived strongly from color—a lesson Matisse especially has taught us—then Italy released Turner's supreme colorist impulses. As Jack Lindsay shows, Turner's first Venetian oils of 1833 also come close to the beginning of his late, major effusions of color.[13] As Henry Fuseli said, "Venice is the birthplace and the theatre of color," a statement that neatly connects the site and the eye.[14] One approach to the impressions that led to Turner's late landscapes—rich and at the same time as though aerated as they are—is not just through Venice and not just through one Venetian painter, but through the use of color generally in that tradition, an airy and light-suffused color applied to scenes that do not receive an airy and light-suffused treatment from those painters. Tintoretto taken by himself comes close, but holding his renderings of Venetian waters against those of Turner reveals how far "heavier" the Venetian painter is.

Indeed the presence of Venice, once Turner had carried through his deep intent of focusing on it, neatly poses the question of the relationship between "reality" or representative fidelity and "imagination" in art, to use the terms of Lawrence Gowing's title. Ruskin's handling of Turner serves to underline how inextricable "imagination" and "reality" remain, even under the sort of intense scrutiny to which Ruskin, and also Gowing and his predecessor Stokes, have subjected the two aspects of both painting and vision.

Turner, of course, though he did some religious, allegorical, and historical painting, was more predominantly a landscape artist, and one can attribute to his preoccupation with landscape the difference in the handling of tone, as it results in differences of signification from Titian. Ruskin notes, contrasting Turner and Titian: "Turner . . . will not sacrifice the higher truths of his landscape to mere pitch of color as Titian does."[15] Ruskin amplifies what he means by "higher truths" when he says that "all true landscape, whether simple or exalted, depends primarily for its interest on connection with humanity, or with spiritual powers."[16] Ronald Paulson forcefully outlines the social and emotional, as well as these religious, amplifications that are implied in landscape painting.[17] He further connects landscapes to cityscapes, asserting that landscape follows cityscape just as country house architecture follows town house architecture—a series that would have the effect of making Turner's Venetian scenes, which are both landscapes and cityscapes, a bold coalescence of modes that in any case echo each other. Yet Ruskin asserts, "From this great Venetian school of landscape (Titian, Tintoretto, Palma) Turner received much important teaching—almost the only healthy teaching which he owed to preceding art."[18]

Actually, landscapes are always put in the background in Titian's paintings, more or less prominently so. And Turner has little affinity with the faintly crepuscular clarities in the setting of *Sacred and Profane Love* (about 1515) or the even sharper mountain scene behind *The Presentation of the Virgin in the Temple* (1534), where the landscape could be described as sub-Giorgionesque. Rather, Turner's bold smudges, which somehow suggest vast distances and even illuminations, come closer to the work of a much later Titian, the painter of *The Rape of Europa* (1560) or of several works after 1570—*The Flaying of Marsyas, St. Sebastian, Nymph and Shepherd,* and *The Crowning of Thorns.* An intense swirl of Turner-like blurs accommodates the central figure in these last two works into what seems an engulfing world.[19] Indeed, this approach may be seen in Turner's pre-Venetian works, notably in *Snow Storm: Hannibal and His Army Crossing the Alps* (1812). This work presents a swirl of dark grey cloud taking over from the sun. The snowstorm is a deluge of light flooding on a slant across nearly the whole left of the canvas into a valley and then circling round in the foreground—a premonition of the flooding light of the later canvases, a colder and more elevated *Rain, Steam and Speed.*

Here we may have a true affinity in the absence of influence, because at the time few of Titian's late works, as it happens, were located where Turner could have seen them. The Titian of his possible viewing, with a couple of exceptions, was the early and middle Titian.[20]

In Turner, when we look for some causal connection or source, we cannot discriminate between Venice and the Venetian painters[21] or give real priority to either, even though Venice was clearly prior in its visible presence. It was through the city, but also the city as seen by the Venetian painters, including Canaletto as perhaps modified by Claude, that Turner was able to prove, to himself and to us, that intensity is not incompatible with lightness as both draw on the coalescence of expectation and eye.

As for expectation, what Turner saw in Venice poses a question, across time, of nearly, or occasionally, anonymous public perception as it surfaces in commissions for architecture, which is then realized within a setting. The anonymity falls away in the perception of a native great painter, Giorgione or Titian, and then of others like Canaletto or Guardi—even if a Ruskin cannot see this for a Canaletto. It works across the stretches of time and space upon a foreign great painter, Turner. Across these centuries of the time that we conventionally set into periods, and across media from stone to paint to words, with the help of Ruskin and of Stokes, we are brought to perceive Turner's intensity-in-lightness and may speculate on why it should often be especially embodied and represented in a particular city. Indeed, those speculations themselves could simply be engaged through further abundant quotation of Ruskin and Stokes, who register, evoke, analyze, focus, and praise, both the painting and the architecture of Venice.

On the one hand, Turner looked penetratingly at what he saw. As Ruskin demonstrated at vast length, he can be counted on to render tree and leaf, cloud and sky, field and rock and mountain, as well as light and color, with a fidelity rarely if ever equaled. It is no contradiction for Ruskin, any more than it is for Kant or for a painter in the act of painting, to place this stress on representation, on "reality," while at the same time emphasizing the necessity of a nearly religious sublimity in painting. Indeed "sublimity," if it be allowed its old near-synonymity with "imagination," is all we go to painting for. And like Kant, Ruskin saw this sublimity so embodied in the outer world, and even in such hieratic special places as Venice, that it became something like an act of religious as well as visual discovery to bring the representation onto the canvas, a supremely counter-Platonic act: the painted object is not at Plato's three removes from the idea but brings it into ideal presence through the painting. As Ruskin says, "If you can paint *one* leaf, you can paint the world."[22] It is only a footnote to these demonstrations of Ruskin to notice, as John Gage points out, that the Venice of Turner, for all the shimmer of its rendered look, has detailed topographical accuracy—something that the young Ruskin had noticed in one of his earliest comments on Turner, and then specifically about Venice.[23] Yet the visual becomes so evanescent, so "impressionistic" in Turner's works—after Venice, so to speak, has had its effect upon them—that they turn us toward "poetry" or "imagination" or preoccupation with paint, rather than toward "reality" or "truth."

These terms, indeed, are no vaguer than the terms that Ruskin uses to supplement them, terms like "sublimity," "contemplation," and "delicacy," to go no further. Ruskin tends to amplify such terms, as he notably does in the seven loosely coordinated abstractions of *The Seven Lamps of Architecture*. Thus pervasively through his work does he try

to spell out, and to account for, that in paintings which he would want
to associate with a moral, and even with a religious, impulse. As many
recent commentators have shown, the term "sublime" carries a richness
for Turner that can be extended to the painterly practice and philosophical theory of a fairly grand array of his predecessors.[24] The play
of contradiction through Ruskin's abstractions need not detach us from
attending to his several points, which are like readings from various
angles, even though individually they can also not be pinned down. In
spite of this tendency toward roughness of vocabulary under the guise
of precision, Ruskin does keep extremely and complexly in view the
"reality" side of Turner and the "imagination" side as well. "Imagination" and "reality," we may see, are bridged somewhat, as well as fused,
if we divide "reality" into the representation of a stable scene and the
representation of momentary visual impression (while bracketing all
the paradoxes of mimesis and its object, and so forth). The "impressionism" of Turner has, then, aspects of both "reality" and "imagination"—though the "paint" of Gowing takes it too exclusively from the
side of "imagination" and tends to see the terms as an opposition rather
than as a paradox. Thus Gombrich, also, forgets too quickly Ruskin's
unimpeachable lengthy demonstrations of Turner's accurate representation of "reality."[25]

Indeed, we can grasp what Ruskin means, and even partially assent
to it, when he insists that contemplation, or signification as we would
say, necessarily inheres in landscape. Certainly the Venice of the Venetians at any time, and the Venice of a nineteenth-century Englishman
aroused by landscape, is saturated in significance. The city is inseparable
from significations, both of itself and of those in the paintings of it and
from it. Ruskin only generalizes these significations when he classifies
landscape, beyond mimetic representation, into the "heroic" (Titian
being his example), the "classical" (as represented by Poussin), the "pastoral" (for him, Cuyp), and the "contemplative" (supremely represented
by Turner)—adding to these various hybrid and "spurious" possibilities, like the "picturesque," which he classes, the way we might, as a
degradation of the "contemplative," even though we might choose examples other than Canaletto and Guardi.[26]

By whatever route we approach what Turner's landscapes signify,
something in Turner's perception is "already there" early in his career,
a sort of fusion of lightness with intensity that comes to magnificent
realization in his last works. But those qualities are both fused already
in early Nottingham scenes that curiously resemble later Venetian paintings.[27] Of his lightness, Stokes says, "Architecture in some very late
Venetian paintings serves no more than as a grandiloquent sail amid
the suffusion of sea with sky."[28] And for what I have called intensity,

Stokes rests, if evocatively, with a psychoanalytic explanation: "Clasping natural immensity, Turner lent a hard-won grandeur to the distance, so irregularly spanned by each of us, between self-destruction and forget- ful, infantile love." The assuredness with which he has executed them, it would seem, provided the intensity; and his openness to experience, his on-the-spot sketching and his readiness to travel, provided the light- ness. Even in the lightness of such late Venetian watercolors as the *Riva degli Schiavoni* of 1840, there is a kind of intensity as the wash of blue- green, variable water seems to weight down the greyish sky, to possess more solidity than the airy buildings that divide the two, and to arrest the many boats sketched in the foreground, angled so that it is hard to see these fleet craft in any kind of motion that would not work against the motion of other vessels. And in *The Dogana and Santa Maria della Salute, Venice* of the same year (fig. 1), an overall lightness in the lemon yellow of the sky and the greenish yellow of the canal as it centers to blue, allows the gondolas to marshal almost with the solidity of the large but airy buildings sketched out beyond them. *The Sun of Venice Going to Sea* (1843) shows the boat of that name exhibiting its variegated sails in an endless shimmer. *Procession of Boats with Distant Smoke— Venice* (1845) is almost indistinguishable from other late paintings. In it black, white, and reddish figures are wrapped and blurred in light. Earlier, in the oil *Staffa, Fingal's Cave* of 1832—just before his most decisive Venetian exposures—Turner subjects the light airiness of this cliff that seems to rise toward the sky to a wash of dusky whites like an aborted rainbow on the left side. The dark greenish-brown slab of the sea cliff and the sea are overshadowed by a variable line of white foam that shades up to their pinks and oranges. All these color effects attain intensity as they dwarf the small pink-rimmed yellow sun sinking into a dense brown sea at the right. The lightness of the sea seems to recede into weightiness in *Stormy Sea Breaking on Shore* (1840) and *Wreckers off the Northumberland Coast* (1834).

Venice drew out and encouraged such effects, the effects of Titian and Tintoretto, even though certainly the Venice of Canaletto, if not "false" in Ruskin's attribution, gives an impression of more fixity and sharper outline. Yet the Venice onto which Turner extrapolated, so to speak, the sweep of Tintoretto and the shadowy wholeness of Titian seems, as a city that from certain angles is surrounded by water, to be a splendid vehicle for what Ruskin calls "the fullness and mystery of Turner's distances."[29]

Indeed, that fullness tends to expand for Turner, and to produce an effect of all-roundness that needs the anchor, however light, of the Canaletto-like line of Venetian buildings to center it. In the limited compass of his single late canvases, Turner achieved something like the

FIG. 1. Joseph Mallord William Turner, *The Dogana and Santa Maria della Salute, Venice*. Courtesy of the National Gallery of Art, Washington. Given in memory of Governor Alvan T. Fuller by the Fuller Foundation.

effect of those early nineteenth-century "panoramas," where a viewer would pay an admission price and then enter a room to be surrounded on all sides by a continuous landscape. This effect is akin to Turner's "embracing or enveloping quality," which Stokes connects to his "indistinctness."[30] Turner tends to let the edges of his canvas strongly carry into a sort of sameness, whether of mountains beyond mountains or open water beyond water on both sides. And open water attracted him as much as enclosed water attracted Constable. The Staffa of *Fingal's Cave* offers a concentrated presence in the middle of vast waters and skies. *The Burning of the Houses of Parliament* locates the large fire at the center of waters that pick up and blend its colors much more than do the majestic buildings that thus lose prominence, white and small on a shimmering horizon. City, it may be said, is a kind of opposite of water in an iconic dictionary, where solidity is suggested by the one and fluid transience by the other.[31] But again, an overall effect is obtained when cities by the water, preeminently Venice but also certain angles of London, are rendered so as to fuse city and water, combining intensity and lightness, amplifying and significantly centering the space on the canvas.[32]

This overall effect is hard to define, and it is attained by various means. It can be felt almost in the absence of representational renderings, as in Turner's late *Light and Colour (Goethe's Theory)*. Titian's paintings, unlike Turner's, usually center themselves so as to contain the spaciousness they suggest, but in *The Rape of Europa* the wash of blues and the flowing clouds are handled openly enough to launch the large white bull into an impression of flight that could go almost anywhere, though headed initially off toward the upper right on an angle steeper than that of the clouds, while definitely at an ascending tangent to the shadowy swirls of color on the uneven ground. Turner could have seen this picture, since it was in a British collection through his lifetime, exhibited by its owner, Lord Darnley, at the British Institution in 1816, and before that in London as part of the Orleans collection in 1798–99.[33] Turner did two Europas himself, one for the *Liber Studiorum* in 1812 and another, arranged very like Titian's, in his last decade (1840–50). In Titian's painting the bull's large forelegs are bent for swimming, buried in a foam-crested wave. A reddish dogfishlike monster, reminiscent of one in the later *Sunrise with Sea-Monsters* of Turner, swims below the bull's belly and the red robe on which the whitegowned Europa precariously rides while holding a posture of something like repose. This fish, like the obscure figures in the water of some of Turner's other paintings, seems to merge with the dark waters, as does the large silver-finned one in the wake of the bull, ridden by a rainbow-winged, up-looking cherub. Beyond and behind all these, the water is a calm blue-green, murky still but clear enough to reflect the reds and whites of the distant persons running along the opposite shore. The shore continues brokenly into the distance, first lightening when it reaches the yellowish brightness at the foot of the abruptly high mountains. These contours vaguely rhyme with Europa and the bull at the center of the picture. Above them are two close-flying cherubs against the sheer blue of the sky, which vanishes into a reddish yellow haze where the outlines of cloud and horizon are lost in a Turneresque dazzle of obscurity. Castle and port are distinctly perceptible in their distant indistinctness, again an effect like Turner's. The two upper cherubs are continuous with the rosy red garment Europa furls, distinct and close against the distant, more orangish cloud-filled sky. The purplish brown stormy sky in the turbulence of the upper right reflects and varies the turbulence of the lower right waters. These two rough triangles are broken by the greyish white bull and his rosy white burden, whose flesh is emphasized by the agitated loosening of her drapery, with a nipple prominently exposed.

Europa and the bull stream with colors that merge them into a tremendous landscape, one not quite of terribilità but certainly evoking the terrors of the sublime, which these figures are swept into far more than is usually the case, for example, in Tintoretto. For Titian the gist of the mythological reference complicates and also diffuses these landscape effects, which are immersively intensified in Turner's late work.

In Turner's *Rain, Steam and Speed,* if the train, "rushing headlong out of the picture,"[34] seems to come forward toward us and thus to round out the whole field behind the viewer, it also has the almost palpable effect of widening the scene in the intense blurrings of rendered shore and land on both sides of its narrow bridge, to the blue wash of water sky and cloud dominating the far distance and filling a good two-thirds of the canvas. Strangely arrested, tipped up almost to the port of a gondola, is the only other vehicle in the picture, a tiny open boat that rides up and down slowly forward, pointing in the opposite direction, its lines suggesting an open triangle as it stands for a counterpart to the straight-moving speed of the dark, enclosed train. There is more cloud than steam in this painting, and hardly anything that would be distinguishable as rain if we did not have the aid of the title. The blurrings of the work itself reinforce the gaps in the title—as it were, they leap over those gaps—since rain and steam are visual presences that often accompany each other, whereas speed is an abstract characterization of the movement of objects that the canvas by definition arrests. Moreover, rain and steam rise and descend, often slowly, in a single spot, whereas in the world of Turner speed moves horizontally, at a rate that a rainstorm cannot attain without changing its name to hurricane or tornado.

Impressionism, as I have said, points toward both "imagination" and "reality." It points toward "imagination" because of the heavy paint and the dominant attention to the painterly act in work like Turner's and that of the French impressionists. Impressionism also points toward "reality" because it captures a moment in the supreme flux of a perceived but overwhelming light and dazzle. This much is implied by the anecdotes about Turner tied to a mast so as to observe a sea storm, or gazing avidly and continuously at another storm out the window of a railway carriage.

Further, though, impressionism contributes forcefully to the overall effect I have been attributing to Turner, and more so than in any of the French impressionists. We have learned through Gombrich and others to understand constructive sight, the conventional selection of details from the visual field and then their organization, both in perception and in execution on a canvas. There is also what may be called immersive sight, the immediate sense of being overwhelmed by the near infinity of visual details, and by the overall strength of light in an environment, before any details in it are selected and organized. Mountains and three-dimensional buildings, or paintings of these objects also evoke such an immersive sense. Indeed, mountains, seas, and imposing architectural monuments, all lead to an immersive sense in the beholder. The Greeks and others often set their temples, themselves conducive to three-dimensional immersion, in the further immersion of a mountainside or a seashore. Mountains, seas, and monumental buildings comprise most of what attracted Turner for representation.

Stokes, who finds carving or invasion of the surface and modeling or smoothing of the surface present in all successful art, effectually provides the terms to begin explaining why immersion has so powerful an effect, and why architecture, either in a visible city or in the painting of one, may serve as a model for an immersion. And immersion can come about more fully because he finds that even the effects of color may be classified as either "carving" or "modeling." An additional inducement toward the immersion of the eye is the persistent tendency in the great colorists toward an effect of backlighting, so that the colors not only shine but shine forward.

In general the bits of representation in Turner's late paintings are overwhelmed by light, and this light spreads out past the canvas so evenly that we cannot even say that Turner has broken the frame. Such an effect is one impression a person may have while standing in Venice with the openness of water and the labyrinthine channeling of water both in view round and before the dazzle of whites and pale colors on the faces of buildings. The eye sees all these as rising from water, punctuated by the few strong details of brightly painted poles and dark-curved gondolas. Turner's representations of Venice are organized so as to open the city out, in contrast with those of Canaletto or Guardi, where the waters are firmly bounded by chockablock lines of serried buildings. One *Venice* in the Victoria and Albert Museum has a Campanile not only elongated but cut off just above the Doge's Palace by a misty extension of a cloud. In *The Grand Canal* of 1840 (Hyde Collection), the canals disappear in two directions round a dazzling Salute. The four grounded gondolas at an angle in the foreground are overwhelmed by the heavy washes of silvery and golden light, sealing and opening water into sky at key points. It is as though the central church stood in a vast openness instead of in a city. In the *Grand Canal* of 1838 (Metropolitan), the converging center puts the Salute on a par with the Piazza San Marco, and balance is maintained by an added building to the right and an untrue elevation of the Campanile on the left. So balanced, the buildings seem not solid blocks but part of a general airiness, where at the central aperture the blue-green water flows through to an infinite distance of sky beyond. Stokes also connects Turner's effect, interestingly, to "the old-fashioned viewpoint from above . . . the bather's deliberate contemplation from the diving board. We are given the opportunity to linger there, and through our own volition we are thereupon immersed and enveloped by the scene."[35] Wilton's description of Turner's combination of breadth and depth well accords with an "immersive" effect: "Views through arcades, avenues of trees, tunnels of rock, even vortices of dust or storm, create an arrow-like retreat through the picture-space that is often at odds with the calmer perspective of the principal view."[36]

The city and the painter offer so much that they carry us with them, beyond the constructions we may make subsequent to our first, immersive impression. Our elation, our artistic response to imagination or "sublimity," depends on our being overwhelmed immersively, and the constructions we subsequently make are but necessary leverages to sustaining and explaining that end.

Lightness increases and also intensity increases, in late works like *Sun Setting over the Sea* and *Sunrise with Sea Monster*. These works are inundated in paint beyond the latest of Monet. They are all awash with yellow, light rendered as color; but they retain their representational force also. Recognizably akin to Turner's impressions of Venice a decade before, they ground his perceptions in a displaced and concentrated version of the perceptions of Titian; and they ground the perceptions of Ruskin and Stokes as well, in a series that we cannot close but also cannot relativize without losing the ground that has been splendidly gained through saturating it with significations by builders, painters, and also writers.[37]

All the various displacements—Ruskin's mistaken attribution of limits to Turner's childhood, the disappearance of the actual Venice in which Titian lived, the conventions that the architects of Venice followed, the template of sublimity set down upon a landscape that is also a cityscape, the limiting predilections of Turner, the abstracting turn of his painterly practice—all these result not in displacing the viewer, and not in tipping Turner preponderantly just toward mimesis or just toward vision, but rather in evidencing the complexity, and therewith the significative coherence, of the vision in which he is swept up and immersed.

THE DIMENSIONS
OF COLOR

Chapter 3

I

Color is direct in so many ways that it seems to vanish as one looks at it. Color surrounds the viewer, and if he closes his eyes he sees not a blank but more color. Color flows uninterruptedly across the visual field, and yet it attaches itself firmly to objects, permitting their recognition as they draw and break up the light. Colors for the modern person who has long been able to name them come in the thousands.[1] But we know that earlier peoples classified them into a handful of names, sometimes as few as three.[2] In early cultures dark and light tend to be differentiated before color is.

The colors, then, seem to present in a pure, or at least a schematic form, the paradox that they cannot be seen before they are named but cannot be named till after they have been seen. As various modern philosophers have reminded us, color also presents a special form of the paradox between the abstract and the concrete, or the general and the particular.[3] The reds we see dissolve into the concrete, particular objects to which we have learned to attribute the name, which in turn seems contradictorily to take on an abstract and general sense that subclassifies all instances of itself. This happens with the sort of immediacy that can be declared to a color-blind man but not explained.

All the complications of color, even before it is coded, lead back to the fundamental experiences of this directness and immediacy, endowing color with the power to induce in the viewer a feeling of immersion that has emotional effects, again immediate.

Color decorates, seals off, touches base, flows across objects or spots them or differentiates them. Color energetically enlists contradictions and resolves them into harmonies, as Goethe remarks; he forcefully compares to electricity, oxidation, and musical tones, the power of color to appear in manifold polarities and its availability to mixture.[4] Cézanne spoke of color as "the place where our spirit and the universe meet."[5] Color words sublate all these functions into a syntactic order, and color in painting differently abstracts such functions into the displaced and inevitably simplified organization of a demarcated visual segment. Shape-defining and code-referring, color is reassuringly reposeful and also mysterious. It is tempting to follow Apollinaire's generalization of Delaunay and base the effect of painting primarily on color, "artistic sensations uniquely owed to the harmony of uneven lights [*lumières impaires*]."[6] Adrian Stokes, following such a line of discussion, defines color in painting by analogy with sculpture. Using a terminology that might embrace what is implied by Apollinaire's phrase, he distinguishes these harmonies of uneven light between forms that "through the medium of their colors have come to an equal fruition," which he calls "carving," and the "plastic superficiality of vast tonal contrast," or "modelling."[7]

The perception of color and the artistic management of color perceptions, in their relation to the forms to which they are attached and to other colors, are further heavily qualified by the culture-bound codes that they evoke. These codes are not simple. Even the emphatic red, often the first color to emerge in nomenclature, means assertiveness, blood, and in liturgical convention, sacrifice. It takes some ratiocination to subsume these notions under one heading. And they remain culture-bound: the Chinese saw red as indicating joy, perhaps more pronouncedly than we might, and for them white, not black, was the color of mourning.[8] Such specificities as these are two-edged; they are abstract insofar as they relate the perceived color to a concept rather than just to a perception, but they are concrete insofar as they tend to bind the color to a particular object, a ribbon or an issue of blood or a fire engine—or rose, rust, cherry, and flamingo, in Ezra Pound's list derived from Fenollosa's reading of the Chinese ideogram for red.[9] All these intricacies are subjected to the further intricacy that, in visual art at least, the perceptions and the codes are bound together and interact.[10]

As for the codes, the fact that the early Chinese series of red, yellow, blue-green, black, and white coincides with one set of "natural" or "fundamental" primaries in color perception neatly highlights the tendency toward convergence between perception and lexical coding.

Among the Dogon the color coding introduces a dimension of time.[11] First came white, the color of cotton, and then saffron yellow, a dye turning garments the color of earth. Next came blue-black, the color of vestments for the dead. The earliest men, the red ("*banu*"), come somewhere at an early point of this series. And green, worn by women, is associated with the body and ornaments of one stage or apparition of the god Nommo.

As the regular and nearly mat assignment of colors to objects in Egyptian frescoes may indicate, the coding of color seems to have been heavily systematized in that culture. The god Menthu-Ra has a white crown and a green crown.[12] There was an early worship of a black bull (1:26). The colors take on geographical meaning in reference to the "Red Land" and the "Black Land," or the land of the Egyptians and the land of the black people (1:304). Memphis is the City of the White Wall (2:148). "The Book of Unas" refers to a red crown that conveys knowledge and power (1:39), and the "Book of the Pylons" refers to an underworld peopled by "red souls" (1:203). The derivation of Greek conventions from Egyptian ones is unclear, but we cannot distinctly separate such conventions about gods and the afterlife from the Greek persistence at putting red and black on vases that were sometimes connected with funeral practices, changing figure and ground when moving from red-figured vases on a black ground to black-figured vases on a red.[13] But these dominant colors, themselves associable according to Stokes,[14] are more distinctly and boldly isolated in their complementarity than are the Egyptian assignments of color. And at the same time they remain comparably schematic.

The Greek coding is, however, qualified by a strong attention to values. In Homer terms about light and dark predominate over actual color words.[15] Irwin further emphasizes the Greek attention to play of light and movement, and in this connection one could find play of light implied even in words she does not discuss, like *poikilos*, which suggests "light-dappled," or *perknos*, "dark-dappled." And in fact *poikilos* codes with the honorific or even the royal, an unusual semantic function for a word indicating variegated play of light, when more usually simple hues like red, purple, and white—or for the Chinese, yellow—are coded to royalty.

It is arresting to find such a small palette and a relatively light coding of color words in Homer, together with the marked sharpness of vision that his similes especially indicate.[16] The sharpness of vision, the predominance of light and dark, and the relative inattention to color coding (which a long inert conservation of Egyptian codes would allow)

all add up to a way of perceiving space and a powerful means of con-
ceiving its abstract implications, both notable in Greek philosophy from
the pre-Socratics on. It could well be that the lost frescoes of Polyg-
notus, known for their mimetic skill, were most remarkable just for
that, and that the loss of paint for the most part from statues does not
change their signification as much as one might think. Certainly it is
hard to see a difference in coding between the monochrome amethyst,
or jasper, and the variegated agate in Greek gems; the colors of these
stones function almost exclusively as simple ground for the sharply
perceived mimetic delineation of animals, men, vegetation, and the like.
Almost the opposite case is presented by the medieval symbolism of
gems, deeply coded for color, as well as for their origins in Aaron's
breastplate (Exodus 28) as adapted and revised by Revelations 7.[17]

By the time of the New Testament the Romans were already expanding Greek practice in their large palette of color words with fine
shadings. As it happens, they were correspondingly resuming a firmer
and more elaborate coding for colors.[18] E. Wunderlich, going back to
Greek usages as well, finds a wide range of implications coded by the
Romans into red, in association with sunbeams and blood for the
Golden Fleece, with royalty as it shades toward purple in the red-purple
of *porphyrios/purpureus*, with marriage and death and mourning and war,
with beauty and sacrifice. Red is connected to magic in agriculture and
medicine, and it has an apotropaic force against demons.[19] This richening Western tradition paves the way for a richening use of colors in
liturgical practice, and for the personal inventions of theologically in-
ventive writers like Hildegard of Bingen[20] and Dante.[21]

Runge, who theorized about the visual properties of the colors he
used in his painting, held related notions, which perhaps motivated him
to his other theories about the significations of color, possible and
actual:

> As we handle the colors of heaven and earth, the changes of colors through
> affections and perceptions among men, in the operations as they proceed in
> the greatest appearances of nature, and in the harmony—so far as certain
> colors have become symbolic—in the same way do we give to each object
> of a composition, its own color, in harmony with the first deep perception
> and the symbols and the objects therefor . . .
>
> Longing, love and will, that is yellow, red and white (blue?).[22]

And Scriabin was not the last who in his color symphonies took
colors one by one as the full code-complement to successive universes
of perception and thought, so much so that he tried to transcribe them
into music.[23]

2

It is not only the visual properties of color, then, that give it the sort of participatory power well indicated by Luce Irigaray as she confronts Merleau-Ponty's notions of the visible and the invisible: "However, color is linked to the fugitive more than are many other visible objects. But this fleeting thing belongs more to the flesh of the visible—and is difficult to take into the memory—than is the punctuality of the form and of the concept. Red, the color, belongs more to the domain of *participation* than to the solitary emergence of the concept."[24] The possibilities in the deployment of color and colors are so rich that they justify the effusions of Stokes and the rapturous attributions of Ruskin, whose vast claims for color seem pardonable and almost just:

> As colour is the type of love, it resembles it in all its modes of operation; and in practical work of human hands, it sustains changes of worthiness precisely like those of human sexual love. That love when true, faithful, well-fixed, is eminently the sanctifying element of human life: without it, the soul cannot reach its fullest height or holiness. But if shallow, faithless, misdirected, it is also one of the strongest corrupting and degrading elements of life. Between these base and lofty states of love are the loveless states; some cold and horrible, others chaste, childish, or ascetic, bearing to careless thinkers the semblance of purity higher than that of love.[25]

The painter by arranging colors and by isolating them among the shapes and forms of a delimited space both reminds us of all these uses and evokes them for us in a direct state. The direct state, though, by being excerpted from the larger and more various flow of color in our world of living, provides the enlarging comment of purity and exalted understanding upon them. The hues, in all their definition of tone, value, brilliance, and saturation, and in all their contrast, body forth a world, just as some paintings try to do, reposefully highlighting two dimensions in such a way that this simplification of the third dimension throws over it, as well, a mantle of corresponding repose. And in the same act the codes are evoked. Can a Westerner look at green, even in nature, without some sense of the coded meaning of hope? At black without some hint of ideas connected with death?

Inside a medieval cathedral the potentiality of color to suggest the surrounding and significance of the visual field is powerfully evoked, and then usually divided in blocks large enough to make an impression. Rich blocks of a prevailing color, the blue of Chartres or the red of Bourges, provide a tonic uniformity to the strong primary chunks of color in the individual panels, and panels within panels. Sometimes aloft, for part of a wall, the blaze of color is unbroken, and it can create a haze over the glow of a single window, like the purple rose window of Notre Dame. In Sainte Chapelle bright stained glass takes over the whole church, and the division from window to window is scarcely more prominent than the lead separations between panes. These windows simultaneously occupy the vision and put it at rest by reassuring a viewer that he need scrutinize it no more than he would a throng of red robes or a bouquet of purple flowers. Sainte Chapelle suggests that an equivalent for the scale of a large cathedral has been attained by the enrichment of such nearly unbroken organized segments of color.

3

The Venetians have long been admired as colorists,[26] and in the profound practice of Titian the sensory and the significative attributes of color are further fused, etherealized, generalized, and transformed. In his late paintings, as the prevailing yellows darken to brown, Titian acts in harmony with a remark Louise Nevelson makes somewhere: "I have always maintained that black contains all colors." Titian, like Turner long after him, almost subverts the natural allegiance of color and form by nearly decomposing these late forms into shadowy airiness. But unlike Turner, he at the same time contraverts this lofty process by stamping a strong and sometimes puzzling iconography upon the picture.

Light reds wash over the prominently foregrounded couple in the Vienna *Nymph and Shepherd,* and these reds continue off into the flaming twilight of the somewhat devastated landscape that stretches beyond them. The Nymph looks back, just slightly, at the intent, robust Shepherd, who seems to be just finishing the music on his strongly grasped flute so that he may lay it down and couple with her. Her bottom is already bared and her left leg is raised slightly in anticipation as she nearly looks back up at him. The animal skin on which she lies is a luxurious one, but the slight splotch of red on it at a point almost directly below the jointure of her thighs hints at the pathos of the kill that produced it. It hints, too, at an analogy to devastation by lining up with the head of the animal skin the most prominent figure in the landscape—a dark brown, blasted tree, the only one on the horizon, sketchily outlined by streaks of red. The tree under which the Nymph and the Shepherd sit is in full foliage, but of a dark brown. It might well not shade him, and if it does shade her, almost her whole body protrudes forth from its protection. The flesh tones of her body are so light that the red splotches on her feet and her cheek seem pronounced. The Shepherd, by contrast, has almost uniformly ruddy limbs and face, but with no approximation either to a healthy flush or to a robust tan. Sexual excitation and the landscape of turbulent tragedy here are touched into near proximity by the unevenly applied but highly dominant reds. Color as well as imagery isolates these pastoral figures in a universe more natural, grander, and more sinister, than what pastoral would seem to allow.

Yellow is more prominent, red more subdued, and the figures seen at much closer hand, in the Vienna *Tarquin and Lucretia*. The lower half of Tarquin's face is almost invisible, while Lucretia's eyes are almost shut as she is caught in a flailing attempt to ward him off, with one arm gripped by his hand and the other too weak to hold back the thrust. The swirl of color brings their bodies into great clouds of yellows, reds, and browns, against a dark brown background. The color washes them into a single catastrophic universe.

In the Venice Accademia *Pietà* (begun by Titian; completed by Palma), the yellow of the nearly statuesque Moses and the Sibyl of the Hellespont, figures flanking the three who attend the dead Christ, stands midway in value between the yellowish pallor of Christ's body and the golden yellow of the Byzantine half-spherical hollow arch above him.[27] This arch is devoid of the figures usually placed there, as though it is waiting for the further, certain triumphant moments of the Christian story. A putto angel seems to be flying out of this arch, since his right foot laps almost into it, and his body is a healthy flesh yellow just touched with red, picked up in the pale red of the kneeling Saint Peter and the darker red of the Virgin's skirt and veil. Another putto at the bottom of the extreme left raises an urn, his body tones matching those of the one above, whose ruddy torch echoes the red gold of the arch. Gradations of yellow across the canvas are distinct, and yet they are enough alike to match the yellows of the living flesh to those of the arched chapel, and to those of the sculptured lion-faced pedestals on which the flanking figures stand. The sallowness of death and the gold of Resurrection retain their coded significance while merging into the larger "revealed" homogeneity of a picture offering a tonic signature that contains them and places them. Leaning against the lower jaw of the right lion, only half inside the picture frame, is a tiny canvas, on a light yellow ground; it represents dark-clad saints approaching the Virgin of the Assumption, who is seated on a red-tinged cloud, with the body of the dead Christ still across her lap. Here the iconographic set is transposed, along with the colors, but both the colors and the iconographic constituents fuse into one another. Hetzer says of this painting, "The colors fill up the breadth of its surface as an endless vibration."[28]

Yellow is the lightest of the colors, as well as being a primary. Titian expands its lightness by letting its association with light leak toward the lowered intensity and heightened value of brown, and in the other direction toward the lowered value of a dull, pallid near-white. Both these hues, for all their difference, are rather depressive or overbearing in emotion, but the gradation that carries them from one to the other can also move toward the elatedness of an intense yellow or the solemn celebration of a gold. The omnipresent fineness of these differentiations in shading tends to unify the picture into a comprehensiveness that the iconography would seem to forbid. A Pietà is rarely so strong in its suggestions of triumph, and the other works of Palma, who completed this one after Titian's death, do not continue this emotional range for the color. The yellow, here and elsewhere, is allowed to verge on the strongest of the primaries, red. The blazing torch of the putto angel holds a red-gold aloft without touching on any intermediate orange. Nor does the red-gold of the hair, so characteristic that Titian gives his name to the color, take on any distinct orange or carroty tinge.

The colors thus contain the possibility of transfusion into other colors, and the transfusion takes place before our very eyes, with all the charges of signification for each color, and all the connections through the close gamut of colors. As Ruth W. Kennedy has said, if perhaps unintentionally in too negative an emphasis (she is speaking of the Borghese *Venus Blindfolding Cupid*), "No color is what it seems to be. The white robe of Venus is really made of yellow and brown touches with lesser touches of a brickish red."[29] In this vast canvas, though, the shadings of one color into another, the lightenings and the darkenings, are emphatically punctuated by the strong red cloak of the rapt, breast-bared woman who holds the quiver and the red cloak of the more fully clothed woman behind her. In *Sacred and Profane Love,* too, a much-folded large red cloak is draped over one arm, down the nude side, and under the partially nude buttocks of Profane Love, contrasting with the white of her body. The slightly larger puffy red of the large sleeve revealed under the brown-yellowish-white of Sacred Love's dress, a red that Hetzer calls "too weak" (92), sets up another contrast. These stretches of color are almost Bellini-like in their simplicity, but here their function of emphasis contrasts with the shadings elsewhere in the picture, while being enigmatically significant for many senses of red—passion and assertion and royalty and fullness of the moment. The two women marked by red are alike at least in this marking, though very different in the way they are marked. And the reds aid the interpreter to a series that moves this elaborate work in its signification away from the deeper mysteries of Giorgione, even in this most Giorgionesque of Titian's paintings. The distinct hunting and pastoral figures are far smaller than the shepherd and his flock in the *Concert Champêtre,* and they are washed in a brown that shades to near yellowish white, as though to assert the simplicity of their obscured activities and their merely genre-illustrative relevance to the painting.

Its large simplicities of contrastive connection hold in abeyance the possibilities of dialectical combination. Its mysteries are so constructed, through the interaction of figure and color, that they are poised between the possibility of the simple presentation of two suggestive figures in a landscape. The landscape itself is somewhat abstract, and so it is inconceivable as a natural possibility for their presence. It would also blur the sort of allegorical scheme such a presentation might imply.[30]

A continuity of color, dark brownish highlighting to gold, runs along the nearly horizontal line between the four objects handled by these three figures—the flowers held upside down in the clothed figure's right hand, tilted so that the dark leaves are most prominent; the largish bowl loosely held by her left hand; the shallow bowl, standing beside two loose flowers and a small leaf that Cupid might be using if he were not looking down while idly trailing his left arm deep in the water; and the smaller flaming bowl held aloft by the nude figure. These two women are graced by tresses of a Titian reddish gold, and they resemble each other so much they could be sisters, or even variants of each other. Their tresses are equally modest, at the other end of the scale from the abundant hair streaming around and shielding the *Penitent Magdalene* of the Uffizi, a painting that this common iconographic attribute dominates. The flow of color through the whitish yellows and gold-to-brownish reds of the dominant Magdalene keys or contrasts with the echoing darkish red of the upper right sky, the even darker town to the left, and the blue, green, brown, and yellow of the upper right sky.

In *Sacred and Profane Love* the contrast between the schematism of the colors outlining the two women and the low tones of nearly all the other colors makes this distinction a predominant one. The dominance of this contrast blurs nearly into ornament the mysterious horse and the active figures on the right of the sarcophagus, the man beating the buttocks of a prostrate figure on the left center, and the distinct nudes on the far left. These two nudes around a central pole or trunk could even be Adam and Eve in the Garden. They resemble in outline and posture the Adam and Eve of Michelangelo. If so, however, the repose of both the clothed Venus and the nude one would be relieved of reference to the Edenic pair. The brownish greys keep the figures on the sarcophagus subdued, just as the sharp reds, brownish-yellowish whites, and light flesh tones of the Venuses keep them prominent, and centered. They are frontally juxtaposed but as unschematized as the large tree over Cupid's head that provides a dark separation for them while he furnishes a light. Indeed his own activity is so random and childlike, so simple in iconographic reference, that it, too, gives the cue for refraining from strong allegorical structures. He is almost at the dead center of the picture; the dead center, in fact, is occupied by a dark vacancy, the darkness of background foliage, with Cupid's open bowl breaking that vertical line.

So the possibility of allegory easily coexists with a holding back before its schematization, and color predominates to cue this intermediate realm of assuredness, in which the color itself is held, so to speak, midway between its perceptual and its significant roles, coming into fullness by the unallegorical harmony of their fusion. The same process, combining differently, may be seen in the *Venus of Urbino,* where the classically reclining Venus Pudica almost fully occupies the whole horizontal center of the picture. The reddish brown highlights of her flesh tones, continuing out to the Titian red-gold of her hair and the brownish white of her pillows and large rumpled sheet, are picked up in the blouse of the attendant woman of the background, and in the dress, hair, and even shoe heels of the little girl kneeling into the *grotteschi-*ornamented cassone. The floor and lower molding of the area between Venus and these background figures continue her colors in a browner tone. Her colors are most wholly picked up in a single figure, the reddish-brown-spotted white spaniel curled asleep or nearly asleep at her feet. This congruence of color for a pet that just adds a touch of genre to the picture gives us the cue not to try to lock the three women into an order. One cannot detach from the randomness of a genre episode the girl deep in the cassone, perhaps fishing out more of the draperies for the maid, who seems to be rolling up a right sleeve to hold more of them. Vertically, the whole upper half behind Venus is covered by a vast gold-bordered green drapery, except for a pillar and a part of the window that spreads across the middle of the picture. The window is shared by the little girl and the maid, behind whom are red, white, and brownish black drapes not too different from those slung over the maid's left shoulder. Aside from the broad white areas, the most prominent color rhyme is the repetition of red from the flowered bolster on which Venus's pillows lie, the red flowers falling on it out of the bunch lightly clasped in her right hand, and the large red dress of the maid. The failure of these reds to enter any other order, and their contrast in distinctness with the solid green of the drape behind her, again holds these figures short of schematized significance while at the same time not wholly releasing us into a mere genre scene. The central figure looking out aslant, with eyes almost the green of the drapes behind her, must be Venus, for whom in this context the modest left hand of the traditional Venus Pudica itself seems to be moving toward genre. The organization of color here shades Venus over into the ordinariness it dominates and heightens.

As Panofsky says, "Titian's space constitutes itself by a sequential arrangement of colored shapes rather than by means of geometrical construction. He builds it from objects instead of distributing objects *within* it."[31] Yet Titian also distributes objects within his paintings. His objects are endowed with a proportionateness and a spaciousness by the interaction between their emphasized demarcation and their coloration as it suffuses through the rest of the canvas. In Theodor Hetzer's words, "Color is not a means for Titian but the primal ground of painting."[32]

This powerful fluidity in making the significations in colors converge is accomplished from the early work on without much recourse to a main means of the Renaissance painter, to chiaroscuro, as Robert Longhi notes.[33] In *Portrait of a Musician* (Spada), the simpler whites are made to serve a disharmony, between the white collar and puffed shirt at the belt that is picked up in the crumpling folds of the Musician's music sheet. On the other hand, the shadings from red to gold are shown as falling from the heavens themselves onto the central figure of his *Danae* (Naples). They spread through the canvas to the body of the shying Cupid, whose foot is lost on a solider red and gold coverlet, folded on a flatter brown blanket that contrasts one end of this range with the other by being laid atop the sheet that is whiter than Danae's body or anything in the sky between the lighter brown pillars. Behind her is a lighter red curtain, which is set off by a darker brown drape. The showering pieces of gold themselves emerge from a gold-brown cloud. The Prado *Danae* is more somber, sharper in contrast, and wider in its range of reference, since below Danae is curled a very small brown dog, while straining forward in the place where Cupid stands in the other picture is a wearied, almost masculine-faced, bare-shouldered maid, whose white cap and loose shirt pick up some of the blue of the sky; she holds up an apron of the same brown as her skirt, to catch the brighter pieces of gold. These colors at once celebrate and qualify the felicity of Danae.

Richer browns run the whole length of the Berlin *Venus with Organist, Cupid, and Dog*. This dog, a Maltese, is the whitest object in the picture, except for the pillow of Venus. The brown runs from the garments, hair, and skin of the organist, across to the duskier reds of Venus's hair, Cupid's hair, and his wings. This wide loop of color is balanced by a dark, almost brown-tinged, gold-bordered purple robe on which Venus reclines, a purple slightly contrasted to the lighter red of the drapes above her at the extreme right, and at the extreme left to the still lighter red of his sleeve, his girdle, and his scabbard. The shining silver-metallic organ, a not quite symmetrical pyramid of ten separate pipes, is echoed nowhere in the painting, and the Musician strains fixedly away from them, his hands off the keys. Nor is there any match for the black vents in a punctuated horizontal line across the pipes, splendid and self-subsistent and silent in discordant homage to the large brown-nippled body, with its brown pubis visible through the nearly sheer stuff painted across it. A brown tone qualifies even the lips of Venus.

Less melancholy, though more menacing, is the Borghese *Venus Blindfolding Cupid*. In this work the strong reds carry across the picture and up into the sky, as well as more lightly onto the cheeks of the three women: the somewhat austere red-lipped Venus, the archer with one bared breast who looks up transfixed in passion while clasping her quiver, and behind her the observant, pensive, nearly running figure clasping her bow forward, her hair done up like Venus's, though Venus wears a crown. The hair of the rapt gazer flows in loose curls to her shoulders, but all three women have hair of the Titian red-gold, while the hair of the two Cupids is brown. In the National Gallery painting of the same subject, there are only two women, and from the upraised arm of the serving woman a reddish yellow is smudged through the blue sky almost to the nearly matching hair of Venus. Another reddish yellow smudge below her arm to the ground unnaturally and pervasively extends the shadows and clouds of color into areas where they would not be perceived.

Strength is suggested, and gloom thereby qualified, in the coloration of late mythological works like *Venus and Adonis, Diana and Actaeon,* and *Diana and Callisto,* even though iconographically they share a negative image of the hunt.[34] In the Munich *Crowning of Thorns* a turbulence of color sustains our perception that for all the sadness of humiliation of this scene a nearly athletic Christ, albeit with closed eyes, seems to be dominating the staves, whose uniform color and thinness seem to be breaking in vain across the color-playing health of his powerful body. He is somewhat flushed but less ruddy by far than the arms and faces of the stave-wielding pair over him, while the face of the foreground figure looking back to beckon the others is pallid by contrast, except for the slight flush at the edge of his cheeks. A candelabrum of open, red-gold blazing lights stands above the scene at the right, completing a line that runs diagonally from Christ's extended foot, its colors as well as its presence calmly and, as one may say, unreachably functioning as an icon of worship as well as an aid to torment.

4

Released largely from the iconological extensions and given plots to which Titian applies his polyphony of color is a Turner who broaches still another yellow-dominated polyphony, achieving with his yellows a quotient of light that, according to Ruskin, far surpasses that of any other painter. Turner's yellows suffuse and flood a single chosen landscape or city. Claudette Columbus finds an "extra-fused" enigmatic color in Turner, especially in his late work.[35] In Turner's *Light and Colour (Goethe's Theory)—The Morning after the Deluge—Moses Writing the Book of Genesis* (1843), a swirling yellow sun engulfs the whole picture, and the comprehensively iconic subject implicitly assigns a special role to this dominant color among the others in the work. And here the yellow is also mysterious. Columbus says that *The Morning After* is "painted in primary colors, notably red and yellow . . . yet . . . is as negative in its way as the bluish *Evening of the Deluge* . . . And so *The Morning After* upsets general conventional color attributions and questions Goethe's in particular." And more particularly of color that Turner attached to Venice:

> In *The Sun of Venice* (1843), color comes as close as possible to verbalizing the rhetorical figures implicit in it. Traditionally and psychologically, yellows and golds represent life's brighter aspects. But in this painting, the yellows and golds of Apollo offer antithetical perceptual adventures in color interpretation. The sun-yellowed sky, the sun-gilded water, the flying pennants, the flying boat laden with potential revellers seem unequivocal expressions of sunny exhilaration. Yet a counter sign is imprinted on the sail: a mimic sun, a mimic Venetian sky-and-water line, and the boat's name, Sol di Venezia (the "z" and "a" unclear), a mirror image. The painting exhibits dichotomous qualities in the revealing and/or deceptive properties of yellow, in addition to what Borges terms the "perishability" of colors, the sense that the scene is imperilled by an inevitable change of light, eclipse in the air. Nature seems, temporarily, to be saying one thing—whether truly or falsely is open to question, as is the question whether the terms "true" and "false" have relevance in a world of appearances—and the sails seem to be saying the obverse . . .

"*From the Giudecca Looking East* [is] set ambiguously between tenuous blue and blue as *The Sun of Venice* between deceptive yellow and yellow." Yet the yellows of *Light and Colour (Goethe's Theory)* induce not a negative, really, but a positive of such intense immersion that the eye falters before it. The theory of color is to exceed color, as the comprehensive conflations and disjunctions of this expansive title indicate. A millennial writer and an epochal moment are first lost and then found in an effulgence that is also an engulfing blaze, a moment of a day so archetypal that its colors run all together in one blinding yellow. Color is

caught, and also spreads beyond, a large sunlike circle, inside which can
be discerned, presumably, the Ararat of the Flood, since the quotation
from his long poem that Turner appends to this painting names and
dwells on Ararat. Yet the mountains so dominant in his Alpine paintings, dwarfing human settlements in the Grisons or Hannibal's entire
army, are themselves here dwarfed before the color that overwhelms
them, the loose geometric figures that contain them, and not biblical
writing but the evoked image of biblical writing—itself, in turn, appended by the title to a theory of color.

The interiors of Turner's watercolors of Petworth draw on and transpose sometimes strange symbolisms of color. Yet in his open-air oils,
especially after his last exposure to Venice, the color yellow does heavier
and heavier duty for all perception. And it does not digress into such
symbolisms as the watercolors show, or as are employed by Titian, van
Gogh, and Matisse (among others). Yellow, representing the light to
which it stands closest on the spectrum, gathers into itself a fullness of
chromatic possibility that is the chromatic dimension of immersion.
Thereby color and space become versions of each other. Turner in his
elaborate composite title combines the notion of color with the sort of
religious subject matter that was taken for granted by Titian. And landscape swallows the religious scene in this *Light and Colour (Goethe's
Theory)—The Morning after the Deluge—Moses Writing the Book of Genesis*. The remarkable play of signification across the four elements in
this title, a sort of condensed equivalent for the long passages from
his own poems and others that Turner attached to his paintings, comes
to a single confluence of dazzling visuality, represented by "light" and
"colour" in the title. John Gage shows that Turner attended more to
the visual and the pedagogic properties of Goethe's *Farbenlehre*, sup-
plementing them by further attention to light but reducing them by an
inattention to the symbolic properties of color that he did enlist in
watercolors.[36] In his marginal notes on Goethe, Turner clearly attends
to the representational aspects of color, which his *Light and Colour*
emphasizes, and which the reference to Goethe seems further to frame.
At the same time the rest of the title applies the color, and the significations in it, to a converging pair of events: the morning after the
Flood, when there would have been water everywhere, and Moses'
writing at the moment when he is well embarked on an earlier part of
the Book of Genesis and should be thought of as imagining visually
what the world would look like surrounded by water and at the same
time inundated with sunlight.[37] What we are shown in the painting has
to be Moses' vision of what Noah would see, a convergence that parallels
the convergence of Turner's presentation of color and his reference to
Goethe's theory. In such works the color calls forth predominantly

visual complexities to fuse, rather than to signify, the complexities of the title.

Ruskin calls color a "beautiful auxiliary" to Titian's chiaroscuro and declares that "he paints in color, but he thinks in light and shade."[38] The colors thus contain the possibility of transfusion into other colors, and the transfusion is made to take place before our very eyes, with all the charges of signification for each color, and all the connections through the closely graduated gamut of colors. What Stokes says of the Venetians, with special reference to Titian, also applies preeminently to Turner: "It is as if the range of illumination were borrowed for the independent otherness of colour, even though it be colour reflected from one object on to another, characteristic of a rich Mediterranean light, that is largely exploited for this end."[39] One could apply to these late works of Turner Hetzer's remark about Titian: "Color is not a means . . . but the primal ground of painting."[40]

5

Schizophrenia, or some other diagnosis, which is sometimes associated with van Gogh's predilection for or indeed dominance by yellow, does not explain that predilection or dominance any more than the old allegation of El Greco's astigmatism would explain his perspective. Nor does schizophrenia by itself, whatever the correlation, explain the attention van Gogh gave to color, an attention paralleled by the theories of his friend Gauguin, in whose work the yellows function differently and less dominantly.[41] Even when stressing the reds and greens of the late *Night Café* (frontispiece), van Gogh brings in the yellows that cover a larger space in that work than the reds and the greens taken together:

> I have tried to express the terrible passions of humanity by means of red and green.
> The room is blood red and dark yellow with a green billiard table in the middle; there are four citron-yellow lamps with a glow of orange and green. Everywhere there is a clash and contrast of the most disparate reds and greens, in the figure of little sleeping hooligans, in the empty, dreary room, in violet and blue. The blood-red and the yellow-green of the billiard table, for instance, contrast with the soft tender Louis XV green of the counter, on which there is a pink nosegay. The white coat of the landlord, awake in a corner of that furnace, turns citron-yellow or pale luminous green.[42]

And there are still other yellows, not derivable from the light source in this painting: the hats of two or three patrons, the pool cue and two of the balls, the face of the clock, the bouquet at the center of the bottles on the yellow-green cabinet, the chairs, the kitchen revealed beyond, two picture frames and the blank face of one picture, the glasses—too much to account for by natural coordinates of perception, or by any system of signification other than some mysterious overall endowment of keyed unity to the scene.

"Light so that the whole becomes blonde," van Gogh says of another picture (110). And when speaking of "kindred colors" he includes "a citron yellow against a chamois yellow" (252). "When I conceive it as a symphony in yellow," he says of an autumn landscape, "what does it matter if the fundamental color of yellow is the same as that of the leaves or not?" (254). Here, perhaps echoing Gauguin's principle of color free from assignment to objects, van Gogh is announcing a significative, unifying force in his colors so strong as to dominate individual objects in the painting. In a sense he chose the color for his very lodging at Arles: "I have rented a house, painted yellow outside, whitewashed within, in the full sun" (290).

Since the religiosity of van Gogh strained to identify his activity with the devotion of the peasant, the shoes he painted at least five times, though of a predominant brown, can be associated with yellow by the matches of shading, and those strong earth colors matter more than the ownership of the shoes, whether attributed to Heidegger's peasant or to Meyer Schapiro's artist. Nor will semimetaphysicalized psychoanalysis of the openings and laces of the shoes, with Derrida, detach their fundamental stoutness of shape and color from the central emphasis we receive in looking at them; they are poles apart in signification from the shoes of Magritte.[43] Moreover, the shoes in the Meyer Collection show much subdued, dull yellow in the background. And on the ones that Heidegger wrote about, the *Boots* (Baltimore) of 1887, there are touches of greenish yellow in the left background, as well as across the light brown sole of one boot and the upper of the other, accentuated by being shown on a blue field. Thus in the browns, and in the touches of yellow, the key signature of that prevailing color is to be found in most if not all of the five separate paintings of shoes. The touches of yellow suggest not only the smearing of earth but the commonality of the sun, and the detachment of the shoes from their owner frames them as monuments of wear rather than as fetishes of any kind. They announce their robust utility, as Heidegger argues, and the range of colors, yellow to brown, deepens the stolidity of that utility, in a large realm of perception that is comprehensive enough easily to admit the celestial suggestion of the blue field of the Baltimore *Boots*. Under the aegis of a yellow that in these paintings is varied, considerably shaded, and only intermittently present, van Gogh pulls earth, sky, and sun into an arbitrary unification, persistent while understated.

While van Gogh's yellow always retains a prevailingly perceptual base, and is therefore never wholly iconic, as is the gold sky of Giotto; at the same time its range of application is too wide, its gradient too restricted by comparison with Titian's, to admit for our reading one area as "sallow," another as "splendid flesh," still another as "gold," with corresponding significations. Yet still less will this overall yellow allow our reading in it the simple affirmation and celebration of a Rubens. Even the flowers in van Gogh's late *Sunflowers* (1888, National Gallery, London) are too dense, too shaded into brown in their wide, dominant pistils, merely to affirm the sun. While they refer both metaphorically and metonymically to the sun, and while they are shown against a soft yellow background that encloses them in an equivalent for subdued sunlight, in fact all these flowers are browner in color than they are usually seen, as brown as the base on which sits the jug that holds them. They are shown by proximate contrast to be a darker brown than the brown of the upper half of the jug. Moreover seven of these flowers have wholly lost their petals; their denuded brown, not to be dissociated from an assimilated somberness of mood as of color, surrounds a core of brownish green. These sunflowers are the most prominent, and of the others only one has nearly retained its petals. The foreshortened center of that one is painted in a brown so dark that it is nearly black. And the petals themselves are a browner yellow than the plain brown-tinged yellow of the background against which they stand.

In such paintings the dominance of yellow, taken together with the compound coding of the color, creates an effect of intensity. Here the visual world is pressed, and pressed over a whole canvas, to reveal its approach to hypostatization, an approach in which exaltation and groaning effort seem to be merged, through the compacting whose signature is the yellow, at home and abroad, indoors and out.

In *The Road Menders* strong swirls of yellow extend up between and beyond the plane trees. The broad, deep roadbed that runs the entire length of the picture sets a rough yellow base for the upended whitish blocks that are to be laid into it. In *Road with Cypresses,* the triangle of a yellow wheat field is rendered in long, nearly vertical brush strokes of yellow, merging into green, brown, and black. The nearly horizontal field is bisected by a single very large cypress, whose swirls of green are broken by punctuations of yellow swirl, as is the road on which two peasants, and a carriage some distance behind them, are moving toward the viewer. The very small cypresses in the background still retain touches of yellow. There are touches of yellow in the blue of the sky, and at the top the haloed sickle of what has to be a moon, though its orange-rimmed yellow is so bright, as is the whole canvas, that one takes it for effectually a sun. In this key, the whole painting approaches the iconography of an apocalypse where night is as day. The swirls of the lines substantiate, and elevate, the omnipresence of the color, though no single object or area in the painting is mainly yellow; even the wheat fields are too brown for that.

In van Gogh's last painting, *Crows over a Wheat Field*, many have been tempted to speak of the anguish of the painter on the brink of suicide, and if his effort here is indeed more "intense" than in other works, there is still control and organization, as Meyer Schapiro points out.[44] If all three fundamental primaries are present, in the reddish brown of the road, the blue of the sky, and the yellow of the field, all merge into secondary colors, the yellow into brown and swatches of nearly pure green, the red into a near-brown, the blue into black at the very top and into whirls of nearly white blue-green in proximity to the wheat field (Schapiro reads these whitish blue-green swirls a shade overspecifically as clouds). The black of the crows, like a concentration of the painting, is so schematized and so simple in execution—bent wings only—that it also seems an intrusion on the painting, except that reading from top to bottom these crows seem to have broken off from the near-black of the sky. And while the roads give the clue to vanishing perspective, the crows seem to escape such coordinates, so much so that it is hard, if not impossible, to tell whether they are flying away from or toward the viewer. In any case the field's yellow dominates the painting. That is what the black crows punctuate. The yellow is of an expanse larger than the sky, and of a brightness that seems to derive from some imputed interior light; since, given the darkness of the sky, there is no source to produce such a golden dazzle. Indeed, by a kind of inversion, the bright yellow of the field, intensifying as it approaches the dark sky, seems to have taken over the power of the sun that should be in the sky but is not.

In *The Enclosed Field* (1889), an even larger field carries dashes of green to qualify its yellows. A further contrasting color is a red that becomes purple to line the stone wall of a farm, purple in the hills beyond. But here the whole sky, what can be seen of it, is a yellow so sunny that the sun itself is only a yellow-brown outline, unnaturally large, at its center. In *The Factory Yard* (Barnes Foundation), a road that narrows toward the distance is strewn with yellow "sand," in streaks on both sides that are broader than the central blue-red.

Van Gogh not only inhabited a yellow house; he painted *The Yellow House*. The title is ambiguous: does it point merely at visual perception, or is it meant also to be significative? As in all these works, the restrictedness of the color and its firm link to visual possibility or actuality expand the range of the signification; and at the same time they centralize the signification, so much that one cannot inventory a lexicon of separate meanings for it. *The Sower* (1888) has yellow wheat, yellow sky, and a yellow sun, coordinating the earthly agricultural cycle with a primitive sense of the spiritual, and yet abstracting such coordination into an intensity for which painting is only an instrumental approach. "The *laws* of the colors are unutterably beautiful, just because they are *not accidental*," van Gogh says (218; italics van Gogh's). *Haystacks in Provence* (1888) assimilates a natural subject for this display of yellow, as does *Cornfield with Mower in the Sun* (1889), which is allowed to be nearly all yellow. "Their faces a magnificent yellow," he declares (285)— of the patrons crowding a brothel! He singles out the yellow of Vermeer (306), almost as Proust was later to do. And he strikingly emphasizes, somewhat against critical expectation, the yellow of Rembrandt, speaking of a "Rembrandt gold" (308).

In *Starry Night* (1889), stars the size of suns, flecking houses and hills and trees with yellow, stream in yellow swirls that bring sky and hills alike to an almost daylit blue. A yellow too bright for the single lantern, far outshining the spaced stars decking the blue of the sky, covers the entire upper wall and slanted open roof of *Pavement Cafe at Night* (1888). In *Vincent's Bedroom*, the heap of books is yellow, as is the bed itself. *Self-Portrait with Straw Hat* tops him with the yellow that is always pronounced in his portraits of himself, and of others. The *Peasant Girl* of 1890 has a broad-brimmed yellow hat and a wide yellow skirt, against a yellow-green ground. In *Madame Roulin and Her Baby* (Philadelphia Museum) the figures are shown against a yellow background, and yellow highlights stretch across their green robes. In the Metropolitan's version the background is a strong orange gold. *The Loom* (1884) is brown, against a broad yellow background, with a yellow-white fabric in the foreground. The technique of this earlier work is more subdued, but the yellow already has the defining function of the late works. *Still Life with Oranges and Lemons* (1889) shows the prevailingly yellow fruit—we must look twice to distinguish oranges from lemons—in a straw basket on a yellow ground. All the fruit is yellow in *Still Life with Lemons, Pears and Grapes*. In *Still Life with Flask, Lemons and Oranges* (1889), the table and the fruit are yellow, the background yellow-green. And there is much yellow in *Still Life with Plant, Tobacco, and Pipe*.

With all this it is no wonder that in van Gogh's two late imitations of Delacroix, the *Pietà* (1889) and *The Good Samaritan* (1890), yellow runs across and unifies the picture in a simplification, but also an intensification, of the work of a painter who himself theorized about the possible effects and uses of color.[45]

6

In his own way Cézanne expressed an interest in the free play
of color that his contemporaries van Gogh and Gauguin exemplified:

> I think of nothing when I paint. I take my pains, I rejoice in transporting
> them the way I see them onto my canvas. They arrange themselves in their
> little pleasure the way they want. The man [is] absent but entire in the
> landscape. The big Buddhist machine, nirvana, consolation without passion,
> without anecdote, colors! colors!

> Je ne pense à rien quand je peins. Je vois des couleurs. Je peine, je jouis de
> les transporter telles que je les vois sur ma toile. Elles s'arrangent au petit
> bonheur, comme elles veulent . . . L'homme absent mais tout entier dans le
> paysage. La grande machine boudhiste, le nirvàna, la consolation sans pas-
> sion, sans anecdotes, les couleurs![46]

In this, of course, Gauguin was looking backward as well as forward.
Early cultures abound in examples of the nonmimetic, iconic use of
color. And in Gauguin's *D'où venons-nous? que sommes-nous? où allons-
nous?*, there is one patch of yellow at the top left and another at the
top right; these are so unattached as to be merely iconic. What they
stand for, indeed, may owe something to the intensity of van Gogh's
yellow, since the painting refers to a natural cycle of human life at once
simple, inclusive of religion (the idol in the painting), and mysterious.
Picasso may be said to follow essentially van Gogh's usage in the prevailing colors of his "Blue" and "Rose" periods.

Matisse, of course, goes much farther. And the modern abstractionist
who follows or parallels the theories of Kandinsky, Delaunay, and Klee
goes further still, making his spatial art rigorously atemporal and self-
referentially iconic just because it eschews the object-coded associations
of iconicity. At the same time modern abstract painting looks very far
backward to decoration as it looks very far forward, or at least with a
clear horizon oriented to the future because not visually rooted in present shapes. "Color is an ideal dimension," says Apollinaire, ". . . It no
longer depends on the three known dimensions; it creates them."[47] The
rapture over color, as it goes beyond mere sublimation, is well described
in one of Rilke's many effusions about color in Cézanne:

> my memory of the great interdependence of color of 'The Woman in the
> Red Armchair' is as little repeatable as a number of very many figures. And
> so I have stamped her in me, figure for figure. In my feeling the consciousness
> of her accessibility has reached an elevation that I still feel in sleep; my blood
> describes her in me, but speaking goes somewhere past outside and cannot
> be called in . . . Before an earth-green wall, on which a cobalt blue pattern
> rarely repeats . . .[48]

Klee theorizes a great deal about color; in *Land of Lemons* (1929,
Phillips Collection), there are largish patches of yellow distributed

throughout the picture, but no lemon trees and no lemons. The only lemon shapes are assigned colors other than yellow. The title points to a color whose presence and whose absence are both thereby mocked, and Klee here uses color to follow his frequent practice of energizing both the significative and the perceptual aspects of his painting. Kandinsky, who attributes spiritual dimensions to color as Klee does, plays as Klee does with their combinations, and even with their interaction against names. In *Two Green Dots* (1935) one of the dots is actually violet because it is covered by a rectangle of another color, thus using, and transcending, the abstract effects of Albers, who in his theoretical work leans heavily on the perceptual manipulation of color.[49] Hard-edge painting and "color field" painting play back and forth in their own way between the perceptual and the significative. Mondrian thought of his work as extensible in both a natural and a spiritual direction beyond what the casual observer might think. The "op" artist, if not a mere trickster, forces the observer to be less than casual, and also depends on all this prior abstraction for colors. To abstract color still extrapolates it into the prior signification which is inescapable for colors when they are used in an artistic act communicated from one person to another, and especially when they are detached from objects. The "op" artist is in his essence also a "conceptual" artist.

One could go back to slightly before van Gogh, however—if not to such overall brownish reds as those of Pompeian wall painting—for a color that suggests significative summary while holding short of offering it. Dark brownish yellow washes over many of the works of Albert Pinkham Ryder, as in *Siegfried and the Rhine Maiden*. Yellow has a pointed presence in Vermeer, as Proust declared for even a tiny patch on a wall. Yet the ermine lining of the splendid yellow-gold gown worn by the writer in *A Lady Writing* points the color further toward an explicit celebration of the glory of sunlight. That almost royal glory is rooted in the quotidian, and in the captured moment of shifting light, with the lay of yellow-tinted light precisely indicated from its invisible source, as with the *petit pan de mur* in the *View of Delft*.

The blacks of Kline absolutize both the absence and the presence of color. Absence and presence are signaled since both the black as figure and the white as ground may indicate absence or presence or both taken together. Pollock's *The Blue Unconscious* (1946) is predominantly yellow, with here and there faint traces of blue among its iconically suggestive forms. The title, like the *Green Dots* of Kandinsky, both names the unconscious and declares it to be omnipresent while concealed, since the largest areas of this painting are not blue but its complement yellow. *Blue Poles* has more blue than just the poles. And *Yellow Islands* (1952) has sprinkles of blue as well as blobs and smears of yellow.

The yellow areas in this painting are uniformly associated with smaller lines of red, completing the triangle of the fundamental primaries; the "yellow islands" are thus singled out, at once arbitrarily and imperiously, to swirl in a sea of red and blue; they too are primary colors, but they are not singled out for the special significance the title assigns to yellow.

A letter of the alphabet has an arbitrary signification. It designates an arbitrary relationship to a single (complex) sound, combined in a series that is globally meaningful if all sounds fit together to correspond to an entry in the lexicon of the given language. In English "glut" is meaningful, and so is "glum." "Glet" and "glit" and "glot," "glem" and "gloim" are not. The letter of a word used as a signifier is even in value; no one letter is more important than another, and no one letter can take up appreciably more space than another. Color, by comparison is not arbitrary in this way. Red is perceptually red anywhere on earth, however many puzzles may inhere in the individual's identification of a particular red. Nor is color, consequently, just a signifier; it is also a direct perception, once the eye has constructively received it. But one color can be made more important than another, and the significances of colors are consequently uneven. The green on a stretch of grass means less than the coded green on the robe of a saint, the ruddy yellow of the Magdalene's hair more than a ruddy yellow rim on a lamp. The letter "g," however, within a given language, always has the same value; it designates a sound to be formed.

The painter manipulates his colors by tone and intensity of hue and value, warm against cold, toned against pure, dark against light, causing interactions among them within the sphere of perceptual color. But he also, and concurrently, manipulates the special effects of their directness on the one hand and their coded unevenness on the other, restoring in his particular way to the colors on a given canvas a special balance that the imbalance between the direct and the uneven both subverts and enriches. The composer has some sort of scale, an arbitrary prior organization of sounds. The notes on it are discrete from one another. The shading of color in a painting need not be discrete, as in the demarcation of reds in *Sacred and Profane Love*. It may also be continuous, as in the flow of reds and yellows across *The Repentant Magdalene*. The painter, so to speak, chooses his "scale" with each work; we recognize the painter partly by his palette. He also chooses his particular adherences to the continuous and the discrete in the application of paint.[50] In order to restore such balance to the area of which he is painting, the painter must do far more than follow principles of color harmony. The "diction" of individually coded colors must enter the "syntax" of his statement. At the deep level of colored utterance, and overlooking other mimetic structures, representationality is only a surface feature, and Pollock may resemble Rembrandt, Kline, Sassetta, at the deep level of colored utterance, where at the same time, in spite of stylistic resemblances, Titian is utterly different from Giovanni Bellini or Giorgione, van Gogh from Gauguin. It is color, perhaps above all, that gives the sense of their identity and harmonizes their significations.

THE WILDERNESS
OF MIRRORS

Chapter 4

I

Mirror is a form of color, since a mirror takes on the colors it reflects. Or else, since it is colorless itself, it also uncannily catches a form of the absence of color. Like a painting, in whatever shape it may have, a mirror frames off a colored segment of the world and merely but uncannily doubles it by giving it back to a viewer.[1] Leonardo in his notebooks singles out mirrors for special attention and compares the painting to a mirror. All dark, the mirror gives back darkness; all light, it flashes; it can burn, in the trick the child learns to play. It can also be made to direct a flashing beam of light into the eye of a perhaps unwary bystander. Burning glasses were an early technological discovery, the mirrors of Diocles. In legend they are an aid to seeing, as Perseus saw Medusa obliquely in a shield. And in science they are an aid to seeing also, notably in the large ground mirrors of modern astronomical observation.

The notion that figures could be projected on a flat surface like the wall of a cave or a palace or a temple, and the world thereby doubled so as effectually to be interpreted, is itself, without reference to techniques of representation, a discovery of enormous power. This discovery was made, independently it would seem, by paleolithic artists, by the Egyptians, and by the Chinese. To do this with a mobile polished or backed instrument, so as to mime the effect that even dogs notice in standing water, is a still more advanced discovery, and one that has been adapted deeply and variously in human cultures.

The mirror draws colors into itself, but it is uncannily itself without an initial coding. The completed painting is a mirror too, since it gives back the world and arrests the viewer into a social set (the function of painting in that society), and perhaps also into contemplation. In a painting, though, the mirrorlike image is already fixed; it doubles the world, but not the face of the viewer, except by the implication that a doubled object *means* only what the "face" of the viewer can bring to it while standing in the absence of what the doubling frame, the mirror, can usually give him, a direct representation of his own face. The window, by contrast, gives on part of the wide world beyond, or stains some of it out in the stained glass window, or curtains off much of what a private world within has organized, if the window is seen from inside. Two-way mirrors are a trick, but two-way windows are normal, and they must be specially curtained and angled if they are not to permit an excessive intrusion on privacy. Unlike the mirror, the window does not seem to be a surface or to allow for such radical changes of perspective.[2]

Mirrors and windows entered Western painting early in the Renaissance and at about the same time. Both were quickly assigned the generic functions we may derive from their optical attributes. The window tends to open on a world beyond the frame of the organized scene foregrounded in the painting, suggesting a real order larger than that of the small scene before us, but an order congruent with the smaller scene; the window is itself a sort of frame within the frame of the painting. Art organizes life; and so it can be taken to organize the larger life beyond the painting, shown in some expanse like the mountains, valleys, and distant towns that are frequently the scenes shown through windows in Renaissance paintings. Larger, though, through art, is contained in smaller: the window in the painting through which the expansive scene is represented, constitutes, in fact, only a segment of the painting. All these functions differ from those of the stained glass window, which proportionally segments the world into separate ordered scenes while it shuts out other shapes and admits light. In addition, the stained glass window coordinates and spatializes, often, the temporal order of a narrative.

The mirror in Renaissance painting would in principle function as a failed window, aesthetic in its significations since it would refer us back to the painting. In practice the self-referentiality of the mirror tends to be assumed within the painting, as early as van Eyck; and it tends to be angled toward still other meanings. Here Parmigianino's *Self-Portrait in a Convex Mirror* is a salient but moderately simple example. Even without a mirror, Rogier van der Weyden's *Saint Luke Painting the Virgin* anthologizes such effects. The saint works at a painting he has barely started—almost as blank as an unreflecting mirror—while Virgin and Child pose for him. Between subject and painter a large semi-Gothic porch-embrasure gives on and segments the distant town, itself segmented by a river and joined by a bridge. Below a stained glass medallion window, two pillars trifurcate the large embrasure and frame the winding river, at which a man and a woman—she to his left as the Virgin is to Saint Luke's—look out, their backs to us. In a partially blocked, further narrow embrasure, a tall window is vertically trifurcated. Its top is of stained glass, its center open on a little more of the town, and its lower third is paned in lozenges of translucent glass. On a tilted lectern below the window is painted part of a book, which looks as though it is a Bible.

As for mirrors outside of paintings, a profound and compendious analysis of functions in a culture would be required to ascertain why a given culture assigns importance to certain objects that we would call aesthetic objects, as the Etruscans did to mirrors, or the Chinese. But the early Irish chose the large brooch, of which the Tara brooch is a signal example; the Ashanti chose gold weights; and we have ourselves for centuries given much attention to an easel painting whose importance is paralleled by an attention to the mirrors that in the thirteenth century began to undergo large production in Venice.

Mirrors, in any case, appeared fairly early and were accorded the importance of religious usages, as the Persians incorporated them into New Year festivals. The Indians used them to decorate objects in religious processions. Mirrors had cosmetic purposes in the Egyptian Middle Kingdom, and they are traceable in Egypt as far back as the third millennium B.C. They appeared in Greece as far back as Mycenaean times. Mirrors were used in a Dionysiac and Orphic context, for divination, magic, and prophecy, from the sixth century B.C. on.[3] Bronze mirrors with human figures as handles are found in the Harappa culture of prehistoric India at the end of the third millennium.[4] Among the Huichol the mirror was the equivalent of the sacred lake used for divination, a use many cultures have made for reflections in water, as Frazer remarks.[5] The Mayans had a Smoking Mirror God who is represented in the sculptures of Palenque. The name of the Mexican god Tezcatlipoka means "shining mirror." Mirrors were important in later Dionysiac rituals, and they were used in Tantra initiations.[6] Initiates in Tibet reflect a sacred sentence in a mirror for twenty-nine days running to purify it.[7] The Japanese used mirrors for divination and venerated them in Shinto shrines. They were part of ancient imperial regalia. In the Indian Chandogya Upanishad (1, 6–7) the soul (*purusha*) mirrors itself, as God himself mirrors himself in the *zimzum* of medieval rabbinical mysticism. Tang mirrors are illustrated with significant ritual designs, and mirrors go back in China at least to the Sung Dynasty. The mirrors of the Chou and Sung dynasties have diagrams on the back that encode the universal cosmology of the culture, a square in the center of a circle, the square standing for earth and the circle for heaven, repeating the first two figures of the *I Ching*. At the same time they are inscribed with letters that indicate the area of a cosmological game played round these figures.[8] Only coins and houses repeat this square-within-a-circle, which is not found on ritual vessels or other artifacts. The Siberian shaman wears around his neck a mirror—of a type that shows Chinese origins—in order to capture in it the souls of those he encounters on voyages to the underworld. They have dragons on them sometimes, and inscriptions indicating that they are a gift, to be used as a good luck charm.[9] In the Egyptian and Hittite languages there is an etymological connection between "mirror" and "life."[10]

The Etruscans could have invented their mirrors, and not got them from the Greeks.[11] In any case, they quickly adapted them to their own uses and gave them a more prominent function in their culture. The Greeks, to begin with, ornamented the handles with figures and usually left the backs bare, whereas the backs of Etruscan mirrors are graved with scenes in fine lines. Turan (Aphrodite) is prominently represented, and there is a natural erotic association for mirrors in any culture; yet Hercules is also prominent, and in a third-century mirror at Florence one legendary figure teaches another the art of divination by entrails. All mirrors come from tombs, and as von Vacano says, "this fact points to a significance extending far beyond cosmetic needs." He remarks, too, that children frequently appear on them, which would make them icons of the family, like the tomb sculptures themselves. Yet the Etruscan tomb sculptures, even when they are mythological, show a range of subject different from the mirrors, as Etruscan ivories show still another range, representing statues of women, heads, sphinxes, banquets, animals, warriors, and scenes of violence.[12] And fibulae show still another kind of subject matter; their animal decorations are more in tune with other miniature art in the Mediterranean, like the seventh-century fibula with sphinxes facing a procession of lions. Etruscan mirrors abound in mythological subjects, but the only known mythological subject in Etruscan tomb painting is the scene of Achilles lying in wait for Troilus in Tarquinia's *Tomb of the Bulls* (mid sixth century). These virtuoso displays continue in antiquity, sometimes eventually incorporating mirrors, as in the Pompeian wall painting *Thetis in the Workshop of Vulcan,* which shows Vulcan, left, holding up in the center of the mural a large shield that almost completely mirrors Thetis, who stands to the right.

The cultural assignments to mirrors can be quite simple. The fetishes with mirrors in their bellies from the Yombe culture of Zaire are said to be "peaceful" as opposed to the "dynamic and aggressive" nail fetishes. In our own perspectival use of mirrors since the Renaissance, the mirror serves as both a simple cue or repetition of the virtuoso perspectival representations in the painting, and as a privileged means of amplifying and doubling its theme.

2

Indeed, there may be an obscure relationship in painting between the use of mirrors and the directness of religious associations. While easel painting was becoming secularized and turned gradually away from its medieval service as an aid to devotion, the perception of the private viewer got emblematized and enlisted in the presence of mirrors that are constructed into the painting even when, as with the Vanitas motif, they are at the same time allegorically rejected. The Vanitas motif carries far, into various popular works of the nineteenth century, adapted by Goya in a small series of graphic works where a woman looking in a mirror sees a serpent, a man sees a monkey, and the like. And the mirror of the Unicorn Tapestry, into which the Unicorn appears to be tamed, signifies something like purity, the opposite of Vanitas.

In connection, perhaps, with both purity and Vanitas, mirrors tend to increase as Virgins tend to diminish from the sixteenth to the seventeenth century, if we compare Titian and Velázquez to Michelangelo and Botticelli. Yet the situation is a fluid one. Virgin and mirror are combined in the convention of the "Spotless Mirror," one image for the Virgin herself. This icon appears in at least four paintings by Zurbarán of *The Virgin of the Immaculate Conception.*[13] Giovanni Bellini is already notable for the secular use of mirrors in one painting at least, and in a famous early mirror painting, van Eyck's *Arnolfini Wedding,* secular in its subject and in its presumed circumstance of being a commissioned double portrait, the prominent mirror is circled by the Stations of the Cross. Leonardo is predominantly a religious painter and his notebooks abound in discussions about mirrors.[14] Still too, his preoccupation with technique so engrossed him that it carries the secular accent of his science.

Just within the techniques of perspective, a mirror in a painting, like a window, helps to double and angle the visual deployments. And Piero della Francesca, who wrote on perspective but includes no mirrors in his paintings, not only shows mirror effects in water but gets an effect of what might be called a blurred sharpness, a mirrorlike cast to his figures. In Piero these water reflections are inconspicuous, insofar as they blend with the landscape; they fit easily into the checkerboard of color segments, and they take up little space. At the same time they are arresting, since the winding streams in the Arezzo *True Cross* frescoes and in the Duke of Urbino diptych help produce a visual maze the reflections seem to solve by freezing. And the pooled water at the feet of Christ in the *Baptism* seems, through its sharp perspectival foreshortening, too small to hold the little world of its reflections. The mirroring water begins to act like a window.

As the strangeness and freedom of mirrors in any culture indicate, however, there is more to the mirror than perspective, and the perspectival mirrors from van Eyck on are usually handled in such a way as to engage and expand a picture's other iconographic and representational strategies. The mirror in *The Arnolfini Wedding* deploys a sense of preciousness, but also of religious mutability in its objects, just because it is convex. And, as the circle of the Stations of the Cross around it indicates, it locates the mirror itself in a repertoire of religious meanings. All the objects in this lucid painting are coded, as Panofsky, Baldwin, and others have shown.[15] Concord is indicated by the central joined hands of the wedded pair, domesticity by the shoes on the floor and the little dog below their hands, and a conventional religious-hymeneal celebration by the candle in the shiny chandelier above their heads and between them. Into this plenum of allegorical assertions the convex mirror intrudes with a validation, since in the mirror are seen the two traditional witnesses to the wedding, but also a suggestion of another world, since the witnesses will walk back through the door while the bridal couple stays in this domicile. The convexity is emphasized by the convex reflection in it of the same large light-admitting window that stands in undistorted rectangular form to Arnolfini's left. While the window is distorted in the mirror, the bride and groom are reversed; their backs are shown in the mirror, though they stand full-face before us, as does the second pair beyond them in the mirror, whom we deduce to be approaching them in the room. Here mirror, the doubled reference to reality, and window, the portal on a further reality, are compounded to an interreference that sharpens and organizes their competing clarity.

The Stations of the Cross that circle the mirror are the most pronounced religious element in the entire painting; they stand as manifest and immediate by comparison with the latency and mediation of the other religious codings such as the chandelier, which is also blurred and distorted in the mirror. But they also stand as pictorial by contrast with the "real," since these Stations of the Cross are pictures within a picture—that is, they "mirror" a mirror—while Arnolfini and his bride are "really" there. In this start toward an infinite regress of relations between the real and the represented, the transitions are not distinct. But it is the mirror, along with its emphasizing convexity, that focuses and carries this painting's paradoxes of representation. One can, indeed, adapt to the mirror the remark that Panofsky makes of van Eyck's portraits generally: "They are descriptive rather than interpretive. But since with him the process of description amounts to *reconstruction* rather than *reproduction* they transcend the limits of their category and constitute a class by themselves" (195; italics mine). The mirror, too, counts among the objects of the picture, but along with them also; it constitutes a class by itself, in its power at once to resume and to transcend the strong plenum of the picture. The mirror, by its displacement and its distortions, supplements, contains, and also transcends the painting, which is nothing if not otherwise pointed and direct in its centering convergence.

Furthermore, the figures in the mirror are small; they are miniaturized far more than normal perspective would allow. And that throws an air of enchantment, mystery, and even distance over them—just as, differently, the Stations of the Cross frame the mirror with a world of the legendary past rather than the present, and of the Mediator's suffering, suffering that takes the whole of Catholic theology to bring into congruence with the joy of a celebrated marriage.

The fact that one of the two witnesses recorded in the mirror is the painter himself opens another tangent of reflexivity for the created reality of the painting. To be sure, the painter is not alone; there is the other witness. The painter has two functions, to paint and to witness, while the other witness has only one. Painters had to use mirrors in order to do self-portraits, but van Eyck has elided his self-portrait by miniaturization, and also by displacing it into the witnessing function. So, too, has he displaced his signature in a declaration of witnessing. "*Johannes de Eyck fuit hic*" ("Jan van Eyck was here"), substituting this for the usual "*pinxit*" declaration of having painted the work.

But where is this "here"? Is it at the moment of life, which is a constructed moment, since the painting would take a long time and the wedded couple already would have set up housekeeping by the time it is completed? Or is it in the painting itself that he is "here"? The witnessing function declares the former, the painter's function declares the latter, and both are contained and differently signified by the containment of the visible witness-painter in the mirror. The mirror gathers and emphasizes all these paradoxical possibilities, something that happens much more simply in that much-discussed mannerist work, Par-migianino's *Self-Portrait in a Convex Mirror*, where the artist has chosen to paint into the painting the very mirror he must use for a self-portrait, and to do so archly and saliently by also choosing a convex one that allows him to render hand and arm pronouncedly in the foreground.

Velázquez left behind ten mirrors at his death.[16] A notable one in his painting, which has been taken—too limitedly, in my view—as the key to a veritable system of perspectival repertoires and paradoxes, is the mirror in *Las Meninas* (fig. 2), centered on the wall behind the repre-sented painter as he pauses, brush in hand, before an enormous fore-ground canvas on an easel. In that mirror, as Michel Foucault empha-sizes, is reflected Philip IV with his queen, the very king whose authority sets this miscellany of persons into an order while he is himself absent from the represented scene. The absent king, Foucault well re-marks, may be thought of as lining up with the spectator of the paint-ing, at once organizing and estranging the sense of the painting: "The function of this reflection is to draw inside the picture that which is intimately alien to it." This circle was perfect, Foucault says, and he takes the work as a model of what he calls classical representation.[17] It would serve such a function, even if careful calculations of the painting's perspective would show its lines of mirror-centering to be less than symmetrically convergent. And *Las Meninas* does run the circuit, often more pronouncedly than does van Eyck's painting, among items on-tologically different with respect to its act of representation, going from the canvas of which we see only the ribbed back, to the painter, to the various courtiers present, and then to the mirrored but absent king, to the finished canvases over the mirror on the wall, and to the figure in the open door. The conjunctions of all of these in their particularity offer possibilities of signification as well as the general paradoxes of picture viewing that are spelled out in John Searle's extension of Fou-cault's perspectival deductions.[18]

We begin with the figure through the open door, the figure with one foot on a step as though to walk away imminently from the scene rather than to approach it the way the king and queen seem to be doing—this figure is the one most distant from the viewer, but he is also the one among all those shown who most resembles the painter in dress and features. Moreover, he bears the same name as the painter (though he is not related to him), Velázquez, and he holds for the queen the same office that the painter does for the king. He is an *aposentador*, a kind of majordomo whose duties include scheduling events and arranging the furniture and supervising passage through the sort of doors here represented—and also commissioning paintings (!). This doubling, without reference to the mirror, posits an uncanniness

FIG. 2. Diego Velázquez, *Las Meninas*. Courtesy of the Prado, Madrid.

of repetition among like-named *aposentadores*. There is a further uncanniness in the giant similar portrait—or is it just a play of shadows?—accidentally showing in the arrangement of light and dark areas on the middle panel of the back of the canvas that the painter in the painting faces.

Nobody is looking at the painter except possibly the other Velázquez in the lighted door. The others are supposed to be looking up attentively at the king and queen according to many commentators. Yet, on the contrary, they may be seen as totally, and randomly, preoccupied with their personal affairs, rather indolently, in the fashion of the couched dog almost asleep in the foreground. In fact distraction, inattentiveness, self-absorption, insufficient arousal, unfulfillment, and inconsequence dominate the mood of the individuals in this painting. The formidable logic of possible certainties in its representational strategies seems to be mired in the shadows of the only partially connected isolation of these participants. The heads of king and queen are vividly colored at the center of the mirror, but they are also surrounded, and as though suspended, in its murky clouds. This murk is in striking contrast to the bright lighting of the door at the back that frames the figure in it, where in the mirror the light clouds up. It clouds up below and above the royal faces and the red drapery hung above the king's head, which lacks far more clarity than it does definition. Again, the cloudiness is remarkable in a painting that emphasizes exact passages of light across sharp satins and other fabrics in the foreground, in which Velázquez has picked up even the glitter of threads in a dress.

Or one could contrast this small, cloudy mirror in *Las Meninas* with the large tapestry that covers most of the background of *Las Hilanderas*, where cupids are shown swimming in a bright light of almost specular silver clarity (and this comes up especially strong after the 1984 cleaning).[19] The aristocratic ladies in the background who enjoy the tapestry and each other's company are set against the busy workers in the dark foreground. These aristocrats enjoy a large light, in comparison with whom the king and queen of *Las Meninas* are virtually disembodied by the mirror. They are not dominances but small and cloudy, therefore almost ghostly, presences.

And what is the painter painting? Most critics, in their effort to close the representational circle, would have it that he is doing a portrait of the king and queen who appear in the mirror. *Las Meninas* is already a portrait of the infanta, indeed, surrounded by her attendants and ladies-in-waiting. It is natural that the queen's *aposentador* would be involved in arrangements for such a conventional group portrait. And it is also natural that the king and queen would drop in on one of the sittings. So it is distinctly possible that Velázquez is not painting the king and queen, just as it is possible that he is in the middle of a sitting with them, for some unusual painting of which we have no example; in this case they would have been there a while, which would account for the relative relaxation of the infanta's entourage. Indeed, given the paradoxes outlined by Searle (see note 18), Velázquez could be painting *Las Meninas* itself,[20] and while pausing to notice the impromptu arrival of the king and queen he could be holding the brush and deciding to inscribe himself into the very painting before us. Of course he is at the same time in that case facing away from his subjects, but the king and queen, as the mirror shows them, are a little distant to be posing. Difficulties abound, whichever way we look. As Searle and Foucault have remarked, the king and queen are in the position of spectators as well as centered and represented mirror figures.

What they are observing, though, is not any actual painting, and certainly not this one, since the back of the canvas stands toward them, as toward us, and since the painting is still in the making. The painter cannot have had time to render them into the mirror where they are shown for "this moment." In the light of Velázquez's many paintings of infantas, this one could be an unusually amplified portrait, perhaps built around a sketch taken at the accidental moment of the preparations for a sitting. If so, it both is and is not a painting of the infanta, who in any case is somewhat isolated in the painting and less centered than her somewhat shadowy parents. Kahr connects it somewhat elaborately with the genre of the studio painting in the Low Countries and elsewhere, but there are really too few paintings here for that, and the central mirror helps to deflect that possibility.[21] The painting, then, has the fixity of the portrait along with the casualness we later associate with the photograph. Its momentary character is emphasized by the pausing other Velázquez in the lighted door frame, by the raised brush of the painter, and by the shadowiness of the mirror image of the king and queen, who must be thought of as moving toward the scene. *Las Meninas* might also be taken, with some commentators, as a census of the court, ordered around the figures in the mirror, though it is somewhat restricted to royal family and retainers; however, its order is too large for such comfortable classification, containing as it does someone in the dress of a nun, both a dwarf and a midget, and the large, prominent dog in the extreme right foreground. In this collection the royal figures are reassuring as well as mysterious to the viewer—and the viewer can be thought of as the king and queen, without undue paradox, since they see not only the assemblage we see, but also their own images in the mirror, which we dimly see.

The mirror here, with its reflection, spans almost the whole distance of the painting's represented depth, plus the unrepresented depth of the viewer's area in front of it. It indicates a powerful three-dimensionality, like the mirror in *The Arnolfini Wedding*. Taken two dimensionally, the mirror is one of four framed objects along the entire back wall. If the queen's *aposentador*, the other Velázquez framed in the lighted door opening, is counted, then the total of framed objects rises to five. And among these framed objects we have three categories: a "real" man, a mirrored royal pair, and a group of three canvases. (The categories rise to four if we count the framed object of *Las Meninas* itself.) We have four measures of dimension, since two of the canvases are about equal in dimension—but we get a fifth size if we include the canvas on which the painter is painting. The three canvases divide into two groups: the large pair on top (which we can see) and the smaller, more vertical rectangle beside the mirror, which is blocked off by the head and shoulders of the painter himself. The two paintings we can see are alike in being mythological, alike in representing legends about artistic contests, and alike in offering a double homage to the painters of the Low Countries. These are not only copies of works by Rubens and Jordaens. They are copies of *copies* of works by these great painters, the first of whom did spend time in Madrid. He is here honored by an imitation of his *Minerva Punishing Arachne*. The Jordaens is a copy of an *Apollo and Pan* done by a relative of Velázquez, so that the painter himself, if distantly through family connection, is once again brought into the significative frame. The size, the very darkness, of these paintings throws the royal pair visually out of the limelight that their central position gives them. So are they differently obscured by the brightness that entirely frames the proximate *aposentador* on the step. They are mysterious, distant, as though surrounded by misty darkness, and at the same time penetrating without being truly resolving or resolved. The mirror gives them all these attributes, drawing the sense of the complex picture into itself—without ordering it into Foucault's representational plenum or even disposing it into the schematic paradoxes of Searle. The royal pair look at us, but they are too far away to be commanding as an ordering center, the way they have been taken by commentators who look here for an impossibly simple principle of organization. The other figures are variously arrested in their attention, or preoccupied, or in some cases looking away. Even the painter's eyes are a little downcast as he holds his brush slightly poised. He stands too far away from his canvas to be painting for any effective time, especially as the figure of a crouched lady-in-waiting is interposed between him and the canvas. He stands to the mirror, indeed, as we stand to the canvas; his back is to the mirror; the back of the canvas is to us. But these are only three of the many objects in the painting, and through the shadowy distance of the mirror they stand in a richly schematic relationship that each of them at the same time richly transcends by the reference to, and the random ordering of, other objects in the painting. The mirror, especially, is central but too small and murky to conclude the large transfers it does suggest. Picasso's copies of this painting make sport of such suggestions, while enlisting them in a bravura they themselves have made possible.

3

The mirror in *The Rokeby Venus* is the essence of simplicity, but also the essence of mystery. Venus's lovely curved back is presented to us, coiled for action yet in repose. We see her face unnaturally enlarged in the mirror, marvelously blurred and as though transported into a passion-saturated sleep. She looks without gazing into the mirror tilted before her by a serious and pensive Cupid. The body is svelte; the mirror-expanded face, the only one we see, is the opposite. Puffed up between the center of her body and the mirror is an almost lacy part of her sheet, which prevents more than her face from showing in the mirror. A random pink ribbon dangles down over Cupid's arm onto the mirror, into the image of her hair. The real of the body and the ideal of the face are made to join in their opposition through the very severance that the mirror holds poised for her. This big object is central and yet angled, enlarging the face to a puffiness quite alien to the trim body: here the mirror makes the reflex of art and reality join, and split, on the conflux of body and spirit, flesh and gaze.[22]

Giovanni Bellini's *Nude Holding a Mirror* (Vienna) may be said to invert this process. We see here the back of a small round mirror held by a lady of whom we have a nearly full frontal view. She is adjusting a coiffure in the other hand, and the lovely white forearm crosses the darkness of a large round mirror behind her head but visible to us. The jewels in her hair are clearly reflected in it. A window open on a serene landscape behind her undraped shoulder balances the two mirrors. More powerful than the mirrors, but also more distracting, this window includes the whole in a spacious world, whereas the world of *The Rokeby Venus* opens only into the internality and passion of the face in the enormous mirror; it is entirely, but unperversely, enclosed in the domain of the lithe reclining Venus. The look of this Bellini is emphasized and, as it were, totalized by the enclosure of the room in the *Comtesse d'Haussonville* of Ingres. In that painting the formally gowned subject faces us pensively at nearly the same angle as Bellini's subject, while the nape of the countess's neck, her shoulders, the red ribbon in her hair, the lace trim on her collar, along with the vase and bouquet on the mantelpiece behind her, are all sharply reflected in a large, simply framed mirror flat to the wall, its grey-blue tones echoed—a mirroring beyond the mirror—in the unadorned wall coloring and in the grey-blue of the highlights on the subject's dress.

Almost always the mirror in a Renaissance painting does more than just give a scope to perspective patterns. Convex mirrors in Flemish painting, such as one Panofsky notes (174) from the Master of Flémalle, include a reference by implication to the signal work of van Eyck himself. The *Saint Eligius* of Petrus Christus is shown weighing gold for an attentive couple in a neatly arranged office-studiolo, where jewels and reflecting vessels are prominent. He performs his weighing beside a convex mirror that reveals, in mysterious miniature perspective, another pair talking outdoors before houses with a sky above. The colors in this reflection rhyme with those on his shelves. And the mirror seems just one of the many objects of this interior, as does the much-ornamented mirror, complete with tiny supporting caryatids, in the *Diane de Poitiers* attributed to François Clouet. Diane here is not looking at the mirror at all, while it registers just part of her profile; she is as busy choosing and arranging her jewels as the kneeling maid through the large open door is in arranging the fabrics in an open chest. In Gabriel Metsu's *Lady at Her Toilet* we see only the back of a round hand mirror. Nothing shows of the face in the mirror in Pieter Codder's *Lady Holding a Mirror.* She holds its rectangle tilted on her knee but does not look into it.

In Caravaggio's *Conversion of the Magdalene,* the Magdalene is better dressed than the woman with whom she converses, but the white flower she holds to her breast is more prominently centered and highlighted than the large convex framed oval mirror across which is spread her puff sleeve, as though to make it casual. She seems to support this mirror without at all looking into it, and of her it reflects only her fingers, part of her red sleeve, the green of her gown, and an intense rhombus of radiant light that seems to represent a window nowhere visible in the plain background, a green that picks up a dark red shading to brown, colors that harmonize with those seen in the mirror.

A mirror effect can be drawn from almost any bright surface. A window is mirrored on the armor of Pontormo's *Alessandro dei Medici* and also on the armor of Montefeltro in the Brera *Madonna.*[23] Vasari has Giorgione remark to Verrocchio that a fountain may be used as a mirror to show at one view the many sides of the body.

Mirror effects in Dutch painting are accorded the smallest objects, like the pearls of Vermeer, which, however, reflect no other objects than the source of light. Mirrors are rare, and sharply distinguished, in Vermeer, like the one in *The Music Lesson,* a tilted mirror that reflects the top of the lady and a segment of easel against a clearly laid out section of the checkerboard floor. The Dresden *Woman Reading a Letter* shows an ephemeral mirror effect, the glancing reflection of the woman's face in a pane of the half-open window. In the *Woman Holding a Balance* the woman is shown full-face with a brown picture of the Last Judgment behind her, while at some distance from her a mirror on the wall stands at such a sharp angle that we can see nothing in it. There is a mirror-globe in *The Allegory of The New Testament.* Such mirror effects, in which the mirrors or mirroring surfaces are manipulated with such skillful ostentation, point up the aestheticization of each picture's representation of reality. The mirror effects help to show the visual world as a surface that is—instantaneously and also perpetually—on its way to becoming depth. This moment is mysteriously both caught and also created by the painter in a triple balance of the visual, the allegorical, and the enigmatic.

The mirror in Tintoretto's *Susanna* shows only her hanging garment, and it stands in great darkness. The eyes of the Elders are not seen at all, but she stands in light, by a wall of roses, her leg shown almost transparently at the center of the water, jeweled as though in a bedroom, with a swan swimming in the distance. Only one eye shows in the mirror of Rubens's *Toilet of Venus*. The mirror is small, and it seems to have inspired Rubens to an uncharacteristic alteration of scale. And in fact all these examples, random as they are, do demonstrate through various styles and centuries a pronounced tendency to manipulate, to proliferate, and even to obscure, the functions of the mirror—without respect to the considerable iconic implications of mirroring, and beyond the mere permutations of perspective.

A striking example of such manipulated occultation is the clear round mirror whose face is shown in the depths of a canopied bed that is to be occupied by the absent bridal pair of Sodoma's *Marriage of Roxanne and Alexander*. Every inch of this large mural is covered with representations, and there is much for the mirror to reflect (fig. 3). But the mirror shows something that cannot be imagined as derived from any angle of view in the painting, and especially not at the back of a bed. What it shows is a single pillar (fig. 4). We are beyond any kind of realistic perspective. This mirror purely asserts an alien, perhaps a prophetic, presence. The pillar shown in it looks as though it were the top of an altar, but it stands alone in the mirror completely without perspectival source. It has nothing to do with the putto above the bed who holds his head in its curtains. The pillar draws off all the rest of the painting into some stern ideal having vaguely to do with empire, an idea that could not be formulated. Perhaps it has something to do, too, with the *trompe l'oeil* often employed in villas, and this painting is in the Villa Farnesina. Pillars also are a frequent component of "perspectives." Yet here perspective has been sternly removed at the center of the very instrument that has been taken to double it. Love, war, empire, luxury—the rod of the pillar in the mirror quietly rules them all through its casual and total unassimilability, which at the same time divorces from them all.[24]

As a kind of inverse of *Las Meninas*, in Vuillard's portrait of himself and his friend Varoqui, only the doubled bottle in the bottom right

FIG. 3. Giovanni Antonio Bazzi [Sodoma], *The Marriage of Roxanne and Alexander*. Courtesy of Farnesina, Rome: Scala/Art Resource, New York.

foreground, and only a certain overcast to the painting, allow us to infer that we are looking at a mirror image. In Degas's *Dance Lesson* (1879), the small mirror in the rear is nearly black except for hints of green and the outline of wall, leaving the eminently mirrorable dancers unmirrored. Indeed it is notable that given Degas's mimetic skill, and even allowing for the quasi-impressionism of his late work, he would choose to blur his mirrors rather than to enlist them for perspective commentary; the blurring, then, is the commentary. In the late *Woman*

FIG. 4. Giovanni Antonio Bazzi [Sodoma], detail from *The Marriage of Roxanne and Alexander.* Courtesy of Farnesina, Rome: Scala/Art Resource, New York.

with Towel (1898) the large blurred mirror in the upper left background is given over to washes of white, brownish yellow, and greenish blue, colors that are also spread over the virtually abstract right surface that represents the wall. And in *At the Dressmaker,* the mirror is thinned to a third the breadth of the principal woman, whom we see from the back, and it shows a nearly uniform gray as an indication, rather than as a representation, of her reflection in it. Painterly illusion dominates, and yet "recedes" before the presence of the actual woman at a magic and transitional moment.

In Manet's *Bar at the Folies Bergères,* the mirror stands behind the dreamy barmaid, her reflection slightly out of perspective line, giving back the entire scene behind her, the bustle of throngs at a busy theatrical moment. She, though, is alone, isolated in her function behind the bar in the semidisplay of her low-cut dress, and the mirror behind her makes it seem as though what stands there behind her head is what she is thinking of, when it has to be what she is looking at if her eyes are truly taking in that crowd instead of dreaming. She is more aware of them, since she is immobilized, than they can be of her. It is we, the viewers, who are aware of her, and arrestedly, by having all the rest of the crowd relegated to the mirror behind her. She herself looks straight out; her perceptions dominate ours as we must simultaneously look at her and at the mirror behind her. We are forced to organize its scansions while she may hold them behind her in the "mind." In Picasso's *Woman in the Mirror* the woman and the mirror interpenetrate each other.

Mirrors take on broad effects, incidental but encompassing, in the work of Bonnard and Matisse. In Matisse's *Interior with Eggplants,* a curved-top large mirror in a thin yellow frame is blocked on the left side by a modified continuation of a brown and violet floral pattern, flanked by a darker one, used as a support for a green rectangular portfolio, and overlapped by the continuation of a white-scrolled green screen it cannot possibly be reflecting. The screen continues from its position at its right, and so the mirror is rendered either with the properties of a window or else with those of the canvas hanging just above it—empty but for the brown and violet wallpaper pattern inside a large yellow frame, which surrounds a small yellow frame empty but for the ocher ground. The window itself in this room, on the other side of the screen, gives a simple schematic rendering of pinkish brown fields, green hills, brown mountains, sky of a pink that is echoed in the door or opening behind the screen. Indeed, none of the objects seen in the mirror is reflected unchanged in the painting—so that the mirror would be a painting itself, were it not for these overlaps, and also for the skewed reproduction in it of the table it faces. In the "mirror" the table is rounded rather than square and holds eggplants done in one rather than two colors, and closer together than those on the "real" table. The mirror table is covered by a simple instead of a swirling-decorated cloth (though the cloth seems to continue in first an open checked pattern, and then a white, which has no original in the "real" scene). It bears a simple teapot vase rather than a larger, somewhat ornate one. Except that the mirror table lacks a small statue and a plate of two pieces of green fruit that the "real" table carries, these are, in other words, the same objects, but they have all been scaled down, and variously. This mirror dissolves into its background in the process of being turned into a paradoxical emblem of representation and the redeployment of color. But this is only a mirror, which is quizzically made to behave like a canvas. Rearranging and reducing, it gives back table, eggplants, tablecloth, and teapot, but altered, as though by a painter (and indeed *Interior with Eggplants* is a painting), rather than just reflected, as by the mirror (which it is).[25]

In Lucas Samaras's *Mirror Room* at Buffalo—an enclosing room where ceiling, floor, and four walls, entirely composed of mirrors, enclose a waist-high table and chairs entirely faced with mirrors—the viewer is at the center of a perspectival infinite regress, at once lost and dazzled. In the mirror paintings of Pistoletto the viewer is casually included as just another participant in the small life-size group already represented on the face of an actual mirror. Even a baroque convention for the mirror seems to persist in the popular folk object of the heavily distorted fun house mirror.

4

In these later uses we pass to an abstract painterly use of the mirror—beyond the thematics that have engaged the mirror in medieval and Renaissance codings. The mirror in many cultures other than our own, of course, has attracted erotic associations for obvious reasons. Various permutations of the self and of Eros find a mythic locus in the story of Narcissus, who mirrored himself in water. So the mirror becomes a figure of consciousness in an "impersonal" aesthetic, in the very drowning of self-reflected preoccupation. The splendid women who have recourse to mirrors in Titian, as in *The Toilet of Venus,* carry this identification beyond any possible perversity. So do the mirrored women of Bonnard, resplendent in the illumination of baths that their mirrors pick up and extend, as imperially as the earlier Mirror Room of Versailles and all its imitations. These effects are naturally, as it were, picked up in the imperviousness and plenitude of a self-celebrating and self-delectating, a narcissistic, court. In Jacques Lacan's extensions of Freud, narcissism is not only the base from which the erotic life must proceed; the knowledge of the self begins with "the mirror stage" in which the child sees his whole body, and can see his whole body, only as "other," thereby activating, in Lacanian terms, the "two narcissisms": the first, the love of self, and the second, the love of the object in the mirror as it is dialectically, and hence "symbolically," related to the self.[26] The *Narcissus* of Caravaggio shows water in the lower half of the painting mirroring knee and hands exactly, but the puffed sleeves are puffy

angles, and the face itself is quite shadowy. The natural and the perversely self-indulgent are fused when Utamaro shows a full-face nursing
mother, the lines of her exposed nipple quite pronounced, who looks
at herself in a mirror of which we see only the back, as though to
emphasize the privacy of the narcissism in her mothering. Of course in
a Christian context such Eros can be a temptation, as in a Saint Chris-
topher at Antwerp where a mermaid holds up a mirror.[27] The devil's
backside is a mirror in Bosch's *Garden of Earthly Delights*.[28] Plato, on
the other hand, refers to the beloved as a mirror (Phaedrus, 255d6). A
mirror stand of 500 B.C. in the Boston Museum has Erotes and an
Aphrodite who holds forth her right hand and holds her garments
forward in her left, an early sophistication.

Since the image in the mirror is even more transient than the body
being reflected, the mirror on the negative side has a strong iconographic association with vanity—the vanity of love, or of all earthly
things. The mirror helps to associate these two, and sometimes, as in
Georges de la Tour's *Madeleine à la Veilleuse,* it is hard to distinguish
them. This central plain mirror, which reflects her not at all, must
indicate by its blackness a renunciation of the world as well as of love.
In Titian's *Vanity of Earthly Things,* however, doubt has been removed;
an outward-facing mirror reflects coins, jewels, and an old woman.
However, a young woman through a door holds out this mirror to us;
while austerely dressed, she holds a ring; she is not reflected in the
mirror, and so she herself may be said to combine prudence with the
vanity that is her lesson as well as the title of the picture. Here, as
elsewhere, Titian effectually uses the mirror to permute the relations
among personages in the painting, as Jean Paris notes.[29] There are many
more clear-cut and overdetermined cases of Vanity; in Sassetta's Saint
Anthony predella a Vanity holding a mirror faces Avarice in nun's dress.
Vanity holds a mirror of which we see the back; she sits on top of a
wild boar and seems to be drowning. Profane Love combines Eros and
vanity in unstable measure, as in Paulus Moreelse's *Allegory of Profane
Love,* where a girl is shown with a mirror tilted outward before a table
loaded with fripperies, while a nymph is about to be raped by a satyr
in a background canvas. The mirror-gazing ape is a figure of love.[30]
This image is reversed, and the iconography complicated with positive
associations, in the *Vanity* of Hans Baldung Grien: the gold-rimmed,
deeply convex mirror that this nude figure holds up shows an ape's
face, but she treads on a serpent, and a seemingly mated pair of deer
move peacefully in the left background.[31]

But the mirror is "blank" enough to be associated also with prudence,
and the dark mirror of Georges de la Tour's *Madeleine* may contain
some such hint. This association appears strongly, of course, in the

long-standing medieval and Renaissance tradition of the "Mirror for Princes,"[32] in which the object in the mirror is not predominantly erotic but rather an ego-ideal—though the two notions, if clearly distinguishable, are virtually inseparable, as Lacan demonstrates. The Mirror Scene in Shakespeare's *Richard II* combines vanity—in the objects contemplated—and prudence—in the one contemplating (who at the same time is invincibly vain and self-centered). Prudence is so strong an association, indeed, that one may trace it in many places where it is not explicitly indicated. Jan Emmens even sees Prudentia, "The Mirror for Princes," in the mirror of *Las Meninas*.[33]

Prudence sees things as they are, but the mirror in its deep connection with practices of divination may be cast in the role of a prophetic instrument, sometimes ambiguously.[34] The mirror used for prophecy is hard to distinguish from the mirror as a revealer of the soul, nor need the cosmetic function be divorced from this prophetic function. It is cosmetic mirrors that are associated with tombs, and the frequent association of mirrors with tombs, as Hartlaub notes, must derive from their employment for magical and spiritual purposes.[35] What does it mean when a mirror shows a mask in a wall painting of the Villa of Mysteries at Pompeii? What exactly is signified in the hanging scroll of Hokkei (a pupil of Hokusai) when a boy writes a Japanese character on the misted surface of a mirror as his mother watches behind? This is, of course, prevailingly a genre scene. At the opposite end of the iconographic spectrum, but equally mysterious, is the fusion of divination, prudence, the miraculous, and Eros when a Virgin holds up a mirror to a unicorn. This traditional scene in the Cluny tapestries is keyed to an allegory of Sight, but its signification is as wide as the scope of that sense which the visual arts powerfully enlist.

5

The mirror as an object of contemplation actually transcends Lacan's distinction between, and even his identification of, the two narcissisms, that of the inner self and that of the outer object. It does so, one may say simply, because the "mirror stage" is only one of its possibilities; the mirror reflects indifferently the self (as other, as self-as-unconscious dialogue of the other, and so on) or some other object. And so it assimilates the self in the real world to other object choices, as well as becoming a means to enlist the imaginary in the service of the symbolic. So far as the mirror's surface is concerned, there is absolutely no difference between a real bouquet of flowers and the bouquet of flowers illusorily mounted in a vase by managing a mounted arrangement of convex and flat mirrors in the optical experiment repeatedly invoked by Lacan.[36] The mirror serves to locate the self among others because in the topology that Lacan makes of his abstractions, the mirror both refers to and "interprets" the self's inclusion in the world. The mirror forbids our separating—or identifying—art (or language) and reality. One does not have to invoke Lacanian terms explicitly, indeed, to see an abstraction of the phallus, and not the phallus itself, in the single pillar mirrored within the small round mirror deep at the center of the canopied marriage bed that Alexander and Roxanne are about to enter in Sodoma's mural discussed above, and especially since there is no possible "real" pillar in or outside the picture that this pillar could be mirroring. Lacan's remarks on his own diagram seem almost like a description of this mirror: "this is only the broadening of the break that can be said to reside in the chain of signifiers, insofar as it is the element [of the subject] which is most radical in its discontinuous sequence, and as such the place where the subject assures the subsistence of the chain."[37] Given empire and prowess as these staple notions dominate the painting, Lacan's "bared phallus" and mirror would provide a revelatory angle but not a full solution for a work in which Sodoma has centrally emphasized the presence of the "pillar" while perspectivally emphasizing its absence.

At once canny and uncanny, the mirror cannot be reduced to perspectivism or to iconic allegories. As an image of consciousness in art, it remains ambivalent towards the experience that at the same time it indicates—and is included in. In Picasso's *La Toilette,* where a clothed woman holds a mirror whose back is alone visible, "the mirror is both palette and canvas."[38] Magritte's *False Mirror* shows an eye with a cloud in it, pointing up the mirroring function of the retina. In Paul Delvaux's *The Mirror* a clothed woman, indoors and in back view, sees her naked self front-view by a sort of portico with alleys of tall trees leading to small buildings and towers. Delvaux says that "the unusual presence of a nude woman or an unexpected personage not only depersonalizes the scene and despecifies the place, but it also, and that is the important thing, offers for viewing a spectacle which, although resting on a faith in unequivocal appearances, traverses both time and consciousness. In that it is signifying *beyond appearances.*"[39]

CONFRONTATIONS
The Agonies and Fusions of Goya

Chapter 5

I

Goya does not test his strong and strongly trained powers of visual representation, as Turner does, to immerse the beholder in the created scene. Instead he presses the representation into a confrontation with ideas and moral imperatives so that they fuse and extend his powers of signification in the direction of a radical questioning new to painting. Like his close contemporary Blake, but without Blake's accompanying armature of theory, he exacts from his work an expression of a spiritual confrontation between image and idea so as to put the image at the service of testing the idea. The work becomes strongly indicial in Peirce's sense: it points at a state of affairs. It does not just match to complex preexisting icons (in the more general sense) as its total effect induces a registering of a state of affairs that has a moral force without yielding to the construction of moral solutions, as in Blake. The visual forces a stark confrontation of the mental without providing the terms for ratiocination.

Into a wide, and in some ways conventional, range of subjects and techniques, Goya introduces through the middle of his career extensive series of etchings and drawings, the "Caprichos" (1799), the "Disasters" (1810–23), and the "Disparates" (1819–24) which press very hard Blake's kind of deep questions about ultimate psychic motivation. Goya carried out this questioning almost wholly through the visual means that for Blake tend to be largely supplementary. In such graphic works, which number in the hundreds, he starkly simplifies, rather than complicating, the centered images of the Napoleonic invasions that had taken place some time before, turning them into observations of memory on single events that compel their being taken for typical. But beyond this the typicality is presented in such a way as to probe the relations between the deep psyche and the common life.

"Values" in painting, and in the visual arts generally, mean the relative darkness or lightness of the areas represented. Goya concentrated on "values" in this sense in order to throw into relief, as we might say, the values that the theoretician of ethical rightness and justice addresses. A great colorist in the first two decades of his career, and later as well, Goya turned to the black and white of etchings and drawings in order to center his work on hard ethical cases. These cases call for an ethical settlement he provides only in a sort of proleptic, summary, and sugges- tive fashion. Yet he does so in ways that test the boundaries of signi- fication that art had confined itself to before his time. Instead of just conveying a vision to the mind by a vision that can be seen by the eyes, Goya, again like Blake, implicitly presents these etchings as a moral claim and a moral test. They work to rival, or at least to supplement, the religion he serves in his commissioned work, while deeply satirizing it in what began as private work.

Goya's practice heavily extends a canon for visual art so deep that it governs all, or nearly all, of Western practice from antiquity to his own time. Pompeian wall painting is a reminder, a visualization, a decora- tion, but not a substitute for the probing of ideas, which are rendered in words by the ancient philosophers, even if this art can be given analogical connections to Epicureanism. And the same is true not only of all medieval painting in its relation to Christian doctrine, but of Renaissance painting, however complex and ineffable.[1] Powerfully in- novative as they are for the diction and the syntax of the images in their paintings, Botticelli, Giorgione, Carpaccio, and Bosch do not push, as Goya does, beyond the visual boundary of the painting. Nor do the mannerist painters who play with and force that visual boundary without at all inducing the viewer to the confrontation of a moral question that some proverb or even theology cannot contain. Even Blake does not force the visual representation to do such intellectual work. He assigns such definitions to the powerful sequences of lyrics and prophetic nar- ratives, and his engravings and etchings then fall into the conventional, secondary place of illustrations or supplements of various kinds.[2] But Goya makes the work a test of the mind, most obviously in the "Ca- prichos" and succeeding etchings, but pervasively also in his other work.

The satires of Hogarth or of Callot, to take two examples, must relate to a norm, as all satire must, to be recognized as such. In apprehending the social norm in such works, the viewer is thrown back on the play of visual rendering and observation: the viewer admires the graphic artist. But in Goya's graphic work the norm is so deep, and the work is so confined to simple contrasts, that the single event or collocation he registers cannot be referred to any norm more specific than "the truth" or "human decency" or "the ideal." To use the terms of Michael Fried, the viewer's "absorption" must be total so that "theatricality," which does grip him, remains in the service of the questioning and confrontation that the work evokes, and the viewer is never thrown back just to content himself with the play of the visual renderings, remarkable as is Goya's achievement in this domain.[3]

Goya provides, further, an interaction between visible and invisible such that the strength of what he presents may imply both an ideal and, in the light of the ideal, the possibility of still stronger sights. The title of one of the "Disasters," *So Much and More* (*Tanto y más*, no. 22), could be generalized to provide a general principle for Goya's confrontational strategy.

Of course finally, as in all visual art, the interplay of signification and sight is a single compound act, and in some sense I am here separating the two overschematically. I am doing so, however, to get at the particular, the unique attribute of Goya's abiding confrontation, and its profound revision and extension of the canons under which artists had universally assumed they were working.

There is an immediate visible presence to painting, but there is also an access to the invisible, to the processes of mentation that we associate with signification. Mind, eye, and the act of painting are inseparable in Turner's representations of Venice. In color itself the visible and the invisible belong together, and it is therefore not surprising that great colorists like Titian, Matisse, and also Goya demonstrate a powerful sense of access to a special vision that involves something that cannot be seen.

This vision, thanks to the achieved visibility of the painting, does not immediately and rationally schematize its invisibility. Goya said, "The sleep of reason produces monsters." Blake schematized such a monstrous notion of reason into the figure of Urizen. Goya broached on the canvas itself a transmutation of the relation of the visible to the invisible so that his visual creations would face and express what monsters mean rather than just how they enter a cultural discourse. He raises them to harrowing confrontation between visible effects and invisible motives.[4] These works are so forceful that they succeed in becoming test cases for any wakeful spiritual orientation to love and justice. The technique of painting falls into the background, in a sense, as Goya moves from splendid color to a preoccupation with black and white. Mirrors, for example, he uses only for satire. Goya's few mirrors, instead of permuting questions about art, as those of Velázquez do, directly draw a line and a connection between the visible and the invisible. A gallant looks in a mirror and sees an ape; a well-dressed man sees a garroted man in his mirror; a constable sees a cat; a student, a frog; a woman, a serpent wound round a sickle. The last work takes a conventional Vanitas theme—the death's head in the mirror—and complicates it with the theme of evil, in the primordial version of the serpent tempting Eve. This serpent is wound not around a tree but instead around the handle of the sickle, an instrument conventionally given to Father Time or to Death the Reaper. But this serpent is also Eve as well, since a serpent wound around a sickle is what the woman sees in the mirror; and in this series what everyone sees is his inner likeness.

Goya here takes the protocartoon of his contemporaries Gillray and Rowlandson and turns it into a vehicle not for social but for spiritual satire, thereby deepening the normative or normalizing values on which satire always relies.

In his paintings Goya, sometimes wholly and always partly, by what seems the pure power of his visual penetration, accomplished fusions that take him beyond the easy plenitudes of his eighteenth-century context, and also beyond all but the most visionary of romantic artists, visual and verbal. There are some hints of this visionary power in his considerable body of religious painting, but it appears more markedly in the paintings of the 1770s and the 1780s that forthrightly adopt the pastoral conventions while deeply transforming them. The people in these early paintings belong to a sunny pastoral world, but they are also thrust forward into a larger one, a world where finally the fusion will breed the agonies already foreboded in the random accident of *The Wounded Mason* (*El albañil herido*, 1786–87), and more mutedly in the openness to nature and to danger of *The Fall* (*La cáida*, 1786–87).

Goya early transcended the technical mastery that had earned him a preeminent position as a court painter, though his increasing transcendences, if not his temperament, played hob throughout his life with any official security. Already in the genre paintings that were cartoons for proposed tapestries in the royal palace, he went beyond not only such predecessors as Watteau, Tiepolo, and Mengs—as well as his associate and brother-in-law, Bayeu—but beyond the painters he might have seen near the end of his career at the Paris Salon when he visited there in 1824: the high polish of Ingres' *Vow of Louis XIII*, the powerful but contained pathos of Delacroix's *Massacre of Scio*, and the various landscapes of Constable and Bonington.[5]

The Swing (*El columpio*, 1786–87) takes a pastoral icon from Watteau and Fragonard and enters it in a wilder context. In an earlier work of the same title, the pastoral is eased into its genre comfortably (1779), and the lightly swinging girl is surrounded by children and women. In this later one the dress of the woman being pushed on the swing is not composed into the delicate order of the aristocrat playing in the country. The man pushing her, his face only partially visible, works so intently that he has lost any aura of playfulness. She seems a little frightened; the man centered and facing her holds wide his arms in a dismay that could be either mock or real. Some of his clothes have been shed and lie on the ground, red and black, unheeded by the two women at the left; they are engrossed in conversation and casual music. The swing itself is perilously improvised at an obtuse angle from one tree to the branch-stump of another. Behind the swinger, nearly framing her, runs a broad, torrential river whose foaming waters fill the center of the painting. Beyond it is a somewhat elevated city, a setting carefully excluded from more conventional pastoral paintings; above the city are blue mountains, whose distance is neatly framed by the bunching green leaves of large trees that lean over the river. The nascent excitation of the swinging woman and the two attendants in front of her and behind contrast with the posture of the third gallant, who lies, complete with hat, soporifically on the ground, propping a pensive head on hand-and-elbow. These three couples must be in the country for some courtly erotic purpose, but that purpose has been heavily dispersed in the randomness of their attitudes.

Beyond such privilege, though, lies a world of labor through which the coaches of aristocrats may heedlessly pass, and in *The Crockery Vendor* (*El cacharrero*, 1779), a young lady in her prime, beautifully dressed, is still not noticed at all by two gallants, whose backs are to her, nor by any of the four attendants of the passing coach, who are also turned away. She, in turn, seems not to focus on the young man who reclines in the foreground, back to us, gesturing toward her. And the old lady beside her, a polished brass plate tucked inside her breast, looks off sternly into the distance.

Fred Licht stresses the early inventiveness of Goya. He says of *The Parasol* (*El quitasol*, 1777), "Goya has disturbed the relationship between figures and setting—a relationship that in the Fragonard was still logically coherent and harmonic."[6] A little black dog curls on the lady's white apron in a posture of repose, but his eyes are anxious. The single leaf-bearing tree or branch behind the cavalier is blowing as in a steady wind. Indeed, he seems to be using the parasol to shield the lady from the wind rather than the sun, since the source of light seems to be pouring from behind him, so strongly as to blur more distant foliage.

Behind her a brown mist begins to the left above the wall where the parasol is pointed. It is not clear why, in any case, it should be pointed nearly horizontally rather than vertically. He holds it, in fact, more like a sword than a parasol. She holds up a fan she would certainly not need in the wind, and indeed the fan is held shut in her fist; but at the moment that the painting captures, the fan would be superfluous. She is against a wall whose detachment from a structure Licht comments on (and somewhat exaggerates). She looks at us; he looks down at her; the dog looks nowhere. The three figures are suspended in a swirl of light and shadow to which the prominent parasol contributes only echoes of color. But they are considerable echoes, ranging from her dress and the ground beneath her at the lower left to the blue-green sky at the upper right and the foliage along nearly the whole right edge of the painting. The figures themselves are presented frontally. They are so close to the picture plane that proportions are lost in the swirl of perceived light; the moment is both emphasized and transcended.

There are similar effects in other works of this time, as in the simpler *Shepherd Blowing His Horn* (*Pastor tocando la dulzaina*, 1786–87), where the lone figure lies reclining, absorbed in his horn, beside a sapling with one long bough, against a lit landscape. His figure is so close-up and so large that the coordinates of pastoral have been painted away, along with the implications of their proportionateness. *The Fighting Cats* (*Los gatos riñendo*) arch isolated and huge atop a rectangular fragment of brick wall, against a background of blinding light. In *The Kite* (*La cometa*, 1778) all look up toward the kite as it flies in the intensely lit sky. A hazelike light, subtle and pervasive, washes over *The Grape Harvest* or *The Vintage* (*La vindimia*, 1786–87) (fig. 5). A blinding light thrown by the huge lantern beside the firing squad centers on the man being executed in *The Third of May*, and the light is caught in his eyes. Whites stand for a comparable light in the graphic works, for example, the large white spaces in the red chalk drawing associated with the "Disparates," *Persons Covered with Sackcloth* (*Personajes cubiertos con sacos*), or in the "Disasters," the white of the shroud in *The Beds of Death* (*Las camas de la muerte*). In *The Witches' Sabbath* (*Aquellares*), the light is too bright to come just from the quarter moon off over the right shoulder of the huge-horned goat. This light, strong though pale, spreads over and brings up the faces of the surrounding women. The drunkard in the painting of that title (*El bebedor*) sleeps against blinding light.

The strong light that envelops these figures and expands beyond them cannot be paralleled in genre or pastoral painting. It is most reminiscent of the blazing sun in the ceiling skies of Giambattista Tiepolo, such as that of *The Apotheosis of the Spanish Monarchy* in the Palacio Real. It is

FIG. 5. Franciso Goya, *The Grape Harvest (La Vindimia)*. Courtesy of the Prado, Madrid.

as though Goya had transported this blazing sun from allegory, divinity, and religious transfiguration, and accorded its light to the lives of ordinary people. Goya, indeed, in his own ceilings departs from tradition by putting the angels on the rim below his personages rather than above them.

Goya's cartoons, Jutta Held notes, are brighter than his earlier religious pictures.[7] Later Goya inverts this fusion by putting somber events in idyllic settings. Even the early work shows a hint of somberness as in *The Straw Mannikin* (*El pelele,* 1791). Why should these girls be so intent in tossing into the air from a circular tarpaulin a life-sized masked puppet? The fictitiousness of this figure is emphasized by the posture into which Goya has set him, his straw legs and body twisted beyond even a tortuous possibility for a human being. He is upside down and distorted and lone; the girls are upright, intent, at their ease, and calmed in the circle that has formed to play this curious but traditional game.[8]

The Grape Harvest centers a group of four on a rise above an active grape harvest. This symmetrical group, in a somewhat pastoral setting, is turned from the erotic to the familial by the presence of the child in back view, reaching up as the man transfers a large bunch of grapes to one woman, while a slightly more rustic woman behind him bears on her head a large basket full of grapes. This transmission seems to draw on the genre icon in Dutch painting of food transmission in a family setting, but such Dutch scenes take place indoors. The harvesters over the rise below are as separated in space as they are in social class from the finely dressed man and what seems to be his rusticating family. All are framed by the range of blues in the background, where the inverted blue triangle of the sky almost merges with the blue triangle of mountains. The man in his yellow silk suit is seated on a robe of richer blue. His reach extends a huge bunch of blackish grapes, his other arm looped through a basket of leafy grapes. Colors in this painting generally, as Jutta Held points out, are bound with especial force to the persons in it.[9] The stretching reach of the little boy whose back is to us extends upward to the basket borne on the head of the peasant girl, and then upward to the mountain—a contrast to the downward leaning of the harvesters, one of whom, red-jacketed, stands up to his knees in vines. They cannot partake of the little boy's gestural expansion toward the largeness of the mountains. The symmetrical four contain balance, removal, and also a certain loftiness. And these people, in their expansiveness, are also self-absorbed; the man does not quite look at the black-clad woman—his wife?—to whom he is handing the bunch of grapes.

Goya's vision squarely locates his people in a situation that marks

their social class but does not confine them to it, opening out to a full
humanity of a sort that only novelists like Dickens and Dostoevski
would later find a way of expressing. In Goya's time a painting of
beggars was called a *murillo,* and some of his figures, like the hard-
beset group of *The Snowstorm* (*La nevada,* 1786), are only a step beyond
beggars. *The Wedding* (*La boda,* 1791–92) contains more than a hint of
Hogarthian satire in the ugliness of the bridegroom, and the peasants
may be mocking him, but the procession takes its horizontal way un-
deterred in the open air as an intense if transitory social collocation not
focused to point any Hogarthian morals. This marriage neither is nor
is not "*à la mode.*" The significations insist on their complexity along
with their actuality.

Ranging across ages as well as social classes, Goya portrays adults in
childlike games, even the aged in the two late sketches of an old man
and an old woman swinging. Children partake of the masquerade that
adults have not abandoned in a work of around 1800, and also in the
series of six paintings of children's games (1777–85). Yet at the same
time, for this sombre figure who lost a number of his own children in
infancy, the child can show a haunted face. The son whom Saturn
devours in the late "Black" painting is almost adult; his face, along with
his whole head, has been eaten away. The children horribly enlisted by
the witches in the "Caprichos" are horribly obliterated, and their faces,
too, tend not to appear.

One of Goya's most elaborate portraits, almost exceeding Velázquez
in that vein, is that of Don Mañuel Osorio, a young nobleman not
much more than an infant, whose brave, bright red garments and luxurious ruff do not tame for him the wonder that shines through his
eyes. He is surrounded by enough darkness to appear lost in the hier-
archy that has led to the very luxurious commission that has brought
him here to be rendered. More than a hint of darkness operates in the
background creatures, so distributed that they do not hit his line of
sight. He holds loosely on a string a bird who carries in his beak a card
bearing the signature of the painter. The bird, too, seems not to see
that he is being glared at from behind the boy by three huge cats, one
deep in the shadows. Cats eat birds and are, as it were, constantly on
the watch to pounce. Don Mañuel, caught in the light that shows off
his luxurious costume and looking frontally ahead, is unaware of such
possibilities, "literally" here and "metaphorically" at his time and station
of life. So much sinister drama in the background of a child's portrait
departs, of course, from the conventions for that genre, in which animals are just agreeable pets. The child's oblivion to dark forces serves
to strengthen them, while the oblivion and the forces combine their
significations for the syntax of this painting.

The children in Goya's paintings may or may not be shown as so childlike. The boys in *Boys Playing Soldier* (*Muchachos jugando a los soldados*, 1779, The Prado) are dreamy and peaceful, but in another painting on that theme (Lázaro Galdiano) they are almost too serious. Numbers of boys are fighting, and the central one tumbles back, bare-bottomed. His assailant holds a basket on his head, fashioned into a bull-puppet. All these boys stand under a dark arch, with a monumental building in the light behind.[10] They are approached and observed by a little tonsured "monk," whose tonsure would be unlikely for a child; and so he stands, unnaturally, for the adult world they are duplicating.[11] On the adult side, in *The Card Players* (*Los jugadores de naipes*, 1778) men are idling in the open air, but their eyes and postures are excessively strenuous for the game, as though their adulthood will not release them for easeful leisure.

The participants in *The Greasy Pole* (*La cucaña*, 1786–87) are mostly clustered below the perilously high and leaning pole as it extends up into the sky across the sharp vertical of the painting to the cock and leaves tied at the top. Those below may be classified into spectators, bystanders, and interferers, while the two participants intently shimmying up the pole are among the youngest present—subverting any easy exclusions between childhood and adulthood. In *Blind Man's Buff* (*La gallina ciega*, 1788–89) the figures range in age from early to late youth and from near immobility to strenuous contortion in their posture. The most balanced is the blinded gallant at the center who points his long spoon at a faintly smiling, ducking, white-clad maiden. The scene here too opens them out. The blue surrounding mountains, the clouds massed white across the picture, and the green foliage, all are blurringly mirrored in the abysslike lake immediately behind these sporting dancers, who maintain their circle in what seems to be a terrain too close to the wilderness for such pastoral activity. The late *Milkmaid of Bordeaux* (1825) shows its central figure entirely in the open against a background of strong hue, a dense color-swirling sky of blues and greens; her milk can is barely distinguishable beside her to the left.

2

The faces of these people tend to be obscured into a mere pointing of the attitudes of their bodies, but Goya was a portraitist in great demand, and portraiture bulks large in his oeuvre. At another extreme, though, in *The Meadow of San Isidro* (*La pradera de San Isidro*, 1788), a whole city of people, it seems, is shown too small for any attention to their faces. These people are strung out in the coils of a horizontal procession on the banks of the river opposite the steep city.

The city is far away from them, though visible, much farther than city from people as they are shown on the banks of Velázquez's comparably structured *City of Saragossa*. The distances and particularities captured in Goya's painting are remarkable for its small size (44 x 94 cm). He has got whole companies of people in, like a super-Boudin, and at the same time he has opened them out. Across the river and above them towers the city, like some rude version of the celestial Jerusalem. The crowd is enormous, the city seems empty, separated not only by the river but by the assignment of colors, darkish green for the throngs of people, whitish for the city. Comfortably seated on the highest rim, aristocrats are strung out in comfortable converse above the winding throngs below, the white of their dresses and two parasols echoing the distant white of river and city. But all these faces are just sketched; they and their blues, whites, and yellows blur into each other. There is just one bit of marked color in the woman bowing to the far right.

In a later painting, *The Burial of the Sardine* (*Entierro de la Sardina*, 1812–19), the centrally dominant figure is a large banner held aloft at this festival procession. A large face is prominent on the banner, too high and too gross to have comfortable religious associations. It also harmonizes too much with the faces of those in the procession below to move over into the grotesquerie of the carnival masks some are wearing. Goya's portraits—like that of the sinister erotic intriguer, political bungler, military bully, patron of the arts, and the queen's lover, Manuel Godoy—can be devastating. Goya tilts him backward in his seated posture, with the result that his face appears all at once as masterful, inattentive, and immobilized into sloth. As Licht points out of the *Naked Maja* (*La Maja desnuda*, 1798–1805), however open she may be, her face is not a welcoming one: "Between the body and the face . . . there intervenes an unsettling shift in meaning."[12]

The large *Royal Company of the Philippines* (1815) carries satire further than Rembrandt's group portraits and dissipates satire in a kind of vapidity that the browns of this large, disorganized, posed group convey. These overdressed, lost, discordant committeemen look ahead to Courbet, and even to Francis Bacon. They are gathered around their large table in what seems an invincible isolation, emphasized by the dark background above and below. They are caught in the process of facing decisions about an extravagantly conquered chain of islands, which they have inherited, standing in the great, other sea half a world away from the very country that members of their class have bungled repeatedly into repression and disaster.

In *The Family of Charles the Fourth* (1800–1801) the paintings on the wall, both the large violent painting to the left behind the king's head and the smaller segment of a landscape to his right, do not really help to define this court. Nor does Goya, seated in the background at his large easel, compose this group, however complexly, as Velázquez's painted presence may be said to compose the group of *Las Meninas*. Charles IV's head, distracted and impotently determined, falls in between the other figures, singling him out spatially but not characterologically from the others. In the open-air portraits of Maria Luisa alone, in a mantilla and on horseback, her solitude is emphasized by the strong and rapid distancing of the mountains beyond. She is far more isolated than the frontally celebrated ladies of Reynolds and Raeburn. In the Velázquez royal portraits against a mountain landscape, like those of Philip III and Margaret of Austria, the horse on which they are mounted sets them up imposingly against the landscape. The domestic look to Goya's Maria Luisa seems to involve her diminishment and her incapacity, and perhaps all the more so by contrast with her actual role of power and intrigue. Her humanity seems lost or misplaced in the faint, decentering traces of perversity and obsession. Velázquez, however, gives his very buffoons a full humanity by framing them not so differently from the way he frames his kings. It is the dwarf whose look outward most resembles Velázquez's own in *Las Meninas*.

Jutta Held has it that Goya's "faces all have a similar stark look, poor in expression."[13] And there is a half-truth to this characterization; yet something in these faces verges on the profundity of chaos that Goya has them register. At another angle, or in another light, as Ortega says, "The faces are not faces but masks."[14] Goya's full-scale portrait of Don Francisco de Borja sets the man against a dusky, light-shot mountain landscape, above a river. The nobleman has left his horse slightly below in the care of a servant who looks up toward him, and he has placed his top hat on a rocky outcropping for an incongruous juxtaposition. He is engrossed—again incongruously—in reading some sort of document that he holds in his right hand. In his left he suspends vertically (and curiously) his whipstock, in such a way that the whip dangles down, its red-tipped end curling like a snake on the ground. In the portrait of Pedro Mocarte (1805–6) the subject's coat is open on a gold and green waistcoat, and on a snowy white silk shirt, but a black scarf cuts off and defines a look of some force, which could be sneering or pensive or even weary. The countess of Altamira and her daughter in their double portrait sit on a highlighted, simple green settee with clearly visible gold legs, against an otherwise brown background that isolates them above the elaborate, nearly funereal inscription Goya has painted onto the canvas. The countess's spread pink skirt and haunted face dominate the work as she holds her little daughter almost upright. The greyish white of the daughter's little dress rhymes with the mother's sleeves and neck trim, but her look, while equally stark, loses her in some other world than the one that the mother seems confidently to confront, for all her isolation.

In *The Blind Man with a Guitar* (*El ciego de la guitarra,* 1778), the eyes of the central figure are large blotches. The crowds around him are mostly inattentive to him, except for a (perhaps hostile) soldier and a seated boy who looks up at him. The two prominent rouge-spotted, white-masked dancing girls on either side of the banner in *The Burial of the Sardine* have on their masks an almost childlike stare. In the memory-painting of a signal chaotic political event, the *Third of May, 1808* (1814), the face of the man being mowed down by an impromptu firing squad blazes in its light. His transfigured face fuses self-obliteration, erased and insistent questioning, extreme agony, appeal, defiance, resignation, and spiritual persistence—while the faces of the dominant soldiers who are annihilating him are not visible at all. Yet in *The Second of May, 1808* (1814) the eyes of the man stabbing another emit and receive a light similar to that in the eyes of the victim in *The Third of May.* So comprehensive is spiritual exertion on either side that it evens out the bodily reaction of a participant—and presses heavily upon the interpretive construction of a viewer.

The faces exceed the presented occasion in the works of Goya, unlike those of his contemporary, Caspar David Friedrich, who often presents only the backs, in full figure, of his central persons. Friedrich's characters look out in immobilized solitude upon intensely simplified, deeply contrasting landscapes, doubling and getting engulfed in the scene that is presented to the viewer, who cannot see the faces of these other viewers.[15]

In a much later panorama winding near a city, *The Pilgrimage of San Isidro* (*La romería de San Isidro,* 1820–23), the throngs are in no order. They are shown startlingly close up, only touches of white in their dress punctuating the engulfing blackish browns. Out of these emerge faces that are flinching, stunned, agape, grisly. Each is individualized but all are similar in the affliction for which their collective mission gives no grounding correlative, except that for pilgrims the passion of Christ must distantly figure in the signification. The foreground faces are anguished; the persons in the middle distance are fully draped; and those in the background are gradually swallowed up in the obscurity of the brownish green murk that covers most of the painting. All these visible faces are as if roughed out in some quickly hardening reddish material. These faces leave all the years of portraits behind to a world in collusion to repress the fierceness that their haunted impenetrability unleashes.

In Goya's album of some eighty etchings, his "Caprichos," the faces are confined to black and white. They are released to wondering expressions at their confinement. The nearly innocent, maidens and children, are entrapped, while the voluntarily implicated are enslaved. The witches, officials, monks, and soldiers, as we read on their faces, luxuriate in spiritual self-indulgence and spiritual oppression. The agonies and fusions of this satiric work have been intensified over what it partially overlaps with, the genre scenes of the Sanlucar Album and its Degas-like softness of observed intimacies. Goya said, "I have succeeded in making observations which there is scope for in conventional works and in which caprice and invention do not get expanded."[16] More explicitly, in an inscription on a piece preparatory to no. 43, he says he wished "to perpetuate with this work of *caprichos* the solid testimony of truth." If we take together the "Caprichos," the "Disasters," the "Disparates," and the six albums that contain comparable works, Goya produced hundreds and hundreds of these separate, single, nearly unbearable confrontations of harsh reality. *One Can't Look* (*No se puede mirar*) is his title for an India ink–sepia wash scene from the late Album C (1814–23) of a man trussed upside down to a dragging swing. *Don't Open Your Eyes* (*No abras los ojos*) is the title of another, which represents not a horrible scene but just a white-clad woman with her back against a spread of black that could be either bed or chair. She does have her eyes closed; if she opened them, she could perhaps see the viewer himself.

Goya has inverted and extended the "capriccio" of his immediate Italian predecessors, editing the fancy out of the genre; "capriccio" implies "arbitrary fancy" and therefore something framed as unreal. Goya's "caprichos" are meant to use this faculty of artistic fantasy to cut through to visual confrontations of essential truth—a thrust to something real, something close to intolerable because it refuses to be taken as evoked just by fantasy. Goya indicates the force of his personal artist's stamp by putting his own face and name firmly on the cover. His own face fills the plate, in a profile whose single eye seems to look faintly askance, belying the formality of his dress. Not until no. 43 of the "Caprichos" series does the motto that might be applied to all of them appear, "The sleep of reason produces monsters" ("El sueño de la razón produce monstruos"). "Sueño" means "dream" as well as "sleep," and Goya in his initial sketches for this series labelled them *Sueños*. They operate between the erasure of reason in a sleep and the awareness in a dream of a spiritual universe beyond reason. "Life is a dream" in the proverb that Calderón dramatized, but Goya's nightmare "Caprichos" anchor themselves in a grainy harshness very different from the associations of such proverbs. Indeed, the ambiguity of Goya's expression cuts differently either from its analogue in the Spanish tradition or from its parallel to the Urizen of Blake. Blake condemns all exclusive rationalities, whereas Goya's expression could mean either "when reason is asleep" one gets monsters (but when it is awake, not); or "reason itself is a kind of sleep to which monsters accrue because it is of necessity asleep and one must be awake (and seeing) in order to hold them at bay." What supports the first reading is the stupidity, and sometimes the correctability, or the injustices, of the figures shown. What supports the second is the occasional association of books and wisdom, or the very process of justice itself, in a total, uncorrectable world. In *That Dust* (*Aquellos polvos*) both the charlatan defendant in the dunce cap and his judges seem to be comprised in the categorized mockery of Goya; within that frame, neither the fraud nor its detection would escape the designation "sleep of reason." Only the vision of the graphic artist who focused on them in their collocation and brought them to the sharp black and white of his art could claim such a freedom from the monsters he is facing.

The "Caprichos" proceed in thematic groups, beginning with a marriage that *is* à la mode (no. 1), and with the dangerous practice of using a bogeyman to frighten children (*Que viene el coco,* no. 2). By such juxtapositions these etchings introduce agonies that go beyond the simple fusion of the fantasies and the satires that can be found separately in the work of Goya's immediate predecessors. These themes expand almost at once from the reasonable framework of satire to monstrosities of behavior—to abduction, witchcraft, prostitution, the physical punishment of children, the murdering of infants so their parts may be used for witches' brew, the bad advice of old women to young, and the dominance of devils. One can connect all these activities by implication to the first two plates, the "Bad Marriage" and the "Bogeyman." Hence the given scene is simultaneously confined to its own world, which the proverb or proverblike caption emphasizes, and related to a whole "black-and-white" existence in which constricted or perverted purposes pervade the whole spiritual life of society, so that "none escapes," in the terms of no. 19, *All Will Fall* (*Todos caerán*). This spiritualization of ordinary oppressions recalls the poems, but not the graphic art, of Blake. Like Blake, Goya here seems to intend not just a condemnation but an encompassing vision from the dark side of existence. The original title on the frontispiece of the "Caprichos" was "Ydioma universal."

In no. 43, overcome by the monsters to the point where the etcher is not using his eyes, Goya lays his head flat to his desk. The monsters throng up at the wall behind, whereas in a preparatory drawing for this plate only a large man stands over the sleeper. In Goya's own comment, the whole psychology of society and the artist is juxtaposed between the negative and the positive effects of such a sleep: "The sleep of reason produces monsters. Fantasy, abandoned by reason, produces impossible monsters: united with reason, it is the mother of the arts and the origin

of their marvels"[17] Goya's term "impossible" will not really bear examination; it pushes to the logical breaking point the difficulties of the
world he has here portrayed. "Fantasía," indeed, runs the gamut in its
associations from the positive power of imagination to the negative
distractions of fantasy. The painter is haunted by the monsters his imagination is controlling as he gives graphic visual expression to the fantasies that dominate his subjects. These fantasies are reciprocal; if the
powerful are visioned as asses, the powerless accede to carrying them
on their backs (*Thou Who Cannot* [*Tú que no puedes*], no. 42). One ass
is pupil to another who is the master (*What If the Pupil Knows More?*
[*Si sabrá más el discípulo?*], no. 37). Lust conceals hostility and exhibits
foolishness. (*Where Is Mother Going* [*Donde vá mamá*], no. 65) shows
a fat, aging woman being spirited away naked by a whole company of
animal-like devils.[18] In another etching the stocking of the prostitute
(if it is certain that this young woman is one) is "well pulled up" (*Bien
tirada está*, no. 17) in the treacherously admiring comment of the old
bawd—for an activity that will make the prostitute entertain the illusion
that she is "sitting pretty." The foolishness of such feelings take visible
form in the strange game entitled *They're Sitting Pretty* (*Ya tienen
asiento*, no. 26), where the prostitutes are not seated but standing and
exhibiting themselves half-naked to ogling men, carrying useless chairs
on their heads and looking away foolishly from the men who inspect
their nudity through transparent garments. Since *tener asiento* can also
mean "clinch a deal," and "to be established," the title ironizes their
lack of establishment when their financial profit is limited by the tran-
sitoriness of the situation. In their topsy-turvy precariousness and use-
lessness, the chairs are turned into ridiculous burdens instead of
supports on which the women might "sit pretty."[19]

The women have their turn at hostility-in-lust: *There They Go Plucked*
(*Ya van desplumados*, no. 20) reduces the prostitutes' customers to tiny,
plucked man-faced chickens whom a group of women in casual dress
fiercely drive away with uplifted brooms.[20] Brooms, here carried by
prostitutes, are the insignia of the witches who will emerge in later
caprichos. And in the immediately following counterpart to this etching,
sternly moralistic but diabolical cat-faced judges suspend by her wings
a poor bird-woman-prostitute, her white breasts dangling helpless in
the center of the etching, *How They Fleece Her!* (*Qual la descañonan!*,
no. 21). This term,, too, gets its counterpart in *Le descañona* (no. 35),
where a woman barbers a man and is understood by her observing
friends to be using his immobilized position finally to "fleece" him.
Goya's note on no. 21 underscores the reciprocity of hostility between
the sexes, a grisly "give and take": "So the chickens encounter hawks
that fleece them and even for that reason it is said 'Where they give

they take.' "[21] These etchings are preceded by *All Will Fall* (*Todos caerán*, no. 19), in which three witches gleefully put a frightened, plucked man-bird on a spit while other such birds are flying in the distance or perching on the tree above, gaily and heedlessly pursuing what seems to be courtship, oblivious of the pitfall trap nearby that will deliver them to such fates.[22] The later female match to this scene is in *They Have Flown Away* (*Volaverunt*, no. 61), in which a well-dressed young woman, a contented look on her face, floats aloft, borne up by demons whose faces sternly and gloatingly scan the air. This is a possible later moment to no. 72, which also completes and counters *All Will Fall*; in *You Won't Escape*, (*No te escaparás*, no. 72), devils with intent faces fly closely round and behind a maiden whose face and posture show a nascent fright that bids fair to extinguish her resemblance to the gentle figures in the Sanlucar and Madrid Albums.[23]

The sexual episodes, here and elsewhere in Goya, singularly combine arresting anecdotal occurrences and strong implications for universal obsessiveness both in those who court and in those who exploit. In *Disparate Triple* the "triple folly" would presumably include both the man and the woman in the match, as well as the group who have advised her—a "triple folly" of forces in all directions, visually indicated by the complicated chain of hands held in the work. In *The Duchess of Alba and Her Duenna*, the duchess almost attacks the duenna, coming forward at the old lady, who leans on a cane with her right hand while holding in her left a cross that the Duchess has thrust past. Goya's near-nudes are unlike those in other paintings, where some joyous or sorrowing air clings to the nudity; here the nudity becomes at once a visible gambit in an invisible game, without being arrested into the visual attributes of nudes from antiquity to the present. Even the *Naked Maja* (*Maja desnuda*) exists not by herself, but as a counterpart to the *Clothed Maja* (*Maja vestida*). Juxtaposing the two works sets up a dialectic of presentation, anticipated joy, social participation, exploitation, blank self-assertion, and visual subjection.[24] The juxtaposition is emphasized by the fact that the poses of the two paintings are identical, and the pillows and bedding nearly are, but the couches are not. Anything the nude means can be countered by what the other suggests. And the *Maja desnuda* taken by itself is extremely confrontational for a nude, even without inferences about the disjunction between face and body. Nudes almost always turn a little away, hide somewhat, lean or occupy themselves or drowse or accede to the boudoir setting. The *Maja desnuda*, in an unusual pose that is at the same time odalisquelike (or rather, like a lady playing an odalisque), presents her body squarely and frontally, her hands behind her head so that the breasts are thrust directly at the viewer, and she also looks at him directly. The genitals, too, are not highlighted by being exhibited, but neither are they concealed by the closed legs. The boldness of the posture plunges this body beyond nudity to a question of what nudity can mean when nakedness has such power. But the *Maja vestida* holds the identical pose, exhibiting the same power in a more dangerous and more implicated concealment that the clothes contextualize. This pose enlists the superpastoral convention of the aristocratic lady dressing like a gypsy girl (a *maja*), but the *desnuda* overlaps and transposes the containment into artifice of such games.

In the "Caprichos" themselves, each of the titles cuts sharply into the situation it summarizes. This is so not least for the overall title, which not only stretches but ironizes—again like Blake—its implied assertion. The "Caprichos" deny the *capriccio* or caprice that clings to this label. These scenes portray hard social fact, with an invisible counterpart. "We wrestle not against flesh and blood, but against principalities, against powers, against the rulers of the darkness of the world," (Ephesians 6.12). So says the very Scripture whose debased representatives Goya mocks in this series. The quotation is one that Blake puts in a key position. Goya, however, does not spiritualize directly; what he does instead is to let the spiritual beings, the invisibles, gradually emerge behind the agonizing pressures of his visible scenes, as the witches and devils and transmogrified asses take over the later frames in this series.

The sexuality here is located, as the series progresses, in an ambiguous realm between visible and invisible, because it is increasingly associated with a witchcraft much discussed in Goya's time but to which there is no firm evidence that Goya gave credence.[25] The witches are sometimes clothed in religious habits (nos. 10, 49, 79, 80), and so they are made to overlap with acts approaching witchcraft on the part of the clergy.[26] Indeed, in a previous wash drawing, *Witches About to Fly* (*Brujas á bolar*, 1796–97), two singing clergy, agape in dunce caps, are deferring to a lean, sow-faced muscular witch who sits naked facing them astraddle an upward-looking, braced, naked devil. They hold a missal open for her with two pairs of tongs. At the hooves of the devil is a death's head, and the covering of the altar shows three larger faces even more agape. The engorged witch, the mamá of no. 65, is persistently and perversely sexual in her reliance on the many demons who carry off her dropsical body. She mingles dreaminess, intentness, stupefaction, and satisfaction in a face that has stopped asking why her special needs of transport would be accorded such special attention. She would be out of balance, did not their throng balance her. The question "Where is mama going?" links her to a normal life that she is leaving, a background of which the title and the distant city are the only traces in the etching. That normal life would presumably absorb and tend toward the spiritual dropsy that the devils can only be imagined as exploiting—the devils whose existence enters the visible realm of the etchings without any necessity for mediation, but without any other grounding than the invisible, the "dream."

In *A Fine Teacher* (*Linda maestra*, no. 68), an old witch rides ahead of a young one on a broomstick and presumably teaches her. The young witch's eyes do not look; she hides her face in transport or fright behind the back of her grizzled, intent teacher, while an owl-devil with spread wings looks down on them in their wide segment of night light. The broomstick is shown cutting through the naked genitals of the young woman, and also presumably of the old. It would be painful for a woman to bear her weight down on such a pole without any protection, but sexual pain here merges into sexual thrill. The possibility of further fright finds expression in the next etching, *Blow* (*Sopla*, no. 69). The command is given by many devils who gather in a night coven next to a brazier while one of their number uses the body of a naked child as a bellows, forcing flatulence from his anus by pumping his heels so that the flames will flare up, in a trick children learn to play with matches.[27] Above them a witch ominously cuddles other children. Goya's note suggests cannibalism. A shaggy satyr-devil performs a similar trick with a naked figure he seems to be holding aloft by the ankles in *Ups and Downs* (*Subir y bajar*, no. 56). The perilously balanced figure holds flames in the left hand and a flaming head in the right; his hair seems to be in flames. The sketchy sword at his left side could not be used to counter the gravitational effects of Fortune, as the commentary holds— a Fortune (if it is indeed that) unconventionally allegorized as a satyr. The satyr is seated across the saddle of another overturned figure, and a third figure topples away in the dark distance.[28]

3

Darks and lights play across these black and white etchings in ways that seldom delineate a source of light. The whites and near-whites lie in a totalizing garishness over the figures, usually over the sufferers, a sort of whiteout where ennoblement of transfiguration gets lost in the concentrating eclipse of a violence unrelieved until the blazing sun that stands behind Truth and her visitant in "Disasters" ("Desastres") no. 82. The shadows of Rembrandt have been further darkened as the psyches are further darkened. And correspondingly the sense of the participants' subjection to physical forces is imagined in their subjection to forces of gravity—or perversely to its opposite, flotation. Many of the witches and demons are borne aloft by sinister supernatural forces in the night sky, a sky often crossed by strange swatches of white that can only be some unnatural light.

In *Sleep Overcomes Them* (*Las rinde el Sueño*, "Capricho" no. 34), the capitalization of the last word links it to the title of the whole series. This etching shows prisoners in a deep dark against a large grate that shows much light but does not let it through. Two prisoners, hooded in white, lie not quite prone on the ground. A third in white is sinking as gravity overtakes her body. A fourth, clearly a woman (as then the others must be; an echo of no. 32), centered above them in shadow, leans on her arm and will clearly soon sink down too; she is the only one whose face at all shows. As a work from a later group of etchings (1810–20) clearly indicates, the criminal (if indeed he is one) and the jailer are caught in a common bond of subjection to dark forces: "The imprisonment is as barbarous as the crime," this work reads; it shows a man hobbled and shackled into place.

Goya himself in "Capricho" no. 43 lets gravity bring his head to the desk while "the sleep of reason produces monsters"—black-winged monsters gathering to circle against the grey background above his head. If taken with the desk, this background indicates a wall, but if taken with the monsters, it indicates some kind of sky. In this general suggestion of space there is a great range in Goya's work. *Now They Are Sitting Pretty* plays with gravity. One of these two women almost entirely in white, one is standing. Both bear chairs on their heads, so the proper control of gravity has been inverted. Yet the chairs look light. The basket full of infant corpses tilts as though rocking on its base while shadowy demons fly behind the grey witches in *There Is a Lot to Suck* (*Mucho hay que chupar*, "Capricho" no. 45); and the oblivious greed of a ritualized infanticide-cannibalism is as though blown through by an evil wind.[29] The witches are shockingly involved in assailing these children with their mouths, and one in the close background is fellating a larger child of whom only the torso and sexual parts are visible. Psychic burdens are crushing physical ones; asses ride men in *Thou Who Canst Not*. The top demon of *Where Is Mama Going* floats with the aid of a parasol, and the whole sweeping train seems to be skimming along on a rising field above a city.

The suggestion of such possibilities for bringing gravity pointedly into the space of the picture appears less grimly in other works. *The Balloon* (*La mongolfiera*, 1812–16) depicts a swaying balloon aloft against mountains with a crowd below—a scene that Goya had done twice a dozen years before, in chalk and in sepia ink, and then with a huge crowd on a flat field below the balloon. The tall pole sways in *The Greased Pole* (*La cucaña*), as does the pole holding the banner in *The Burial of the Sardine*. In *The Kite* (*La cometa*, 1778) the people are de-

ployed up a gradual rise, the topmost one with arms slightly raised
looking upward against light, as the kite rises off to the upper left. In
The Manikin, (El pelele) the circle of girls tosses the gay-masked manikin
up, and he is shown in air above their tarpaulin. The figure itself is
lighter than a man, less subject to gravity; it is made of straw. *The
Parasol* sets its people on a slope that suggests at least a psychological
soaring. *The Stilts (Los zancos,* 1791–92) sets two men high above the
crowd; they are pointedly struggling to balance on these tall narrow
stilts, and gravity emphasizes the contraposition of pleasure against
awkwardness. In *The Pitcher Girls (Las mozas de cántaro,* 1791–92) two
women easily balance large jugs on their heads against a wall and a lit
sky beyond, while a third walks dreamily behind, and a short boy in a
hat (they are bareheaded) leads them. In the cupola of San Antonio de
la Florida, representing the miracle of Saint Anthony of Padua (1798),
all the participants are gathered round a balcony, low in the representation but lofty in their looks at the standing saint, all as though caught
in the swirling force of the sky with its central, small, light-surrounded
dome.[30] The actual light in the dome of the church where this work
has been painted comes from the window at the top of the dome. Saint
Anthony is painted as looking up to this light, while the other faces
look at him but not at the light; each is isolated in the stolid singularity
of an undeviating look as the saint blesses those nearby; their looks are
only slightly transfigured. In a way reminiscent of the "starry floor" in
the "Introduction" to Blake's *Songs of Experience,* all the angels are below, rather than conventionally above, the human beings. Putti occupy
sections in each of the four supporting arches, in the four ogives over
the altar, and in two segments beside each of the side windows. The
painted railing aligns the saint and those surrounding him with the real
window; it also grounds them, but high in the church. None of the
angels below them, contrastingly, is grounded. They float in the air of
a sky that the coloring only occasionally suggests, and they pull aside
drapes given so little spatial location as to assimilate them to the mansions of heaven.

In *The Grape Harvest* the elevated figures, washed in strong light, are
extended upward at each of the four points of the near-diamond that
they form. The workers below are earthbound, even the one who holds
his hands down to continue working while he looks up at the central,
elevated four. The arms of the yellow-suited man, as he leans back
slightly to look up and out, are spread as if to soar, though his right
arm is counter-weighted by the large bunch of grapes it holds and the
left reposes on his basket. The black-dressed woman across from him,
his wife we may say, is slightly more elevated than he and leans back
slightly, as though to sustain the weight of the bunch of grapes. The

red-belted, green-suited little boy between them, seen in back view, stretches his body and his hands upward toward that bunch, or else even higher to the bunches in the basket on the head of the servant who stands centered and above them all, against the open sky. She easily balances her grape-laden straw basket with her upraised right hand. In all this, elevation plays as a possibility through the group and expands its celebrating composure.

Gravity lightly subjects the washerwomen in *Las lavanderas*. One walks in the background, her head weighted with a bundle of clothes. In the foreground a woman in a gold-striped green dress is weighted on her left by a sheep, as well as by another woman on her right who leans across her lap to the sheep.

In *And Still They Won't Go Away* (*Υ aún no se van*) the dead struggle vainly to push up the slanting weight of a rock slab. *The Wounded Mason*, indeed, demonstrates graphically how the living are constantly subject to gravity—as well as to the sort of spiritual counterpart of gravity for which joy, licit or illicit, would have the spiritual counterpart of lightness.[31] In *The Fates* (*Atropos,* 1820–23) those mythological beings are bunched together and suspended in air, as are the seemingly frightened pair who point at a towering city threatened by attacking horsemen from below in *Asmodea*, from the same series of dark paintings in the "Quinta del Sordo" (the "Villa of the Deaf Man"), which Goya, the deaf man of the name, set on the walls of his own house.[32] Elevation, like everything else, has the double face of uplifting release from normal gravity and dangerous suspension of infrangible rules.

4

The "Caprichos" are narrowed and intensified—*enfáticos*—in *The Disasters of War*. Goya did not assign this title to the later work, though he may have had a hand in the description that links it to the "Caprichos": "Fatal consequences of the bloody war in Spain with Bonaparte, and other emphatic *caprichos*."[33] Where the earlier "Caprichos" had jumped from subject to subject, the sort of dark forces they depict are fully unleashed in a war; and in the "Disasters," the "Caprichos" do indeed become emphatic; the series of murders, arbitrary executions, mutilations, rapes, and mass burials is unbroken. The dark forces have taken over so fully in this representation of a persistent if intermittent human dedication to total destruction that the preternatural birds and demons do not appear till nearly the very end.

This series begins with a plate that shows a man kneeling with bared chest and outstretched hands that could ambiguously signify either prayer—his head looks upward—or resignation. Yet the time of the work's reference is not the past but the future, as its caption indicates, "sad presentiments of what is to happen" ("tristes presentimientos de lo que ha de acontecer"). The man is done in greyish white on an almost completely black background. Prevailingly the suffering or dead are accorded the white areas in these darknesses, as though to hint faintly at the possibility that truth may triumph against all odds, as it does in what may be the final plate (no. 82).

The space is too small or too vast, the light too ambiguous or too glorious, to contain these intensities, to justify these deaths. Even the violence of the deaths, though it cries to the heavens, escapes, for all the "emphasis" of this certainty into the unknown; so much is indicated by no. 69, in which the foregrounded corpse, his head already nearly a skull, has written "Nada." The title, too, emphasizes the finality and uncertainty of this frame—*Nothing. It Says So(Nada. Ello lo dice)*—a conclusion so severe that the official publishers modified the caption.

These captions leap out, more strongly even than such titles as Poussin's conventionally severe death's head in a pastoral scene, *Et in Arcadia ego*. Often they emphasize the horrifying sameness of the frames: *The Same (Lo Mismo,* nos. 3, 21, 23), *Likewise (Tampoco,* nos. 6, 36), *And This Is Like It (Y esto tambien,* nos. 25, 43). Finality may be stated: *And There Is No Remedy (Y no hay remedio,* no. 10), *What More Is There to Do? (Qué hay que hacer más?,* no. 20). Now and then, bare condemnation: *Barbarians (Bárbaros,* no. 22)—but this execution is far from as barbarous as the sword castration of the naked man in no. 20. Condemnation alternates with irony in *Charity (Caridad,* no. 14), which portrays the burial of dead, perhaps violated women. In *He Deserved It (Lo merecía,* no. 29), a man is being dragged in a death no one could possibly deserve. The two representations of garroted men get different titles, one general—*Why (Por qué,* no. 32)—and one an ironic statement of disproportion—*For a Knife (Por una navaja,* no. 34). In an earlier drawing of a garroted man, to his right a large ecclesiastical candle stands almost as tall as he is.

Toward its conclusion the series erupts into further extravagance and allegory. In *The Carnivorous Vulture (El buitre carnívoro,* no. 76) a huge bird marches away, wings spread, either sated or headed for further corpses. Only in its size is this bird preternatural, unlike those of the "Caprichos." And it is not accompanied by others of its flock. Moreover, a redundancy in the title may itself contain a hint; all vultures are carnivorous.

Almost at once thereupon, in nos. 79, 80, and 82, a bald set of allegories takes over, a centering on truth: *Truth Has Died (Murió la Verdad), Will She Live Again? (Si resucitará?),* and *This Is What Is Truth (Esto es lo verdadero).* In the last one a shaggy, bearded man confronts a pointing woman with dog and basket at her flank. His head and her whole body are set against a sunlike radiance, and her breasts are bared in the convention of Fertility, Liberty, and Charity (but less often of Truth). The cap and the counterargument and the mitigation have been placed on the uncontainable, and inarguable, the immitigable. Taken with the series, this triple invocation of Truth puts all the horrors of war in a contingent rather than a necessary relation to the essence of life. It sets as broad and inclusive an ideal as possible against the persistent and painful distortions of human actors.

Goya hovered around Truth as an allegorical presence, setting *Truth, Time and History* in his fairly conventional series of six allegorical paintings (1797–1800)—so conventional that this large generality is not really congruent with the others: *Agriculture, Industry, Poetry, Science,* and *Commerce.* Goya has an interesting late *Truth Recovering from Illness,* as well as *Time Flying with Truth* (1797–98), a work that may be taken, with Gassier and Wilson, as belonging to the overflow from the "Caprichos," and which deeply modifies the sinister flights of witches and demons in many of those plates.[34] The veins of deep evil and deep virtue are brought together in a sepia work of the later Album F, *Truth beset by dark spirits,* where the demons crowd frontally toward the viewer as though to assail and overpower a white-gowned, oblivious young woman—Goya's standard representation of Truth—in ways reminiscent of the young women who will be overpowered by demons in other works. But here the rays of light above Truth's head seem to be holding the assailants firmly at bay. And of the "two friars" (*dos frailes*) in the "Black" paintings Goya arranged in the "Villa of the Deaf Man," one seems gross, stupid, and evil, while the other, into whose ear the first one whispers, holds himself in a posture of not attending, with a clear face that seems to betoken long-earned virtue.

In both the earlier "Caprichos" and in the "Disasters," the plates tend to center not on such transcendent allegories, which conclude, supplement, and ground them, but rather on a one-time but typical violence. Both of these sets of signification differ from the martyrdoms that were painted during the previous two centuries, since those have a built-in doctrinal explanation, and indeed a principle that in their conception elevates them to prayerful acts from which all mankind could benefit. Religious practice provides for them a context that is removed from Goya's most emphatic works.

Goya rarely treated martyrdoms in his considerable body of religious paintings, and then not with the intense focus of the "Caprichos." But in his work all victims have the look of martyrs. The central figure in *The Exorcised* (*El exorcizado,* 1812–20) is prostrate and almost corpselike in his exhaustion. The "Disasters" resurrect such horrors in memory some years after the Napoleonic wars, providing the single social setting that will explain them. They have been purged of the detail of Callot's war engravings, and their rudenesses of depiction and extravagances of lighting insist on the typicality of their horrors. Men, it may be inferred, tend toward individual and collective madness. And indeed, a step further provides the group of the "Disparates," the various "follies," each of which gets an adjective of description—"cruel," "feminine," "furious," "clear," "known," "matrimonial," and the like—as though their typicality is so apparent that each striking scene will be understood with such simple labels, and without the explanatory captions of the "Caprichos."

Such a perpetual straining of values, such a skewing of them, could drive men mad, and madness enters Goya's work more directly in representations of those who are incarcerated because of their madness, the *Pen of Madmen*, (*Corral de locos*, 1793–94) and the series of drawings of *locos* (1824–28), who are more fully classifiable than the "Disparates," in that they are not only pegged by a single adjective but given the permanent designation of "mad," when the actors in the "Disparates" might conceivably turn to other activities. The label "mad" arrests the image into the residue not of a single imaginable episode, like the atrocity in a war, but of a large irrecoverable series of events in a life, a complex plot. The result: the represented figures stand starkly before the viewer.

Equally mad seems the painting of double hostility outside a tavern, where men in one group are pulling at and clubbing one another, and another pair is rolling on the ground, the lower one biting the arm of his assailant. These episodes are common and yet obscure; their obscurity points at the persistence of human violence. Of the two dogs present, one merely bares his teeth, while the other sits quiet. A madwoman in a black chalk drawing of Album G (1824–28) is shown selling pleasures, health, and dreams ("Loca que bende los placeres, Salud, Sueño"). A blind man palps the hernia he is in love with ("Ciego enamorado de su potra") in a sepia wash drawing from Album C (1814–23). The title of *What a Misfortune* (*Qué disgracia*) orients this drawing of a very fat man in the madness of his obsession. The horror of the drunkard at his own obsession is depicted in *Grimaces of Bacchus* (*Muecas de Baco*) by transporting his reaction away from the visual in which the viewer is caught: he holds his *ears* before the bottle and the glass on the floor before him. A painting in the Museo Lázaro Galdeano shows flagellated men in Inquisition dunce caps, naked to their waists, blood soaked into their skirts, under a dark arch, with women (nuns?) praying behind and below them.

The activities in the *Corral de Locos* are under a double and convergent constraint. The central figures are naked wrestlers, but their keeper, who swings back a whip to force them apart, enters the same system, a graphic depiction of what Michel Foucault effectually characterizes as the implicit homology between incarcerators and incarcerated.[35] The top of this work is a white, which must be a wall, though it is bright enough to leak a bit of yellow into the green of these walls. All the figures here, the standing one with arms folded, the one in the door with upraised arms, the one half-recumbent, and the one seated on the ground, stare fixedly ahead, agape or agrin in an amusement or a terror that engulfs them in some nameless state of emotion beside which Géricault's head of a madman is merely clinical.

Foucault compares the treatment of the insane at this time to the treatment of animals. In Goya's works animals are neither accorded just their conventional places in the order of things, nor merely enlisted into allegorical frames. Goya runs the gamut from tame to wild, from natural to supernatural, and from manlike to wholly feral in the animals with which his work abounds. In it are found apes, bears, bats, a range of birds, boars, bulls, butterflies, cats, chinchillas, crocodiles, dogs, donkeys, dromedaries, elephants, fish, fleas, foxes, frogs, goats, horses, lions, lynxes, mice, oxen, panthers, pigs, rams, serpents, and wolves.[36] Most of Goya's still lives are of dead animals, or in one case the parts of a dead animal, the head and joints of a sheep. The dog is sometimes a household pet, and once he is a monstrous animal reclining and disgorging the whole human corpses he has eaten (*Fierce Monster*, [*Fiero monstruo*], "Disasters" no. 81). A man picks fleas off a dog in one late drawing; in another a dog preternaturally flies. A dog cart arrested the aging painter in his French exile enough that he not only rendered it but put a caption on it similar to some in the "Disasters," *I Saw It in Paris*. In *The Witches' Kitchen* (1797–98) the most prominent of the excited figures in this underground room is a large doglike naked woman or devil leaning over the cauldron.

"Man is a wolf to man," but the inclusion of animals in Goya sometimes spreads the violence across the line between men and animals. In one *Nightmare* (*Pesadilla*), a simple small black dog is leaping up on a woman. Goya has blurred the distinction between visible and invisible, a distinction that is clear in the *Nightmare* of Fuseli, where the white body of the sleeper is visible and the devil squatting on her chest can be inferred to be invisible, like the head of the glaring-eyed horse peering round the curtain at the foot of her bed.

Violence, too, since it is everywhere, easily crosses the line between animals and man. One of the "Disparates" shows a horse biting a woman. Another work shows a woman attacked by a bear. The animal may breach the boundary of the natural, as in *The Flying Dog* (*El Perro*

Volante, 1824–28), the sketch of a donkey on his hind legs, and that of
A Literate Animal (*Animal de letras*). "Those who spend their lives with
animals" come to resemble them in *Con animales pasan su vida*. All
these works go beyond the fierce but conventional representation of
men as asses and the like. Animals shade over into the supernatural, of
which they are often images; so the horrifying birds of the "Caprichos"
and the bird-masked batlike flying men of a later work, *Way of Flying*
(*Modo de volar*, 1815–20). The devil is conventionally represented as a
goat, and Goya twice shows witches gathered round a large goat, fully
animal from horn to hoof—in *The Witches' Sabbath* (*El Aquellare*, 1797–
98) and in one of the "Black" paintings, *The Great He-Goat* (*El gran
cabrón*, 1820–23).

Bulls carry the conventional power of mysterious force. The bullfight,
of course, ritualizes the power, but also the violence, of men who by
their skill can put these large animals to death. Goya many times rendered bullfights, in Spain with one series and again with another series
during his last years in Bordeaux, where the bullfight would not have
been so centered in the folk consciousness as in Spain.[37] In one of his
paintings he renders a double bullring, as though to extend through
repetition a suggestion of the expandability of this absorbing ritualized
violence. One of the "Disparates" (*Toritos*) is of small flying bulls, who
are suspended in a group reminiscent of the witches and devils in earlier
works.[38]

In *The Dog* (fig. 6), the most arresting of the "Black" paintings, an
animal's head looks up from what may be quicksand if it is not the odd
angle of a mound or the slope of a hill, or even a brown curtain. Indeed,
the wash of brown is very heavy to the right just above the mound, as
though this part of the "sky" entered into some undifferentiated, intermediate state, like the mound on which the figure in *La Leocadia*
leans, in another of these paintings. In this plain work elevation and
gravity have been elided into each other; hope, trust, death, the mystery
of suffering, the transience of the natural creature, and the fellowship
of creatures, all enter into a suggestion that has concentrated on the
single head in an intensity so great that it allows only a partial and
frustrated purchase on the spiritual. This dog is overwhelmed in an
environment that at once exceeds and expresses him, like Caspar David
Friedrich's *Monk by the Sea*. Dogs don't partake of the spiritual in conventional theology, but they may be seen in a work like this to border
on the range of feeling that men undergo, and the perception of the
painting—especially as it may partially echo others here in the "Quinta
del Sordo"—would bring a man to the verge of facing the sufferings
whose sense theology centers in the supernatural.

Goya, as Held's book testifies, was a great master of color. It is all

FIG. 6. Francisco Goya, *The Dog*. Courtesy of the Prado, Madrid.

the more remarkable that he would devote himself so protractedly to works in black and white. And that he would declare: "In art there is no need of color; I see only light and shade." Certainly in his late work a somberness falls over the great chromatic triumphs of his earlier achievements. Held describes this change as an ascription of the same significance to all colors, so that they seem like the colors in still lives.[39] *The Dog* seems to compass the achievements, and the significations, of both the great years of color and the strongly visionary blacks and whites of the "Caprichos" and the "Disasters." Except for the slate-blue head of the dog, modulated in values, the whole large painting is a wash of colors, mostly warm ones, from the dark brown of the mound that cuts its head at the neck and the brownish tinged yellows of the upper two-thirds of the painting to the greenish blue that begins to appear in the upper right. The color is a nondescript background for the dog, but it also overwhelms the dog; it fills out a sameness and steadiness that at the same time isolates the partially seen animal in a sinister finality.

There have been many attempts to read an order into the "Black" paintings arranged through the rooms of the "Quinta del Sordo" (1820–23), but on the one hand their agonies are too separate, and on the other their fusion too complete, to turn them into a syntax. They comment by reverberation. Next to *The Dog* on the first floor may have hung a painting of witches, and its theme would be reinforced by the painting to its left on the wall before the other door, *Asmodea,* in which two devil-like beings are suspended over groups of attacking and firing horsemen, who approach a city on a mesa so very high it looks impregnable. To the right of the door hung *Atropos,* in which four, (and not, as conventionally, three) Fates are suspended in a whirling circle. Of these the one on the left holds out an unveiled, double-faced baby, the one on the right holds up snipping shears, the old one centered at the back door looks through a round object like a loupe or small mirror, and the one centered at the front merely gawks, her hands behind her back. These two paintings are alike in representing the sort of dark powers before which the dog may be going under. At the opposite point across the room, though, are two women (or perhaps a couple) grinning sickishly and widely at a man, doubtless a village idiot, who is probably masturbating—and psychoanalytically, undergoing a self-castration symbolical of the annihilation that the son of Saturn in a painting on the floor above is really undergoing. The mockery of the women watching the masturbator, shocking as the collocation is, seems episodic by comparison.

By the other side of the door stood the painting of a group of men of various ages reading, presumably for a collective political purpose, the activity therefore oriented away from the private or devotional toward possibly a better but certainly a violent future. Here the subject of the reader is freed of the genre suggestions for this act in eighteenth- and nineteenth-century painting. The masturbator, the mockers, and the readers, taken together, both duplicate the dog and transcend him, since they like the dog are entrenched in activities that may ruin them, but he cannot by his nature engage in any of their activities. On the other segment of wall, corresponding to *Asmodea* and *The Fates* respectively, is a duel of men fighting each other (to the death?) with cudgels. Like the dog they are immersed, but only up to their knees. The threat they face is one they have locked themselves into; they too both resemble the dog and differ from him, but in any case they differ from the figures of the readers beside them. The scale of the work makes the men look like giants against the background landscape, and indeed there is nothing to prevent our assimilating this work to Goya's other representations of giants. Seeing these fighters as giants puts the hillocks on which they stand into natural focus and puts into perspective the bulls, otherwise impossibly tiny, running in the field between and behind them. In this case though, if the bulls are a measure, the giants seem to be sinking into the ground to a depth of twenty feet or so, and their combat would have created a cataclysm in nature.

Opposite them a group of *The Holy Office* (*El santo oficio*) is a sort of shorter version of *The Pilgrimage of San Isidro* (*La romería de San Isidro*) in the same position upstairs, but the agony of religious affiliation is no longer traceable here as some simple folly. The faces are rapt, and the figures, like the dog, are fused into the totality of their absorptions. It both resembles in possible violence and differs in collective unity from the *Duel with Cudgels* (*Duelo a garrotazos*), which stands opposite.

At the entrance to the ground floor, right, stands the portrait of a dressed-up, veiled, vaguely melancholy woman, *La Leocadia*, Goya's companion in his last years. Her posture derives from a convention of women mourning at tombs, but what she leans on cannot exactly be discerned as a tomb. It is a large rocklike mass of yellowish-tinged brown that takes up more than half the picture, resembling the mound of quicksand in *The Dog*. Beyond her are a balcony railing, trees, clouds, and blue skies, which begin to assimilate the work, if distantly, into the open-air pastoral conventions of Goya's early tapestry cartoons. Her look is soft enough and dominant enough to modify the anguish and fright that screws up the faces in *The Pilgrimage of San Isidro* and the comfortless, stupefied-fearful rapture that obscures those in *The Great He-Goat,* works that are set opposite each other on the central longer walls. Yet she is herself modified by the two works on the left of the entrance, *Old Men* and *Old People Eating*, figures isolated and absorbed, their faces as grim in extreme old age as those in the *Pilgrimage*, and still more skull-like.

The corresponding wall at the other end of the room matches a dynamic *Judith* and a *Saturn Devouring One of His Sons*—a supremely justified and a supremely unjustified violence, on the part of a legendary woman on the one hand and a legendary male deity on the other. Saturn patently gains nothing from his bloody meal; he is not part of a Hesiodic sequence but locked in the horrible finality of this act, even though he repeats it. His face exhibits the most extreme anguish to be observed in all these paintings. His eyes are huge with what seems more anguish than hunger, his lean shanks wiry with strength but exhibiting a need for this insatiability. He has begun by biting off the entire head of the son, a savagery that would in fact reduce the son's suffering. Saturn's giant head is entirely covered by a growth of shaggy white hair. We may measure his intensity and focus by Rubens's unconvincing painting on the same subject, which Goya could have seen (it is now in the Prado). Rubens's robust Saturn leans over to pull away with his teeth a fold of flesh from a plump, terrified baby in his arms. Or we could also compare it with Goya's less intense red chalk drawing on the same subject, in which an unhaunted, rather contented Saturn, of whom only hand and head are seen, has eaten first the leg of one son while clutching another son in his other hand.

The spiritual extensions of these works can be read into paintings other than these "Black" ones that were set to enclose the reclusive life of the painter. Their old people and harried pilgrims are echoed in *I Am Still Learning* (*Aún aprendo*, 1824–28), a black chalk drawing of a very old man with two canes, emerging white from a simple, undefined darkness. In another drawing, *So Do Useful Men End Up* (*Así suelen acabar los hombres útiles*), an old man on crutches is unrewarded, but still alive. In *The Last Communion of St. Joseph of Calasanz* (1819) the light from some unperceived dome sends a shaft down through the deep darkness to stop just short of the saint, so aged that he can barely hold himself in the kneeling position, his eyes closed in what could be read as either rapture at communion or an utter fatigue that, on the threshold of death, blends into rapture. The saint is shown full-view, while the faces of the spectators are sketched roughly (and his face is indeed somewhat rough). His garments are black, those of the priest prevailingly white. The priest's face is virtually invisible, turned three-quarters away, while the saint's face is turned three-quarters toward us, whereas in a natural perspective for such a scene the two men would be facing each other directly. Over the spectators to the left, at least in the smaller, preparatory version of the Musée Bonnat, there looms in almost total obscurity from the wall what appears to be a painting of a huge head of the Virgin or a female saint.

The eyes of Goya himself are closed in a work of 1820 that shows him sinking back into the arms of the doctor who is propping a cup up toward his lips, and the long inscription of this large painting, serving as a title, records the aging Goya's gratitude to the young doctor. In a more conventional iconography, monstrous figures throng at the chest of the impenitent in *St. Francis Borgia at the Death Bed of an Impenitent* (1788). The black-haired impenitent lies dead or near death, uncovered to the waist in a garish red light, his mouth gaping and his eyes also shut, ignoring the black-haired vigorous saint who holds up a cross. The intensities and exertions of ordinary labor show up, beyond even the glare of Joseph Wright of Derby, in such works as *The Forge* (1812–16), where three men, isolated against a brown background, concentrate in dangerous proximity to a glowing forge, one clenching a tongs, another raising a sledgehammer, and the third operating a bellows, leaning his white-haired head down upon it. Gassier and Wilson print in conjunction to it the similar concentrated postures in a drawing of three men digging (1812–23).[40] This same intentness dominates the contraband activity (as forbidden by the French) of *Making Shot in the Sierra de Tardienta* (1812–14), again a memory from a decade earlier rather than an observed recording. The play of lights and shadows over the many people in the heavy forest catches up the participants in the countertensions of military preparation under constrained circumstances. Indeed, ordinary labor tends to get caught up in systems of diabolical fantasy, apocalypse, or just simple, if extreme, strain. In an India ink wash drawing from Album B (1796–97) an oil-seller beats away masqueraders with a whip. In "Caprichos" no. 18, a mat-maker, as the note tells us, returns home drunk and burns down his house while giving good advice to his oil lamp ("y dando buenos consejos a un candil yncendia la casa"). In no. 40 a doctor at the bedside of a gravely ill man has an ass's head, which suggests that he will not be able to answer the question of the caption, "Of what ill will he die?" ("De qué mal morira?") and a drawing related to it shows "witches decked out as ordinary doctors," also with asses' heads.

Goya verges on allegory but he cannot be confined to it. The giant in *The Colossus* (1808–12) may represent some great phantom, like the monsters of the "Caprichos," or a naked Gulliver turning away from frightened Lilliputians. In harmony with such an interpretation would be the later *Great Colossus Sleeping* (*Gran coloso dormido*, 1824–28), a black chalk drawing in which a head with the closed eyes of Goya's later work takes up nearly the whole frame. This head is swarmed over by hordes of midge-sized human beings who are atop it or mounting the forehead on a ladder in a manner quite congruent with an illustration for *Gulliver's Travels*. In a mezzotint of roughly the same period (1810–18) a colossus sits naked by night, turning his gloomy head round, on an undefined horizontal, his face turned so as not to see the sickle of a moon above it. On the slope below his rump tiny horizontal clusters of what must be cities are spread out, their sharp outlines made visible in the darkness. The assimilability of such figures to human beings on a large scale is hinted at by a *sueño* drawing (1797–98) that depicts the dreams of growing to huge size after death ("crecer después de morir"). Goya often approaches the gigantic; Saturn is a giant, and an earlier work, *The Little Giants* (*Las Gigantillas*, 1791–92), takes a colloquial expression about boys adding to their height for unstable combat in what strains past a genre rendering of childhood.

The Colossus in the "Black" series could also be taken for some great god. Green sky and clouds run through his middle, brown over his head, shoulders, and fist. He swirls away from the people he has finished devastating (or at least grazed so near that they have been panicked into exile). We can no more deduce why his back is turned, and how any such event relates temporally to the wind-swept moving throngs below, than we can attribute either sinking or rising to *The Dog*. With his back turned and moving, the colossus is engaged in the same motion as the people below, and he is more naked than they. But his motion seems more assured and slower than that of the long trains of men and animals, complete with a group of galloping bulls and some galloping horses, streaming in all directions in the obscured darkness below him. Perhaps he is invisible to them or they to him; or the whole canvas, in all its detail, could be a vision of a spiritual state beyond the eye. The presence of what has to be a plotted set of events is locked into the absence of an explanation for them.

The Colossus, like many other works of Goya, both hovers between the visible and the invisible and brings about their fusions, whatever agonies it holds itself bound to make visible in the process, at once raising and transcending questions of final value.[41]. The relationship between what the artist presents starkly before the viewer's eyes and the dark, often irrecoverable source or explanation for it calls for a superaddition of the moral to the aesthetic. Yet this reconciliation at the same time deplores, as it were, the impossibility of mitigations, while steadying the viewer in these strenuous assimilations.

MODERN INSTANCES

Part Two

SPACE, TIME, AND THE UNCONSCIOUS IN THE COLLAGE NOVELS OF MAX ERNST

Chapter 6

I

This century's radical testing of modes of signification in both the verbal and the visual arts has made us aware of the possibility of inducing one mode to enter into some convergence with the other. Freed from the necessity of mimesis and iconography, the modern painter liberates the mystery of the visual toward the referentiality of the verbal, in order to draw further on the mystery of the verbal, to complicate, mystify, and set up further intercommunication between visual and verbal. Drawings within texts and verbal snatches inside paintings—or arch, unrelated titles for them—are actually among the simplest of the composites that have been brought forward by such testing. The conceptual art of the past few years has produced many versions of such compositions.

In one profound act of testing, Max Ernst's collage novels subject a mode and genre of verbal art to the canons of nonverbal presentation, to a sequence of pictures. These, in turn, complicate their syntax for being collages; their interreferences make them mutely analogous to the syntax of a sentence or paragraph. Further, they refer back to words by being excerpted as illustrative material for written texts, some of which were fictions and all of which exhibit the fictiveness of the unconscious.

Here Ernst has succeeded at grafting a form of visual art upon a form of verbal art. These collage novels serve the more as models of possible fusions by making their individual frames, the focused referents in the sequences of these novels, not only graphic plates but collages, composites which, at the time he fashioned them, were a fresh means for the visual artist. The collages of which Ernst composed his novels turn out to be central to their conception, but in principle that kind of juxtaposition is not necessary for visual frames to be mounted into a narrative sequence.

"Max Ernst's designs," Ezra Pound says, "send a great deal of psychological novel writing into the discard."[1] Pound said this in 1934, when the collage novels were still fresh. *La Femme cent têtes* (1929), *Une Semaine de bonté* (1932), and *Rêve d'une petite fille qui voulut entrer au Carmel* (1930), undertake to perform a version of sequenced narration by a series of composite pictures, of collages, in which the element of the explicitly verbal is reduced to a caption or a title. With his assemblage into numbered page sequences of single-page collages that had themselves already been assembled, Max Ernst powerfully projected a linear time dimension on these arresting collocations in space. By calling them novels he also added the expectation of causal sequence to that of temporal sequence, while at the same time frustrating that expectation by the very linearity of the sequence, a sequence unexplained in the glosses on each collage while arbitrarily connected in the pattern that links one to another. The continuities from frame to frame come soon, in these works, to appear persistent in their repetitions but haphazard in the pattern of their appearances. Sequence and cause, within the repetition of single iconic constituents, are set off against one another at the same time that they are called into play.

Here this process of juxtaposition is combined with irresolution. The overall combination projects upon the arbitrary and archly presented time line of the novel the comparable juxtaposition and irresolution of the single pages, each of them offered more conventionally in space as a visual work. One image is juxtaposed to another, and then another. A man has the head of a bird pasted where his head would be; then he is shown holding up his hands while a dressed woman lies face down in a pool of blood; then a mirror and pitcher are set in the background on a dressing table under a canopy; then two roosters are present, one on the floor looking away from her, and one on the bedclothes under the canopy of the bed, looking toward her. Just in this one page (*Une Semaine de bonté*, 153) a number of irresolutions obtain before (or rather while) some central perception of the relation between conscious and unconscious takes over. Has the man-bird killed the woman? Is he raising his hands in horror at discovery? What is his relation to her? To one or both roosters? To the bedroom? Does she have a prior relation to any of these, and if so, what? How do she and they relate to the central title, which names one (or all) of the three bird figures "The Rooster's Laugh" ("Le Rire du coq") (fig. 7)? We have roosters here, but roosters do not exactly laugh to begin with, and it is hard to see this man-bird's posture as including laughter. What might settle the question is the exact nature of Ernst's tone toward this single page, but that is a question to be settled before the other questions are settled.

As for tone, there is a dominant contrast between the cruelty of much that happens in these pictures and the "kindness" announced by the overall title, "A Week of Kindness." The three roosters run a gamut from routine barnyard pride (though this is not a barnyard) to arm-raised apoplectic surprise or horror. The woman lies face down in a wash of blood to which the man-rooster seems to be responding, setting an episodic tone that leaks away from the cock-perched canopied bed, and still more from the mirror at the center of the canopied dressing table. This mirror, the central object in the frame, reflects nothing, not even the calmly perched pitcher and bowl of Victorian night toilets, orderly and enigmatic and evasive, as the figure behind the agitated man-rooster is also evasive, and somewhat focused, perhaps differently. Are we to associate him with the calm mirror or the grisly death?

Looking backward does not help us decide. Page 152 has not one woman but two, both reposing in unusual circumstances, both nude, one awake, the other asleep. Another figure, probably male, is shown on a plinth, nude except for a loincloth, from which a stream of firelike urine (or urinelike fire) pours into a small urn. Consulting this scene are two all-but-oblivious man-roosters, who seem to be in confabulation over a garment. None of the other details (top hat, cane, religious arches, relief sculptures) does more than qualify the tone of page 153. Nor does what follows it, a man dressed almost like a woman in a baggy version of evening dress, pressing his back against an armoire in order to hold a man-rooster inside a closet, while a woman who tends an open fire looks on at his effort in what could be either sadness or alarm.

Moreover, such irresolutions pervade this work, irresolutions that are intrinsic to the way the collage elements are presented. Printing of its nature erases the lines of suture that show in a constructed collage, unless the collagist allows them to be seen. The erasures have the effect of aligning into a simple surface the separate parts of the clipped engravings that are themselves already complex and become still more complex through this juxtaposition. Their seamlessness also emphasizes

FIG. 7. Max Ernst, *Le Rire du coq*. Courtesy of Dorothea Tanning.

the bodiliness of the figures whose rendering has been so completely transposed and so successfully remounted.[2] The simple, even surface heightens the oneiric overcast of so much complexity.

In the erasures of the page in question, has Ernst glued three disparate elements together here, or five, or six? And it would seem that behind the man-bird, entering through the same wide crack in the door, is the Easter Island idol on whom is centered the second half of this "Thursday" section of the "Week of Kindness." The Easter Island idol appears nowhere else definitely among the sixteen collages of this "first example." That "second example" of "black" bears the title "Easter Island," raising through sequence the question raised in just this one collage, what the rooster has to do with the Easter Island idol. Black, in fact, is general for *Une Semaine de bonté* as well as specifically named and foregrounded here; all these collages are black and white. The Easter Island idol was itself, before Max Ernst adopted it, a famous unsolved puzzle at the center of a primitive culture whose writing we cannot read and of which we know nothing. Ernst used the term "totem" in titles, and he often includes totemlike figures in his separate works of art.

Time comes into question here too, because in selecting materials for collage from nineteenth-century engravings, Ernst in one gesture both refers to time and erases it. There are no traces other than general iconographic ones of his sources, though diligent art historians have traced some.[3] In themselves the single iconic constituents refer to a story, as well as to a time in history, but they have been removed from the story, leaving only hints of their origin in such documents as accounts of the sort of sensational murder that always rivets public attention. The particular nineteenth-century accounts that Ernst cut up for his collages had a prominence that had faded by the time Ernst sought them out, a prominence accorded them by their arresting hold on the unconscious, with its tendency to identify sexuality and violence while displacing and sublimating them in ways these collages and their sequences bring to our own attention. The action of the collages is more violent than we would usually admit to ourselves to being, and in that way too, by bringing old or unconscious material to a present surface, they give a meaning to time sequences for which both their muteness and their irresolution offer no explanation. Nietzschean "biocentric" affirmation and the denials of sublimation are here mounted into a single mysterious convergence.[4]

In these single collages, since the elements are cleanly cut so as to be left whole rather than broken (as in other collages), violence somewhat disappears in the imperturbable murk of a dreamlike surface. Violence persists, as a constant emphasis, a realization, a cry, in the continuation of sequences, as it gradually comes almost clear to present itself as a constant in any such assemblage of psychic elements. It has the permanence of the violence in the world of Goya, and its connection with the unconscious makes it even more irrecoverable, as also far more muted, than in Goya's work. The care in Ernst's découpage comes to resemble that of the sadist or the anally repressed—except that deep material has escaped and is organized into free recombination. Ernst has, so to speak, done the violence of cleanly, "surgically," cutting from

his whole sources and contexts pictures of incidents that have themselves a preponderance of violence.[5] The "surrealist" elements and the
"Dadaist" elements are themselves set into juxtaposition, and prominence is given neither to the unconscious celebration of the one nor to
the near-nonsense of the other.[6] Ernst speaks of "the chance encounter
of two distant realities on a frame that does not fit them" ("sur un plan
non-convenant") and also of a "systematic alienation" ("dépaysement
systématique").[7]

In these novels the repetitions, and the causal connections, are at
once simpler and more abstruse than the structures of repetition and
connection in dreams as Freud interprets them. A woman and a man,
with hints of Adam and Eve, are more persistent in each of these three
novels than figures tend to be in dreams. In the first "cahier" of *Une
Semaine de bonté,* the "element" is "mud," which is not one of Aristotle's
four, yet it may be said to combine "water" and "earth," the titles of
the second and the third "cahiers" respectively. Mud may also suggest
the primeval slime out of which the creation on a Sunday might take
place. In the first section the corresponding "example" is *Le Lion de
Belfort,* a statue commemorating a victory in the Franco-Prussian War.
The logical connection here is pronouncedly surrealist, to be super-
seded in the second "cahier" by a logical identity: the element is "water"
and the example is "water." Instead of a causal connection, present or
absent, a whole scale of connections is here offered through the repetitions from frame to frame, and from the constituent of one collage
to the constituent of another. A lion appears in most of the frames of
the first "cahier," but he is usually a walking lion in a man's clothing,
or rather a mobile erotic man with the head of a lion. Water appears
in every one of the seventeen frames of the second "cahier" and so do
women, unless the single figure falling from a railroad bridge of the
first frame (page 41) is either male or androgynous. He/she, too
wrapped in clothing for us to tell, begins a series that continues from
the first "cahier" over a range of clothing from near-total nudity to
complete robing (as here). Somewhat less than fully clothed is the figure
of the third frame (page 43) who stands booted above lapping waves
in a revealing stage costume, ruched and plumed, over the prostrate
body of a man with a rope around his neck, the first definite man in
this "chapter." She leans against a large cathedral clock, which is the
first and last appearance of such an explicit reference to time measurement, though just below the clock and the man is some strange swiv-
eling object on a pole projecting from the waves. This object looks as
though it measured something, especially as it rhymes with a tiny lighthouse projecting on a point. Both of these refer to the motif of voyage
by or over water, and they repeat it, just as the enlarged church can be

taken for a detail of the town that appears in page 42 and the architectural structures that appear in page 41. But between the head of the man, just above the church, and the lighthouse is a jagged silhouette figure that has to be taken for a blurred Rorschach in contrast to these clarities, for a single random element as opposed to these repetitions, because it has too many angles to be either a gargoyle or another man. It is so puzzling as to stand in surrealized contrast to any nonrepetitive elements, like the tiny army marching across the collapsed bridge in page 42. The possibilities of causal connection in all this have been both obscured and multiplied.[8]

Freud characterizes the unconscious as "dynamic" and therefore involved in constant sequences of interaction with the ego that has been reclaimed from it by the dynamic process of getting past early object choices. The superego allows for still more dynamism, as well as for a kind of stalemate, when it turns an introjected ideal figure, father or mother, into a permanent censor. In Ernst's *Rêve d'une petite fille*, the father is ambiguously a censor, a suitor, and a sponsor for her taking the veil; the priests in that work exhibit an analogous ambiguity. From the beginning of the insinuating work, Death figures too, alongside a blatant, wholly sublimated sexuality, and we are in the very period of Freud's most emphatic statement about the death wish, *Beyond the Pleasure Principle*. The very first frame of *Rêve d'une petite fille* shows skulls on bent sticks surrounding something like a fountain enclosed, inside its rim, by a giant sugar shaker, with dragonflies clinging in a circle to the top of the rim, all under an umbrella suspended from the center of a thatched roof. Distant references to the Dance of Death here permute with references to the sacrificial or ancestor rites that result in skull-studded thatched huts in a tribal primitive village. This scene has little to do, except subliminally and ultimately, with the little girl, her father, the Church, or "The Academy of Sciences," which is the heading for this particular initial collage.[9]

In line with all this juxtaposed symbolic material, the collage novels of Ernst, by following time sequences, but also by altering the set of relations for a sequence, do not just exemplify or illustrate the unconscious, as Dali does. Ernst says that the surrealists are "painters of an oneiric reality in perpetual change; by that we must not understand that they copy their dreams on the canvas . . . it signifies, rather, that they move freely, boldly, and quite naturally at the frontier of the interior world and the exterior world."[10]

This kind of transgeneric novel manipulates reactions and changes the ground of its manipulations, including the relation between verbal titles and the collages subsumed under them.[11] Crippled word helps crippled image; this work empowers none of the interaction between word and image managed by Klee. The last section, "Saturday," of *Une Semaine de bonté*, has been reframed, to begin with, by being included with "Thursday" and "Friday" in a single "cahier," whereas the four earlier days had been given a cahier each. Part of the puzzle discussed above between the cock and the Easter Island figure in "Thursday" may be derived from the fact that this day alone of the seven has two subsections and two "examples," "Le Rire du coq," and "L'Ile de Pâques." The "elements" have parted from Aristotelian substances, though the fourth, "Wednesday," has already shifted from versions of air, water, earth, and fire to the Aristotelian humors, to "blood." The "element" for "Saturday" is the most remote of all, "inconnu" ("unknown"). It is not even "l'inconnu" "the unknown." But its "example," "The Key of Songs" ("La Clé des chants"), more than any other, promises explanation as it parodies one-volume nineteenth-century occult treatises. This key, we may infer, turns out to be a woman, because a woman in close perspective dominates each of its ten frames, in only one of which does any other human figure appear. This surface of the focus for Eros is countered by the depth of the caption, and a different interaction between surface and depth is found in the "Friday" section, under the rubric "The Interior of Sight" ("L'Intérieur de la vue"). There, suddenly, as though for summary, the narrative recedes, and the collages, of bones, flowers, and the like, take on a more static and emblematic character, as though explanation had surfaced to plot the depth of this interior. The repetitions from frame to frame of these "three visible poems" are at first greater and then less than in other sections, as they gradually condense from five frames for the first to four for the second and then two for the third. Expansions and condensations, repetitions and novelties, play through these novels to demonstrate the power of the unconscious and to offer a version of an explanation for what cannot be directly explained. The enigma of the visual reasserts itself by enlisting and paralleling the enigma of the verbal.

So for "Wednesday" the element "blood" finds its "example" in "Oedipus," and yet the frames, in staying closer to human figures than does Ernst's single work of that title, still manage to subvert easy identifications of the personages. In a resolute widening of the connection between visual work and verbal title, the Oedipus frontispiece has a plane-tree leaf folded within a sheet of thin paper. The *Oedipus Rex* of 1921 shows giant fingers pierced by an instrument, clasping a large walnut out a bricked window with two large bird heads isolated on the terrace nearby and a balloon elevated in the far distance. This work is complete in itself, rather than enforced into the sequences that the collages of the novels present. It would lend itself to various constructions of animal, vegetable, and mineral, as well as the evocation of commonality between man and animal in the "biocentrism" that Margot Norris reads into Ernst's work.[12]

The first of these frames in the "Wednesday" of *Une Semaine de bonté* (page 117), shows an imperious middle-aged woman pointing a masculine figure to a door that opens on an abyss of pure blackness. In the Oedipus legend she can only be Jocasta, since Merope, the foster mother of a younger Oedipus, did not dismiss him. Neither did Jocasta, however, at any time. The female figure who did command men to the abyss was the Sphinx. This was indeed the fate that Oedipus averted, sending her to the abyss instead. The man here carries a strange, cumbersome wing-frame cape on his back, an echo of the wings of the Sphinx. And he carries the head of a bird, making him a composite of human and animal, as the Sphinx also is. The third figure in this frame, a giant grasshopper at the feet of the woman, also holds a horizontal posture reminiscent of the Egyptian Sphinx. It can be said that the story, such as it may be present, is completely skewed here, while the carrier of the riddle, the Sphinx, is echoed in each of the three figures. In an ornate frame over the woman's head is a picture that could be a whirling landscape or a diagram of Oedipus's mountain roads or a mechanical contrivance in dazzling light (somewhat echoing the ribs on the man's wings)—or simply a badly cracked and broken mirror.

The explicitness and the narrative implications of "Oedipus" are deployed, as though compensatorily, into condensations and confusions. The bird-headed man, who carries through all of "Wednesday," anticipates the bird-headed man in "Le Rire du coq." He is alone in the next two frames, shot in the fourth, and presumably hung in the fifth, though now the bird head has expanded to a fat wattle as the hand of a man breaks into the frame to cup the breast of a young woman with her eyes closed. Where is the Oedipus of Ernst's title here? He gets more remote still as he converges upon the courtship/sexual violence scenes that turn this section, too, increasingly into a repetition of what has gone before. In one (page 123) there are two bird-headed men. In another (page 126) the woman has a bird's head. In page 128 a bird-headed man and a bird-headed woman carry the dead or unconscious body of a girl (Antigone?). Indeed in page 137 the Sphinx itself, direct and unmistakable in giant closeup, stares through the window of a room/railway compartment. The final frame here has no figures but just a heap of skulls.

In this novel the verbal elements all work just to classify. In the earlier two, Ernst had recourse to the language of caption, sometimes of greater poetic complexity than the collage it pretends to explain. This is the case with the first frame of chapter six in *The Hundred Headless Woman* (*La Femme Cent Têtes*), where a fairly simple scene of watchful and busy seamen approaching distant land is qualified only by the most usual of elements, a statuelike woman emerging from the hold, a little girl in dress and lace petticoats pointing off to the distance, and a mysterious hand grasping the rail. The caption, which of course obscures rather than explains, equates through a colon a supple and abstractive hanging participle with the condensed, evocative refrain that runs through the work—"Plus isolée que la mer, toujours légère et puissante: Perturbation, ma soeur, la femme 100 têtes" ("More isolated than the sea, forever light and powerful: Perturbation, my sister, the 100 headless woman"). The last phrase closes on identity with the title of the novel, and as though it were describing the picture.[13] And indeed the pasted-on elements of this frame are almost certainly the two women and the hand of a possible third. Three already begins the count to the round and emblematic number of one hundred.[14] Thus one can make the end of the phrase resoundingly explain the picture. To do so, however, is to leave the initial phrase hanging and to elide the equivalence indicated by the colon, an equivalence more explicit than that between words and pictures, particularly these words and this picture.

The novel and the collage in combination have been brought to qualify mysteries with a multiplicity and an economy it would have been hard for either to do alone. The unconscious, as it were, falls between them and illustrates a dynamism that keeps the cryptic from being simply automatic.

The viewer of a picture pauses to look at it, and thereby he arrests himself into the attitude that highlights the picture as the thing beheld. What the viewer sees in the picture relates to his subjectivity by immediately schematizing it, and in this light *La Femme Cent Têtes* is an object for protean subjective transformation along lines of the Mother. But the reader of a novel in some way identifies with the protagonist, as he enters the stream of discourse silently. The protagonist is not only an object but more pronouncedly an analogous subject.[15] And in this light the woman who can be isolated in each of the frames of *La Femme Cent Têtes* is also a subject, emphasized as such by the novelistic temporalization of her spatial presentation. This interactive process, where spatiality and temporality permute objectivity and subjectivity, gives a strength and salience to the collage novels of Max Ernst. They boldly thrust upon us the impression that a solution has been arrived at, with the clutch of images precisely mounted and sequenced, in the very act of effectually declaring a mystery. The procedure is nuanced by the heavy enclosure of the young protagonist of *Rêve d'une petite fille* in our sense that she and all the participants are drowning in the honey of the unconscious. *Une Semaine de bonté* resubjects these nuances of the unconscious to a dark plot or series of plots, to the strenuous partial realizations of what could be erotic fulfillment. As we turn these pages, time sends us back to space and space to time in a powerful cycle that is also a series, a new vision of the interaction of both.

The directness of a picture subsists between the suspension of the dream and the unambiguous pointing of a Peircean index. In verbal language, and especially in the language of literary works, an indirectness can easily come to the fore, since such works do not enlist—other than indirectly or contingently!—the various performative functions of ordinary language. Ernst sets the directness of a picture that has been blurred by being composed of other unrelated pictures in a collage that is usually an impossible visual scene (which all collages do not have to be). In doing so he has made the visual frame adhere to a sequence that, moment for moment, is simpler in its movement than would be likely in a sequence of narrative sentences. He creates in the blurred complication of the collage a virtual equivalent for the indirect compounding of words, while at the same time retaining the air of flat inevitability that both dreams and pictures share. Such novels test the very limits of social causality while reassuring the reader-viewer that sequences may continue unabated and the most sinister intrications of action turn out to be susceptible of some form of mastery after all.

THE SIGN IN KLEE

Chapter 7

I

In Klee's work the composite sign that constitutes the painting is presented in an ambiguous dimensionality that is made to interact with the verbal signs that label it, the title, in a dynamism or *Bewegung*, to use one of his favorite terms.[1] Such a possibility, of course, had been opened up through the programmatic complication of the painting itself by his contemporaries. And also, somewhat correspondingly, the signs within the painting are asked to work harder than simple icons or simple visual presences usually do. Klee evolved an elaborate theory of how lines in particular combination, points in particular combination, and colors in particular combination could guide the eye of the viewer.[2] These theories, surprisingly, are aimed also to explain what happens through line, point, and color to the spirit of the viewer, as of the painter. Now a certain discontinuity obtains between the visual and the spiritual in Klee's treatise *Image-maker's Thinking* (*Das Bildnerische Denken*), still more than in Kandinsky's treatise of a dozen years before, *On the Spiritual in Art* (*Über das Geistige in der Kunst*). Yet Klee worked, by the careful manipulation of visual and verbal signs, to bridge that discontinuity in a way quite different from Kandinsky's. Klee's way would open into tonalities that are quite alien to the fairly set mood of

Kandinsky, who stayed contentedly on the even pitch of his late works while Klee engaged himself almost with each work in the strenuousness, in what he called the "sparks" (*"Funken"*) of his perception.

As Lyotard has shown us, the sense and the reference in painting work somewhat differently from their corresponding functions in language.[3] Without precisely sifting Lyotard's particular attributions here, it is possible to say that Klee offers both a simplification and a complication in what is initially a fourfold set—two each for language and for painting—and finally a much more complex one than that. While complicating the possibilities by bringing language and painting often into explicit juxtaposition, Klee simplifies them by making them converge on what he clearly sees as a single act of constructive perception involving both space and time. As he put it, "Tension is connection" ("Spannung ist Bindung.")[4]

Klee's investment, as a theoretician, of so much energy or *Bewegung* in the point may direct our attention to the ambiguous role of the dimension in his painting, an ambiguity that intensifies rather than just relativizes the viewer's participation in it.[5]

For Seurat, by contrast, the point or dot was a means of systematizing a visual effect. Seurat took upon himself the task of modifying impressionism, structuring the moment on a single geometric principle, just as Cézanne spoke of handling nature in accord with the cones and other geometric figures that might be taken to underlie visible scenes and objects.[6] Beginning with the point, Klee aims for a direct and energetic local effect, while at the same time leaving uncertain the viewpoint, and the dimensions, within the work. From the dynamic single dimension of the point he moves to two dimensions so dynamic that they leave open the perspectival possibility of a third. In the terminology of James Bunn, we cannot say that any one of the three dimensions is either highlighted distinctly by itself or suppressed; and if one of them is "torqued," the others are too.[7]

Cubism, it has been said (most recently by David Hockney), involves the body by highlighting three dimensions in the engagement of a perspectival relativism.[8] The postcubist Klee inverts this process by forcing the viewer to bracket such problems, to use Husserl's terminology, and thereby in the bracketing to experience an intentional participation that provides a comparable mutual reinforcement of figure and ground. Thus Klee becomes the rich man's Escher, and the resultant visual ease becomes itself highlighted in the playfulness and poetic probing of the title labeling the picture, and sometimes also of the letters, hieroglyphs, signs, and indecipherable figures that are allowed to invade the work. Like Plato and some romantics, Klee thus engages in an irony that contains no element of self-refutation, no endless regress. His irony remains positive as well as tensile, returning the viewer, so to speak, to the assurances built into the painting.

Klee has found a way to work these constructive gestures into an interaction of word with visual image by further playing them off against one another. The titles of his works perform the sort of poetic transmutation of the subject matter that has by now become commonplace in modern painting. In his earliest works Klee gives us a distant but distinct version of the languidities of Gustav Klimt and the mordancies of the early Blaue Reiter, as well as of the satirical element that is pronounced in Jugendstil generally. But already in his notebooks he distinguishes himself from the Blaue Reiter in the person of his friend Franz Marc.[9] His adaptation of pointilliste techniques does not just employ dots as points of visual representation, as Grohmann has noted.[10] Dots in Klee have an abstracting as well as an organizing force, as he claims for them in *Das Bildnerische Denken*. The dot is usually both visual ("*bildnerisch*") and conceptual (involving "*Denken*"). But Klee remains free to manipulate this means too, and in such a work as *Cliffs by the Sea* (*Klippen am Meer, 1931*), his use happens to approach Seurat's in its preponderantly representational visuality. Both representation and abstraction hold for the *pointilliste Insula Dulcimara* (1939), where clouds of color are punctuated by a ship outline and a face. This abstract ideal place with a bite, *Bittersweet Isle,* was originally called *Calypso's Isle*. Even in such works, as often more pronouncedly, his paintings illustrate the maxim with which he began his "Creative Confession" ("Schöpferische Konfession," 1918): "Art does not reproduce the visible but renders visible" ("Kunst gibt nicht das Sichtbare wieder, sondern macht sichbar") (BD, 76).

Pushing further Lyotard's formulation that Klee "represses difference to sublimate it into opposition" (223), we may say that the oppositions are also easily but powerfully surfaced into unity: "Spannung ist Bindung." A chief opposition is that, I have been asserting, between the verbal and the visual. What Lyotard calls a "between-world" ("entre-monde," 224) in Klee is also a forced perception of this world. Klee confronts head-on the double hiding and revelation that Lyotard argues for the visual with respect to the verbal (19). In this way even the abstraction of pure color and design encapsulates a significative force while at the same time transcending one by eliding the differences between the natural and the conventional. Klee wrote a great deal separately about nature.[11] In such a painting as *Once Emerged from the Gray of Night* (*Einst dem Grau der Nacht enttaucht,* 1918), traces of "nature" appear only in the arbitrary colors of the squares, which have been allowed to bleed a little into one another. The squares organize and "illuminate" the text of a poem that in no way can be conceived of as referring to them—except that the middle belt of space in the painting that divides the stanzas of the poem is of a gray to which this first word of the poem and the title could refer:

> Once emerged from the gray of night / Then heavy and dear / and strong with fire / Evening full of God and bent // Now ethereal showered round with blue / Floats off over snow peaks / star-browed to ring.

> Einst dem Grau der Nacht enttaucht / Dann schwer und teuer / und stark vom Feuer / Abends voll von Gott und gebeugt // Nun ätherlings vom Blau um-schauert, / entschwebt über Firnen / zu klingen gestirnen.

The text is given twice—once in Klee's handwriting as an entire title, and once in the lettering of the painting. The title, then, is coextensive with the painting, the name functions partly as the work, the whole as the part, and vice versa. In neither version are the line breaks indicated, though in the written version the stanza break takes up an exaggerated place at the center of the painting. Normal traditions of calligraphy and illumination have been abstracted, and also bypassed, by moving toward the advertising sign and all its contexts of convention, here fused into the conventions of "art object," in convergence with, and at the same time in disjunction from, this text. For its romantic afflatus and diction, this text, indeed, is far more fulsome than the lyrics Klee was writing in his notebook even earlier than this. But it is freer and more obscure in its main reference than a romantic text would be. And so satire shadows the verbal statement, or a satire that is in turn overwhelmed by the abstractions, the disjunctions, and the very hyperbole of this part or whole of a poem. The straitjacket of the small visual squares and lively colors organizes and celebrates the statement while it is gently being mocked.

This interaction between verbal and visual components happens often in Klee's work, as with *Script Pictures, (Schriftbilder,* 1928), and *Secret Writing Picture (Geheimschriftbild,* 1934). In *Villa R* (1919) the large R is imposed on the representation of the villa. In *Color-constructed with a Black-graphic Objective (Farbig gebaut mit schwarz-graphischen, Gegen-ständlichem,* 1919) the only "object" is a letter, nearly abstract, on colored trapezoids and rhombi, the letter R. *Salon Tunisien* (1918) shows small people, their backs to us, by or under spaced palm trees, with the letters of the title painted unevenly through them—a sort of oxymoron: the open-air salon emphasized by the painting. Almost like a greeting card, in its conception and in its title, is a pen and water drawing of 1918, *Memento Leaf (to Gersthofen) (Gedenkblatt [an Gersthofen]).* Here is an all-yellow house or room marked in black lines and seen from above, complete with stovepipe. Printed above the drawing of a heart is:

Thou still alone
You monster
My heart is yours
My heart is thine.

Du still Allein
Ihr Ungeheuer
Mein Herz ist euer
Mein Herz ist dein.

Display Window for Ladies Underclothing (*Schaufenster für Damen-unterkleidung*, 1922) mixes irrelevant names and two languages with the usual advertising signs in the writing for the "entrance": "Anna Wenne Special Feste Preise Eingang Entrée." Yet much is made visually of the bulbous-waisted, somewhat abstract manikins. The watercolor *Alphabet Picture* (*Buchstaabenbild*, 1924) shows mostly indeterminate shapes, red on red. An X and a D are discernible, upon them three E's, a P, and a T. Alternate titles indicating the verbal and the visual are given for *Composition with Windows* (*Komposition mit Fenstern*) or *With the B* (*Komposition mit dem B*) (1919). In this work are indeed many windows, with plants prevailingly in reds and greens. The B, brownish black against violet red, is almost concealed by a larger brownish black square. In *Analysis of Various Perversities* (*Analyse verschiedenen Perversitaten*, 1922) the letters are set quizzically to do the work of identifying birds and various abstract machines, one labeled "R," one "P," with another free R below and a P atop the head of a hirsute stick-figure whose right hand holds what seems to be a manipulating lever that might have some corresondence to the act of labeling. In *Tree Nursery* (*Baumgarten*, 1929), tiny trees are arranged on close-set bent "ruled" lines to seem like letters or musical notes. Such interactions reach a dead heat in *Abstract Script* (*Abstrakte Schrift*, 1931), where all that remains [only the visual effect] of a script a visual form, is the visual effect; the sense and reference of script, which hinge on its sign-function, are here withdrawn. In this work Klee points to the oxymoron between visual and verbal for a script that is so abstract that it cannot be read but can only be perceived as four columns of nonscript, something indeterminately located between scribbles and the signs of an unknown language. In *Signs Solidify Themselves* (*Zeichen verdichten sich*, 1932), too, the work is done simply in blue ink and with no discriminable letters. The signs are abstract. The combination of letters and numbers, as well as a potential signal for error, is built into *Seventeen, irr, 17* (*Siebzehn, irr, 17*). Here the number 17 and the letters IRR are printed on one red and one black arrow by a weeping woman's eyes, nose, and mouth. Her eye is red, her tears, black.

An interaction holds, too, for the indeterminacies or archness of a title, as in the case of *The Twittering Machine* (*Die Zwitschermaschine*, 1922), a device that works only if the birds really stay on the wire, and it does not seem that they would when the crank of the machine is turned. They might fly rather than twitter in that case. Indeed from their open mouths and extruded tongues they already appear to be twittering, an interpretation validated by the original drawing that corresponds to this painting, *Concert on the Twig* (*Konzert auf dem Zweig*, 1921). The wires or the branches, in fact, are close to the musical staves not infrequent in Klee's work at this time, and the aura of blue surrounding the birds, itself enclosed by purple, suggests that this penumbra "makes visible" the chorus of the birds. This title approaches a simple labeling of a complex operation using natural faculties but suspended to one side of nature. As such, like the illuminated poem, it draws on a freedom with respect to the visual work that permits it to function, if intensely and comically, in a conventional way. Both these uses differ from the algebra of Magritte in *Ceci n'est pas une pipe*. Magritte's title for a picture of a pipe allows one, with Foucault, to extend a paradigm at some length, but always proportionally, and always maintaining the verbal and the visual in a distinctness that allows for their permutation.[12] Now the chessboard, too, is a sort of plenum, according to Klee's strictures for the areas of horizontal and vertical demarcation on a picture space (BD, 222–29 and passim). And he characterizes as "passive" a bounded space filled in by color. So the chessboard, or a comparable series of squares, is a particular extreme for abstraction, one to which Klee often had recourse.

Superchess (*Überschach*) invents a term to describe a painting that turns the term into a description of the process of the painting as well as of what is seen in it. This particular work shows a strange chessboard on which the pieces are on two different scales, "super" in that sense. There are just three pieces, so that if a game does remain on the board, it must be some sort of transcendental endgame. This chessboard also has too many squares, and the squares are of uneven shapes, with lines bent and skewed. In his theoretical writings Klee discussed at great length the directions, shapes, and combinations of lines in painting. The line has visual effects that lead to psychological and even to spiritual ones. The painting *Superchess* offers an example of various lines that organize to combine, cancel each other partially out, and return the viewer to an act of viewing, which itself, too, can be defined as a superchess. The title, in the light of Klee's theories and demonstrations about lines, triggers such ratiocinative acts. The title here breaks the connection between word and picture in a way that paradoxically reaffirms and intensifies it. "Superchess" as some new metavariant of a game we know and "superchess' as a hint about the painting so titled, if we attend to what we see, cannot really be reconciled, but they need not be: the zaniness of the invented "game," for which no rules are provided, gives us that clue. Chess we can play, "Superchess" not, without provided rules; we can only look at a painting that plays its lines into our perception, a "superchess." Klee's comic tone carries all this off in such a way that it is not so much puzzling as reassuring, while also being self-spoofing. The rational substructure always present in comedy has been brought to the surface and resubmerged in the double stroke of applying this comprehensive title to the picture. The comic note is carried through in the depiction of the chess pieces, which are not only out of scale with respect to each other but more rounded and skeletal than chess pieces usually are, recalling the abstract birds of other Klee works.

More simply, the title turns what would be an odd and distorted view of an ordinary chess game into a kind of chess game on a different plane. The title asserts that the bent lines and out-of-scale pieces, the oddly numbered and shaped squares, all make sense in some superior realm that is so far not known, one that the spoof of the painting tells us does not yet exist except by the author's fiat. The title compresses and expands the picture ("Spannung ist Bindung") as it does also in other works where combinations and fusions of visual elements are effectuated or at least mock-validated by the title.[13] *Cacti* (*Kakteen*, 1912) densens its color to make its cacti look also like men. *Hat, Body, and Small Table, Sheet of Pictures*, and *Hieroglyph with Parasol* arrestingly collocate random, well-delineated objects. Klee's last painting, "Still Life," floats in an undifferentiated space a semicubic table surrounded by objects not usually included in still lives—the drawing of an angel, plants that look like musical notes or hieroglyphics, a moon, and something like a crumpled horn, along with a truncated African statue on one table strewn with hieroglyphs beside a large pitcher. On the other, smaller table-space something like an upended truncheon sits crowded against one of three differently shaped vases. The title *Around the Fish* (*Um den Fisch*) poker-facedly declares a unity to obtain in a situation that its flatness implies is not unusual, when around the fish we usually have simple water, and maybe a few rocks and seaweed, or else a platter, but not in addition to these a quarter and a full moon, an upended flag, an arrow, an exclamation point, a cat's cradle with a leaf extension, a suspended cross, an inverted and unnatural shadow, plus other geometric objects hard to define.[14] We do not expect to see *A Woodlouse in an Enclosure* (*Assjel im Gehege*, 1940). The title names and locates but also flatly joins what we could not even have identified, so abstract is the painting. The visual and the verbal converge to neutralize what is not neutral in our social context, the woodlouse. This insect is objectionable but so small as not to have built for it any sort of enclosure, still less to have it painted. But this is no Dürer beetle. The miniaturized subject is presented in unminiaturized fashion by being freed of any coordinates of scale, and the verbal and visual flatness allow the disgusting to shade over into the comic. In one sense there is a "divisionism" here, and Grohmann makes much of the term in Klee's use (283–86). But in another sense a union is effectuated. The conjunction of the verbal and the visual does not so much suspend these alternatives as render their opposition secondary to the intensification carried through by the picture once it is joined to its title. As Klee says—and he repeats the statement in abundant variation throughout his work— "Duality is treated as unity" (*"Dualität als Einheit behandelt" [BD, 15]*).

2

The seeming directness of comic presentation in Klee's painting is not an illusion. It derives from the convergence of elements, in which the verbal plays a large and mobile part, as well as from the occasional isolation of a clownlike figure or the depiction of a situation with a funny side. The horrifying, the comic, and the enchanting are brought together through the title and the suggestively monochrome convergence of color and line in *Dance, You Monster, to My Sweet Song* (*Tanze, du Ungeheuer, zu meinem süssen Lied*). Diana is not normally, and perhaps not ever elsewhere, a funny figure. Klee's *Diana* (1931) (fig. 8), done almost entirely in dark dots and blue lines on a light grey background, seems to be moving in clownish solitude through a bare landscape. Her usual cluster of companions and her usual forest setting by a pool have been set at odds. A violet half-face peeks out, composed of a single slant-line nose and two dotted eyes, from what looks to be a scalloped scarf. The figure of the usually beautiful and semidraped goddess is entirely obscured in what can be taken for scalloped garments. She is dominated by the sort of spatial overlays that, again, Klee discussed in *Das Bildnerische Denken*. She seems to be holding a bow down and somewhat at the ready. And she seems to be kicking like a child, or moving in unison with, a largish cross-striped ball at her left foot. Yet over her head, parallel to its flattened top and of a length more than half the height of her body, flies a huge arrow that covers two-thirds the horizontal dimension of the painting. This arrow bears at the center of its side, uniquely and untraditionally, an eye almost the size of her entire head, not done in dots but fully delineated. The title *Diana* forces us to make all these iconographic deductions and arrests the figure away from mere childishness or mere clownishness. An uncomic figure has been set in a comic situation. Unseen by her flies the

FIG. 8. Paul Klee, *Diana*. Private collection, Saint Louis.

arrow over her head, while unseen by her the ball rolls at her feet. Both are seen by us, and we must mute into a sense of the enigmatic our sense of fun over this cosmic banana peel.

The Rope-Dancer (*Seiltänzer*, 1923) similarly transmutes the comic. Is he pathetic, daring, desperate, lonely, determined, heroic, or merely professionally skillful? Rendering him against a plain background away from the genre setting of the *fin-de-siècle* fascination with clowns has the effect of foregrounding and conflating all these possibilities. The rope-dancer dances, too, atop a structure far more complicated than even the most spectacular circus arrangements for such acts. Klee makes much of what he calls weights and counterbalances in painting (BD, 197-216), using *The Rope Dancer* at one point for illustration. One curled line, the general linear arrangement, and the plain background of his act tend to make him an allegorical rather than just an actual being. The curled line and the brownish color of the lines match those in Klee's frequent combinations that use musical notation for suggestion. Even more obscure is the plain white cross that entirely bisects this lithograph, the bottom of its horizontal axis running coextensively with the dancer's rope.

If the figure *Lomolarm* (1923) has a compound name that is transposed into the second main Swiss language ("L'homme aux larmes"), then his absorption in tears moves into another lexical possibility. The combinatory energy applied to his name has also affected his very face. His eyes are too huge; their tops seem to extend right out the top of his head. His nose fuses with his mouth, and the outline of his head disappears in a reddish penumbra, while his green chest is open to show what cannot be a heart—it is dead center. It resembles a sketchily drawn open gloriole, again illustrating Klee's discussed principles for rendering short ray-lines around a curved figure. Birds have individual names only if they are individualized pets, but no human beings surround *The Bird Pep* (1935). The name in Klee's painting individuates him and then sets him in an environment that questions the ground of that individuation. A sun shines down on him but does not penetrate his red penumbra. He walks through plants that might be tall—perspective and species differentiation are not sufficient to indicate firmly. And he walks right out of the painting, beak pointed proudly high almost to the left edge of the picture plane. Without the title we would have something close to a late Odilon Redon; with the title solemnity is sapped by comedy, but to an increase rather than a decrease of mystification. We do not quite have grounds for allegorizing the bird Pep as a human being, but neither can that possibility be withdrawn. Klee, in fact, questions beings by releasing laughter over the residue of enigma that prevails when word and image converge and collide at the same time. The resultant beings, displayed in the pictures, are the slaves of such near definition, while masters of it for their capacity to move freely and collectedly in a world composed of shuffled elements from ours. Diana, the rope dancer, the bird Pep, and many others are notably on the move, virtuosos of an abstract and directed motion.

I have myself been moving toward the evocation of Klee's arrows, and I have already cited one arrow, that in *Diana*. It is an atypical Klee arrow, being feathered, eyed, and of a simple, thin shaft. The others are abstract, and comic first of all for their quizzical presence. Their comedy itself shades into abstractness, as I have been saying that comedy in Klee generally does. Indeed the arrows taken by themselves function in many ways as signs, the way writers on Klee have taken them.[15] They are icons in Peirce's sense, models of themselves. And also indices in Peirce's sense, pointers at something. And also symbols of something—if of nothing else than the possibility of symbolization. In all three of these Peircean modes they are a convergence par excellence: *Arrow in the Garden* (*Pfeil im Garten,* 1929) lets the arrow into the title, and in that painting the arrow is an intrusion as well as an indicator, whereas in combinations where its name does not appear in the title, it combines with too many other disparate elements, usually, to be singled out as a particular intrusion. In *With the Dove Flying Off* (*Mit der herabfliegende Taube*), an arrowlike tower is prominent at the bottom of the work. Indeed, in a context where Klee's announced subject is the visual appearance of particular lines, he moves over into the complexities of the psychological, the philosophical, and perhaps also the spiritual. He says, under the rubric of "the arrow as an active treatment with respect to the movement-manifold of the whole-spatial":

> When positionings have a central tendency, this has its psychic basis. The rational and the less rational are mixed. The sense of the law is as follows, that a natural and simple view area is given, and that with this natural view area something special is emphasized. The loading of the center emphasizes the divergence from the norm.[16]

Taken dynamically, the arrow is an especially strong locus of the sort of motion whose graphic possibilities Klee analyzed at still further length.[17] It tends to be, in the title of another painting, a *Labile Direction Pointer* (*Labiler Wegweiser,* 1937). Taken statically, the arrow is a collector and displacer of attention, an organizer of constituents to which it pointedly does not belong. It disrupts the painting and skews it in a direction, as the fat, differently colored arrows do for *The Wild Man* (*Der Wilde Mann,* 1922), where a red one with a brown one beneath and below it hangs down in place of the penis an African statue, say, would have.

3

What evens out such works as *Poster for Comedians* (*Werbeblatt der Komiker,* 1938) is the lack of arrows. Comedians and signs are topsy-turvy in this work, in alternation with each other. The center of the painting displays a large stick-figure comedian in a jumping posture much like that of *The Wild Man,* amid all the signs that seem to jump. Their visual jumpiness does not here blur their sharp outlines, however—or identify most of them. The title first of all pretends to locate them in a matrix where communication would entail identity for the signs, and they are seen gaily to refuse that. These compositional strategies deeply differentiate this work from the painted bark cloth from Zaire that it superficially resembles, displayed with it in a show of the modernist debt to primitive art at the Museum of Modern Art in fall 1984.[18] Picasso's visual intent is far closer to such "sources" than is Klee's, because only the value and orientation of the signification, not the relation between visualization and signification, have been changed much. In Klee the value and orientation have changed. The figures on the bark cloth are schemas for mythical entities in a cosmos. Klee's entities, because their principle of combination is free, and even because they are tied initially to the casual context of the poster, while released directly from it by their indecipherability, remain submythic while being supermythic. They triumph over myth for their very refusal to enter the mythic, where Picasso, again, gives evidence of recombining, through visualizations, myths of erotic power and presence.

By occurring in a visual environment, arrows and comparable signs raise the question not only of what their particular function is in a given picture but of what general role such designations might have. As such they are not only abstract in themselves—rarely are Klee's arrows more than simple pointers, rarely are they the sort that one might pluck out of a quiver. Their intrusion into a domain where they are not expected also raises the general question of what their abstraction amounts to. And their plotted direction at the same time settles that question. Just as Klee's many hieroglyphic pictures often cannot be deciphered, so the arrows cannot be assigned an explicit target for their pointing. They spread semi-enigmatically across the picture.[19] *Secret Writing Picture* (*Geheimschriftbild*) doubles the enigma by naming it as well as by inscribing it across the picture plane. *Initial Landscape* (*Buchstabe-Landschaft,* 1932) locates its signs midway between the illuminated initial and the sketched landscape. Thereby it manages a reference to the convention of writing, and to the convention of drawing, doing both and neither at the same time. *A Leaf out of the Book of Cities* (*Ein Blatt aus dem Städtebuch,* 1928), turns out to be a cuneiformlike series of rows of linear signs, set out beneath a dark, round, sunlike figure above, much like the one that is set above the abstract lines of a painting that announces its conceptuality, *Limits of Understanding* (*Grenzen des Verstandes*, 1927). *Chosen States* (*Auserwählte Stätte*, 1927), sets out groups of checkerlike trapezoids below a checkered sunlike figure, and visually the painting most resembles Klee's many paintings of imaginary cities. It, too, approaches a visual reference without reaching one, since the "states" or conditions are abstract, and the painting presents itself as only a record of a mental process, the act of choosing.

Osterwold says, "The dynamics of this sign-speech consists in the analogical character of its elements, which stands between the reality they designate and their formal and objectified self-sufficiency."[20] Yet at the same time the dynamic of these signs propounds a possible unity while "standing between," a unity that stands in the future of the viewer and the painter, since the painting suggests it rather than fully effectuating it. Neither visual nor intellectual closure is offered, and rarely is the painting completely abstract in the manner of Kandinsky and Mondrian, to say nothing of the hosts of later abstractionists. Nor is it ever completely schematic like the paintings of Miró or Dubuffet.

Color patterns are a kind of abstraction, and Klee often painted works composed entirely of color squares or blocked segments. Yet never, or almost never, were these matched by the sort of abstract title that Pollock and Albers used. Like *Glass Facade* (*Glas Fassade*, 1940), the title tends to move the segments of color part of the way toward representation. Thereby the interaction between the title and the kind of depiction replays the interaction between letter or indecipherable hieroglyph and visual figure in works where these graphic elements invade the picture space itself. So too, between title and color, if more conventionally, *Churches* (*Kirchen*, 1940) looks more like a stained glass window, the synecdochic abstraction of a church, than it does like church buildings, though a few triangles like simple towers are inserted in its segments. Thus it can offer, as perceived, a "synthesis of spatial-plastic representation and movement" ("Synthese der räumlich-plastischen Darstellung und der Bewegung") (BD, 194).

Color in an abstract way is made to interact with hieroglyphs in the abstractly titled *Signs in Yellow* (*Zeichen in Gelb*, 1937). And for Klee the abstract is never just analytic but always a spiritual indicator. In his syntax the traditional connection of color significations with a spiritual code, in liturgical colors and their echoes through medieval and Renaissance painting, is itself abstracted beyond the loosening of color from representation for tonal effect in Gauguin and Matisse. Klee astonishingly criticizes as more sensual ("*sinnlich*") than spiritual ("*geistlich*") the colors in Botticelli and Titian (*Tagebücher*, 127). He sees his identity as a painter in terms of color: "I and color are one. I am a painter" ("Ich und die Farbe sind eins. Ich bin Maler") (*Tagebücher*, 306). Color is compared with music, notably in the comment about *Fugue in Red* (*Fuge in Rot*, 1921). Unlike Albers, Klee does not really produce practical and perceptual notions about color beyond those of Goethe, Runge, Delacroix, and Kandinsky, all of whom he cites in his fairly extensive discussions of color in *Das Bildnerische Denken*. But he persistently mixes spiritual deductions into his conclusions. Color pairs are called "witchcraft" ("*Hexerei*") (BD, 473). Of color he declares, "Our creative capacity can meanwhile help us also here over the deficiency in appearance to a synthesis of the perfection of otherworldly existence."[21] And yet such "synthesis" is in turn also defined in terms of an abstract pattern, a "canon." Of an expanded color wheel surrounding grey and expanded by black and white he writes: "This unified representation allows us well to recognize a three-voiced movement and easily to follow its course. These voices order themselves in the manner of a canon . . . This new figure one could call the canon of totality."[22]

Klee, indeed, preferred the term "absolute" to the term "abstract."[23] When he spoke of the abstract, he implied the absolute and the spiritual—and he managed to fold suggestions of them into the painting itself beyond the austerity of the theosophist Mondrian. "Purity is an abstract domain" ("Reinheit ist ein abstraktes Gebiet"), Klee said (BD, 72). *The Light and Something More* (*Das Licht und Etliches*, 1931) hints at as much while allowing that possibility that the "something more" could be identified with the tiny outlined shapes and lines spaced across the pointillist field of dots in this painting. "The question means life or death, and the decision rests with the small arrow," he says of a diagram in the *Pedagogical Sketchbook* (36). This remark takes a leap so wild from visual to spiritual that it seems to mock itself, and yet in the context of his work it cannot be said to cancel itself out. Klee saw the very point, the smallest constituent of spatial representation, as a manifestation of the ego ("*Ich*") (BD, 192–96). At the same time, in more usual fashion, he identifies the ego with the largest attributes of the painting, "Material and dream at the same time, and thrown in wholly as a third thing, my ego" ("Materie und Traum zu gleicher Zeit, und als Drittes ganz hinein verfügt mein Ich").[24] And he brought the ego into schematic connection with the actual process of painting when in his pocket calendar he speaks of a "productive ego" and a "receptive ego," both defined in terms of the arrow "with its movement in a single sense" ("mit seiner eindeutigen Bewegung").[25] He posited an "identity of way and work" ("Identität von Weg und Werk") (BD, 168) to put the creative process on a spiritual path that involved the dimensions of space and time he constantly refers to. A whole section of *Das Bildner-*

ische Denken treats of "becoming" (*"Werden"*), the means of getting the temporal process into the painting more pointedly than just the diagrammatic arrow, the dynamic as opposed to the static, or the constructive act of the viewer. The point, again "is seen dynamically as an active force" ("Der Punkt, dynamisch gesehen, als Agens") (BD, 22). "Not the work that is but the work that becomes" ("Nicht das Werk, welches ist, sondern das Werk, welches wird"), he says (BD, 433). And more obscurely in a context where he has been discussing abstraction, the transitory, the object, and the world, he declares that "polyphonic painting is overlaid through and through with music as the temporal is here more something spatial" ("Die polyphone Malerei ist der Musik dadurch überlegen, als das Zeitliche hier mehr ein Räumliches ist" (*Tagebücher,* 380). And he explicitly corrects Lessing when he declares "Space too is a temporal concept" ("Auch Raum ist ein zeitlicher Begriff ") (BD, 78). *Allegorical Figurine* (*Allegorische Figurine,* 1927) shows a figure blocked out in rectilinear segments, with backward-pointing Egyptian feet and a headdress suggesting wind motion, against a plain red background, as though running but with hands held up as though stopping. Klee speaks—somewhat contradictorily if we take it just negatively—of an aoristic ("aoristisch") or time-free element in painting, with reference to nature on the one hand and the need to remove oneself from particular conditions on the other ("sich abheben von Zuständlichen") (*Tagebücher,* 236, 239).

Klee is not contradicting himself when he uses the term "aoristic" to characterize the painting here and then elsewhere speaks of time as being a component of the work. "Aoristic" means not atemporal but rather unbounded with respect to time; it is a temporal term. Since a painting must be looked at a while, and must be constructively assimilated, both the action of the eye and the pausing repose of the mind engage it in a temporal process, one that is highlighted when the painting includes words, which are apprehended in a more exclusively temporal sequence, or even hieroglyphs or loose letters, which suggest a sequence they cannot fulfill. But they do not here disappoint; the loose letters and hieroglyphs take their places, static or dynamic but always also spatial, within the picture space.

Another approach is to include results of temporal change or the process of temporal change in the painting without attempting either the shimmering moment of high impressionism or the quasi-cinematic motion-diagraming of the futurists. *The Twittering Machine,* curiously, offers an exact moment that could occur before or after the operation of the machine. Klee assigns "color harmonies" to the five vowels uttered by the singer Rosa Silber in the painting entitled *The Vocal Fabric of the Chamber Singer Rosa Silber* (*Das Vokaltuch der Kammersängerin*

Rosa Silber, 1922) (fig. 9), but in fact this painting has more than vowels on the rough surface of the fabric or "cloth", and its checkerboard pattern that suggests the time-free plenum of more abstract paintings. Moreover, the seven letters on it—the vowels plus the initials of the singer—have different time values, since conventionally a person's initials are embroidered on his handkerchief, but the vowels she has sung can only have got there, allegorically so to speak, by being imprinted as she spoke them or even breathed them through the cloth. What is a "vocal cloth"?[26] It is an invention of Klee's, by analogy with the veronica, (*Schweisstuch*), the napkin that wiped the sweat from the brow of Christ in Christian legend and in long-standing iconography. As it happens, this term occurs unmodified, and with musical fusions, in the title and representations of another painting, *The Sweatcloth of the Violinist (Das Schweisstuch des Geigers,* 1930). The violinist's sweat is natural, and it involves an agony only by the kind of connection to the spiritual life that Klee seems very much to wish to suggest without overtly declaring it. While a violinist would put a sweat cloth under his chin, "*Schweisstuch*" is also the German term for the veronica, and in this work Klee follows the common iconographic convention of showing the veronica flat and unfurled, taking up almost the whole of the picture plane. The hanging cloth is bordered by narrow, uneven strips of blue on four sides, as though the background were the sky. The alternate title of *Schweisstuch,* however, is *Fruits on Red (Früchte auf Rot),* and the orange-red cloth has drawn (or "sweated") upon it some widely spaced fruits, flowers, and seeds, all growing on elongated, thin stems. At the extreme right of the cloth a small treble clef is also growing on a stem. On two of the flowers are designs, a star and a cross. It is as though Klee, a dedicated and nearly professional musician, were presenting a rebus to suggest that the artist in the form of the violinist goes through spiritual struggles, which in the case of the artist produce invisible growths that may be detected in the physical record of his struggles, on his sweat cloth.

4

The contrast between "aoristic" timelessness and the manipulation of time through space more pronouncedly suggests the spiritual life in works where the title points to a temporal process that precedes or accompanies the action indicated but not depicted in the painting. As Grohmann says of *Intention (Vorhaben,* 1938), "the black symbols lie on a vermilion ground on the right-hand side and on an olive green ground on the left-hand side of the picture; they are edged respectively with white and red. The smaller section on the left, with the figures

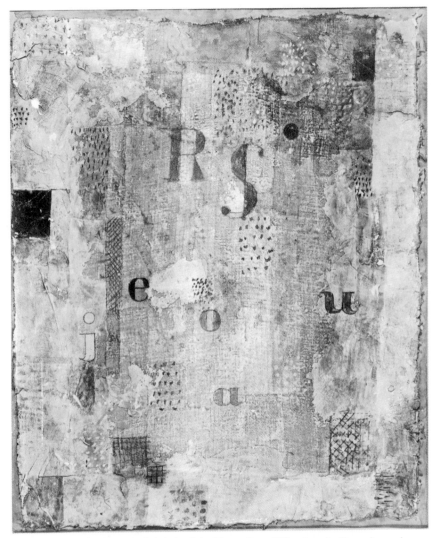

FIG. 9. Paul Klee, *Vocal Fabric of the Singer Rosa Silber* (1922). Gouache and gesso on canvas, 20¼ × 16⅜″ (irregular). Collection, The Museum of Modern Art, New York. Gift of Mr. and Mrs. Stanley Resor.

and animals, the little flags and trees, seems to represent the past; the project is centered on the brighter right-hand side, which is dominated by the large shape that divides the picture in two. The past is clear, the future full of riddles."[27] The eye of the man stands out, while the rough ground of the burlap seems to emphasize provisionality. Yet since riddles of firm outline proliferate in works of Klee that have no particular temporal orientation, one could as well reverse Grohmann's attributions, making the present full of confusions and riddles, while the future would clearly focus on the intent of a single consciousness. In a further dialectical extension of the matter, both clarity and obscurity characterize our actions—past, present, and future; to exhibit both clarity and obscurity in a single frame, under the title *What you have before you (Vorhaben)* or *Intention* produces a spatial sign for a temporal process rather than for a temporal moment, one carrying with it both its clarities and its obscurities.

In the painting entitled *Atrophy* (or *Dying* or *Withering*; *Schwund*, 1940) the visual work broaches the disappearence of conditions that would make it possible. The title moves it away from our vision, so to speak. Something like this is depicted in *Death and Fire* (*Tod und Feuer*, 1940), where a white cartoon mask is shadowed by a large stick figure in the background, as well as by simple lines and colors, and the process of dying is imaged in the alternation of possibilities for these two figures, who could be a dying man at different stages of burning to death or a dying or dead man and, facing him, the allegorical figure Death (who could be either represented figure). Something like this happens in *Little Hope* (*Wenig Hoffnung*, 1938), in which a "disappearing" outline is cut through green plaster. Contrastingly, *Man of the Future* (*Der Künftige*, 1933), could also be entitled *Man in the Future*. The title hovers temporally between a representation in the present of a future being and a mock-divinatory peek into the future to see the being that would be present there.

Still more problematic in their temporal dimension, and also in their reference to theological ultimates, are the many angels Klee painted in his later career, a conventional icon isolated from the elaborate surroundings accorded Saint Michael or the throngs of angels in medieval and Renaissance paintings, so as to suggest a new context and an "aoristic" freedom from time. These, as much as any works of Klee, also resemble children's drawings and associate last things with the life of the child, as Kafka did, and the romantics generally. In these angels the world of fairytale (*Märchen*) and the world of eschatology reaffirm their old connection.[28] Each might have been given the title he gave one of them, *Angelus Novus*. Their gaiety and lightness make them simpler, and at the same time more obscure, than the angels of Rilke, who are nameless, whereas nearly all these have designations—and a nameless, seemingly casual angel or angel-like figure, a cross at his middle, is sketched on what looks like an up-ended scrap of paper isolated between the tables that hold disparate objects in his last *Still Life* (fig. 8).[29]

The notion of the angelic outside a theology tests and marginalizes the relationship between art and a possible religious cosmology. Blake broached such a conception by expanding theology so that art, both visual and verbal, could radiate at its center, through the substitution of quasi-allegorical beings for fixed concepts. The beings had the look of fixity, especially in his engravings, but they take on in his Prophetic Books an actual mobility in their combinations of narrative action.[30] In a still more advanced development Klee's near contemporaries Rilke and Wallace Stevens, differently but comparably, take simple recourse to the naming and invocation of angels from whom full credence is at the same time withheld. Fictionality does duty for apocalyptic consciousness, and the use of the limitations of language to suggest transcendences of language dispenses with accompanying theory (Stevens's "The Necessary Angel" comprising comparable equivocations), even at the hands of dexterous theoreticians. The whole process is carried out simply through the adduction of the word "angel."

In Klee the word "angel" enters the title, and the representational status of the sketchy beings carrying the label "angel" suspends itself into a possible abstraction that elides the barrier between visual and allegorical, to make limitations permute with possible transcendences. This significative gambit complicates the process of Kandinsky, for whom the colors themselves in their "harmonies" invoke participation in something like an earthly bliss. Line and color in the angel pictures of Klee are at once more problematic and still more celebratory. The comic tone provides the fusion.[31] Self-questioning becomes self-assertion, which becomes a visual-cum-verbal equivalent of a smile that participates in a sort of apocalypse, one that at no point admits the possibility of the definite solemnity of an assertion.

Klee's angels dominate and float in a large, undefined space. An aspect of the self-reference in Klee's works is the indeterminacy of perspective in them, combined with a marked and elaborate attention to visual effects within them. Klee speaks of a "wandering viewpoint" ("wandernde Blickpunkt") (BD, 168). Perspective is variously loosened in Klee, but it is usually not abolished, as it is in more thoroughgoing abstractionists, who rest contentedly with the two dimensions of the picture space. Klee at once heightens the possibility of closure into these two dimensions and confronts that possibility with its contrary, the illusion of the three dimensions traditional in Western painting. Yet the absence or uncertainty of scale for the three dimensions—combined with an extreme activity for point, line, and surface—sets the two possibilities against each other, to interact often with a third element, the title. This triple interaction intensifies and enriches while it avoids illusionist skepticism by the firmness of its comic stance, assertive and optimistic in its gaiety even when it touches a wistful chord. Thus Klee goes very much against the grain of either a simple programmatic surrealism that would celebrate the mere unconscious or a simple Dadaist promulgation of the absurd.

Rather, Klee engages head-on, and overdetermines, the phenomenological task of perception. His work simply refuses in its approach to disjoin, as Lyotard declares it must do, from "transcendental activity."[32] In the very act of relating the disjointed domains of the verbal and the visual, Klee's work approaches a synthesis, which it celebrates, between the space of the picture and the constructing space of the eye, as well as the temporal dimension in which the continuum that the painting envisions takes on meaning. This synthesis is the overall sense, as well as the full "syntactic" reference, of the painting. It not only, in Lyotard's words, performs the function of the modernist painting, "an object in which is shown the engendering of objects, the transcendental activity itself" ("un objet où se montre l'engendrement des objets, l'activité transcendentale même") (28). The painting also suspends that activity by keeping the object dynamized, with respect to its visible properties, and concurrently with respect to the segment of discourse, the title, with which it is aligned.

So, in this canny act of supplementation and self-qualification, it avoids the flat figurality that would keep it, in Lyotard's terms, linked to the exteriority of the symbol.[33] Klee has managed in his painting, as have Husserl and Wittgenstein in their theories, to make "exterior" and "interior" considerations that are secondary or irrelevant. And the possibilities actualized in these works throw a comparable light, by analogy, on any painting whatever.

Klee locates his work spiritually between unconsciousness and certitude: "Art plays with last things an unknowing game and yet still attains them!" ("Die kunst spielt mit den letzten Dingen ein unwissend Spiel und erreicht sie doch!" (BD, 80). His plastic invariants, as Lyotard implies, never accord with the harmonious Renaissance principles of the Golden Section or of D'Arcy Thompson's structural-functional abstract symmetries in nature.[34] There is in his work a play of symmetry against asymmetry, as though to make symmetry itself a step in the dialectic of spiritual realization through sight, rather than its analogue and fulfillment.[35] Klee early says, "[An] abstraction of this world is more than a game and less than a breakdown on this side. Thus it is between the two" ("Abstraktion von dieser Welt mehr als ein Spiel, weniger als ein diesseitiger Zusammenbruch. So dazwischen") (*Tage-bücher,* 286). In Klee's practice, as in his theory, his work is associable, and even extrapolable, into many of the categories and problems that have occupied modern philosophers.[36] Such paintings carry us beyond such considerations, while pointedly evoking them. One could speak, indeed—while bracketing the considerable further problems raised when one attributes notions and gestures to a viewer—of a phenom-enological amplification to accompany the phenomenological reduction validating our knowledge of an object in cases where the object is so full as a painting. The two processes energetically supplement each other in assimilating a painting of Klee, which puts the viewer in more of a position to repose in the rich square of color than he would be in looking at a sandwich, a telephone, or even a desirable body, where his desire would tend to engulf the object in sublimations not so dialectical as those engaged when he looks—properly we may say—at a painting of a nude. Klee emblematizes such a process by jarring the repose further into constructive acts that often involve another set of com-municative structures, the directly verbal ones. The final result is not an endless jitteriness before the work—and still less an ironic with-drawal from it—but rather a participation in it.[37]

THE "META-IRONY" OF
MARCEL DUCHAMP

Chapter 8

I

"Irony is a playful way of accepting something. Mine is the irony of indifference. It is a 'Meta-irony,' says Marcel Duchamp.[1] The contradictions in Marcel Duchamp's work are not put at the service of *vases communicants,* of André Breton's goal, to put the dreaming life and the waking life in fluent touch and creative equivalence. Nor are they mounted in the spirit of Max Ernst's narrative hide-and-seek with the unconscious. Rather, Duchamp's contradictions question both the communication and the vessel, while at the same time retaining rich reverberations in each of the disjunct semantic fields he enlists. Even the visual and the verbal stand at interactive odds, as against the moderate abstract convergence into near nonsense of Schwitters, or the well-poised communicative parable offered by Magritte in works of high and conservative visual finish, or the firm quotations and juxtapositions from nineteenth-century graphics set afloat through collage juxtaposition and arbitrary narrative sequence in Ernst's surrealist novels. Duchamp differs from all these by combining persistent sense with persistent questioning, even so early as the *Nude Descending a Staircase* (1912), where the oldest of icons is set in a position and a frame more arresting even than the *Demoiselles d'Avignon* (1907), whose location is the defined space of the brothel. But is Duchamp's nude an imperious woman above the viewer, like the bride above the bachelors in *The Large Glass*? Or is she a figure scandalously appearing beyond the dressing room, something like the demimondaine dancer who would have been maneuvered into such a position by men? And is she posing on the stairs or falling down them in lively but stumbling *danse macabre*? Her actual visual rendering complicates and displaces these questions, since she is shown in an impressionist flash, in a cubist deconstruction, and in a pre-Dadaist spoof anatomy, all at once.

Duchamp's "Readymades" make the inertness of a foregone cultural context part of the question. Duchamp pointedly does not revise his Readymades in a visual direction the way Picasso turns the found object of a bicycle handlebars and seat into a "bull" by foregrounding an underlying visual metaphor. The visual is at once inert and elaborate in the nineteenth-century practical engraving of Duchamp's *Roulette de Monte Carlo,* while the verbal is at once straightforward and endlessly questioning. The photograph of the dignitary on this bond is none other than Duchamp of course, in the center of a roulette wheel and wearing goat horns. Or what look like goat horns. The effect has been achieved by having Man Ray soap Duchamp's hair and arrange it in tufts. The two officials who countersign the bond at the bottom are none other than Marcel Duchamp and his transvestite alter ego Rose Sélavy.[2] The fiscal Duchamp and the sexual Duchamp are one. This collapse of self-reference can in fact be extended into the world of finance, where interlocking directorates produce an equivalent of the same man signing several times under the guise of committee decision, and where stock can be watered to the point of valuelessness. Since Monte Carlo produces nothing but the increment on money gambled away, even a real Monte Carlo bond would typify the rarefaction and ultimate sterility of some highly profitable enterprises. Yet unlike munitions manufactures, such activities take place in an unreal world of pure play. The world of pure play has certain analogues to the world of art, where a valueless piece of paper, a fake Monte Carlo bond, can have high value conferred on it by a few strokes of the pen.

In a sculpture like *Fresh Widow* (fig. 10), the pun on "French Window" sets many interactions going, since the actual sculpture is a miniaturized French window fully labeled at the bottom as an art work. The panes of glass have been blacked out by leather, and the connection to the title leads the viewer not to play over the sculpture visually but rather to draw significative inferences. Conceptual art has begun, but not on its later direct satirical course. The widow is in mourning, and she is also the opposite of a transparent window; nobody knows what is happening inside her, and yet she might be inferred to be entering

FIG. 10. Marcel Duchamp, *Fresh Widow* (New York, 1920). Miniature French window, painted wood frame and eight panes of glass covered with black leather, 30½ × 17⅝″ on wood sill, ¾ × 21 × 4″. Collection, The Museum of Modern Art, New York. Katherine S. Dreier Bequest.

the widow's scandalously proverbial state of sexual readiness, a reading
that the veterinary sense of "fresh" would reinforce.[3] Something in the
relentlessness of an animal response to death makes a widow prover-
bially "fresh" or ready again for sexual activity. On the contrary, however, if a widow whose nose was stuffed up from weeping over her
dead husband were to try to say the words "French window," what
might come out would be the utterance "fresh widow," an embarrassing
reversion, through dreamlike and body-distorted Joycean punning, to
a self-reference that could be taken as scandalously undermining the
inaccessibility of her willed presentation. "I am a new widow, and the
fact that I have been weeping actually reveals rather than conceals the
fact that I am or am soon to be scandalously 'fresh.' I can't help saying
all this, and my very helplessness becomes an appeal with sexual over-
tones that makes me transparent in a way that the particular French
window I am trying vainly to indicate is not." And so on. The whole
set of possibilities here is doubly qualified by literary law and transvestite mockery in the further designation painted on it of the title "Copy-
right Rose Selavy, 1920."

Where is the sculpture in all this? One cannot see through it, but
one can walk around it—a fact that again easily lends itself to significative deduction about the widow but does not really add much to the
visual sculpture. This piece seems, in the fashion of other sculptures of
the period, to be reducing three dimensions to nearly two. Duchamp
interested himself explicitly in theories about the fourth dimension long
before executing this work.[4]

Further dimensional puzzles and further virtualizing of the visual
element in a sculpture are presented by another "window" piece of
roughly the same period, *La Bagarre d'Austerlitz* (1921).[5] Taking one
of the projections of the portmanteau title, the "Gare d'Austerlitz" in
Paris, throws us back on the realization that this flat window, bricked
and with the typical French handles removed, cannot be entered for
business. Still less can it be visually expanded into the complex three-
dimensionality of a real *gare*, with its vast *salle* and its further three-
dimensional extensions of track. Three dimensions collapsed to two in
a sculpture can suggest four dimensions collapsed into three, as in
Edwin Abbott's *Flatland* and in Duchamp's own remarks on the fourth
dimension. In any case there is no way of entering this *gare*. It is closed
for business anyway, or ready for business only in the future. The loops
of whitewash that Duchamp has put on the panes of glass are a French
workman's sign that a house is not yet ready for entry. Or are these
hints of the figure-eights soaped onto windows by bands of American
children in the destructive fun of a Halloween night? The archness of
the title, and part of its other extension, as well as Duchamp's trans-

atlantic existence, allow our reading the whitewash loops in the direction of that kind of *Bagarre*.

On that projection of the title, we have not a railroad station but a battle, one of the great victories of a legendary French ruler, Napoleon. In a militarist ideology—but Duchamp was resolutely antimilitarist—it would be called *La Bataille d'Austerlitz*, not the *bagarre* or brawl that an antimilitarist cynic would want to call any battle, however glorious. The single portmanteau word has a single lexical meaning and becomes a portmanteau only in combination with *Austerlitz*. *Ba-* is not a possible prefix for a *gare* in the sense of railroad station, and *bagarre* degenerates and unmasks *bataille*. The process of construing the title, or relating it to the sculpture, is also a *bagarre*. A contradiction obtains between the visual and the verbal: between this sculpture of a bricked French window and either a railroad station or a battle. There is also a contradiction between a railroad station, which organizes people to travel long distances alone in peace, and a battle, which immobilizes them to fight in a great crowd in war. The references back and forth to the visual window, however, do not contradict but reinforce and pick up aspects of railroad station or battle—but do not ever square the nest of contradictions. At the same time there is nothing inchoate or obscurantist about any of them taken separately.

There is the further sense that society strangely persists not only in warring but in glorifying great battles. It does so by displacing the normal rules for forming the nomenclature of a French railroad station, in the instance of this actual station in Paris, named for where you are rather than, as often, for where you are going. The glory of the battle stops the title rather than pointing it in the direction of Lyon, the east, or the north, where the trains would be going, from stations that take their names from the direction to be taken. To be sure, other stations are named for a location in Paris, but these names are rather more benign, with religious associations or classical, Saint Lazare or Montparnasse. Austerlitz is a place in Austria where a battle was fought. The real Gare d'Austerlitz will never provide a train to or from Austerlitz, and Duchamp's sculpture advertises both the elaboration of its signs and a disappointment of recursive meaning in them, a procedure different from Breton, from Dada, and from Joyce.

The train is of course a surrealist, as well as a futurist, icon. There are trains in Breton, as in Apollinaire, and in Paul Delvaux. But no trains are present either in the sculpture or the title of Duchamp's work. These specially significant and especially cryptic procedures are even more elaborate in the vast late works, the *Large Glass* (1915–23) and *Étant donnés: 1° la chute d'eau, 2° le gaz d'éclairage* (1946–66). In all these Duchamp is what Char calls him, a "distillateur des Écritures."[6] It is an *écriture* that cannot be said to deconstruct fully on the one hand, or to respond fully to or offer *transformateurs* (pace Lyotard) on the other.

Such a work as *La Bagarre d'Austerlitz* does not visually enclose a syntax of discordant signs, as a surrealist painting might. In a Miró we relate star, bird, and woman to a group of abstract configurations that the near abstractness, or even the sketchiness, of the particular delineations within the painting have already suggested. In a Magritte we visually register that a painted sky differs from a "real" (painted) sky, or that a woman's shoe has fused with her actual foot. In a Duchamp the work itself offers us no discordancies: a brick wall with a window that contains windows whitewash-scrawled by the builder can be found in an actual French city. The title taken by itself offers just a simple pun produced by fusing three ordinary locutions, *La Bataille (Austerlitz)*, *La Bagarre*, and *La Gare d'Austerlitz*. As we move from the representational mystery of the fenestrated wall to the nesting signifiers in the verbal title, an interaction is set up just because the discrepancy does not seem obviously discordant; the signifiers seem to belong to domains that do not stand in any sort of simple opposition. Within the verbal realm, this kind of illogical connection also follows surrealist practice: Breton's "le revolver à cheveux blancs" offers domains that are not even opposable to one another, since revolvers do not grow hair nor are they in any immediately obvious antithesis to hair. Duchamp takes this surrealizing practice of Breton's and extends it to the partial discordance between the verbal and the visual realm, stretching the viewer into producing the discordances, for which the work serves as a kind of exercising cause rather than a result. The miniature size of *La Bagarre d'Austerlitz* and the difference between the door on one side and the window on the other hint at the artistic nature of the work—as of course its title and its gallery situation also do. The removal of the handle—according to an ordinary provision in such French doors—from the vertical lock system on the door side hints at the necessity for exercise to "unlock" the work.

Duchamp in the title begins by offering puns of the sort printed in the collection *Rrose Sélavy*, an anthology of puns built on the punning transvestite name of the artist himself.[7] Some of these puns break the class mold of high art by seeming to be drawn from low-life dialect (Cockney rhyming slang and argot puns) or child language (naive scatology or pig Latin). Like the puns on the several pun-discs he painted, these are verbally complete in themselves, whereas the sense of *La Bagarre d'Austerlitz* can be obtained only by shuttling back and forth between the verbal and the visual. Thus is set up an area of assimilation that has a powerful completeness from its enclosure of two realms normally complete each to itself. At the same time the viewer is both removed from "full" aesthetic apprehension by the verbal title's energetic appropriation of the visual artifact and sealed into an active discontinuity for the incompleteness, never resolvable, of the title. The visual window and wall stop both verbal railroad and verbal battle. The verbal railroad and the verbal battle both force the signification of the visual window and wall beyond the threshold of even a constructed visual coherence. Arturo Schwarz quotes Duchamp as saying that his aim is "to transfer the significance of language from words into signs, into a visual expression of the word, similar to the ideogram of the Chinese language."[8] Or into a dynamic version of the Chinese ideogram—begun, we might remark, around 1915 at almost exactly the time that Pound was adapting the Chinese ideogram for what would soon become a central place in the *Cantos*. Duchamp's ideograms, however, surpass the Chinese by being more comprehensive (they keep the visual interacting) and more arbitrary (they are personal; and the senses keep multiplying).[9]

In this way Duchamp makes the verbal ironize the visual and the visual ironize the verbal. Irony usually activates the response of an addressee by calling attention to contradictions in the utterance or in the posture of the addressor, as Socrates forces self-questioning by obliging the addressee to deal with his proffered doubt.[10] But Duchamp's irony circuits itself back through the work. The visual-and-verbal in the work thereby calls attention to the context in which it is exhibited, out of which it has been created. "I have forced myself to contradict myself in order to avoid conforming to my own taste," Duchamp declares, underscoring the obligation he has triggered in the spectator to deal with the artist. In the process he provides a statement that can be applied back to itself in an endless regress: "Any idea that came to me, the thing would be to turn it around and try to see it with another set of senses."[11]

L.H.O.O.Q. is not the title of the *Mona Lisa*—a painting that strictly speaking lacks a title and so may have one provided. The work of Duchamp is not the *Mona Lisa* but a reproduction of it modified by a beard and mustache crayoned on it. The archness of this childish desecration of a hallowed artifact begins as a Dadaist gesture, and it is replicated in the irreverent reading of the cryptic alphabetical title, putting a French slur on the Italian painting: *elle a chaud au cul*. The irreverent sentence gives a transient and demystifying explanation of the smile by referring to a part of the sitter's body not shown in the painting. It does not at all explain the beard and mustache, and they remove her from erotic appeal to de-eroticized transvestite masquerade. She has been turned away from art object into desecrated reproduction, as a sort of reverse Rrose Sélavy. A common Duchamp theme, the gap and the ensuing contradictory connection between eros and high art, has been reillustrated by calling attention to a desecrator who shifts the values placed upon each, and upon the relation between them. Trivializing and modernizing become the same act, and the irony has lost the twist of hurting by not leaving the addressee open to explore the contradictions further than the work posits them. The verbal sense here stops, losing auras and intimations, because it has been recycled back ironically through the visual. It is not only that "Duchamp has brought the tools of chance, humor and ironic indifference into play."[12] He has done so in a way that removes the normal props of them all. Chance comes to have a sort of rigidity; a Monte Carlo bond has a value that is in turn questioned. "I would like to force roulette to become a game of chess," he said. Humor is arrested in its bodily response: the joke offers no cathectic release, and the effect of the interplay between beard-and-mustache and *elle a chaud au cul* may be said to deprive both of the laughter that either would evoke singly. Ironic indifference in this situation comes to exhibit alertness to mysteries it is neither deploring nor exploring.

One can attribute to Duchamp himself an attitude he attributes to Kandinsky, who as the author of *On the Spiritual in Art* cannot be imagined so free of the unconscious and the emotional: "Tracing his lines with ruler and compass . . . it was no more the lines of the unconscious, but a deliberate condemnation of the emotional: a clear transfer of thought on canvas."[13] Duchamp says this with reference to *Tu m'*, the large work that organizes outlines of his own prior works on one canvas. The blank to be filled in for this title *Tu m'(emmerdes)*[14] does indeed control the painting by thought, and a self-referential thought that slights the very work and works it exhibits—an undertone aside of the artist to himself elevated to the position of a permanent designation and governing the viewer's relation not to him so much as to the work that in turn is governed by its relation to him. The "note of humor," Duchamp declares in a letter to the Arensbergs, "indicates my future direction to abandon mere retinal painting." Still, to put a distance between himself and visual surfaces is not to abandon them, but rather to enlist them in an ironic relationship to himself and to a viewer simultaneously, where a Dadaist work does so successively, and thereby traditionally. *L.H.O.O.Q.* has the initial look of Dadaist alphabetical nonsense, but it turns out to have a straight colloquial sense, and the alphabetical coding has the additional ironic effect of playing this "only" key to the painting under the voice. What cannot be directly stated in the polite company of a group going through a museum is what can be taken for the source of all it enshrines, a bodily effect and an engaged desire.

The title is doubly cryptic, since initials with periods after them usually stand for a sequence of words each in succession beginning with the letter printed. *L.H.O.O.Q.* would be an unusual series in either English or French and would be bound to result in some such outlandish sentence as "Let her outpace others quickly," "Ladle hot onions on quahogs," or "La honte ouvre onze querelles." The right approach of enunciating the letters slowly produces a more normative but also a more indecorous sense: "elle a chaud au cul." This sense further erases the sequence of letters by eliding the second and third, disrupting the series and consigning the resultant phrase to an undertone, since the voice must break up *H.* into *a* and *ch.*

The statement "painting is an olfactory art" performs a comparable irony upon the aesthetic effect. The absurd demystification in this sentence can be made to yield two contradictory senses (at least): "painting is subliminal and intuitive in its production by the artist and its effect on the viewer" and "painting makes either no impression or a nonsensical one." In its form this aphorism adheres to the classical pattern of irony by stating a negative to imply a positive, since smell is the only one of the senses not engaged by some art—sight has the visual arts, sound has music and literature, touch has sculpture, and even taste has *grande cuisine.* "Olfactory" involves us in producing such a series, and even in getting to the questionable fourth sense that leads us to ask whether in some sense *grande cuisine* may be an art. This very question returns us to the indubitable absence of any art connected with smell— other than that of the perfumer, whose task is to enhance the erotic appeal that does have some connection with the mainsprings of artistic expression. The work *Belle Haleine Eau de Voilette* (*Beautiful Breath, Veil Water*) puts this term and a photograph of Rose Sélavy on a perfume bottle. "Breath" replaces "Helen," and "veil" replaces "violet." Helen of Troy is a transvestite joke and violet water vanishes into a nonsense phrase. The relief sculpture *With My Tongue in My Cheek* (1959) solemnizes that indication of humor by confining itself to a simple visual representation of what the phrase physically describes. Duchamp is shown in a side view with a cheek more evenly swollen than a tongue pressed into a cheek could really produce. This excess, indeed, leads the viewer to perceive it as what it feels like, rather than what it looks like, to have a tongue in the cheek. But in both cases it remains physical and "unhumorous."

This Socrates, then, wishes the viewer to look and think his way back to the displacements involved in looking by regarding the seriousness underlying the self-effacement of an artist who has made joking and self-renunciation versions of one and the other. Visual perception cannot seek repose, and verbal expression cannot formulate either propositions or the charmed formulae of an equivalent poetry. The terrain has been bared of all icons but the complex ones that ironically carry out an act of baring. By comparison Oldenburg merely points to a questioning of visual textures and scales by the giant hard lipstick, and Rauschenberg returns the intellectual acrobatics of Duchamp to collage juxtapositions and honorific work-erasures. As a method these approaches have become easy, a classical repertoire.

The effect of Duchamp's irony is often to contextualize the work, and at the same time to suspend it from context.[15] *L.H.O.O.Q.* dislodges the *Mona Lisa* from its Renaissance aura and from its cultural circumstances while referring to those very elements by desecrating them. The Readymades of Duchamp do the same by small but crucial alterations, as in the very first one, *Pharmacy* (1914), where a calendar landscape is altered and enigmatically displaced by a red and green dot placed in the middle of the work and the signature of Duchamp placed at the bottom.[16] The dots, the artistic reproduction, and the signature revolve in a disjunction of nonrelationship. *The Fountain,* a urinal, typically raises a contradictory question (does the water come from urination or from flushing?) and answers it with an absence (water of neither type is seen when the work is set up without plumbing in an art gallery). The signature, "R. Mutt," suggests a man of bluntly humble origins or else a name for a dog that combines the honorific (a dog has two names like a man) and the slangy ("mutt" is pejorative for "dog"). And because of physiology and habit a dog could not use a urinal—a further reason why such a gleaming appurtenance would be consigned to the realm of art (and yet never be created) by a dog— who lacks the realm of art anyway, as human beings should, the Duchamp of that time pretended to claim.

Duchamp said that in 1915 he had a desire to break up forms—to "decompose them much along the lines that the Cubists had done."[17] The act of decomposition proceeds not by visual perspectivizing but by referring the landscape reproduction or the urinal back to the implications of its context through the addition of redefining touches. The touches fail to redefine; the urinal does not become a fountain visually. Nor does it become one lexically: water is not produced, though its relation to water, and of such water to dogs, engenders a thought pattern that sets up three contexts, each of which is a dimension in itself (fountains, urinals, dogs).[18] The social response to the desecrating joke triggers these references. So, too, the red and the green dots do not change the landscape reproduction; they refer it to irrelevance (the dots cannot relate to the landscape), to the enabling art (this sub-Seurat shows where painting, of landscapes or anything else, must begin),[19] and to an art radically different from landscape (patterning, or abstraction, or the color harmonies of Delaunay—anything unconventional). The signature "takes over" the landscape, but impotently. In this sense Therese Eiben is on the right track when she asserts that such Readymades as *Unhappy Readymade* (1919) and *Bicycle Wheel* (1913) offer a tenor and a vehicle but no referent.[20] The space of distance between one referent (fountain) and another (urinal) engendered by the tenor of "artistic act" (mounted porcelain figure) and the vehicle of expropriated object (the installable urinal) creates a giant nonreferent that can only be taken as a bracing, ironic return to a verbal and visual *tabula rasa*.

Dada, by celebrating nonsense, stretches the context, rejects it, and still leaves it in place. The work escapes the cerebration that produced it by consolidating a gesture of assertive rejection. Duchamp's work never abuts on nonsense. In *To be Looked at with One Eye (From the Other Side of the Glass), Close to, for Almost an Hour* (1918), visual modifiers in the form of magnifying glasses, visual design in the form of a pyramidal figure, a visual referral-onward in the form of the glass, all refocus in an "imperial" artistic visual imperative of this work's title. The imperative is so exaggerated as never to be obeyed, but the non-obedience neither rejects context, as a Dadaist work does, nor creates a hieratic context, like the standard work of art. Instead, it liberates its own context through the very mechanism of referring to the manner of its visual apprehension.

More complexly in the same vein, the title of *Why Not Sneeze, Rose Sélavy?* (1921) can refer to its work—marble sugar cubes, a piece of cuttlebone, and a thermometer in a bird cage—only if the imagined sneeze were so strong as to disturb the sugar cubes and temporarily rattle them in the cage, producing a temporary mobile. But no human sneeze could rattle these cubes; they are too heavy. The transition from the lightness of objects in a normal context to the heaviness of artistic objects is figured in the iconic move from light sugar cubes to heavy, enlarged cubes of marble. Sugar cubes are kept in a closed box to keep them moist, not in an open cage, but these sugar cubes have the permanence of art and need no protection. They are displayed rather than shut away. The cubes could feed neither humans nor a bird, since the cage is empty, and in any case is a little too small for a normal bird cage. The piece of cuttlebone, linking the work's sole redundancy of sign, is too big for the cage and protrudes above it, altering the sense of scale. And the thermometer? Its precise measurement sorts ill with the artistic observer, unless he is thought to be running a fever in his transport before the work. Or unless it operates a vain climatic control over the sugar cubes. "The thermometer," Duchamp says, "is to register the temperature of the marble."[21] Or unless its numerical markers are taken to measure not the mercury in the tube but rather the cubes and the cage, the sculptural dimensions—a function it cannot perform in this context. It is useless, in fact, a pure visual display. Before such looseness the alter ego of the artist, the Rose Sélavy in Duchamp, can give in to the random bodily reaction—she can sneeze. Why not? And he can also turn a remark that makes sense only if thought of as muttered to himself into the title of the work. The viewer thus also becomes that alter ego, female to the male of Duchamp, taking his cues and extending his context before the work, which only incidentally "parodies" cubism—or for that matter, constructivism, since this *is* a sculpture that advertises not its rearrangement of planes but its forced coordination of discordant contexts. If you try to lift *Why Not Sneeze,* it creates an effect somewhat mythological, Duchamp asserts.[22] Why? The weight is heavier than the eye expects, and this discrepancy between the body's visual and tactile senses mythologizes not the objects, surely—these remain marble *trompe l'oeil* sugar cubes—but the body of the viewer-holder, become strangely weightless thereby and induced into a realm of hieratic connection.

Duchamp sees Arp's Dadaism as "humor in its subtlest form."[23] And he praises in Dada its exuberant liveliness as opposed to the intellectual tendencies of cubism and expressionism. These angles on an associated provocative posture afford an angle on his own sense of irony and context, where the humor disappears into an intellectuality never separate from it.

2

Duchamp, like many surrealists, exploits the connection between the automatic or machinelike unconscious mechanisms of sexuality and the amorous transport, a connection underlying the visible discrepancy between the soft, curvilinear, rounded body and the hard-edged, rectilinear, skeletal machine. But typically he carries it further even than his own writings do, where the Rose Sélavy texts are more simply surrealistic than any visual work that includes a reference to her. It is Boccioni, who showed rapidly successive views of a moving machine in his work, whom Duchamp calls a "Prince of Futurism."[24] But Duchamp never simply translates Eros into a machine one-dimensionally; he preserves in his most sportive and demystifying efforts the many dimensions of such a virtual connection. The complication appears already in the *Nude Descending a Staircase* series, as he moves past Apollinaire's characterization of him as the only painter still preoccupied with the nude. The tone in which the viewer is to take the *Nude* has been ironically concealed. How great is Duchamp's suppressed distance from the celebratory or even the sorrowing aura of the nude in prior Western painting! Picasso's *Demoiselles d'Avignon* have been set in motion to go a step further. As I have remarked above, we cannot also discern whether the nude is dominated or dominating, anatomically deconstructed or cubistically dazzling. Octavio Paz says, "The *Nude* is an anti-mechanism. The irony comes first from our not knowing if we are dealing with a nude. Locked into a corset or a suit of armor, it is inviolable."[25] Yet the title's first word tells us it *is* a nude; Paz's deduction must be applied not to the visual effect but to our intellectual construction upon it. Are our eyes failing to focus for the erotic dazzle as she descends? Are we seeing through the flesh to the bones underneath, as in the *memento mori* visual motif still alive in the late nineteenth century? These questions, too, are undecidable.

Lacan, who early moved in the surrealists' milieu, centers all psychic interaction in a linguistically defined transaction initiated by desire, one that he repeatedly visualizes as an extensible diagram. The link he offers between Eros and the mechanizable is serious and intricate. So is that of Deleuze, who draws on Robert Lindner's figures of armored erotic objects to illustrate a "machine" of sex and the unconscious he asserts would transcend Freud's formulations, an "*Anti-Oedipe.*"[26] Duchamp, the "merchant of salt," can be imagined as taking with a grain of salt such theoretical extensions of his area of association. He himself sets up a psychology with gaps in it, one where, in describing his *Large Glass,* the "ellipse" of "expansion" ("*épanouissement*")[27] does not connect to the "timid power" or to the "magneto-desire." There is a separation between the "woman" in the upper half and the "man" in the lower half of his *Mariée mise à nu par ses célibataires, même.* Indeed, the woman herself is disjoined into a "female hung object" ("*pendu femelle*") and a "wasp," while the men are even further distributed among various domains in ways I shall discuss below. In the woman's area the "sieve" does not really supplement the "umbrellas." In what Duchamp describes as their slow life ("*vie lente*") vicious circle ("*cercle vicieux*"), and onanism ("*Onanisme*"), they include a "Professor of Beer"—a connection only if it is psychoanalyzed to Eros in general or to this specific machine. This term touches a broad note of humor, but not exclusively so in a Europe where it is possible to earn a doctorate in *Braumeisterschaft.* "The bachelor grinds his own chocolate," Duchamp says,[28] and chocolate does not go with beer, nor is the humor of this double entendre of a commensurable sort. For one thing, it offers a differently angled combination of figurative and literal when a representational drawing of a chocolate grinder figures prominently in the work. Still different in its figurative structure from either of these is the machine that bears the mysterious name of a famous weight lifter and strong man of the period, Sandow.

The *Network of Stoppages* (1914) gathers together into near repetition measuring-rods (*étalons*) that make sense only when taken singly. In a group they resemble, and also represent, the nine malic molds or bachelors of the *Large Glass*. Another sense of *étalons* is "stallions." As in the *Large Glass*, the visual-abstraction of human features into hard-edged forms has the effect of neutralizing—but also of measuring or stopping—the operations of sexuality. The whole is randomized by being provided with a case that is a croquet case—whose mallets have a shape that resembles measuring rods. And the game of croquet, in turn, is faintly sexualized (through *stallions*). The network was created by randomizing to begin with: meter-long pieces of string were dropped from the height of one meter.

The machine of the *Large Glass* itself will not work, since there is a thick, opaque line of separation between male and female, and since it is said to function by "cutting the gases into pieces,"[29] an elementary, impossible violation of the kinetic theory of gases. The conception of this unworkable process results in humor, innuendo, and figurative gambit different from the three areas already discussed.

Yet the work combines all these entities and activities. Therefore their contradictions among themselves condense into a spoof of mechanical operation so intricate, and so rich in its individual parts, as to arrest laughter. In this the "machine" of the *Large Glass* differs not only from those of Tristan Tzara or Breton, but also Rube Goldberg, whose machines will work, but through such extravagant connections among parts that the result induces laughter. The "malic molds" of men in the *Large Glass,* unlike Goldberg's paperclip and shoestring inventions, form a machine that will not work mechanically, and one whose parts are greater, not less, than the sum of the whole—which is simpler (erotic activity) than the disjunct intricacies of its evasions. Duchamp's forcing of an erotic mechanism here into an absurd anatomy comes to a self-ironization that paradoxically leaves Eros and the machine in domains that remain distinct—so the very absurdity hints—while all the time the very connection between them is being analyzed separately in the structure of the constituent parts. Eros is not really being analyzed but only diagrammed. Duchamp's mimetic powers as painter and sculptor are kept especially here in a suspension and placed on a nearly transparent glass that gives its name to the whole creation.

3

As his fragmentary writings connected with them, and also his sketches, make clear, Duchamp was working on his two largest works, the *Large Glass* and *Étant donnés: 1° la chute d'eau, 2° et le gaz d'éclairage,* throughout his lifetime. His postures toward them were so extreme that his own attitudes and the course of the career where he kept them deliberately at the sidelines must be taken into account. The first he fussed over endlessly, letting six months of dust collect on it to be partially cleaned for visual effects, and then allowing the random accident of a breakage in the glass to be incorporated into it. The second work he concealed totally while carrying out the posture of a *"respirateur,"* a human being whose profession was not art or anything else but simply breathing, thus letting his act of silence cover it with his much-bruited anti-art posture. In setting these works against each other, one should begin with their location in his career, to which they also refer.

Publicly Duchamp was permitting the two-dimensional, antirepresentational abstract and multiply humorous *Large Glass* to be exhibited as a work even more comprehensive and crowning than *Tu m'*. Privately he was completing the three-dimensional, scrupulously representational, simply arresting *Étant donnés*. The two works differ initially in their nearly opposing disposition to the mimetic canons of academic art. The superrealistic sculpture of *Étant donnés*, using the unfamiliar material of treated hide for the woman, an actual light for the *gaz,* and a real, mechanically operated waterfall for the waterfall, exceeds the representational resources of Renaissance or nineteenth-century painters of figure and landscape.

Thus *Étant donnés* recalls and outdoes the "valenced" context of traditional high art, subverting it by a title cast in the unconventional form of a logical proposition, a title that fails to mention the work's most prominent feature, a reclining nude. The title, too, sets mechanical art against nature. The *Large Glass*, however, recalls and parallels the "unvalenced" context of Duchamp's contemporaries, Picabia, Man Ray, de Chirico, and Arp, to list those with whom he was affiliated. While among them he had to, as it were, conceal his adhesion to the old modes of art, somewhat adhered to in *Étant donnés*; he could exhibit the *Large Glass* congruously in their midst.

D'Harnoncourt and Hopps remind us of Duchamp's sensitive responsiveness to the challenge of a temporary environment. The *Société Anonyme* (founded 1920), indeed, with the double entendre of its title, would have been another one of these, a semiprivate gallery in this instance. "Some of Duchamp's most fantastic forays into the use of materials were done for huge exhibition areas: the ceiling hung with twelve hundred coal sacks over a floor covered with dead leaves and a real lily pond ringed with reeds and ferns for the Paris *Exposition Internationale du Surrealisme* of 1938; the gallery wound about with yards and yards of string for the *First Papers of Surrealism* exhibition of 1942 in New York."[30] Neither the sacks nor the floor of the first example would have been surrealistic, though taken together they might loosely be conceived as so. The sacks anticipate *arte povera* or Eva Hesse; the lily pond, environmental sculpture; the string-wound gallery, conceptual art or Christo. Or rather, these later developments simplify as well as extend the signs of Duchamp's acts, which, like one of his titles, set up series of comments on a specific and temporary location. *Étant donnés* and the *Large Glass*, having evolved through the life of the anti-artist, are permanent. And they paradoxically require a specially defined artistic space, beyond the usual gallery provisions, to house and exhibit them.

By being "as unaesthetic as possible I would be poetic after all," Duchamp said.[31] *Tu m'* complements these works by offering a third context, not the valences of grand art nor the austere recombinations of modern art, but a context that is none other than this artist's previous work: it includes the shadows of three Readymades, *Bicycle Wheel, Corkscrew,* and *Hat Rack.*[32]

Just as his affirmation of sexuality is more modified and qualified than that of his surrealist contemporaries, so Duchamp cannot be found in the simple, standard surrealist antireligious posture. Nor does he more than faintly effectuate their combinations of sex and religion, as in the Bottle of Benedictine structured into the *Large Glass*. He says of the *Large Glass*, "I am non-clerical and ... the genesis of the 'glass' [has] been exterior to any religious or anti-religious preoccupation."[33]

4

Man Ray's *Gift* (*Cadeau*, 1921), an ordinary domestic iron with a row of nails protruding prominently along its surface, presents a coherent and converging series of implications. By choosing the industrially produced object made of a utilitarian metal, he is celebrating futurist canons while being anti-artistic in singling out a humble domestic instrument, something private rather than the large public vehicles that figure almost exclusively in the futurist iconography. It is genre painting, not sculpture, that draws on domestic implements, and the iron is not ostentatiously mechanical, since it is operated by the hand.

A sculpture has tactile values, but these nails say "don't touch"— something that an iron "says" in any case, since we cannot be sure how hot its surface is. The nails are of course in the wrong place, though they continue the material homogeneously, iron and iron.

This *Gift* is a surrealist icon too, like the fur-lined cup. As such it refers not to the world of daytime activities, but to the dream world that communicates with it, according to Breton's assertion.[34] It therefore suggests an erotic object—an unsuckable breast, a pubis half-shaved, a *vagina dentata*. The nails are "exposed" in the wrong place, direction, and set; normally the heads of nails are visible, not the nail itself. The ordinary has been turned into dream as the nails have made useless the normally useful iron. The appealing and the dangerous, as in sexuality, have been brought into conjunction, as have the utilitarian and the gratuitous—all in a coherent and converging implied pattern that finds no parallel in the significations of Duchamp's simpler works, to say nothing of the vast gaps in the *Large Glass* and *Étant donnés*—which exist in the same general surrealist realm, since in their own way they too draw on sexuality and dream.

Duchamp's highly representational *Torture Morte* (*Dead Torture,* 1959) shares some visual and surrealizing features with Man Ray's *Gift,* but it provides far more "activity" between work and title. It also shows a plain surface, in this case the bottom of a foot, dotted with protuberances in an unusual position, in this case flies crawling on the foot. Yet a modified and somewhat incoherent dialectic is engendered when the parody of *Still Life* (*Nature Morte*) is brought into view. The flies would only torture the foot if its owner were *not* dead. If alive, he would not hold still while the flies crawled there—they could do so only if he were dead. Flies would be likely to crawl in such numbers on the bottom of only a dead man's foot. The photographic character of this work immobilizes—freezes for art—both the flies and the foot. Actually, whether the man is alive or dead, the flies are in any case crawling across the surface. They are "playing dead" for art. Consequently, they offer a "still life" of an ugly and repulsive sort. They do so by enlisting in the formula foot-plus-flies an unusually disconnected part of another large iconographic area, not "still life" but "nude." But nudes usually have some erotic tone, and only a foot fetishist would respond to a disconnected foot. Indeed, as opposed to the wholeness of Man Ray's iron, this foot, shown face up, may possibly be dismembered as well as disconnected. If amputated, even without the flies, it would be still more repulsive (rather than attractive, like a still life or nude).

Even more in Duchamp's work, by contrast, and saliently in the *Large Glass* and *Étant donnés,* there obtains what Lyotard calls an incongruence. This incongruence resists even assignment to different "frames," with Hedges's adaptation of Minsky.[35] On the one hand, the *Large Glass* is all in the same frame, sexuality. So are the two halves, male bachelors and female bride. It is only in the details, and in the large spaces punctuated by such visual groupings as the "chariot," the "oculist's glass," the "milky way," and so on, that discordances appear. These are deeply incongruous in themselves, and yet paradoxicaly they leap their discontinuities of space and logic so as to contribute to the machine of sexual fulfillment.

The incongruity underscores Duchamp's economy of means, as

against the proliferation of simpler entities in such surrealist works as Picabia's *L'Oeil cacylodate* or the canvases of Miró. In *Étant donnés* especially, the nude exhausts that icon both mimetically (it is superrealistic) and in its unveiling (the spotlight built into the sculpture is directed by Duchamp to fall on the shaved vulva that her splayed legs exhibit, and it is one in which some excitation is discernible). Even the fact that the head of the nude falls beyond the viewer contributes to the focus on the body. "Landscape" is a domain not necessarily incongruous with "nude"; nineteenth-century painters and earlier ones put the nude in a landscape, as does the *Déjeuner sur l'Herbe*.[36] In this work, though, the background landscape and its waterfall do not easily merge and fuse with the woman who lies on dead leaves and twigs, while a near forest flourishes greenly beyond her. Certainly the lamp she holds up in her hand–the Bec Auer furnishing the *gaz d'éclairage* of the title— is simply but definitely incongruous to her and to the landscape. All these, as a scene of merging and celebration, are cut off into a fixed discontinuity from the viewer, who approaches a real weathered Spanish door with a crack in it. Such a crack would provide a view not of a landscape, still less of a plein air nude, but rather of an interior— perhaps one lit by gas. The interior is emphasized by an irregular frame of broken bricks around the scene beyond the peephole. Looking through the crack, the viewer not only becomes a "voyeur"; he also posts himself at the intersection of the actual (a real Spanish door) and the dreamlike (to a house that has no interior but opens on a fixed erotic object and a beautiful landscape, combined strangely and incongruously with a gas light held in the nude's hand).[37]

The discussions about the relation of such perceptions to projections into a fourth dimension, by Duchamp and the various writers on him, give a mathematical or logical cast to these significant incongruences. Their force lies not in their resistance to relations among the terms visually offered by Duchamp, but rather to the wakefulness induced as a result of confronting them, a cognitive attainment beyond art. This cognition takes as a springboard, without resting on it, the paradox that most artistic is that which initially rejects art—and most visual that which modifies the visual.

One is reminded of David Burrell's discussion of analogy: "Since we know how to operate with = but have no idea what to do with :, ::, :, the schema a:b::c:d becomes itself an analogy, at once useful and misleading, for analogous usage."[38] Such a logical proviso underlies Lyotard's assertion that the duplicitous wall imagined to separate the *Large Glass* down the middle is analogous to the *dissoi logoi*, the double propositions, of the Sophists.[39] "There are no problems; problems are an invention of the spirit [*esprit*]," Duchamp said to Rudi Blesh.[40] The

"Wilson-Lincoln effect," or seeing one profile against another, is attributed to passing from bottom to top of the *Large Glass* by Lyotard and Duchamp,[41] because the work does not just reside in such visual properties. The effect falls away as one more relational opening in the work, and returns as another incongruity. Duchamp's work well conforms to the difficulties formulated by more recent investigators in perception theory, who find that size, overlap, perspective, density gradients, and other features are both hard to ascertain and heavily dependent on cultural cues.[42] The whole, Lyotard insists, thus moves toward the "positive irony" of Duchamp's assertion, since the lack of connection among constituents paradoxically alows an embrace of their discordancies rather than the ironic dialectic of interqualification.[43] Duchamp himself, indeed, is ironic in a more ordinary sense when he says that he treats the title as an invisible color.[44] An invisible color anyway is a paradox, but the title of a Duchamp work at once orients us toward it and separates itself from it, if only by its partiality. (The nude is not mentioned in *Étant donnés,* only the waterfall and the gas lamp she holds.)

The *Large Glass* has an alternative title, The Bride Stripped Bare by her Bachelors, Even (*La Mariée mise à nu par ses célibataires, même*). Taking it by that description first, it is at once apparent that the glass on which the bride and her bachelors rest is a defining quasi-context, as well as a noncontext for them. The viewer looks through and sees nothing, as well as identifying with them. He may easily look through this transparency, remark on its shattered condition, or approach and see himself mirrored, along with the gallery, across the reflections of its surface.

5

The hints of logical operations that "hinge" the *Large Glass* to speculations about a fourth dimension operate at a tangent to the presented work.[45] Central to such a notion is the interaction between intellectual deductions or failed deductions and the disjunct visual panorama of the work, an interaction already present between the decades of notes and the work's gradual construction. The disjunction is of two sorts: First, the constituents are not representational in the same way. The Chocolate Grinder, which occupies the center of the bottom, male panel, is firmly mimetic, and it virtually copies a Duchamp work of 1914. However, even its components (Louis XV chassis, Rollers, Necktie, Bayonet, Scissors) are variously representational. The bayonet looks little like one, and the scissors are far too big. The necktie looks nothing like one. The Glider next to the Chocolate Grinder, to begin with, is out of scale with relation to it. It is a mere skeleton of a glider (or "chariot"), and one of its main components, the equally skeletal "runners," are actually facing the wrong way for a glider—they are set on the short dimension of its rectangle. If they glided, they would glide right out of the picture in one direction and collide head-on with the Chocolate Grinder in the other. And the Glider contains inside itself—skeletal and out-of-scale—a discordant component: a Water Mill. If the Water Mill worked, it would be moving in place, while the Glider, if it moved, would be fixed while moving. But nothing actually moves; it is not a mobile. And there is no water, only watery glass. Above the Glider and riding on it, the Nine Malic Molds are neither mimetic nor skeletal. They are strangely shaped casings, each a little different from the others, a "Cemetery of Uniforms and Liveries" which is quite abstract.

The second disjunction among such components is not the visual but the verbal or intellectual. "The bachelor grinds his own chocolate," and the Chocolate Grinder stands allegorically for a sexual activity, probably onanistic, mechanistically conceived. The malic molds, while visually abstract, are literalizing in their labels; the nine of them stand for nine males (priest, delivery boy, gendarme, cavalryman, policeman, undertaker, flunky, busboy, flunky). The items in this list also, by bare juxtaposition, suggest connections (priest and undertaker, delivery boy and busboy). All the terms hint at allegories of relationship to the bride but also indicate a persistent bachelor status: the priest has taken a vow not to marry, the busboy and the delivery boy are too young.

One could go through the other thirteen components of the Bachelor Apparatus in the work—though these are the most prominent—and catalogue further disjunctions, visual and verbal. The upper Bride's Domain of ten components, completed and uncompleted, offers similar disjunctions, verbal and visual—though its disjunctions turn out to offer more composedness than those in the Bachelor Apparatus. The strongest separation in the work—the "bride's garment"/"region of the gilled cooler"/"horizon"—which triply divides the upper part of the work from the lower in visual presentation, is also in logical connection the most firmly established: it links (and separates) Bride and Bachelor(s).

In the viewer's normal relationship to any art work, his constructions of perception sink back into a perceptual grounding that establishes an easy immersive flow between him and the work, and also between the visual properties of the work and what may be called the diction of individual images in it and the syntax of their combination. The visual and what corresponds to the verbal, a significative intellectual content, coexist in an easy, mutually enriching harmony. In a mannerist or cubist work the visual construction, by forcing perception to work harder, induces an intensity in the harmony, but the harmony still obtains. In surrealist works the intellectualizations must work harder, and still a harmony obtains. The unconscious may precede the art work, but it must be reconstructed. No viewer of a surrealistic work looks at it with the passivity in which he receives a dream. Rather, he comes specially awake to the dreamlike in the work, to the ultimately harmonious conjunction of huge bows with nudes, of nudes with railway stations in Paul Delvaux, of birds with plants or frames with skies in Magritte, of biomorphic shapes with each other in Masson or Arp.

Duchamp subverts such harmonies by setting the verbal and the visual into more than one kind of contradiction—thereby paradoxically creating a ground for the conjunction in their ultimate apprehension of the way the work operates, rather than in the visual and significative convergences from perceiving the work.

Duchamp's works, even the *Large Glass*, are noteworthy for the economical spareness of their constituents, by contrast with the busy abundance of Picabia, Magritte, or Miró. At the same time the visual disjunctions in Duchamp's works, as they further disjoin from disjunctions of signification, invoke an alertness in the viewer and impel an intensity. William Köller says, "The emancipation from the category of relatedness and the evacuation of substance-concepts connected with it, stamps all modern knowledge and art with differential intensity."[46] Duchamp moves to the center of such differentials, easily handling and balancing the intensity.

Duchamp early articulated such a process. In the *Green Box* of 1914, while beginning the decades-long process of putting his purposes for the *Large Glass* into words, he speaks of "isolating the *sign of agreement between* this *repose* on the one hand (capable of all the innumerable eccentricities), and on the other hand a *choice of possibilities,* legitimated by and also occasioning these laws."[47] The italics are Duchamp's, and he circles in red the parenthesized phrase. What makes the repose capable of innumerable eccentricities is the choice of possibilities. These jog the viewer from his visual repose, but also return him to it, in a perpetual and encompassing experience. Here Duchamp has found a way to actualize a purpose he had described just a year before, "to find a correspondence in painting for (the process of) comparison in literature."[48]

Duchamp turns the *Green Box* itself into such a work by gathering his notes into it, surrounding them with the box, and placing on the lid of the box the single-item collage of a Kodak label, as though inside were either a photograph of his intellections or materials for the future "photograph" of a transparent object which would be the *Large Glass*.[49]

Maurizio Calvesi says that, "the symbols of the imagination, in their mobility, regroup not through analogy but through convergence in constellations of images."[50] These constellations of images, however, are also divergent. They move back and forth between convergence and divergence, much like the "corresponding squares" of Duchamp's own treatise on chess.

The chance of which Duchamp often speaks is kept alive in the possibilities of connection among the constituents of a work and its verbal and visual properties, while the double disjunctions keep the discontinuities of association so firmly in place that the chance never really comes to rest. This process, again, resembles the dynamism in chess that Duchamp speaks of in the preface to his translation of a treatise by Znosko-Borovsky (whom at one point he actually defeated in a tournament): "After the statics of position play there comes in succession the dynamism of ultramodern play."[51] The *Green Box* and other such notes, then, themselves constitute a large amplification, and effectually a temporalizing, of the visual works they move toward.

In the rare instances when Duchamp works without the substantiation and qualifying supplementation of a visual artifact, his writing resembles that of other Dadaists. The poem "The" reads like a poem of Arp's, and one must imagine Duchamp's art works to dimensionalize his puns and punning notes, which rarely attain the length of "The aspirant inhabits Javel [water] because I had my prick/habit in a spiral" ("L'aspirant habite javel parce que j'avais la bite en spirale").[52] No special features enable us to disengage Duchamp's contribution to collaborative literary works, such as *Les Malheurs des Immortels '22* (with Paul Éluard), presenting the adventures of Mr. Knife and Miss Fork, or *L'Homme qui a perdu son squelette* (with Éluard, Arp, Georges Hugnet, Max Ernst, Henri Pastoureau, and Gisèle Prassinos).[53] His *Transformateurs* and *Inframinces,* text lists of small arresting items, are more simply randomized than they might be if they were connected with a visual artifact.[54]

Adcock speaks of Duchamp's "desire to construct what might be called a topological language [which] represents part of the conflation of geometric and non-geometric categories seen throughout his notes and works."[55] Such "topology" comes markedly into play not only in the significations of the visual elements in the *Large Glass*, but in smaller works where words or letters are set on them. In *Unhappy Readymade,* crushed pages of a geometry text to be hung in a household of newlyweds, the geometry is sublated by being both mangled and invisible. "The wind had to go through the book," he says, and indoors this would be an intellectual wind. In *With Hidden Noise,* a ball of twine between two brass plates conceals an invisible and unidentifiable noisy object. All this is complicated by a caption that Duchamp himself declares not to make sense, a scrambled text of French and English where in fact, if easily identifiable letters are supplied, the individual words make sense: "P.G. ECIDES DEBARRASEE/E. D.SERT F.URNIS.ENT/AS HOW. V.R. COR.ESPONDS." The last word gives a cue, while the word beginning "*f.ur*" breaks the pattern by providing an instance where the dot would have to be erased rather than a letter be supplied. As the *Large Glass* (*La Mariée* . . .) does more metaphorically, these letters approach the condition of a French game called "*la mariée,*" in which words with missing letters are set up to be solved with insertions by the players.[56]

The last note for *Le Grand Verre* refers to a "text" whose "exterior form" would itself be a "table of references." It goes on to mention the interlinear translation in "an entirely new alphabet with no relation to Latin Greek or German letters, not phonetic but purely visual . . . to translate the *progressive* deformation of the phenomenon of conventional hieroglyphics."[57] The *Large Glass* embodies such transformations with no words but those that label its visual components—which would be indecipherable without the labels, while remaining quizzically representational.

Other shuffles are presented in *Fresh Widow* and *La Bagarre d'Austerlitz,* where the active title is providing the interqualifications. Powerful shuffling occurs also in another work where both the title and an inscription are operative without converging toward either nonsense or easy supplementation, the "rectified Readymade" *Apolinère Enameled* (fig. 11).[58] This altered advertisement for Sapolin Enamels is among the most mysterious, as well as the most genial, of Duchamp's smaller works. Done in 1916–17 while Apollinaire was still alive (Duchamp says, "I am sorry Apollinaire never saw it"), this Readymade has three texts, only one of which is given by the advertisement. The S is erased, allowing APOLIN to become APOLINÈRE. While the found character of the first three syllables explains their spelling, it cannot explain why the name of the poet is altered in the fourth, creating a termination, *ère,* which is normally attached to an object, like a *chiffonière* or a *bière,* rather than a person. The past participle, ENAMELED, reinforces this misreading, especially since it can be taken to describe the effort of the little girl gracefully painting the white tin bed frame mounted in relief upon the work. Some strange object called an *apolinère* is being enameled; the Readymade is decorating the poet; and the bed—one thinks of Apollinaire's erotic poetry—is being finished off. Of these readings, only one refers to the representational visual elements in the work,

FIG. 11. Marcel Duchamp, *Ready-Made, Girl with Bedstead, Apolinère Enameled*. Philadelphia Museum of Art. The Louise and Walter Arensberg Collection.

which Duchamp has made even more representational by painting the rear view image of the girl's hair, he tells us, into the mirror on the dresser in this curtained bedroom.

But the title phrase interacts with two others, the first a signature of the painter, given the two unusual twists of a composite date and "from" in brackets—"[from] MARCEL DUCHAMP 1916 1917"—with no hyphen between the dates. The "from" makes it like a letter or a postcard, but this object is too large and heavy for either. The "from" retains a mystery, all the more in the face of *Apolinère Enameled*. The third verbal component, lettered on in capitals at bottom right, is still more mysterious: MANY ACT RED BY HER TEN OR ERPERGNE, NEW YORK, U.S.A.[59] Each word of this telegraphic message, instead of effectuating syntactic closure, opens up into further mysteries. "Any act" is generalizable enough, and so far one could take it as a statement of the wide applicability of the act we see the small girl debonairely performing, as she trails a graceful foot in a near dance step and looks closely at the bulb finial of the bedpost she is gently painting. "Act" suggests a sexual or a Freudian reading, especially since Apollinaire is mentioned and she is painting a bed. But "any act red"? She paints with white. Since letters are in question, should we take "red" as a naive misspelling for "read"? *Apolinère* would seem to legitimate misspellings. Or is "red" an adjective, placed in French rather than English position, where even a telegram would not gain from having the normal English order reversed. But if so, what is an "act red"? "By her" does seem to refer to the girl, though normal syntax would make "her" a pronominal adjective rather than a pronoun; "by her ten" would then mean "by those ten items or people of hers." But there is only one person in the picture, and allowing for a foreshortening of normal word order, or normal punctuation, we get a plausible reading of the young girl's age: "by her, ten" or "by her, who is ten years old." And how much of all this, how many words back, does "or" cover? However that question be decided, the sentence concludes with an equation that will not factor. "Epergne"? There is no epergne in the picture. An epergne is a holder for table decorations, and visually the picture shows no holders, no decorations, and no tables, though the bureau holds a number of toiletry objects that would accord in style and period with an epergne, as the decor of the room generally does. However, an "epergne" is not an "act", and "her ten" is not an epergne, in any plausible metaphorical sense relating to this picture. "Epergne" is a French word that turns out to be rarer in French than in English. "New York, U.S.A." seems to belong to the signature rather than to this mysterious, floating series, to which it is attached. It is given in the letter-by-letter sequence of the

series, however, and as such it is equally mysterious. What does this
metropolis have to do with "her ten," with "epergne," with "act red,"
or for that matter with Apollinaire? It has to do only with Sapolin
paints, and with Marcel Duchamp, who is subverted in a dozen directions by the disjunctions among these three discordant captions, and
between all of them and the calm, simple, representational scene they
are set up to qualify.

For all this one is reminded of what Pauline Yu says of images in
Chinese poetry: "they do not permit us to arrive at any unnamed tenors,
for they many not even be functioning as vehicles at all."[60] The indeterminacy keeps such works endlessly dynamic.

So the last word of the title for the *Large Glass* is gratuitous, which
Duchamp tells us by ironically calling it nonsense, which it is not. *Même*
cannot be read as *m'aime* in *La Mariée mise à nu par ses célibataires,
même.*[61] In the "text" that he describes the *Glass* to be, the *"mise à nu"*
of the title is rendered active, and the locutions range from superfluous
(*"même"*) to denominative (*"mariée," "célibataires,"*) and then to "explosive" (*"mise à nu"*) even before the strange labels from the notes are
applied to its various constituents. The term *"mise à nu"* gives us, Duchamp says, the "effects of an explosion." "But," he notes, "the *sources*
of this baring are in the dynamo desire." And a little later he says,
"every decision or event of the picture [*tableau*] becomes either an
axiom or indeed a necessary consequence according to a logic of appearance . . . each of these . . . is an *excrescence* which indeed remains
. . . only *apparent* and has no other pretension than a *signification of
Image.*"[62] This last phrase, denoting a single image rather than a mul-
tiplex one of considerable discordancies, sends out an ironic dare to
the viewer as well as an assertion for the artist at once evasive and
reassuring.

The logic of *Étant donnés,* too, does not follow from its title. "Given
1) the waterfall and 2) gas illumination" you have . . . the nude? In the
first place, 2 does not follow from 1 here. In the second place, neither
has anything to do with the nude except in arbitrary cultural association
(nymphs inhabit springs, nudes happened to be used to advertise the
Bec Auer). In the third place, within this setting, through a Spanish
door, there are no real clues. This Spanish door has other holes that
turn out not to be peepholes, false clues we may say, from the ones we
look through to see this scene. The discordancy between the waterfall
and the gas lamp does suggest that these exist as clues in a detective
mystery. Sherlock Holmes, after all, did disappear at the Reichenbach
Falls, in the same Switzerland from which Duchamp drew this landscape. But is the prominent nude a corpse? If the body is dead, so are
the twigs, and they are very prominent, too, while the waterfall is quite

tiny by comparison. Its smallness throws an extreme emphasis on the merely perspectival aspects of this visual part of the work. The nude's body shows signs of the flattening of inertness, and of being locked into its somewhat unnatural sprawl. Or is she alive? Her prominent vulva shows some signs of excitation. Why is it shaved? Has she been raped and thrown on a sort of trash heap? Or is she just reclining and sunning herself in nature, and are these rough straws and twigs, which would be uncomfortable, to be taken as signs for grass rather than as a bed that would disturb a live person? She grips the lamp with a gesture that looks as much erotic as it does economical for holding such a fixture. And the lamp is the one discordancy in the visual part of the scene. A nude, a waterfall, a bed of vegetation, trees, distant skies in a stereoscopic three-dimensional clarity—all these go together, and the lamp comes in out of nowhere.

"The glass saved me because of its transparence," Duchamp says.[63] But we are not exactly meant to look through it; we also look into it as into a mirror of our psychic processes, an intellectual-emotional X-ray. Its transparence captures and heightens for this large sculpture the principle Duchamp expresses for art generally. Its "principle of contradiction" is that "in general the picture [*tableau*] is the apparition of an appearance" ("en général le tableau est l'apparition d'une apparence").[64] Duchamp does not follow Plato and say that it is the appearance of an appearance. The word "apparition" has a negative aspect; it is something momentary and possibly illusory. But it also has a positive aspect; it is something conveying a vision behind the appearance, Plato's idea as well as Plato's artifact.

The anthropological context of Mary Douglas is somehow appropriate here: "Rituals of purity and impurity create unity in experience." If we substitute coherence and discordancy for purity and impurity, we get Duchamp's work, as we do if we substitute transparence and invisible background. "A ritual is more to society than words are to thought," Douglas also says.[65] And Duchamp's works are an antiritual that carry out some of this ritualistic transcendence for a society of the mobile and alert. To see *Étant donnés* the viewer must assume a ritual position that is at the same time a flagrant violation of the social compact; he becomes a voyeur/attentive connoisseur. He penetrates the wall of a Spanish town twice to do so, once in the door and once in the interior bricking. To see the *Large Glass* he does well to go from part to part, as in a ritual, but also not to force conjunctions among parts, as in a ritual, and not to question the nearly invisible surface on which it is also concatenated—or to question it endlessly. Duchamp has made these two processes much the same thing.

MAGRITTE

The Smoothing of the Mystery

Chapter 9

I

Duchamp demystifies by setting up a dialectic between visual and verbal. By contrast Magritte is, so to speak, initially undialectical, and committed to mystery. He evens out his "mystery" into the visual, abstracting and surrealizing the landscapes rendered as such intense icons by painters of the tradition for which Turner stands. He accepts and incorporates Goya's direct lessons about cruelty; there is violence of various kinds in his work. But he addresses it in what amounts to solemnity, locking it away from the somewhat randomized play of Max Ernst. He sets about a version of Klee's questioning by resolutely representational means, at the same time setting word and image, the verbal and the visual, into still another rich interaction than those offered by Klee, Ernst, and Duchamp—or for that matter by Arp, Picabia, and Miró.

There are many mysteries in Magritte, and the word "mystère" comes up again and again in his many statements about art. The term can be brought to bear on the paintings of Magritte, taken in any of its many senses—as something ultimately soluble, like a murder mystery;[1] as vague and amorphous, like a woman of mystery; or as full but indefinable, like a religious mystery. First of all, perhaps, is the mystery of why the surrealist discrepancies are so few in his work (by contrast with Miró or Masson or Victor Brauner—or even Paul Delvaux), and why they are so little pervasive (by contrast with the de Chirico from whom he began).

At the base of such questions, there is the mystery of why such profundities are presented in a surface of almost obsessive representational fidelity. Magritte attends even more to such accuracies than does Balthus. In this representationality, he is, to be sure, surpassed by the glabrous accuracy of Dali. But Dali's mysteries soon resolve into banalities, and his painterly dexterity into a mere show of prowess. Dali, the Rosa Bonheur of surrealism, quickly reduces to sensationalism, except in works like the *Crucifixion*. Dali's obsessiveness tries to compensate by showiness for having renounced any attempt at profundity. Only in collaboration with Buñuel, in *Le Chien andalou*, does Dali associate himself with profundity; and the other films of Buñuel indicate that in that film, too, the profundity cannot be ascribed to Dali.

Profundity, however, is attained almost uniformly by Magritte, in a model resolution of the rich interpenetrations possible between the visible and the significative. The accurate surface, to begin with, gives us the cue not to follow Foucault and interpret Magritte mainly as a visualizer of logical paradoxes that might involve or translate into words, even if Magritte, the pleased amateur of philosophy, cheerfully endorses such an enterprise in the very act of qualifying it.[2]

Magritte also answered by reference to "mystery" when asked about his representationality: To the question "Why do you paint trompe l'oeil?" he replied, "Because trompe l'oeil allows me to give to the painted image the expression of depth that is proper for the visible world, and because my painting must resemble the world to evoke its mystery."[3] He also said, "Mystery is not one of the possibilities of the real. The mystery is that which is absolutely necessary for the real to exist" ("Le mystère n'est pas une des possibilités du réel. Le mystère est ce qui est nécessaire absolument pour qu'il y ait du réel") (525).

The mystery of the group of works that show a pipe and inscribe "Ceci n'est pas une pipe," consequently, does not simply loop back on itself through the logical puzzles that Foucault applies to them, discontinuous or not. Foucault reproduces two paintings that use this rubric. The simpler one (1928) sets this inscription within the painting under a giant floating pipe, with the title *The Betrayal of Images* (*La Trahison des images*).[4] The more complex painting of nearly forty years later sets this work, framed on a sort of blackboard, on an easel inside a bare room (a classroom?), while another, untitled, larger pipe floats above it. This later painting carries a different title, *Deux Mystères* (1966), but the only possibility of reaching a count of two would be to count the simple pipes, in which the painting of a pipe and the painting of the painting of a pipe would be regressive versions of each other. In that light the two similar objects, pipes or parts of a painting, could be reduced to one mystery, not two. "It's very simple," Magritte said, when asked about the first one, "Who would dare claim that the REPRESEN-TATION of a pipe IS a pipe? Who could smoke the pipe in my painting? Nobody. So this IS NOT A PIPE" (250) Yet "A word can replace an image," and "an image can replace a word," he says at the beginning of a short discourse; at the end he says, "These images are curious" (97). Again, in a surrealist anthology, and with reference to the earlier painting, he states, "Poetry is a pipe" (59).

Magritte plays back and forth between the logic of his paintings and their mysteries, which Foucault cannot approach in all his dexterous multiplication around the logic they evoke:

> There are two pipes. Or rather must we not say, two drawings of the same pipe? Or yet a pipe and the drawing of that pipe, or yet again two drawings each representing a different pipe? Or two drawings, one representing a pipe and the other not, or two more drawings yet, of which neither the one nor the other are or represent pipes? Or yet again, a drawing representing not a pipe at all but another drawing, itself representing a pipe so well I must ask myself: To what does the sentence written in the painting relate? "See these lines assembled on the blackboard—vainly do they resemble, without the least digression or infidelity, what is displayed above them. Make no mistake; the pipe is overhead, not in this childish scrawl."
>
> Yet perhaps the sentence refers precisely to the disproportionate, floating, ideal pipe—the simple notion or fantasy of a pipe. Then we should have to read, "Do not look overhead for a true pipe. That is a pipe dream . . ."[5]

Even more impressively than in his discussion of Velázquez's *Las Meninas*, Foucault here multiplies simplicities in a way that really draws away from the mysteries of the work. Part of the mystery, I have been saying, is the degree of representationality in the work, and in these works the degree is rather low for Magritte. It is still lower in his 1962 etching *Ceci n'est pas une pipe*, a smaller version of the early work with large lines advertising their sketchiness, lines too far apart, really, to serve as shadows surrounding the etched pipe.

Magritte always has some other kind of mystery under way when he presents visual puzzles, and that mystery ties in with representationality, as well as with the verbal-visual interaction his paintings often pose and foreground. In the painting entitled *Representation* (1962), a balcony-frame on the left miniaturizes the scene of a football game that is shown on a much larger scale at the right of the painting; we are brought up square against a perspectival impossibility but also invited to contemplate a landscape, so that even here Magritte cannot be accounted a more representational version of Escher. *Ceci n'est pas une pomme* (1964) is quite different from any of the group of pipe paintings for insisting on the rosiness, the stemmed presence, the virtual tactile rotundity, of his apple, as though to bury the obviousness of the representational paradox in the very triumph of representation. *La Condition humaine* (1935) shows what could be a sheet of glass held on an easel, so continuous is its seeming frame with the sea scene it slightly cuts—except it also cuts into, and cuts away part of, the wall of the building, as a discontinued arch emphasizes.

"That which one sees on an object is another hidden object" ("Ce que l'on voit sur un objet, c'est un autre objet caché"), Magritte says (434). "My paintings 'look like' paintings without answering, I believe, to what treatises of aesthetics designate as such" (435). And he speaks of conducting researches "to find a unilateral, nonreversible, sense in objects."[6]

Magritte, in fact, mimimalizes, and thereby strengthens, the surrealized juxtapositions that are composed into his painted objects. This gives, along with the strong realistic surface, a sense of fullness to them, and of explanatory wholeness, rather than of fragments pieced together (one angle of approach suggested by Foucault). He himself evokes the image of Ariadne's thread as a way to overcome the temptation to facility in meeting the vulnerability of "the most authentic manifestations of the spirit" ("les manifestations les plus authentiques de l'esprit semblent vulnérables grâce à quelque défaut: on s'en débarrasse trop facilement") (82). "But *holding for real* the poetic fact . . . would become a knowledge of the secrets of the universe that would permit us to act upon its elements" ("Mais *tenant pour réel* le fait poétique . . . deviendrait une connaissance des secrets de l'univers qui nous permettrait d'agir sur les éléments"). The paucity of objects allows for a sort of palping of the thread of Ariadne, length by length, an operation not too hasty upon the elements of the labyrinth of objects in the universe. Careful organization, a deliberate plotting of directions, is crucial. "If the dagger is the answer to the rose, the rose is not the answer to the dagger" ("Si le poignard est la réponse à la rose, la rose n'est pas la réponse au poignard") (326). The mind and the sight are linked: "Thinking an image signifies Seeing an image" ("Penser à une image signifie Voir une image") (374). And he speaks of the painting "that touches us," nonetheless, as "a language without thought"—a notion posed in the form of a question that encapsulates the mystery of its own paradox: "Peut-être la peinture qui nous touche serait-elle un langage sans pensée?" But "nothing is confused except the mind" ("rien n'est confus, sauf l'esprit") (593).

In *Portrait* (*Le Portrait*), aside from the title, the only incongruous object is the eye at the center of the ham steak on the plate; that eye, which may be thought of as replacing the marrow, is enough to sur-realize the ordinary glass, bottle, and table setting. In *The Empire of Light* (*L'Empire de la lumière*, 1958), the defamiliarization has been achieved by representing the light of day for one part of the painting and the light of twilight for the other, as Magritte testifies in his dis-cussion of this work.[7] In *Personal Values* (*Les Valeurs Personelles*, 1952) there are just two discrepancies. One is between the framing bedroom and the size of the objects of personal use that are randomly distributed in it. Elements of this fairly large group—comb, match, soap, glass, shaving brush (of mildly discrepant size)—are themselves quite in scale with one another. They are also lexically classifiable together. The other discrepancy consists in the fact that the "wallpaper" is replaced by clouds and sky.[8] Inside and outside are thus both sharply discriminated and wholly confused, a sort of advance on certain paintings of Matisse, in which outside and inside flow simply one into the other.

Foucault points up the significative, and intensifying, strategy in this painting by calling these collocations of images "calligrams," in a sense actually special to himself, since they differ from Apollinaire's play of space against signification in his book *Calligrammes:* Foucault says, "The calligram has a triple role: to augment the alphabet, to repeat something without the aid of rhetoric, to trap things in a double cipher." Condensing this astute but ad hoc census of attributes, we may confidently deal only with the last, looking to the doubleness of the cipher in Magritte's work, while remaining unperturbed by Foucault's observation that "the calligram is thus tautological."[9] Only by staying with the logic that is just an alphabetic—or calligraphic—beginning for Magritte, need we attend, either positively or negatively, to the tautology, except to abide by the tone that the presence of tautology does set for the painting.

Magritte, indeed, sees himself as taking a new step in the develop-ment of painting, tracing it from Courbet through Corot, then to the impressionists, then to the pointillists, then to Cézanne, and finally to the cubists, sketching this survey in 1936 on the occasion of a Braque exhibition (92–93). He declares that the term "surrealism" means noth-ing for him ("signifie rien pour moi") and compares it to the term "God" (269); and he is often at pains to dissociate himself from the "fantastic."[10] Magritte resists validating the dream in full-blown pro-grammatic surrealistic fashion. He says, speaking of popular literature, "the passages that *always* leave me indifferent (and that's strange) are those where acts take place on the plane of dreams, hallucination, and revery."[11] He declares that psychoanalysis is only one interpretation among others, and says—perhaps somewhat disingenuously in a con-nection where the intention to dissociate himself from programmatic surrealism is quite clear—that he does not believe in the imagination. He does not, because "elle est arbitraire et je recherche la vérité et la vérité c'est le mystère" (544). In this light, Magritte would presumably have resisted the assimilation of André Breton, who says of him, still quite suggestively, "His half-open half-closed eyes, endowed with perfect visual acuity, have been uniquely capable of tracking down and then being guided by the precise moment when the oneiric image topples over into the waking state and when, too, the waking image collapses at the gates of sleep."[12]

2

In his short autobiographical sketch, Magritte emphasizes that he began in 1922 as an abstract, nonfigurative painter. There are strong traces of these purely formal considerations in a painting of that year, *The Rider,* where the abstract segments of color are more reminiscent of Klee than of the cubists. These segments of color do, however, designate persons, a discernible black rider moving away on a schematic white horse, while a schematic couple are kissing to the right. (It is tempting to move, here, not only to the perception of noncubist, abstracted figuration but of an allegory in which the two discernible groups would be identified with Death—the rider and his horse—and Love—the embracing couple.)

But as Magritte keeps insisting, using the term "mystery" as his talisman, "light and shadow do not belong any longer to a systematized world that is regulated by abstract laws; they are united in an order that evokes mystery and which forbids thought to satisfy itself by the questions it could ask and the answers it could find in them."[13] One painting entitled *The Key of Dreams* (*La Clef des songes*) short-circuits both the popular dreambooks that its iconography imitates and the Freudian system of interpretation that its intellectualization at once suspends and evokes, while the discontinuities of the work both parallel and negate in their discontinuities the univocal implications of Breton's "communicating vessels" between dreaming and waking, or between image and language. As Magritte says, with reference to his admiration for Apollinaire, the admixture of the "real" (for which we may read the representational, though of course more is implied by "real"), is "a charming reality, sometimes with approaches to the surreal" ("un réel charmant, avec des approches parfois du surréel") (455). The painting *Readymade Bouquet* (*Le Bouquet tout fait*) may illustrate the mix: a man stands with his back to us looking across a balcony at a forest. This scene is already a romantic condensation, a choice of combining person and landscape that may find its strongest analogue not in any surrealist but in Kaspar David Friedrich. At the same time the most salient detail, a touch of the surreal, juxtaposes to this scene the Flora of Botticelli's *Primavera*. In Magritte's painting the reproduction of Flora extends all the way up to the man's nape across the coat on his back. Intellectually, as a painting of a painting, and as the intrusion of a detail from a Renaissance painting into a "real" scene, and as a violation of the proper code for the twentieth-century ornamentation of clothing in the West (though not for the ornamentation of clothing in Edo Japan), the single detail engenders the sort of paradoxical series that Foucault so eloquently elaborates—and could have elaborated entirely upon this painting instead of upon *Ceci n'est pas une pipe*, since the works of that title, while not atypical, are at the verge of this gesture for Magritte. *Readymade Bouquet* refers to the woman as well as to the flowers on her dress, but first of all to the large print on the man's back hinting at the erotic life that centers him and governs him, while standing behind him and accompanying him everywhere (without his knowing it?).

This "readymade bouquet" also functions visually as an incongruity sealed into harmony, a schematism for the single discrepancy that is typical of a Magritte painting. The intellectual is returned to the visual and anchored in the calming representationality of the painting. Here, as generally, Magritte's surrealism can be defined as a redefinition of and an advance upon the fusion of a realistic surface and allegorical moments in the painting of the Low Countries generally. In *The Chateau of the Pyrenees* (*Château des Pyrénées*, 1959) (a title perhaps taken from Ann Radcliffe, though the painting in no way illustrates a Gothic novel) a large rock, pocked as if by volcanic action, is suspended over the sea, a castle emerging from the top of it. Castle, sea, and mountain, are romantic icons, separately and together. Magritte's work not only suspends gravity and floats an enormously heavy object—he frequently floats in air things that would not so float, as though within the painting the sealed smoothness and the suspension of laws are equally within the power of the painter. He also sutures a visual discrepancy, the castle growing from the top of a rock, into a conceptual discrepancy, the enormous floating rock. The conceptual discrepancy is in fact a greater visual discrepancy also. All possible breaks that might indicate a building in progress have been roughed over. We have to look closely and learn slowly that the castle grows on top of the rock and was not built on it. But the eye (since it has recourse inescapably to its bred knowledge of the laws of gravity) is immediately shocked at the discrepancy of the floating mountain.

For the individual image Magritte explicitly rejects the Bachelardian view that would interpret it as having a "depth in the cosmic sense" ("une vue sur la profondeur, au sens cosmique étudié par Bachelard")

(344). This view he labels "scientifico-poétique" (345). In speaking of the collocation of images, he stresses that by changing the ordering of things "a new visage for the world appears immediately" ("un nouveau visage du monde paraît aussitôt) (255). The term "immediately" here is temporal; but for the spatiality of a canvas one cannot rule out also the logical sense, and there is also at least implicitly a reference to the directness in the "nouveau visage." The collocation can be almost schematic, as in Magritte's schematic deductions about putting an egg in a cage, or juxtaposing a landscape and a door in various ways (98). This process, however, must be undertaken so as to disengage the "secret affinity between certain images" ("une affinité secrète entre certaines images") (97).[14] He broaches a sort of transcendental intentionality when he says, "Thinking of an image signifies Seeing an image" ("Penser à une image signifie Voir une image") (374). And he speculated extensively on engaging the collaboration of Heidegger (387–89).

No surrealist brouhaha perturbs the juncture of incongruous images in Magritte's work. The incongruity can be of placement—we would not find a lion crouched in a living room, nor would lion and living room blend into a single rough gray *Memory of Travel* (*Souvenir de voyage*, 1955). Or it can be merely of size—the objects in *Personal Values* could all be found in a bedroom but not one that had a sky for wallpaper or a bed not much larger than the comb resting on it. It can be a combination of shape and placement: coffins are not in the sitting position in our coffin-using culture; cultures that do bury their dead in sitting position do not use coffins. In any case coffins are confined (as they confine dead bodies) to funeral parlors, churches, and cemeteries; they are not to be found "loaded" in the places of open-air leisure, the balconies, where Magritte has placed them in many paintings. Or the incongruity can be of attribute: mountain-size rocks do not float, birds do not root and become plants (though the breast curve of some birds nearly repeats the curve of some large leaves). Men cannot open their chests to reveal that their intestines have been replaced by spare display cabinets.

The effect of confining a work, often, to just a pair of images or classes of image, or just one suture between one domain of image and another, is to force what is easy to the eye into the question of how a comparable ease can be effectuated in accounting for what the eye has taken in. Brass musical instruments do not catch fire (*Discovery of Fire* [*Découverte de feu*, 1958]). The Prometheus in this painting resides in the mind's eye, and in the memory of a legend that is almost wholly discontinuous with the visible scene, except for the title. Magritte declares that this picture "gave me the privilege of knowing how the first men felt who brought flame into birth by striking two rocks together" ("me donna le privilège de connaître le même sentiment qu'eurent les premiers hommes qui firent naître la flamme par le choc de deux morceaux de pierre") (III). He substitutes a mental "*choc*" in the present to recapture a physical shock in the past. It is the two objects that are necessary, and two of them, rather than just the particular objects (though both fire and the brass horn are common icons for Magritte). He goes on to say that he could ignite "a piece of paper, an egg, and a key"—a series setting up, two by two, further incongruities in the language, since the first is very easy to ignite, the second quite difficult, and the third by normal means almost impossible. Indeed in his photograph with a slightly different title but on the same subject *L'Invention de feu,* the object, not ignited, is a bicycle, held in place though slightly off center, on a pedestal at a park balcony, an advertising sign in the background. Three men hold the bicycle: Magritte, his brother, and a friend; Madame Magritte looks on.[15]

There is a kind of parity among images that raises the question of making a distinction on which Magritte insists but which he says is in no dictionary, that between resemblance and similarity ("*similitude*").[16] "It is hardly possible to choose between two equal images if no displaced preference tilts the scale" ("Il n'est guère possible de choisir entre deux images égales si aucune préférence déplacée ne fait pencher la balance") (335). Magritte's whole effort, carried through with consummate aplomb, is to keep the scale from tilting in this connection. Banishing to triviality the notion of "*similitude,*" he places his whole emphasis on what he calls "*ressemblance,*" having purged it of what would seem to be its distinguishing feature, some act of (visual) matching. In this essay he invokes the invisible and "*mystère,*" while at the same time equivocally confining "the art of painting" to the visible. The equivocation permits him not, of course, to construct a hard argument, but to insist at once on the direct representationality and the elusiveness of the artistic act, which he connects with "thought."[17] It is though he were painting under an awareness of the philosopher who shuttled between France and the Low Countries, Descartes, who said of copper engravings ("*taille-douces*") that "to be more perfect in their quality of images and to represent an object better, they must not resemble it."[18] In a statement entitled "L'Art de la ressemblance," Magritte calls the art of painting the art of resemblance (655) and says that it would be stupidity ("*niaiserie*") to try to represent ideas and sentiments, which belong to the invisible through the visible images of painting. But in some sense he is trying to do just that (and playing ironically *faux-niais?*). The distinction between resemblance and similarity is sharply maintained so that it can be elided, just as the restriction of the visible universe to just one or two discrepancies powerfully unites it to (rather than just indicates) the universe of ideas and sentiments. These two universes, in his view, are not separable in this act of perception and so are not to be characterized as discretely indicated. Resemblance belongs to thought, he says, while similarity ("*similitude*") can be verified by different means of measurement. Peas, the false and the authentic, the sky and its reflection in the water of a lake, are all classified by Magritte under "*similitude*," and not, as many would treat especially the example of peas, under "*ressemblance*."

True to his deft but uninsistent philosophical vantage, Magritte does not really press or systematize this distinction. He makes it here unite seeming and being, as well as the near-identity of peas. In the passage quoted above, the distinction becomes a purchase, a quasi-Proustian one (Magritte was a devoted reader of Proust) for uniting the relation of present to past and the relation of visible to invisible. Applying these notions to his paintings, we may say that Magritte's Prometheus is a memory elided in the flaming horn. In the work that is itself entitled *Memory* (*La Mémoire*, 1948) a white marble head stands in its own shadow between carefully drawn curtains, its eyes lidded (as the eyes of statues usually are not). It sits on a balcony overlooking a seascape, a single leaf and a divided spherical bell (a frequent shape in Magritte) sitting on the same balcony, its symmetrical divisions asymmetrically framed in the painting. Rhyming with the curtain in color, over the right eye of the marble head, is a possible but unattributable splash of blood.[19]

3

When anyone is killed, but especially when a woman is killed, erotic connections, as well as erotic motives, come into play. The marble of this woman's head keeps such a story from being formed; one cannot kill a marble head because it was never alive. Yet the blood is there, visible evidence of a preceding story. The head has "*similitude*" but not "*ressemblance*" to the head of a real woman, if one may apply the terms of Magritte's anti-Peircean symbology, where the distinctions among icon, index, and symbol have first been reduced to two and then inverted. The power of Magritte's handling of that favorite subject matter for surrealists, the erotic, emerges from this resolute attention to a resolute abstractness. Magritte's Eros transcends what it imitates, the identification of love with the machine in Duchamp, Picabia, Man Ray, and Max Ernst; the mere glorification of women as an access to the unconscious and the imagination in Breton and Éluard; the fetishization of the woman's body in all these and in followers like Robert Lindner; and the abstracting of rounded quasi-feminine forms into a super-Eros in Miró, Arp, and Brancusi. Magritte abjures the surrealist view of women as simplistic: "The 'surrealistic woman' has been an invention as stupid as the 'pin-up girl' that is now replacing her."[20]

In what are perhaps Magritte's most "fetishistic" works, *The Red Model* (*Le Modèle Rouge*, 1935), and *Philosophy in the Boudoir* (*La Philosophie dans le boudoir*, 1947–48), the very shock in them modifies them away from eroticism. Toes grow out of the very shoes in the *Red Model*, a fusion that allows either toes or shoes to be thought of as predominant. Either feet are collapsed back into shoes (an antifetishism) or shoes take on the attributes of feet (a sort of postfetishism). These high shoes stand free, their tops open and their laces slightly dangling, on stony ground against a plain board fence.[21] A second version of this painting has no red at all. English coins are strewn on the rough ground as a sign that is was painted on commission for an Englishman, Edward James. A torn newspaper on the ground to the left of the feet-shoes reproduces another "erotic" painting of Magritte's that reverses this work, *Titantic Days*, in which a nude woman and part of a black-suited man are in struggling embrace. On the newspaper are the words "*in-utiles*," "*fumées*," "*solitaires*," and "*malgré*." In both works entitled *Red Model*, all such details modalize them away from a simple fetishism.[22]

Philosophy in the Boudoir, of course, cites and refers to a novel by a writer whom the surrealists singled out for attention, the Marquis de Sade. Magritte's painting does not so much illustrate the novel as parallel it. For the novel's sequences of increasingly violent action he substitutes a pair of high-heeled shoes with "real" toes set on a table before a night chemise on a coat hanger, its front ornamented with "real" breasts and bright red, prominent nipples. These appurtenances, in their fusion, can be taken as either preparation or aftermath of erotic activity, and so an abstraction from both that allows the philosophizing viewer to settle on neither. Rather, they identify and philosophize the attention to either true erogenous zones (the breasts) or the fetishized appurtenances of clothing. It is impossible to justify either the differences or the resemblances, and the philosophical conclusion places a seal of "*mystère*" over the represented objects, just because they can be taken as beginning at the point of obvious fetishising. The "philosophy" starts with an elementary lesson, the bold but unresolvable sight of the painting. An earlier version of this scene (1934) purifies and simplifies this motif by showing the night dress alone, with the breasts but without the accompanying high-heeled shoe-feet. The dress, a somewhat silkier one, is hung up in a fine, plain, open armoire, under a completely different title, *Homage to Mack Sennett*, an evocation for the still, erotic painting of films known for rapid-fire sequences in the public streets not associated with love. This title powerfully redirects all the erotic possibilities of the necessarily stationary indoor object to the sign-system associated with a highly mobile outdoor chase of uniformed men. Under the first title, *Philosophy in the Boudoir,* a photograph by Magritte alters the erotic mix once again. A woman shading her eyes is seated outdoors in a garden chair and seems to be paying little attention to Magritte, kneeling in shirtsleeves, his hands either adjusting or making advances under her large striped blanket.[23] In *Les Liaisons Dangereuses,* the fierce erotic content of Laclos's novel is displaced in favor of a mirror or beveled glass held up by a woman's hands. The woman's body is clearly represented, as always. This glass turns her half round "semi-cubistically" from chin to thighs inside the glass, though her head is turned away above it; below it the frontal view of her lower half includes part of her pubic hair. And in *Les Fleurs du mal,* Baudelaire's title is somewhat softened by a painting in which a nude woman between curtains leans on a rock while she holds a rose, with the sea and the sky beyond.

La Dame rounds a female form in the shape of a bottle, but neither direction can be roped off; this is neither the reduction of a woman to a vessel of something that can be consumed nor the elevation of a bottle to erotic status, but rather a use of curve-resemblance to create an intellectual "*similitude*" that moves toward Magritte's version of "*ressemblance.*" It can indeed be taken, with Xavière Gauthier, as a celebration of woman.[24] In *A Courtesan's Palace (Le Palais d'une courtisane),* a nude body in a mirror/box set in plywood is cut off above the breasts and below the navel. A phallic, smooth turnip (?) leans vertically against the plywood.

The philosophy generalizes the erotic interest. Magritte says, echoing Proust, "If you imagine young girls in flower, you can equally well admit a bird in flower" ("Si l'on imagine des jeunes filles en fleurs on peut admettre également un oiseau en fleurs") (260). *The Sky,* (1943) *The Horizon* (1941), and *The Woman* (1932) are all three on bottles. *Le Viol* is *The Rape*; but it is also *The Act of Violation,* in which breasts replace a woman's eyes, a navel replaces her nose, and a hairless pubic region replaces her mouth. The effect is not to associate two things but to elide them by forcing them upon one another so that the person cannot be perceived as capable of hearing, seeing, or speaking. The whole has the appearance of a violent medical graft rather than an act. It is the idea of rape, not a rape; the body fuses over the face, and the identification of the two cries out the impossibility; resemblance being forced to testify to lack of similitude.

A dead woman's body occupies the background of *The Menaced Assassin (L'Assassin menacé,* 1926) (fig. 12). She lies languidly in a vaguely sexual pose on a red couch, her mouth trailing blood. The painting

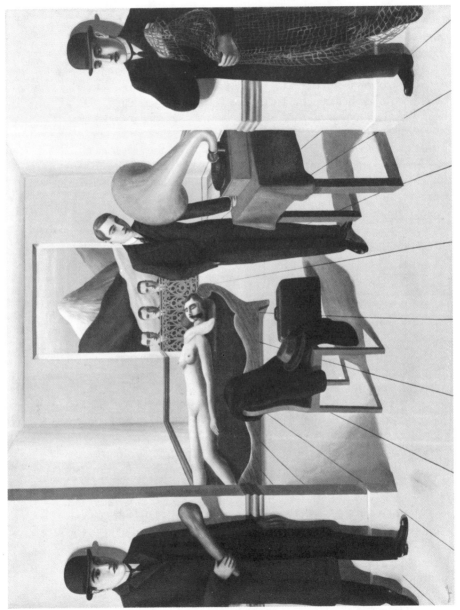

FIG. 12. René Magritte, *The Menaced Assassin* (1926). Oil on canvas, 59¼ × 6'4⅞". Collection, the Museum of Modern

overlays this connection between eroticism and violence with a sche-matization of social definitions and reactions: the obvious criminal lis-tens to a phonograph while behind an alcove at the left is a man with a club, and at the right a man with a net. Three staring observers stand at eye level looking in the window, unobserved by the criminal listener as they are unobservable by the dead body.

The main figure of *Scheherazade* (1947) is suggested by only eyes and mouth, outlined as a wire-work jewelry ornament stand in pearl filigree, set on a table against cloud segments beside a glass of water. Is she herself a sexual object threatened with death, or is she a spellbinding teller of tales? Both these possibilities are somewhat removed, since she does not exist as a person exactly. In another version of this work the filigree is bare of a stand and nevertheless does stand on grass-tufted sand by the sea, while a small bell stands beside her. All of this has distant erotic possibilities, but it also has other classifiable actualities that realign the erotic into the visual mysteries of generalized percep-tion. "Sexuality is compatible only with indifferent reflection," Magritte says (361). This highly paradoxical statement must refer to the contem-plation of Eros, since the character of the human body dictates that the actualization of Eros is precisely incompatible with indifferent reflec-tion. A photograph entitled *L'Amour* shows the intent Magritte, large paint box in hand, daubing the left shoulder of his wife, who stands before him in a black slip.[25] In *Cinéma Bleu* (1925) the incongruities question the prurient absorption implied by the title, since the central figure is a grande dame with a small mermaid tail instead of feet (a motif Magritte uses elsewhere). She wears an equivocal body stocking and has a reverse fan on her arm, standing between huge red curtains against an Ionic facade, while a blue sign with an arrow and the label of the title points off to the right. Under and behind it is set a hori-zontal, giant, two-toned Renaissance chess piece. In *Le Principe d'in-certitude*—I quote Magritte's own description—"A nude woman pro-jects her shadow on the wall in the form of a bird with extended wings" ("Une femme nue projette sur le mur son ombre en forme d'oiseau aux ailes déployées") (175). A demure nude with downcast eyes sits at an embrasure by the sea in *The Magnet* (*L'Aimant*, 1947, the French title carrying "love" in its root).

The imperturbable projection can take on a much greater simplicity, and the Magritte who often paints clothed men from a back view shows in *The Evening Gown* (*La Robe du soir*) a naked woman from the back, facing the sea. The title complicates the work, connecting the notion that nakedness is a form of clothing with the notion that women and the sea have a traditional affinity. Such a traditional affinity is suggested in the lexical entry "moon" ("*la lune*") attached to an empty high-heeled shoe in *The Key of Dreams* (*La Clef des songes,* 1930). In an opposite mode for the equivocation between the body as veil and the body as revelation, one painting entitled *Lovers* (*Les Amants*) doubly shrouds two torsos in a landscape by the sea, first by having them fully dressed and then by completely shrouding their heads.[26] Indeed, they are torsos seen only from the shoulders up rather than engaged lovers. *Eternal Evidence* (*L'Évidence éternelle,* 1930) does split the female body up into five separate and separately framed "pictures." On the one hand, these are inescapably fragmented. On the other hand, nearly the entire body is present, though not quite in identical perspective—suggesting the constructive apprehension of a viewer rather than the whole identification of a lover. But the lover begins as a viewer.

In an opposite mode, another painting called *Lovers* (1928) shows a full woman sitting by the sea being kissed by the floating, turned, and disembodied head of an enraptured man in a posture that may have been borrowed from Chagall, and both simplified and intensified. In *The Seducer* (*Le Séducteur,* 1952) the single dominant object, a sailing ship seen from the side upon the water, seems to be fading from view, since it seems to be entirely composed of the water on which it sails, wavy and light blue. The bottom of the boat merges into the water, indistinguishably. In *Black Magic* (*La Magie noire,* 1935), the title may refer to what the painting has done to a woman, or what a woman does to a viewer, or what a lover does to a woman. Impossibility is made to haunt quasi-allegory in one of the carefully representational paintings of this title, a nude, the upper half of whose body is the blue of the sky against which she demurely stands, while the lower half is of natural flesh coloring. In a sort of adaptation of sexual implication to the entire act of perception, *The Bosom* (*La Poitrine,* 1960) arranges vaguely into the shape of a breast a heap of many pastel-colored house fronts. And the sexuality need not unfailingly involve actual representations of women: *The Married Priest* (*Le Prêtre marié,* 1952) shows two green apples in violet carnival masks, set cheek to cheek against a light night sky and a huge moon. In another painting of this title just one masked apple sits by a seascape against a wall.

4

Much of the energy in such paintings is generated by their titles, and that energy is not only intellectual. *The Bosom* directs the eye to attend to the visual shape, more than to the erotic effect of the heaped houses; the erotic effect is noteworthy here for an absence that the title makes unexpected. Without the title we would have a central incongruity, the near impossibility of ever seeing houses stacked like firewood—or still more like apples. The title adds a further incongruity, or a series of incongruities: between lovers and houses inside which love takes place, between multicolored facades and a flesh-colored breast, between inanimate and animate, between one attractive part and many jumbled wholes. The verbal and the visual, indeed, shadow each other's domains in many modern paintings for an interplay of likenesses and differences about which many constructions could be extended beyond the already considerable body of recent discussion on the subject. It is perhaps such interplay, rather than the "epistemes" of classification, that caught Magritte's attention in Foucault's title, and Magritte's letter to Foucault about *Les Mots et les choses* takes the posture of instructing him. "Painting poses a problem," Magritte says in that letter.[27] Indeed, one of Magritte's frequent procedures with words is to admit words into the painting, as in *The Key of Dreams*. This procedure is to be distinguished from the cubist motif of letting a few decipherable letters show, a mere hint of the assimilability of the conceptual world to the visual. It is also to be distinguished from the inclusion of newspaper or other texts, usually fragmented, into collages, where the visual and the conceptual can be neatly differentiated, as they can also be differentiated in "conceptual art," where the visual is neatly subsumed under the conceptual.

Once again, the *This Is Not a Pipe* group is an extreme case. Its visual bareness matches the relative directness of the included expression, which is identical with the title. Once in that work, twice in the work that splits the title to the general designation of *Two Mysteries*, the paradox is set up between the words and the painting, a paradox between identity and contradiction. The picture *is* of a pipe, and the word nests a form of the paradox of the Cretan liar. Yet, as Magritte says, it is not a pipe but a picture of a pipe—you cannot smoke it. The iconicity of the drawing of a pipe is reduced to the level of arbitrariness that assigns the letters p-i-p-e —as it happens, in English or French—to the appurtenance for smoking tobacco.

In Magritte's usual titles, and even in *The Key of Dreams*, where words also stand inside the painting, this fundamental, extensible distinction moves to the background, to make room for other echoes of discrepancy. *The Key of Dreams* is a fairly direct title,[28] since the visual projection of six boxes with a picture and an "interpretation" mimes the nineteenth-century dream books. In one of its dimensions *The Key of Dreams* masks as a found text, an assimilation of folk art and folk psychology. Magritte's interpretations themselves, however, are on the whole less narrative than are popular dream codes. And they do not allow for Freudianism in the words, though the pictures could nearly all be read in a familiar Freudian way: the egg, the bowler hat, the open-mouthed glass, the open high-heeled shoe, the candle, and the mallet. Moreover, the work is modified from folk dream books by being more visually structured; the six boxes are mounted as though in the panes of a French window. And the writing is a kind of calligraphic version of a schoolboy hand, whereas no popular book would reproduce handwriting; the text would be printed.

As for connections between words and pictures in *The Key of Dreams,* some logical thread can usually be established. For all his words Magritte provides the article; another small discrepancy obtains between each single object in the picture and the general noun appended to it as a "key." To take each case, an egg and "the acacia" are both organic, and beyond that the yellow of the acacia blossoms is the color of the inside of an egg, while the small blossoms may be seen to resemble crumbs of boiled egg yolk. A bowler hat protects from "the snow." Its name in French, not given here, is *"chapeau melon,"* which associates it with something organic. An empty glass may hold water, as "the storm" may bring down water. And there may be some hint of the tempest in a teapot. Not only do a high-heeled shoe and "the moon" both have feminine associations; both also come out at night. A candle does not stand on "the ceiling," but its light easily reaches the ceiling, and will be stopped by the ceiling. A mallet and "the desert" both combine mineral (the head of the mallet; the sands of the desert) and vegetable (the handle of the mallet; the plants of the desert). And a mallet may suggest either breaking rocks in the desert or building in the desert.

But of course mainly there is a stoppage of connection in these identifications, a reference to an oneiric mystery. The key of dreams remains itself a dream, even if associations of visual resemblance can be established between the objects, three of them with large openings to receive something (shoe, bowler hat, glass) and three of them taller than they are wide and without openings (egg, candle, mallet). These visual similarities are randomized in the six boxes, and it would be hard to establish congruences two by two horizontally or three by three vertically for these six objects.

For Magritte's titles there is a distant reverberation between their verbal designations and the complete, discrepant visual scene for which they stand. They are fuller cases of the intimated connections and smoothed-over conceptual shocks established between the single objects and the single nouns of *The Key of Dreams.* And the intimations are intended to remain such, neither to be fully established (as the painting "looks" fully grounded) nor to disappear into a pointed Dadaist irrelevance. Magritte says, "A false idea about works of art attributes to painting the power of expressing feelings more or less precisely and even to enunciate ideas."[29]

In *Le Thérapeute* (1937), a double mystery presents itself. First, this man's figure is headless and chestless, a brown drape shrouding a bird cage where his head and his chest should be, under a straw hat, sitting at the edge of the sea, clutching in his left hand a soft green bag, laced shut, and gripping a cane in his right. How can he cure anything, and what is the relationship between his possible acts of cure and the doves in the cage, one inside and one on a platform outside? Doves have been used for cures in primitive medicine. Yet we cannot establish any connection between this man's looks and the curing function. The man is seated, he cannot see, and his hands are full; all this would preclude his taking steps toward curing. Second, though, in the presence of this radical mystery, we are unable to establish the validity of the possible cures here. The doctor (or is he the patient?) may be a quack, as in Bosch's *The Cure of Folly*. But Magritte's painting is more placid and simpler than Bosch's.

The arbitrariness of such identifications in any case is pointed up by Magritte's use of the same seated, chestless, and headless man with open drapes topped by a hat under other titles and accompanied by slightly different components. In *The Liberator* this figure reveals, not a cage where his chest should be, but a white sheet with four objects in black outline symmetrically represented upon it—a key, a poised bird, a wine glass, and a pipe.[30] He sits not by the sea but on rocks overlooking a river landscape, against a sky that is thick with clouds and filled with rectangular pale blue arches. This man has a snap-shut valise sitting by his right foot; he clutches a bamboo cane in his left hand and the *Scheherazade* ornament in his right hand (is he a liberator because he has a grip on the essence of her stories?). In another variant, the figure appears in a photograph Matisse took of himself in this pose by a house, nothing visible in his right hand, a cane in his left; a white rabbit couches behind. The man is covered by a floppy tam and a striped blanket. His open chest now reveals a canvas with a pebble-strewn ground, a centered, outlined door, and above it two dark dotted clouds.[31] Here the title, *God, the Eighth Day* (*Dieu, le huitième jour*), is even more distant from the work. Finally these works are all drawn on, and given no special title other than *Le Domaine Enchanté* for the whole, in one of the giant frames on the ceiling of the Casino at Knokke. There the man sits on a rock in front of a bush, against a pink wall covered with diamonds and ball-and-triangle patterns, a wall that laps into the next frame till it abuts on a variant version of *The Married Priest*. He has the doves and their cage for a chest, as in *Le Thérapeute*, and he clutches the laced bag. But in his left hand he clutches the *Scheherazade* ornament, as in *The Liberator*. And an important new addition, couched almost on his foot, is a large lion, his neck garlanded with roses.

The principle of repetition with variation, of an underlying possibility of distant echoing, is constantly asserted by the shifts in these collocations of image and title. The procedure, again, is not followed so fully by any other surrealist. Like Vermeer and Rembrandt, Magritte performs utterly within his given conditions while he uniquely transcends them. He himself, indeed, goes on at some length about titles, and speaks of a painting as being "difficult to name" ("ce tableau difficile à nommer") (487):

> There are two kinds of titles:
>   1) "Die of not dying," for example, "says" something about the book.
>   2) "Divagations" does not say something that is indifferent. It makes one thing of the book that "says" something.
>   As a title of the number two kind, "The Free Field" is very honest, without taking it further: you have to read the poems for this title to indicate or recall something. In themselves "The Free Field," "Divagations," are indifferent and say nothing.
>   I prefer the no. 1 titles but, as I think about it, the titles of my paintings are nearly always no. 2 titles: The Tempest, The Art of Conversation, Memory, etc. (The Ignorant Fairy is in the world of no. 1 titles.)
>   But these no. 2 titles become "speaking" when they name paintings, on the condition that they be exactly adequate. Their sense has a force and a charm thanks to the paintings, and those acquire more precision once they are well named.[32]

Interestingly, Magritte here uses as examples only the titles of books (Éluard, borrowed from Saint Theresa, and Mallarmé), just as he often has recourse to book titles for the titles of his paintings. He equivocates between his declared preference for the first kind of title and his adjudicated tendency to use the second. Three converging criteria are adduced—force, charm, and precision. It may be inferred that precision would be lacking if force and charm were not present, and vice versa. This collocation itself redefines precision, and thereby force and charm as well.

Put differently, another paradox presents itself: the title would not fit if it were not distant from the work. To resume the work precisely a title must include a large measure of what seems like imprecision. Along these lines a philosophical dialectic is slightly adumbrated in the title Hegel's Vacation (Les Vacances de Hegel), used for two works, slightly varied, of 1958 and 1959. In these a glass of water sits atop an umbrella. We move back and forth between possibilities here.[33] Hegel does not spill the water and so the umbrella is not needed; it is superfluous. Or Hegel's dialectic orders disparities and keeps the water in the glass atop the umbrella. Or the glass to contain the water and the umbrella to shield against it are overpreparation. Or the glass would have too little water in any case and so the umbrella is not needed. Or the glass will catch some water and the umbrella shield against the rest; all bases are covered. And the whole can be taken not as two objects but as one. Suzy Gablick quotes a remark of Magritte's about the work along these lines: "This object not to admit any water (repelling it) and to admit it (containing it")."[34] Or there is no water in any case, and both glass and umbrella are superfluous. As superfluous as Hegel would be in a world of visual presences and mysteries? But that world also contains philosophical treatises by Hegel and paintings by such as Magritte. Bearing on all these possible extrapolations of deduction is the question of what a vacation of Hegel would be. An overpreparation: he takes along both glass and raincoat? An underpreparation: he takes too much to deal with water, and nothing to deal with anything else? Is the vacation a busman's holiday, and on it would Hegel apply his speculation not to the grandiosities of history but to everyday objects? Or on his vacation does he drop philosophy and act like anyone else, drinking water, walking in the rain? In that instance all the previous possibilities are only a sort of signature to personalize him, through his activity, by providing an emblem for it when he is not exercising it. Magritte says, "You are actually, you say, at the 'metaphysical stage,' 'I hope you stay there,' for that signifies to me: life in the mystery" (433). Here Magritte identifies the precision of philosophy as a form of mystery, and thereby blurs the distinction (which, to be sure, is mine and not his) between works like *This Is Not a Pipe* and works like *Le Thérapeute,* titles and paintings being taken together in both instances.

In *The Explanation* (*L'Explication,* 1954), on a ledge against a mountain horizon stands at the left a bottle and a carrot; at the right, the "impossible" fusion of the two objects in a carrot-topped bottle, the glass growing into the vegetable and sealing over the opening that allows it to function as a bottle. The "explanation" here both fulfills and short-circuits, as do the glass and the umbrella in *Hegel's Vacation.* All that is explained is what is visually demonstrated but mysteriously unrecordable in the visual world where we live; the visible is underscored for its connection to the invisible by the term of the title, "explanation."[35] Somewhat more loosely, as though it were an explanation, *Golden Legend* (*La Légende d'or,* 1956) shows large loaves of bread against a starry sky. Man does not live by bread alone, and his religious life is wrought into types in the medieval *Aurea Legenda.* The Latin title indicates something to read, and here we are asked to read the painting as different from, or as fulfilling, the religious life (sky?) with bread. The *Golden Legend* announces its special character, but it is famous for repetitions, inaccuracies, and the naive ascription of miracles—all attributes that bear on the visual scene of giant loaves of bread floating through the sky. In this particular light one could turn *Philosophy in the Boudoir* away from Eros, detaching it still further from Sade, and align it through the "philosophy" of the title to such possibilities as these.

But "sense is the impossible for possible thought," Magritte asserts (363). The possibility of sense can only exist then, beyond the possibility of thought—in the possibility of collocating the incommensurabilities of word and painting in such a way as to bring them somewhat into view. Or as he says on the more restrictive side, "There are possible similarities and possible differences among things that are separated. These relationships are discovered by the thought that examines, compares and evaluates."[36] *L'Espace d'une Pensée* is the title of a film script by Magritte, a film that confronts a man with a woman in a series of fairly schematic encounters. He declares that propositions make thought too easy: "it is easy to say: a rose in the garden; it is not easy to say: a rose in the universe" (436). Nor is it easy to apply the title *The Tomb of the Wrestlers* (*Le Tombeau des lutteurs*) to a single giant rose in an empty room.[37] Here a discrepancy of mere scale (for roses are often put in rooms) is vastly extended by getting a title of an arresting discrepancy, one that is nearly an opposition, if fighting and flowers be thought of as opposites. Yet if the wrestlers are entombed, they will get flowers like anybody else. And just as bulls in the bullfights of Provence are garlanded with flowers rather than slaughtered, so the wrestler puts on the mere show of force; his "struggle' ("*lutte*") does not lead to real death, like the deaths in combat. To that degree the single flower is appropriate for him. Also, perhaps, flowers are giant for the wrestler because he is both large and overdeveloped. Another work in the same vein, however, is much more obscure: in *The Listening Chamber* (*La Chambre d'écoute*), a giant green apple fills a bare room.

More briefly, Magritte speaks not of the title but of the "relation between the title and the painting" as poetic (259). Thus he locates the sense of a painting between the fullness of an appropriate response and the emptiness of the inexplicit mystery. On the side of fullness: "The poetic title has nothing to teach us, but it must surprise and enchant us" ("Le titre poétique n'a rien à nous apprendre, mais il doit nous surprendre et nous enchanter") (263). On the side of emptiness: "The indifference of stones is doubtless the same as that of nothingness" ("L'indifférence des pierres est sans doute la même que celle du néant") (593). So *Pandora's Box* (*La Boîte de Pandore*) —or any painting—can be taken either way, and so both, a melding beyond either presence or absence. We are shown the back of a man at a bridge facing a quay beside a large white rose. There is no box here. On the one hand, Pandora is the inverse of Prometheus. She opened the box and brought ills. On the other hand, the man standing with his back to us conflates Prometheus and Epimetheus. He contemplates the sealed but open world, both before and after the opening of the box, in a timelessness for which the visible presences, and their discrepancies, are also nascent figures.

"It is difficult to think while thinking of nothing" ("Il est difficile de penser en ne pensant à rien") says Magritte (318). He brings about a comparable state by his act of sealing off discrepancies in his deeply placid surfaces. These discrepancies become large-scale ones because of their paucity. What he says of *La Condition humaine*, the painting where the easel breaks the wall to let the landscape through, brings his perspectival manipulations and his conceptual ones into a grid of identification: "The tree . . . found itself for the spectator at once inside the room on the painting and outside in the real landscape. This simultaneous existence in two different spaces resembles the existence in at once past and present of a single moment, as happens in 'false recognition.'"[38] Usually this state is achieved with the powerful adjunct of a title, in that interaction of word and image which Magritte mediated not only on the canvas but in an ancillary fashion in his sometimes elaborate commentary on the relation between the two. Interestingly, the titles he invents for a show of Pierre Alechinsky are inconceivable as applied to any of his own paintings, except possibly for the fifth: *The Friend of Tetanos, Return of Effects, Legal Extraction, The Pieces of the Doctor, The Amateur's Box, Project for Jam.*[39] But to deduce why these titles do not fit conceivable works of Magritte would require a fairly complete exposition of the internal logic of his paintings, all over again, so to speak.

5

The difference between these titles and his own, lies, among other things, and centrally, in the question of tone. The first and fourth of these made-up Alechinsky titles are too violent, the last too flip, and the others too flat, to lend themselves readily to Magritte's own works. Put differently, they would not permit of what James Thrall Soby calls the "metamorphoses" in Magritte: "interior to exterior setting; deep to shallow; dead weight to buoyancy."[40] Yet "metamorphosis" seems an inappropriate term to apply to Magritte, when the paintings have all the finish of a permanent condition. Even *Golconda*, with its phalanxes of tiny men floating across the air of a city, has not so much changed dead weight into buoyancy as it has created the tone of a psychic realm where miniaturization, weightlessness, and near identity with one's fellows become the coordinates of a new tonal realm where the distinction between dead weight and buoyancy has disappeared. These men are neither sinking nor floating; they are fixed in an equilibrium, and a tone that partakes of both ease and reassurance as well as of loneliness-in-company seems to pervade the painting. So the loaves of bread in the sky of the *Golden Legend* seem to stand in a comparable equilibrium, to suggest the peace, plenty, and simplicity that would combine the staples of earth with the recurrences in the heavens. Interior does not so much metamorphose into exterior as meld with it and comment on it for a visual effect that gets beyond cubism without resorting to the visual fragmentations of that approach to representation. The same would hold for deep and shallow perspective, where a given work, when it "violates" traditional perspective, does so for reasons that are conceptual. Yet the combination of the visual and the conceptual creates the tone characteristic of Magritte, a strong and dominant tone that may vary from painting to painting but that remains marked in a given painting.

The discrepancies between title and painting, and from object to object, contribute to this effect, while the representational surface holds title and painting together, as in *Musings of a Solitary Walker* (*Rêveries d'un promeneur solitaire*, 1926–27), where Rousseau's title is moved to a more somber and ominous universe than that of Rousseau, or even of Kaspar David Friedrich, whom much of the work recalls. In it a derbied, coated man stands against a twilight sky, somewhat stormy in appearance, with its dark greens, its lit bridge, and its slanting stream. This romantic appearance is heavily qualified by a huge body, eyes closed as in sleep, bald, lying to the waist behind him in the foreground. Again *The Difficult Passage* (*Le Passage Difficile*, 1967), modifies the Turner-esque icons of a ship on a rough sea by a balcony, and by crimson drapes that stress the eye on a pillar "beholding" the scene and transfixing the beholder of this work beyond any romantic mergings.

The many seated coffins in Magritte are nothing if not key signatures of a tone that forces a confrontation of death in Arcadia, without any of the hints of Poussin. The confrontation moves to the foreground, sometimes with a touch of gallows humor, as in his re-rendering of David's Madame Récamier and Manet's Balcony with the personages replaced by coffins. *The Domain of Arnheim* (1962) has a bird's nest on a balcony, beyond which stands a purple-grey mountain in the shape of an eagle. This painting illustrates no events of Poe's story, but it does transmute the tone of Poe into something still more menacing. Yet *The Menaced Assassin* remains curiously calm for the fact that its central figure, the assassin menaced on three sides (or four, if the visible corpse is counted), stands unaware of the present threats and the past violence, his ear inside an old-fashioned phonograph, in which he seems totally, if schizophrenically, absorbed. To say that he is calming his nerves here would be to revise the permanence of this painting into an episode. Here only three men look in the window; the motif expands in *The Month of Grape Gathering* (*Le Mois des vendanges*, 1959), where the window, which takes up the whole painting, is filled with a phalanx of derbied starers whose tone of menace undergoes the pacification suggested by this painting's title.

All the room of this last painting is, however, pervaded by its tone, because Magritte sets his starers simultaneously to confront the puzzles of representation and to draw up short before them. Louis Scutenaire well says, "For him reality is the negation of the impossible,"[41] but this is not because the negation is a special act within a painting. It is a general act. And the pipe of "this is not a pipe" continues to float in the face of one impossibility that is quite possible, that we can apply the word "pipe" to such a strangely shaped object and smoke it when we turn away from the painting. The paradox becomes sharpest in this instance when a recourse to the flow of reality in the everyday world is easiest and most trivial. Rooted birds on the mountainside give title to *The Companions of Fear* (*Les compagnons de la peur*). Plant-Bird, the new creature who looks like a metamorphosed one but is really a composite one, is rooted on a mountainside, a companion of fear but not an object or subject of fear. At another icon, under another name, the rooted birds enter a different tonal universe: they bill in a moonscape by the sea, *Natural Graces* (*Les Grâces naturelles*). The painting is constant, the icons repeat, but variation keeps the tones changing. Even sadness, in Magritte's essay, has variants, "Deux Variantes sur la tristesse"[42] and again "Variantes de la tristesse" (410–11).

The painting *The Great War* (*La Grande Guerre*, 1964) tempers and concentrates the effect of that cataclysm by taking as its central image a woman dressed in the high style of the Belle Époque before World War I, a high-collared, long dress, a parasol, and a large plumed hat, all in white as she stands before a balcony by the sea. The note of sadness and impossibility is struck by a bouquet of violets that blots her face. Often, indeed, the note of discrepancy not only mounts a paradox between the visual and the verbal but at the same time revises the tone of the work. In *The Voice of the Blood* (*La Voix du sang*) a tree by a river valley strikes a more than romantic note when it turns out to have doors and compartments inside its trunk. The top one, opening to the right, holds a large ball, a severe abstraction; but the bottom one evokes the pathos of the night city—opening to the left, this compartment holds a small house, its six windows lit against the dark of the trunk's interior. In *False Mirror* (*Le Faux Miroir*) we seem to have entered the "*mise en abîme*" of Foucault. But in this large eye, which naturally sees or unnaturally includes sky and clouds, the dead black iris closes off, frustrates, and asserts the assurance of its dominance, all at once. Of one of his breakthrough paintings, *The Lost Jockey* (*Le Jockey perdu*) Magritte says that this representation of a tiny jockey moving through a denuded forest of black trees was "conceived without aesthetic preoccupation with the unique goal of ANSWERING TO a mysterious sentiment, an anguish 'without reason,' a sort of 'call to order.' "[43]

"It is much easier to terrorize than to charm" ("Il est beaucoup plus facile de terroriser que de charmer"), Magritte says (250). In the economy of visual inventions he somehow manages to do both. In *Nostalgia* (*Le Mal du pays*, with the ambiguous alternative *Regional Illness*), the black-winged, black-suited man whom we see from a back angle looking over a balcony rests his elbows upon it, without having to pay any attention to the lion couched and looking away behind him.[44] In *Time Transfixed* (*La Durée poignardée*) a small locomotive, complete with steam, comes out of a fireplace where normally a stovepipe might be. Yet the menace of the locomotive is contained by its miniature size. It is stopped; its having been "pierced by a dagger" is visibly in the past. Charm and terror have here become one, and the clock on the mantle accords with the strange object beneath it. Magritte lists a series of examples of bad paintings of terror, in a scale going from a scene showing a soldier saving a half-naked, half-ravaged woman, through a knife-wielding assassin menacing a blindfolded passerby, to the same passerby blindfolded but without the assassin (274). In *The Menaced Assassin* it is the assassin who is in a sense blindfolded, since he does not see the three men staring in his window or the two behind the alcove preparing to capture him; nor does he even see the corpse, so intent is he on listening to the large Victrola into which he holds his ear, charm arresting terror for him, and for the viewer. Magritte discerns a weakness of "a 'normal' precipice" ("*un précipice 'normal'* ") in Munch's *The Cry* (443). "The black sun of melancholy' illuminates the Universe" ("'Le soleil noir de la mélancolie' éclaire l'Univers") (386). Thus the tables are turned, and deep depression is turned into illumination, as Magritte both applies and reverses the gloomy line from Nerval. Magritte tells us that he could not hold back his tears when looking at de Chirico's *Song of Love* (367), and his own painting of that title (1948) enlists humor as well as pathos in its two rock-pocked fish-headed lovers—fish don't sing!—seated on a rock as a vague ship floats past them.

Magritte reshuffles often the same icons—the balcony, the bowler hat, the figures from behind, the streetlight, the closed house, the bell, the bilboquet, the blocked sky-modules, the seated coffin, the body with fish attributes, the lion, the rooted bird, the object in flames, the window, the empty room. And he redistributes the elements of his titles, so that the conjunctions of word and image have the air of being at once random and inevitable. In his largest work—the seventy-meter *Le Domaine enchanté*—he had assistants mount eighteen scenes, comprising a partial but liberal anthology of his icons, in eight large panels all round the ceiling of the Casino at Knokke. The whole work provides an image of the symbolic sky that dominates many of his paintings, since the viewer must look up and look round to see it, and yet he is not in the devotional situation of a visitor to the Sistine Chapel but rather in the central entertainment hall of a public building. In this casual but highly structured public space the history of a private iconography is offered to view, under a single and general title. Inner and outer, the visual and the conceptual, are here forced into a larger, and summary, conjunction.

The titles of Magritte, like the titles of de Chirico, try to strike a chord that centers the painting around a single perception, and then to strike a tone that, with the help of the words, it can be perceived to resonate. Thus the supplemental, poetic words of the title both transpose the visual miscellany that is offered and declare its unity with what appears on the different plane of the verbal. The description that is assumed in a conventional title has been implicitly consigned to the single dimension of repetitive amplification: we would recognize the Virgin and Child from iconography, and we would recognize Constable's Wivenhoe Park, perhaps, from a photograph, even if the painter had manipulated the visual elements somewhat. But a white, masklike profile and a glove would never bring us to *The Song of Love*, even though once they had been associated with such a title; those items, even inside walls with a cityscape visible beyond, are as easily coded to love as the lawns and stately facade are coded to "English Country Seat." Magritte puts an even greater strain on the relation between words and the painting than de Chirico does. In his *Song of Love* the lugubrious fish-headed bodies seated together on monochrome tufa with up-tilted heads seem more directly engaged in a song, paradoxical though that would be because fish are, in a classical epithet, "mute." But the relation of these figures to the title is still more indirect than handsome near-profiles and gloves are to the notion of love. Magritte's greater strain between words and images entails and achieves a greater resonance; the wide discrepancy between words and images is bridged, an inverse analogue to the breaching of the few discrepancies within the painting. The leap of association across one or two discrepant visual objects resembles the leap from one or two expressions in a title to the painting that is initially discrepant with it. And the careful representational surface confirms and reinforces the bridging, as it insists on a final, calm, clear anchorage in the visible.

For Max Ernst, in the collage novels and elsewhere, both the words of a title and the visual images assert the interaction of sexuality, the unconscious, and a blurred causality. There is no real discrepancy, in Magritte's sharp way, for Ernst, between the nineteenth-century urban military monument *Le Lion de Belfort* and that title applied to the first day of *Une Semaine de bonté*, with obvious reference to its lion-headed man, who moves through the city on seductive errands. The city of the collages, too, is substantially a nineteenth-century city, and both the erotic and the military conventions of life are rooted in and connected by the unconscious, for which the man's lion head also stands. The lion head at one stroke translates the activity into dream and interprets the dream, whereas Magritte does not interpret the dreams to which he offers a "key." For Klee, who resembles Magritte in mounting a structure of resonances across discrepancies, the recurrences in his work are not mainly of image (though the bird and the schematic man do recur). And the application of widely different titles to substantially the same collocation of images, Magritte's repeated practice, would be inconceivable for him. Klee's recurrences are of line, point, quadrated segment, color—and arrow—and the like, in their suggestive functions as interpreted by *Das Bildnerische Denken*. So *Purpose* (*Vorhaben*) sets, and fixes, a mystery between this term and the somewhat anxious face it directs toward a future, the dimension of time that the space of a painting can only suggest. Magritte, however, always suspends his mysteries—and his smooth surface never permits itself Klee's sketchiness.

Marcel Duchamp's arch arbitrariness of skewing between titles, or title segments, and art works, or elements in them, moves not toward mystery but rather toward the presentation of ironic paradox and incongruity. The "malic molds," a planned constituent of Duchamp's *Large Glass,* retain that title through decades of planning. And the gap between this obscure locution and the obscure construction inside the "bachelor" half of the sculpture is deliberately unbridgeable, even though connections between the type of acid and the chemistry of sexual attraction are presented so that their cast of scientificity cannot hold in any realm of biology. But Magritte's titles do hold, for all their mystery. They hold to the mystery of a visual presentation that they orient and amplify.

THE MODIFICATION
OF THE NARRATIVE
IN ART

Chapter 10

Narrative, in our personal accounts of experience, in our large fictions and in our histories, is itself a mode of understanding that would seem to be irreducible to formulations of abstract thinking.[1] Narrative, interestingly, can be combined as readily with that which would seem to arrest its temporalities as with the implied thought (the symbols in Peirce's sense) that its associations encode.[2]

The constructive apprehension of the art work, Rudolph Arnheim reminds us, in itself modifies the spatiality of its presentation in a temporal direction.[3] The temporality is sequential, and a connected sequentiality is already well on its way to becoming a narrative structure. This process is caught in an incipient state by what Arp called a "concretion," an art work, usually a sculpture, that composes a single shape out of elements that suggest at once a leaf and a bird, or a fruit and a torso. In doing so, such a work raises the question of a narrative explanation for how such a double metamorphosis could have taken place. At the same time its fused realization suspends such questions and the viewer "leaves them behind" to immerse himself in the physical presence of the composite image, which blurs rather than complicates its initial constituents.[4] The image itself is rich, but at the same time seductive and unstable in its reference and in its structure.

There is a challenge to the eye, an uncanniness, an arrest of attention, an incipient inducement to idolatry of lesser or greater intensity, in all attention to man-made visual images. This potentially upsetting and distracting aspect of the visual arts, tamed and somewhat sanctified in our museum culture, finds its expression in earlier cultures when a society bans some, or even all, images. The Old Testament is emphatic about this: "Thou shalt not make unto thee any graven image or any likeness of anything that is in heaven above or that is in the earth beneath or that is in the water under the earth" (Exodus 20.4). The term "graven image" ("*fesel*") emphasizes the act of sculpting, of hewing boughs or cutting stone into the figure of something like an animal. The term "likeness" ("*temunah*") derives from a root ("*min*") that classifies creatures into kinds and species; it contains in embryo an implied notion of mimesis while at the same time comprising a religious orientation to the Creation and perhaps even to the Flood—to a narrative, in effect, that was to be left in the holy words of Scripture.

This iconoclastic tradition did not prohibit the Israelites from elaborately decorating the Temple in Jerusalem. But the spirit of uncertainty about images, as well as the impulse to create them, persists in human society, to be found in the Byzantine controversy around the Iconoclasts, in the Arab prohibition against representing animate figures, and in the Protestant restrictions on images from the Reformation up to our own time. This resistance to specific image can take on a positive power of contemplation in such texts as the medieval *Cloud of Unknowing* and in such nonrepresentational works as Mark Rothko's chapel in Houston.

Image assimilates to narrative in many traditions. The association of iconic figures with myths itself provides a lexicon for the connection between image and narrative, a connection that is to be found in Greek vase paintings, Chinese ritual vessels, Ashanti goldweights, Egyptian coffin lids, Assyrian friezes, the masks of the Pacific Northwest, and many other places.[5] The *alcheringas* of the Australian aborigines carry on their surface patterns that are cues to incidents in a mythical story. The sandpaintings of the Navajos are narrative representations that must be incorporated in a ritual and then destroyed. All these selections from myth, arranged according to the template of rites, refer to the story in a rigorously functional connection. The power in images is such that in our own and in other traditions images come eventually to represent not only composed hieratic subjects of no specific textual reference, like Virgin and Child, but actual moments in narrative accounts from sacred or secular texts, like the driving of the money changers from the Temple and the Crucifixion, or the departure of Aeneas from Carthage. This textual and narrative use of image became so predominant in the Renaissance, and so complex in its significations, that nearly all modern iconologists have assumed that it was then universal.[6] The break from this tradition in modern times, however, has been so strong that it carried with it a depreciation of the narrative painting in the nineteenth century or even earlier, reinforcing the emphasis away from history painting onto landscape at the turn of the eighteenth century. The contrast between Claude and the Turner who began somewhat in his shadow carries in itself this shift of emphasis, since Claude, like Poussin before him, often paints scenes that illustrate a prior narrative, and rarely does Turner turn to a narrative for his subjects. At the same time—in this, as in other respects, like the painters of our own century—he powerfully modifies narrative elements. Yet he does not wholly abandon them. One could even say that the Venice of an Englishman is "storied" in the way that the Venice of a native Venetian cannot exactly be. But there is a narrative interest, as well as a theoretical one, in the title of *Light and Colour (Goethe's Theory)—The Morning after the Deluge—Moses Writing the Book of Genesis.* This title presents an almost irreconcilable conflation of a narrative that refers to an account of Creation, along with a reference to a theory that is embodied but not proportionally illustrated in the extravagant coloring of the painting to which it is attached. In Turner's *Snow Storm: Hannibal and His Army Crossing the Alps,* the reference to a complex story is muted in the painting's compelling absorption by the swirls of a storm and the massiveness of the surrounding mountains. History is swallowed up in a landscape that is rendered with Turner's extraordinary attention to visual detail in "reality," as well as with the centering on his "imagination" on the vivid representation of this landscape icon. Henri Focillon said of Turner's impressionist side, "For Turner the world is an unstable accord of fluids, form is a moving light, an uncertain spot in a universe in flight."[7] These words are evocative for this painting, as for his paintings of Venice. yet the representational paradox of a supreme accuracy in fixing the evanescent impression of a deeply coded scene is resolved, as it were, in the actual presence of the painting, and carries off the corollary of throwing into the shadow, and into something like insignificance, the very story of its subject matter.

The same, indeed, could be said of Brueghel's *Landscape with the Fall of Icarus,* which crosses the genre scene with the scene of legendary catastrophe in a landscape dominant enough to forbid our confinement of a "reading" in the painting just to W. H. Auden's lesson of relativizing catastrophes before the necessary ordinary events of living. Even *Icarus* offers us a scene as well as an event that has been so shrunk, as Auden reminds us, that we are asked simultaneously to attend to it and to attend to what is more imposing in the painting.[8] When the narrative element in a painting is manipulated so as to offer and include "un-coded" supernumerary details in its discourse, this sets up a special confrontation with the viewer, as Norman Bryson has shown.[9] And it also has the effect of evening out the view, for the very fact that the significances are layered into the painting. Thus Masaccio's *Rendering of the Tribute Money*, Bryson's example, is noteworthy for its vivid roughing out and grouping of human shapes, as well as for a complex handling of the integers of its story.

Goya, when he refers to narrative outside his early religious paintings, tends to do so either in an almost enigmatic way, as in the "Black" paintings, where a story is necessary but not fully offered, except in the case of *Saturn*, or in a narrative so clear in its results that we do not need the details. Of some victim in the *Disasters of War*, the represen-tation refers to the end of a story that is part of a larger story, the unleashing of unbearable savagery in the Napoleonic invasion and in war generally. That story is needed for the result exhibited, and some specific set of events would be needed. The specific story is thus referred to, but it is at the same time abrogated in its details before the con-frontational point that Goya's significations are stretching and also sim-plifying. We assume that "the wounded mason" in that painting either slipped or lost his balance; such an event had to precede the state of affairs shown in the painting, but we do not have to know which event. And the complications even of Goya's pastoral paintings are such that they must be taken as asserting the significations of complexities, with-out our being able to unravel just what is happening, or even how the codes combine—connections that are clear both in Fragonard and in the subtler Watteau. Even when he deals with allegory, Goya highlights the element of story. In his *Time, Truth and the Poet, History* (1797), a full-face blonde nude, nearly breastless and prepubescent, stands open armed and seemingly undisturbed, as a winged brown devil pulls fe-rociously at her left wrist. This scene is already a specific story that allegorizes a spiritual sequence. Below this jointure History, seen seated naked from a back side view, has her blonde head turned round. She sits on an overturned pillar. The jointure of hands is just above her head, and the white underside of the devil's wings is lost and darkened to his left, as he leans at nearly a forty-five degree angle. In fact he is virtually held up by Truth; he would fall otherwise, and the represented force here at the joined hands pushes the baroque tensions to a specific point in the balance and enlists them for allegory, as well as for a story that is the more sinister because its details cannot be disentangled. His right wing fades into a white background, and the angle above it shows a dark sky in which a phalanx of full-winged owl and batlike demons flies toward the trio, hinting at the climax of a takeover (or even an ultimate defeat for them) in the future of the story of which the painting offers essential, and only partial, elements.

The abstractionists whom I have not discussed in this book, from Burgoyne Dillard, say, to Frank Stella just on this side of the Atlantic, would offer still greater challenges to deductions about the significations inhering in color than does Pollock, who often enlisted narrative titles for nearly abstract paintings, or Kandinsky, who offers a theory in *On the Spiritual in Art* (*Über das Geistige in der Kunst*) that provides a nascent code, but not at all a narrative, for his paintings. It can be said simply, however, that all these painters have left behind all or nearly all traces of narrative, along with traces of reference to objects. A nonobjective painting is perforce a nonnarrative painting, unless a back-reference to narrative is arbitrarily added in the words of the title. At the same time the nonobjective painter can be seen as both super-iconoclastic, in that he has voluntarily removed himself into an austere absence of image, and superidolatrous, insofar as having done so puts him into a greater concentration on the canvas before him.

Of the artists I have discussed here, only Klee is an occasional abstractionist. And his abstract works tend toward a simple, almost canonical-modern plan. *Rhythmic* (*Rythmisches*, 1930) consists of just black and white squares. *Polyphony* (*Polyphonie*, 1932) repeats dots in squares. Squares, again, simply fill out *New Harmony* (*Neue Harmonie*, 1936), in which I would guess we cannot read a reference to Robert Owen's utopian community of that name in Indiana. Ernst would be an abstractionist in many of his works if his titles did not almost always reorient his abstractions toward (often autobiographical) narrative. Connected with that choice is not only a focus on objects but a modification of that focus in ways that complicate signification along lines different from the great classical modern painters who do not come in for discussion here—Matisse, Picasso, and Braque. Those painters themselves offer, of course, rich iconographic presentations of their own, and they also have various recourse on occasion to narrative or quasi-narrative, especially Picasso. And all three were frequent illustrators of written narrative. Klee's modifications, like those of Ernst, Duchamp, and Magritte, involve special manipulations of what amounts to narrative, in ways that call for the kind of prolonged, deliberate attention I have tried to offer for their underlying structures of signification.

It is, among other things, his relation to an insistent but obscured narrative that gives some of the air of Goya to the early Klee. In *Hoary Phoenix* (*Greiser Phoenix*, 1905), a figure with the posture of a peacock (though his feathers are smaller) stands with a sprig of blossoms and buds beside a footless left leg. The right leg ends in a large splayed claw. Crossed out after the title, as though to reduce the thrust of allegory is "as a symbol of the heart" ("*als Symbol der Herzen*"), and a large further description. Yet at the same time this erasure has been allowed to remain, "*sous rature*" in an almost Derridean sense, except that the erasure is subordinated to the untold story of the function of this bird who either waits, or waits in vain past his time, for the fabled resurrection. What story lies behind *The Flying Policemen* (*Die fliehenden Polizisten*, 1913)? Not an allegory; in these policemen the sinister stands in balance with the comic for an equation the story might resolve if it could be told. The three are of different sizes in their spiked helmets, holding in the air almost a dance pose. The *Musical Society* (*Musikalische Gesellschaft*, 1907) is an imaginary group portrait on an imaginable but unspecifiable group occasion. Does *Genesis of the Brain* (*Genesis der Gestirne*, 1914) refer to Moses and Genesis? We can neither know nor refrain from asking. *Seesaw* (*Schaukel*, 1914)shows the line of a left-tipping seesaw on an uneven fulcrum, heavily weighted with star patterns and other schematic objects. Failing a firm iconological lexicon for these items, our perceptions must suspend them between allegory and the registered result of an undelivered narrative. Such a narrative must lie behind whatever heavily threatens Pinz in the *View of the Heavily Threatened City Pinz* (*Ansicht der schwer bedrohen Stadt, Pinz*, 1915), in which arrows are raining down on a chaos of schemes. "Pinz" is lettered in one area, "Weylau" in another, and we can be fairly certain that hostilities must obtain between these fictional cities, as they do between nearly homonymous real cities. Nor can we locate who delivers the warnings or what the warning is about in *Warning of the Ships* (*Warnung der Schiffe*, 1917). It must have something to do with the line, above which are large birds, an exclamation point, and half moons, while the ships are below it. *The Bavarian Don Giovanni* (1919) suggests a local variant on a pattern story that follows fairly closely the form of the version best known to the musician Klee, that of Mozart. The operatic figure has more style than the little man on the ladder, who wears a German hunter's hat, with names patterned on it: Emma, Cenzl, Mari, Kathi, Therez. This list is somewhat shorter and less cosmopolitan than the original Don Giovanni's "*mille e tre.*" Judging from the expression on his face, there seems to be a story, both a recent and a long-range one, behind the *Degradation: Portrait of an Expressionist* (*Versunkenheit. Bildnis einer Expressionisten*, 1919). The abstract term "*Versunkenheit*" indicates a submerged narrative sequence more than would "a degenerate" for this bearded man in closeup with a little flat tuft of hair on head, his large eyes held shut as though against the memory of events he cannot bear.

China is a real and remote place, Unklaich a legendary one, in a legend Klee has invented. *The Way from Unklaich to China* (*Weg von Unklaich nach China,* 1920), implies a whole history; and given in only visual form, it also makes game of the nonexistence of the route. In this painting the city has two unusual attributes: Unklaich is labeled, and it is like a boat, whereas cities are stationary. An arrow above the boat with an aerial lifeboat points to "China." Rigid on the left, as though itself a boat anchored by, is an island with three trees whose well-like central elevated stonework suggests the Great Wall. The flags on the anchored boat are blowing the wrong way. There are other humorous details, all of which ask to be given the narrative they disappoint, as do the somewhat abstract objects in *Hoffmanesque Tale* (*Hoffmaneske Geschichte,* 1921), with its schematic figures in a sectioned field.

In Klee's handling the very suspension of narrative resolution keeps up an interaction between the temporality of the word and the spatial confrontation of image. The *Annunciation* of Leonardo attends and draws attention to the psychology of spatial disposition between Virgin and angel in the laid-out segments of the area they occupy between porch and landscape. The viewer, knowing the story, arrests its temporal moment and suspends the sequence for contemplation. This state of affairs holds preponderantly even when a painter letters in the scriptural words that Luke has pass between angel and Virgin. Typically, and this is the case in Leonardo's version, the figures are small enough to allow porch and landscape to preponderate. Furthermore details are often added, not uncoded ones for an "effect of the real," but rather details that are coded toward the anecdotal (and so away from the archetypal), in this instance the delicately laid table across which the angel delivers his message. Taken by itself visually, the table with its vessel is an included still life of the sort offered by the table of Leonardo's *Last Supper.* Taken in what its context signifies for humble life, it contributes to a genre scene. Taken in reference to the archetypal scene of the painting's subject, however, the table and its vessels introduce the anecdotal, a small daily event interrupted. The intrusion of the anecdotal underscores a narrative element and points it toward some resolution of a relationship between the archetypal and the quotidian, the pattern event and the episodic event. All these categories are present, but transmuted, in Klee: *The Way from Unklaich to China* (the very title could easily be Kafka's!) sounds archetypal but is scaled to the anecdotal in the whimsicality of its visual rendering. Spatially speaking—and Klee gave prolonged and intricate attention to spatial effects—the viewer is arrested at the particular sportive moment along the way from Unklaich to China. But he is also moving in possible narrative connection along the considerable distance from one of those termini to the other. The work gives a number of visual cues to indicate where he might possibly be, but not enough for him to deduce where he actually is. That situation retains him, so to speak, in the temporal sequence of the deductive process. So, too, with *Purpose* and *The Vocal Fabric of the Chamber Singer Rosa Silber,* and even with the iconographically conventional subject in *Diana,* since she is moving and there are indicators as to where and even why, but no possible solution as to why.

Along the continuum of Klee's work, image adapts word and interacts with it by inducing the viewer to its temporalities; but also, in such creations as *Abstract Writing* (*Abstrakte Schrift,* 1931) word is arrested to the spatial condition of image; indecipherable designations of words are frozen into their character as image and cues are erased in the very presentation of a likeness to what could be—with a few changes—decipherable scrawls in an actual language.

Magritte's paucity of icons in a given painting reinforces his richness of visual representation to redirect the viewer to the spatial presentation and to induce him, often, to a visual repose in the apprehension of the mystery involved. A bouquet of violets blots the face of a white-gowned woman on a balcony. That this is *The Great War* might lead to ratiocination about that conflict, if the conflicting icons in the painting were more turbulent. As it is, the war's modification of the preceding Belle Époque is here itself modified and muted by the viewer's only slightly deflected immersion in the Belle Époque's visual delectations. Only a bouquet blocks his view, and a bouquet is a pleasant icon of love and nature, with all the associations that violets have in a French "language of flowers," supplemented by the rich pacifications of the warm color violet against the expansive white. De Chirico's paintings are more confrontational and more awesome, partly because his icons draw heavily on transience and the nocturnal.

In Max Ernst's collage novels the very sequence he sets up for each of them modifies the individual collages in a temporal and therefore a verbal direction. In his other works he often makes much of the conceptual, the verbal, element in Dada, through his titles. *A little machine dadamax himself constructed of minimax* (*von minimax dadamax selbst konstruirtes maschinchen,* 1919–20) inscribes this title in tiny script at the bottom of a double construction of what look like pieces of tubing, some of them in the form of letters themselves. The signature itself repeats the nonce name, "dadamax ernst." More is added to the writing, which concludes "at the beginning of climacteric and similar fruitless performances" ("zu beginn der wechseljähres u. dergl fruchtlose verrichtungen"). This arbitrary unconcluded title for a tale casts the painter in the alternative designation of an expression condensed enough to become, decades later, the term for a kind of economic calculation, "minimax." If here, in this noun and verb neologism, art has anticipated life, it is the verbal side of this art work that life later imitates. The invented figure "Loplop," a sportive alter ego for the painter, stands at the center of many works in which Ernst casts quasi-summaries of narrative episodes.

Marcel Duchamp also casts himself in his work, as Rrose Sélavy, as the signer of a bond, or as the anonymous randomizer of a recorded action or the validator of an accident, leaving the cracks from a mishap in the *Large Glass.* The gap between one significative icon and another in that work is so great that it imposes a large "empty" syntax of possible narration, an emphasis on the (nonexistent) verbal element so great that it refers to the work—and back again to the sequence of thought. This process is already fully in place for *Nude Descending a Staircase,* to be concentrated later in the women of de Kooning and others, where all the contradictory iconographic associations are fiercely fused together in the energies of visual presentation.

In Peirce's terminology, an image in a painting can serve as an icon, an index, and a symbol, all three at once.[10] A psychoanalytic perspective bears on the sense of art too, in a situation where an object cathexis takes place in the intentional act of dwelling on a painting. But in the last analysis the "rapture" of the viewer, as Freud distinguished art from dreams, takes place in a public context, a context of reality. Psycho-analytic terms are not the message of a painting, as they can be for a dream; rather they are a fundamental part of its code. In paintings like those I have been discussing, in which narrative elements are variously and complexly present, the reality to which they refer ultimately involves the sort of logical process that Freud said dreams cannot enlist.[11] Nar-ration in paintings also involves more than a logical process; it involves the very oneiric absorption that relates them to dreams. Indeed, the mechanisms of dream analysis would serve well to indicate initially the processes to which the images in these paintings have been subjected: as Lyotard has shown, they involve condensations (of ideas of a woman in Magritte, Ernst, and Duchamp, for example). And they involve dis-placements, of image into words if nothing else. But these condensa-tions and displacements, again, enter into syntactic relationships: they complicate, rather than simplify, by comparison with the dream, even if Freud's reading of the dream message is expanded to include an emphasis, with Hillman, Erikson, and others, on the resistant "navel" of the dream to which Freud refers.[12] Ernst's Oedipus in *Une Semaine de Bonté* refers to Freud's; Ernst also includes Oedipus in a syntax that, as it were, refers back to Freud for combinations, while eluding the Freudian readings by holding up surrealistic, but also logical, juxta-positions of complex artifacts from the fading culture of the previous century, whose incontrovertible evidence is visible in the single items from its printed materials that Ernst isolates for his découpage. Ernst's work celebrates, deplores, but only partially decodes, the unconscious, which remains stubbornly and "visibly" in place to remind the viewer of the universe of pitfalls into which the visible may be structured to tell him he is invisibly locked. So Magritte, by referring back to popular dream books in *The Key of Dreams,* is able to do all of this work, sublimating Freud while calmly assimilating him and referring him back to the ongoing life whose oneiric properties these smooth paintings even out into a visibly demonstrated congruence with their more humdrum attributes.

If all the works I have been discussing modify narrative while evoking it, the modification is at the service of intensifying the image. The complexities of signification thereby enlisted recede, or unfold, in the face of a plenary immersion in the perception that a work has brought forward to a horizon of possibility. The work thus, in its actual presence, may be said to envision possibility, and to achieve at once the fruition of a moment and the opening to something beyond the moment, to a rapture that fills out, as it uses up, the dimensions of its signs.

NOTES

PART ONE. EXTENSIONS OF VISUAL REALIZATION

Chapter 1. Rhetoric and Rapture: The Interdependence of
Signification and Depth-Communication in the Arts

1. The status of signs as they relate to consciousness is a complex, still live
question in philosophy. And the question has a long history. Jeffrey Barnouw
says, describing his book in progress on natural signs:

> The conception of natural signs is one of the oldest and hardiest of man's resources
> for understanding his own capacity of knowledge. It was used in the specialized prac-
> tical epistemologies of various particular arts or *technai* in classical antiquity, including
> medicine ("signs and symptoms"), navigation (weather signs), rhetoric and statecraft,
> and divination (where the distinction between natural and supernatural signs was not
> yet drawn firmly or consistently). Natural signs became a basis of divergent theories
> of knowledge in general in the writings of Greek philosophers of the Stoic, Epicurean
> and Sceptical schools, building on suggestions found in Aristotle, with the Stoics
> advancing the broadest and most penetrating claims. They in effect extend the concept
> of indicative or revelatory signs into an understanding of the process of perception
> itself, and establish continuity between sign and inference such that all thinking is
> seen to be "in signs."
>
> This conception does not give priority to language, but on the contrary makes
> natural sign relations, such as are already active in perception, basic to propositional
> thinking. This implies that the use of artificial signs is made possible by the prior
> operation of natural sign relations which constitutes the original workings of mental
> discourse . . .

The Greek Sceptics distinguished two kinds of natural sign. The first, which they not only accepted but made the basis of all practical knowledge, was the commemorative or recalling sign, which was based on prior association. Once two phenomena [have] been observed together, i.e. in conjunction, . . . either phenomenon may serve to suggest the other when the latter is absent. Thus commemorative signs signify what is only temporarily non-manifest, as clouds may signify rain and conversely . . .

The other kind of natural sign is the indicative or revealing sign, which is said to signify what is by nature non-manifest, though it might be fairer to say, what can only be revealed or indicated through such signification. A classical example is sweat as a sign of invisible (but "intelligible") pores . . . the duality of recalling and revealing signs provides a convenient and illuminating framework for tracing subsequent developments in sign theory, particularly in showing how theories have managed to shift their emphasis from one type or aspect of natural signs to the other. (personal communication, 1985)

2. The recent literature on art focused in this way would include the work of E. H. Gombrich, Nelson Goodman, Arthur Danto, W. J. T. Mitchell, and many others, including some semioticians. See the further comments on the limits of such questions in Albert Cook, *Changing the Signs: The Fifteenth-Century Breakthrough* (Lincoln: University of Nebraska Press, 1985), and *Figural Choice in Poetry and Art* (University Press of New England, 1985).

3. In this connection, what Joseph Margolis says is apposite about Gombrich's "conditions of perception" (E. H. Gombrich, *Art and Illusion* [Princeton: Princeton University Press, 1960]) and Goodman's "logical conditions of representation" (Nelson Goodman, *The Languages of Art* [Indianapolis: Hackett, 1976]): "The opposition between the 'conventional' and the 'natural" only makes sense if one denies the realist/idealist symbiosis *and* if one ignores the cognitive problem regarding universals. Within that complex, there is room for both elements—though *not* determinately or disjunctively; and within that complex, it is entirely possible, empirically, to demonstrate that *some* forms of representation *are* more 'natural' than others: either more likely to be closer to original biological dispositions or behaviorally more apt within the space of a particular culture (or even more apt in terms of recognizability within the perceptual practices of an alien culture). But what this shows is the simple fact that the success of spontaneous recognition cannot (*contra* Goodman) be merely an artifact of 'representational systems (or) pictorial purposes alone'" (Margolis, "Puzzles of Pictorial Representation," in *Philosophy Looks at the Arts,* ed. Joseph Margolis [Philadelphia: Temple University Press, 1987], 349).

4. *Republic,* 510d–e.

5. Goodman, *The Languages of Art,* 16.

6. These methods are defined as "seeing them under one idea to bring together particulars that have been scattered in many places" (*Phaedrus,* 265d) and "to be able to divide them again into separate ideas according to the ligatures they have by nature" (265e). These Stenzel calls "the plainest statement of the method of abstraction from particulars that can be found anywhere in Plato" (Julius Stenzel, *Plato's Method of Dialectic,* tr. and ed. D. J. Allan [Oxford: Clarendon Press, 1940], 17).

7. Jean-Francois Lyotard, *Discours, Figure* (Paris: Klincksieck, 1971).

8. Wendy Steiner, *The Colors of Rhetoric* (Chicago: University of Chicago Press, 1983), 68 and passim. See also Cook, *Figural Choice.*

9. E. H. Gombrich, "Icones Symbolicae," in *Symbolic Images* (New York: Phaidon, 1978), 123–95.

10. Naomi Schor, *Reading in Detail* (New York: Methuen, 1987), 131–40.

11. Erwin Panofsky, *Studies in Iconology* (New York: Harper, 1962 [1939]), 4–15.

12. Rudolf Arnheim, *Art and Visual Perception* (Berkeley: University of California Press, 1974).

13. Charles Sanders Peirce, "Logic as Semiotic: The Theory of Signs," in *Philosophical Writings of Peirce,* ed. Justus Buchler (New York: Dover, 1955), 98–119. In Peirce's well-reticulated system

> a sign or *representamen,* is something which stands to somebody for something in some respect or capacity. It addresses somebody, that is, creates in the mind of that person an equivalent sign, or perhaps a more developed sign. That sign which it creates I call the *interpretant* of the first sign. The sign stands for something, its *object.* It stands for that object, not in all respects, but in reference to a sort of idea which I have sometimes called the *ground* of the representamen. . . . In consequence of every representamen being thus connected with three things, the ground, the object, and the interpretant, the science of semiotic has three branches. . . . Signs are divisible by three trichotomies; first, according as the sign in itself is a mere quality, is an actual existent, or is a general law; secondly, according as the relation of the sign to its object consists in the sign's having some character in itself, or in some existential relation to that object, or in its relation to an interpretant; thirdly, according as its interpretant represents it as a sign of possibility or as a sign of fact or a sign of reason. . . ." According to the second trichotomy, a Sign may be termed an *Icon,* an *Index,* or a *Symbol.* (102)

Following out this system, not just in the second trichotomy of icon, index, and symbol, but the first and third as well, could take us, of course, very far, and might turn out to afford a complete, or at least a satisfactorily abundant, set of definitions for the expressive and communicative operations performed by works of art.

14. Such considerations would involve an adaptation of Peirce, turning his "relational" or dyadic icon into his "metaphors" or "symbols"—involving a "third," or an abstract connector between two other points, the land and the set of mapped correspondences to the land. For a discussion of such underlying principles as they govern some maps, see John Seelye, *Prophetic Waters: The River in Early American Life and Literature* (New York: Oxford University Press, 1977), which discusses such unconscious projection of spatial perceptions in American colonial mapmaking; and Svetlana Alpers, *The Art of Describing* (Chicago: University of Chicago Press, 1983), which gives the theoretical background for the principles behind Dutch mapmaking and other science as it relates to seventeenth-century Dutch painting.

15. On this question, see Albert Cook, "The Integers of Giorgione," in *Changing the Signs,* 44–56.

16. Boris Uspensky, *The Semiotics of the Russian Icon,* tr. Stephen Rudy (Lisse: Peter de Ridder Press, 1976), 15.

17. Klee's paintings, however, both constitute and incorporate "icons" in the less restricted common sense (very different from Peirce's) of culturally determined images, as I shall be using the term throughout my discussion.

18. See Cook, "The Range of Image," in *Figural Choice,* 7–37.

19. Cook, *Changing the Signs,* 1–13 and passim.

20. Umberto Eco, *Semiotica e filosofia del linguaggio* (Turin: Einaudi, 1984), 196; translated as *Semiotics and Philosophy of Language* (Bloomington: Indiana University Press, 1984).

21. Longinus, "Ou gar eis peitho tous akroomenous all' eis ekstasin agei ta hyperphua," in *On the Sublime* 1:4. On the Longinean tradition, see Thomas

Rice Henn, *Longinus and English Criticism* (Cambridge: Cambridge University Press, 1934).

22. See "Surrealism and Surrealisms," in Cook, *Figural Choice,* 86–123.

23. For Lyotard, *Discours, Figure,* esp. 239–70. Lyotard maps the mechanisms of Freudian dream theory (displacement, condensation, figurability, secondary elaboration) upon the procedures of art. His set of abstractions, while it does not convincingly demonstrate its own necessity, impressively indicates the accessibility of art to complex structural analysis. For Claude Lévi-Strauss, "L'Ouverture" to *Le Cru et le cuit* (Paris: Plon, 1963), 9–40. The whole of this book is organized under the headings of musical forms: "overture," "song," "variations," "sonata," "symphonies," "fugue," "well-tempered astronomy."

24. Handel and Bach, among others, had recourse to these simple patterns. The term "abstractive correlative" was used by Bertrand Bronson in a lecture describing and discussing the practice. This lecture is amplified in Bertrand H. Bronson, "Some Aspects of Music and Literature," in *Facets of the Enlightenment* (Berkeley: University of California Press, 1968), 91–118. Bronson says, "But, once having accepted the convention of an 'up' and a 'down' among musical tones, we can of course extend the figurative analogies at will. Bach uses the device of dropping to the lower bass to suggest Adam's "fall"; and also to indicate night, and darkness, and hell. Handel, in the Cecilia Ode, writes Dryden's phrase, 'depth of pains and height of passion' as E to A above, to A at the octave, and back to E, the octave leap coming on the word *height*—and such was no doubt Dryden's intention" (98). Bronson touches on several correspondences between sound and sense in music, including "the intellectual significance of the keys" (100). This whole system was criticized almost at its inception by Vincenzo Galilei, *Dialogo della musica antica e della moderna* (1581), who is quoted and discussed by Peter Kivy, "Representation as Expression," in *Philosophy Looks at the Arts,* ed. Joseph Margolis, 319–37.

25. Jacques Attali, *Bruits* (Paris: Presses Universitaires, 1977).

26. Once again, the pitfalls of definition in this domain are vividly evoked by Jacques Derrida: "*Mimesis.* At the same time, I would deliberately set aside the too difficult question announced by this word; it escapes any frontal approach, and the thing I am going to talk about obliges me to consider *mimesis* through and through, as an open-ended question, but also as a miniscule vanishing point at the already sunlit abyssal depths of the mimosa. *'Mimo-:* said of plants that contract when touched'" (Jacques Derrida, *Signéponge,* tr. Richard Rand [New York: Columbia University Press, 1984], 4–7).

27. In this connection see Anton Ehrenzweig, *The Psychoanalysis of Artistic Vision and Hearing* (1953; New York: Braziller, 1965).

28. Roland Barthes, *Le Plaisir du texte* (Paris: Seuil, 1978). The "empathy" or *"Einfühlung"* of Theodor Lipps addresses the connection established between work and viewer, but not the transport (*Leitfaden der Psychologie* [Leipzig: Engelmann, 1906]).

29. Immanuel Kant, in *Kritik der Urteilskraft* (1799; Hamburg: Meiner, 1954), first part, second book, sections 51–59, "Von der Schönheit als Symbol der Sittlichkeit," 197; 211–14.

30. "Judgment of taste bases itself on a concept from which, however, nothing in consideration of the object can be known and proven . . . it attains through the very same [process] at the same time a validity for everyone, because its basis of definition perhaps lies in the concept of what can be viewed as the supernatural substratum of mankind" "Das Geschmacksurteil gründet

sich auf einem Begriffe . . . aus dem aber nichts in Ansehung des Objekts er-
kannt und bewiesen werden kann . . . es bekommt aber durch ebendenselben
doch zugleich Gültigkeit für jedermann . . . weil der Bestimmungsgrund des-
selben vielleicht im Begriffe von demjenigen liegt, was als das übersinnliche
Substrat der Menschheit angesehen werden kann" (ibid., section 57, 198–99).
This is my translation, as are all others here, unless otherwise indicated.

31. "Fine art is an art in so far as it at the same time appears to be nature"
("Schöne Kunst ist eine Kunst, sofern sie zugleich Natur zu sein scheint")
(ibid., section 45, 159). Kant mainly intends here to say that the artistic product
must achieve an appearance of effortlessness, but the reason behind this rests
on the effort to achieve an impression like that of beauties in nature, where no
other is present. The other, of course, is not present, or not in the same way,
when a beholder looks at a real, rather than a painted, landscape. And the
painted landscape draws on some of that sense of beauty—which has cultural,
and perhaps even precultural, determinants, even though they have not been
coded by an actual human artist.

32. Martin Heidegger, *Unterwegs zur Sprache* (Pfullingen: Neske, 1959), 83–
155. The "inquirer" reproduces his sense of the earlier Japanese visitor's definition of "*Iki*": "He spoke of sense appearances, through whose vigorous rapture the supersensual appears" "Er sprach von sinnlichen Scheinen, durch des-
sen lebhaftes Entzücken Übersinnliches hindurchscheint" (101). The Japanese
quickly adds other terms: "Without 'color' no 'emptiness,' 'openness,' 'heaven.'"
("*Iro*, d.h. Farbe, und sagen *Kū*, d.h. das Leere, das Offene, der Himmel. Wir
sagen: ohne *Iro* kein *Kū*"). "*Kū*" is literally "sky" and resists the supernatural
notion in "heaven." The terms tend, then, to combine and to permute, as well
as to evade—just as do Western terminologies in Heidegger's hands, who has
his Japanese soon put the sense and unsense (*Sinnliche, Nichtsinnliche*) on the
basis of language itself, as it combines sound and signification (103). So the
term "gesture" or "glance" ("*Wink*") is adduced (144), and with it a Japanese
term for speech-as-message, *Koto ba*, and since "*ba*" is literally "leaves," "leaves
from the heart" would be a relevant reading. Further, Japanese emphasizes a
special aesthetic term at different historical periods. In the medieval period it
was the pathos-sensibility of "*mono no aware*"; then the "mystery" of "*Yūgen*";
and still later a "*sabi*," a term suggesting loneliness and rust, the extraordinary-
in-the-ordinary, and the sort of age that a patina provides. For this information
I am indebted to Meera Viswanathan and her unpublished article on Heidegger's dialogue.

33. Martin Heidegger, *Der Ursprung des Kunstwerkes* (1935–60; Stuttgart:
Reklam, 1977), 61.

34. Jacques Lacan, *Le Séminaire,* II (Paris: Seuil, 1978), 51.

35. "I spoke of the imaginary; I did not say what drawing is, which is already
a symbol" ("J'ai parlé de l'imaginaire, je n'ai pas dit que c'était le dessin, qui
est déjà un symbole"). The fudging lies in "*déjà*," and perhaps doubly. First,
Lacan had been talking about the imaginary in image, and a drawing is certainly
an image, and so the question is fair and remains unanswered: "It seems to me
that drawing is already an obscure elaboration of the imagined" ("Il me semble
que le dessin est déjà une elaboration obscure de l'imaginaire"). Second, Lacan's
reply seems to equivocate between the minimal use of symbol as a mimetic
representation of something and the maximal presence of his own symbolic
order, which in his terms, of course, is always dominant. Invoking that order,
however, with whatever dialectical and even mathematical permutations he may

offer, will not really serve, as it seems to want to do here, to conclude a demonstrated answer.

36. Lacan, *Le Séminaire*, XX (1975), 21. These diagram the discourse of the Master, the University, the Hysteric, and the Analyst.

37. Lyotard, *Discours, Figure*, 31.

38. Cook, *Changing the Signs.*

39. For examples of this interplay, see Simon Schama, *The Embarrassment of Riches: An Interpretation of Dutch Culture in the Golden Age* (New York: Knopf, 1987).

Chapter 2. Mind, Eye, and Brush: Turner's Venice

1. I do not wish to imply that the term "sublime" has ceased to occur in an evaluative sense. Richard Wollheim, for example, applies it boldly and appositely to the work of Mark Rothko: "one of Rothko's canvases from the Four Seasons Series . . . (Plate 6): to my mind, one of the sublimest creations of our time" (*On Art and the Mind* [Cambridge: Harvard University Press, 1974], 128).

2. Lawrence Gowing, *Turner: Imagination and Reality* (New York: Museum of Modern Art, 1966).

3. John Ruskin, *Works*, ed. E. T. Cook and Alexander Wedderburn (library edition), London: George Allen, 1903–12, 7; *Modern Painters*, vol. 5, part 9, chap. 2, "The Lance of Pallas," 263–78. All notes to Ruskin are to this edition, which will be indicated first by the volume number and then by the data for the particular work being cited. The term "picturesque" covers a broad range in the eighteenth and nineteenth centuries, and it can sometimes shade into its occasional opposite, the "sublime." Ruskin sees the effect as a limiting one, and certainly it was a kind of formula. James A. W. Heffernan says, "Unfixed in its meaning, ubiquitously applied, and hovering somewhere in the space between pictures and natural scenery, the picturesque was just one manifestation of the extent to which nature and art became entangled in the eighteenth century" (*The Re-creation of Landscape: A Study of Wordsworth, Coleridge, Constable, and Turner* [Hanover: University Press of New England, 1985], 6). It is, so to speak, the "space between pictures and natural scenery" that I am addressing. John Dixon Hunt points out how Turner early uses frames like trees and bridges to attain the "picturesque," but gets away from them as he moves more distinctly toward the "sublime" ("Wondrous Deep and Dark: Turner and the Sublime," *Georgia Review* 30 [Spring 1976]: 139–54). Hunt says that Burke's "space, magnitude, imprecision . . . are all applied by Turner in his painting" (143). He quotes Turner's statement to a prospective buyer, as it were answering Hazlitt's reservations: "Indistinctness is my forte" (151). In representing "mystery," "Venice . . . gave a whole new energy and formulation for the sublime."

4. *Works*, 7; *Modern Painters*, vol. 5, part 9, chap. 9, "The Two Boyhoods," 374–88 and passim.

5. Of course Turner has other affinities than just the Venetians. A. G. H. Bachrach stresses his derivations from Van Goyen and Ruysdael ("Turner, Ruysdael and the Dutch," in *Turner Studies* 1(1) (1981): 19–30). Ronald Paulson, *Literary Landscape: Turner and Constable* (New Haven: Yale University Press, 1982), links him to another kind of mediator of impressions, the poet Thomson (67–68), while touching on his use of Titian (72, 133). Ruskin also connects him to Cuyp and Vandevelde and speaks of the British as being "incidentally mingled with his graver study," citing Robson, Fielding, Cozens, and Girtin

among the painters of the earlier British landscape tradition (*Modern Painters,* 3:352). Among the paintings of Turner that do answer to Ruskin's description— not a large number—would be *Abingdon, the Ford,* which has some of this grimy London feeling, and *Washing Sheep* and *Goring Mill,* which bring Turner close to the characteristic landscapes and scenes of Constable. *The Chain Pier. Brighton* and *St. Michael's Mount* also work in some of this feeling.

6. *Works,* 7: *Modern Painters,* vol. 5, part 9, chap. 9, "The Two Boyhoods," 374–88.

7. Adrian Stokes, *Venice,* in *Critical Writings* (London: Thames and Hudson, 1978), 2:114: "[Ruskin] would strive to prove in terms of this stone that an anterior, for all practical purposes no longer existent Venice, a Venice pre- eminently of wood, brick, stucco, paint, terra-cotta and mud, transcended and shamed the Venice he knew. His own magnificent title is sufficient condem- nation of his distorted thesis . . . forget about stone and the beauty of stone and water. This is a Venice fit for horses and mules which are largely employed, a Venice of muddy ways and chained canals, a kind of medieval Rotterdam."

8. Max F. Schulz, "Turner's Fabled Atlantis: Venice, Carthage, and London as Paradisal Cityscape," *Studies in Romanticism* (Fall 1980), 395–417. Schulz ex- pands on the complexities of the idea of the earthly paradise as it is evoked by Turner in painting even such cities as Zurich (396).

9. "Starting in Venice, the eventual Palladian versions obtained a wide cur- rency, particularly in England" (Stokes, *Venice,* 124). Ruskin draws attention to Turner's "drawings of flower gardens and Palladian mansions," when he would later be "disguising them"—preeminently the way his Venetian buildings look—"merely as kinds of white clouds" (*Works,* 5; *Modern Painters,* vol. 3, part 4, chap. 18, "Of the Teachers of Turner," paras. 7–8, 390–92).

10. *Works,* 3: *Modern Painters,* vol. 1, part 2, sect. 1, chap. 7, paras. 37–46, 228– 52.

11. The sharp contrast between London and Venice remains as a sort of aegis over such writing about art as well, and it could certainly be carried into the conditions around *The Stones of Venice,* as well as into the conditions of Ruskin's tragic life. The contrast between the two cities effectually carries forward into the work of Stokes, who used that contrast to justify his own attention to the Mediterranean world, long before he wrote his book on Venice.

12. John Gage, *Colour in Turner: Poetry and Truth* (London: Studio Vista, 1969).

13. Jack Lindsay, *J. M. W. Turner: His Life and Work* (London: Cory Adams & Mackay, 1966), 168–80.

14. Quoted in Gowing, *Turner: Imagination and Reality,* 19.

15. *Works,* 3; *Modern Painters,* vol. 1, part 2, sect. 2, chap. 1, paras. 16–17, 269– 70.

16. *Works,* 7; *Modern Painters,* vol. 5, part 9, chap. 1, "The Dark Mirror," 255.

17. Paulson, *Literary Landscape,* 1–25.

18. *Works,* 5; *Modern Painters,* vol. 3, part 4, chap. 18, "Of the Teachers of Turner," para. 19, 399.

19. Turner admired, as did Constable, Titian's much earlier painting *The Death of St. Peter Martyr* (1526–30), which is now lost. He saw that its "landscape tho natural is heroic"—like his own, and even more forcefully like those of late Titian. "Amplitude, quantity and space appear in this picture given by the means of Trees opposed to a blue sky and deep sunk horizon not more than one-sixth the height of the picture"—qualities that obtain more of late Turner

than of the Titian of this phase. (I quote from and summarize the discussion in Heffernan, *The Re-creation of Landscape*, 81, 131–34.)

20. He could have seen *The Rape of Europa*, then in a British collection, and the *Pietà* in the Venice Accademia. Turner's European itineraries never took him as far east as Vienna or even Munich, and he therefore could not have seen first-hand *The Flaying of Marsyas* in Czechoslovakia, the *Crowning of Thorns* in the collection of the elector of Bavaria, the *Nymph and Shepherd* in Vienna, and probably not the *Saint Sebastian* now in the Hermitage, sold by the Barbarigo family in 1850.

21. Gage, *Colour in Turner*, 90, stresses Tintoretto and Veronese, as Ruskin had stressed Giorgione.

22. *Works*, 7; *Modern Painters*, vol. 5, part 6, chap. 5, "Leaf Aspects," para. 2, 51–52. Ruskin is graphic at this point in specifying the complexity and difficulty of the smallest representation, in this going far beyond the *Discourses* of Reynolds, whom he quotes and admires both as a painter and as a theorist:

> The facility of drawing the group [of leaves] may be judged of by a comparison. Suppose five or six boats, very beautifully built, and sharp in the prow, to start all from one point, and the first bearing up into the wind, the other three or four to fall off from it in succession an equal number of points, taking each, in consequence, a different slope of deck from the stem of the sail. Suppose also, that the bows of these boats were transparent, so that you could see the under sides of their decks as well as the upper;—and that it were required of you to draw all their five decks, the under or upper side, as their curve showed it, in true foreshortened perspective, indicating the exact distance each boat had reached at a given moment from the central point they started from.
> If you can do that, you can draw a rose-leaf. Not otherwise. (48–49)

23. John Dixon Hunt, *The Wider Sea* (New York: Viking, 1982), 80, notes that having specified the exact location of the view, the young Ruskin then declared, "The view is accurate in every particular, even to the number of divisions in the Gothic of the Doge's Palace." John Gage makes the point once again in "The Poet and the City," review of *Turner in Venice*, by A. J. Finberg, *Times Literary Supplement*, February 7, 1986, 144.

24. Andrew Wilton, *Turner and the Sublime* (Chicago: University of Chicago Press, 1980) discusses the range of sources and emphases in Turner's broad use of the sublime. Wilton classifies these under several headings: the classic sublime, the landscape sublime, the Turnerian sublime, the picturesque sublime, the architectural sublime, and the historical sublime. Wilton quotes Turner's manuscript lecture notes on the painter's admiration for Titian as a landscape painter based on Titian's now lost *Death of St. Peter Martyr*: "the sublimity of the arrangement of lines by its unshackled obliquity obtains the associated feelings of free continuity that rushes like the ignited spark struggling as the ascending Rocket with the Elements from Earth towards Heaven; and when no more propelled by the force it scatters around its falling glories, ignited embers, seeing again its Earthly bourne, while diffusing around its mellow radiance in the descending cherub with the palm of Beatitude sheds the mellow glow of Gold through the dark embrowned foliage to the dying Martyr" (71). This passage will readily be seen as even more appropriate a characterization of Turner's own painting than of Titian's.

25. "The status of objects is often quite swallowed up by the modification of the moment—mist, light, and dazzle. Matching wins over making. There is some justification in the idea that he suppressed what he knew of the world

and concentrated only on what he saw" (Gombrich, *Art and Illusion,* 296). Many questions of visual perception are begged here, while some others are being sharpened in this view of Turner, and in Gombrich's work generally, at the service of a psychology of artistic seeing that leaves out or perilously takes for granted some essentials. This statement would make as much, or even more, sense, if Gombrich's "matching" and "making" were reversed. Indeed, Gombrich really seems to be asserting that "making wins over matching."

It cannot be shown, as Gombrich effectually maintains, that the "duck-rabbit" puzzle of Wittgenstein constrains a viewer from attending in one view to both "matching" and "making." The constructive habits of the eye and the conventions of representation within a culture no more split the viewer from direct immersive apprehension of a painting than the phonetic structure of language and the social conventions of communication split the auditor from the direct apprehension of a sentence. Richard Wollheim, *Art and Its Objects,* 2d ed. (Cambridge: Cambridge University Press, 1980), 56–66, further qualifies Gombrich's nominalizing assumptions, which tend to atomize the aesthetic effect under cover of explaining it: "That works of art have this [iconic] kind of translucence is a plausible tenet, and it should be apparent how a belief in a natural expressive ordering of the constituents of art would go some way to preserving it" (60–61). Wollheim elaborates in "Reflections on *Art and Illusion:* "But why does Gombrich assume that we can no more see a picture simultaneously as canvas and as nature than we can see the duck-rabbit figure simultaneously as a duck and as a rabbit? Because—it might be said—canvas and nature are different interpretations. But if this is Gombrich's argument, it is invalid. For the reason why we cannot see the duck-rabbit figure simultaneously as a duck and as a rabbit is not because 'duck' and 'rabbit' are two different interpretations, it is because they are two incompatible interpretations" (in Wollheim, *On Art and the Mind,* 280). For further discussion of the limitations to Gombrich's theory of representation, see Norman Bryson, *Vision and Painting* (New Haven: Yale University Press, 1983), and W. J. T. Mitchell, *Iconology* (Chicago: University of Chicago Press, 1986).

26. *Works,* 7; *Modern Painters,* vol. 5, part 9, chap. 1, "The Dark Mirror," 253–62. For further inferences about the significations of Turner's landscape from a post-Ruskin perspective, see Hunt, "Wondrous Deep and Dark." While Ruskin emphasizes the "picturesque" negatively with reference to the sublime, others often have pointed out that Turner, up to his latest phase, reflects the "picturesque" in a positive sense.

27. Ruskin has pointed out the persistence of "imagination" in Turner's vision of a given landscape by noting the similarity of approach between a very early view of Nottingham and a moderately late one of the same scene ("Of Topography in Turner," *Modern Painters,* 4, v., 27–42).

28. Stokes, "The Art of Turner," in *Painting and the Inner World* (1963), in *Critical Writings* 3:236–55. Further, he notes that "buildings are sometimes treated almost as clouds" (251) and still further, that "awareness of a centre in great space will favor a *rencontre* of contrary factors in whatever sense" (254).

29. *Works,* 4; *Modern Painters,* vol. 2, part 2, sect. 5, chap. 1, "Of Truth of Water," para. 18, "And Canaletto," 513–14.

30. Stokes, "The Art of Turner," 237.

31. The icon of water is amplified in Georges Bachelard, *L'Eau et les rêves* (Paris: José Corti, 1963).

32. Heffernan relates this procedure to certain techniques in poetry that re-

sult in what he calls "the internalization of prospect." He identifies "two contrasting ways in which romantic poets and painters make the outer world express the inner world. One is by representing scenes of enclosure or 'refuge' from the world at large. The other is by eliminating stable or elevated viewpoints" (*The Re-creation of Landscape*, 105). He goes on to distinguish an avalanche painting of Turner's from one of de Loutherbourg's by saying that "Turner's picture precludes spectatorship by removing any vantage point from which the avalanche might be safely viewed" (123). And his statement that "the atmosphere tends to consume elaborate outlines" (147) in *Old London Bridge* is equally true of the late landscapes, beginning with the Venetian scenes. Further, suggestively for the "all-round" effect, "sublimity is a consciousness of *boundaries crossed*" And "Turner's attack on parallel perspective sprang from his conviction that the field of human vision is circular" (196). Among earlier paintings, an immersive, all-round effect that has a Venetian cast is achieved in *The Lake from Petworth House, Sunset* (1828).

33. The data are from Martin Butlin and Evelyn Joel, *The Paintings of J. M. W. Turner* (New Haven: Yale University Press, 1984), 2:302. Butlin and Joel indicate that Turner's own Europas are very likely modeled on Titian's.

34. John Gage, *Turner: Rain, Steam and Speed* (London: Penguin Press, 1972), 45.

35. Stokes, "The Art of Turner," 245.

36. Wilton, *Turner and the Sublime*, 79.

37. Another way to come at this whole question of impressions prior to a medium that they get expressed in would be to compare Turner and Constable with Wordsworth and Coleridge (or Titian with Bembo), as Ronald Paulson does, and more protractedly James A. W. Heffernan. Alternatively, one could move, as some writers have, analogously from Wordsworth to Proust by noting, as Ruskin does, that Turner and Wordsworth have very close affinities—affinities that Ruskin digested and passed on to Proust, who gets the gist of paintings and landscapes, and then the gist of a poetry he may never have read, through Ruskin's eyes. Such a transfer, where Proust got his Wordsworth through a Ruskin whose vision Turner had enlarged, would bring critical prose into the stream of interactions. So Ezra Pound's perception of the Tempio in Rimini was enlarged by his Rapallo neighbor Adrian Stokes—but also by the pervasive impression of white stone in the Venice of his youth. And probably by having read Ruskin on Venice.

Chapter 3. The Dimensions of Color

1. Faber Birren, *Principles of Color* (New York: Van Nostrand, 1969), 50, speaks of millions of colors, limiting those that can actually be differentiated to some thousands.

2. According to Brent Berlin and Paul Kay, *Basic Color Terms: Their Universality and Evolution* (Berkeley: University of California Press, 1969) (as cited in Rudolf Arnheim, *Art and Visual Perception*, 331–32), their survey of color terms in the development of twenty languages revealed that primitive peoples, when they get to differentiating color from the simple contrast of dark and light, tend first to name just red.

3. Ludwig Wittgenstein in his *Remarks on Colour* (Berkeley: University of California Press, 1977) raises many difficulties between the perception of color and the naming of color, dealing especially with nomenclature-correspondence for intermediate colors ("*Zwischenfarben*"). "The logic of the concept of color

is just much more complicated than it might seem," he says (2:106), amplifying puzzles about the perception and nomenclature of color that go back at least as far as Plato (*Lysis*, 217c). "We do not want to find a theory of color (neither a physiological nor a psychological one), but rather the logic of color concepts" (3:188). Yet this last remark points inescapably in the direction of the experiential—and color cannot avoid at least an analogue to the physiological or the psychological if taken in the light of another of Wittgenstein's apothegms: "The color concepts are to be treated like the concepts of sensations [*Sinnesempfindungen*]" (3:72). The German term here leads onto the ground of traditional epistemology, and even of Husserlian phenomenology. The consequent complications are unavoidable, as Wittgenstein declares in the first quotation above. Edmund Husserl, *Logische Untersuchungen* (Tübingen: Niemeyer, 1913), 2:222–26 and passim, takes color as a test case for the necessity of mediating between concrete and abstract when dealing with perceptions. He follows a tradition that goes back at least as far as Georg Hegel, *Ästhetik* (Frankfurt: Europäisches Verlagsanstalt [1842], 114–15, though Hegel's example is blue rather than red; the discussion has gone from a cold color to a warm one. Maurice Merleau-Ponty, *Le Visible et l'invisible* (Paris: Gallimard, 1964), 174, in turn, amplifies such speculations by adding the dimension of time: "[Red] in short is a certain knot in the web of the simultaneous and the successive . . . a red dress [is] a punctuation in the field of red things."

4. J. W. Goethe, *Zur Farbenlehre* (1806; reprinted in *Werke, Hamburger Ausgabe* [Hamburg: Wegner, 1955], 13:314–523; 14:7–269. Remarks are found at 696 (p. 478) and 741–49 (pp. 488–91).

5. As quoted in Will Grohmann, *Paul Klee* (New York: Abrams, n.d.), 143. William Gass, *On Being Blue* (Boston: Godine, n.d.), 1–2, offers a number of speculations and instantiations of one color:

> Blue pencils, blue noses, blue movies, laws, blue legs and stockings, the language of birds, bees, and flowers as sung by longshoremen, that lead-like look the skin has when affected by cold, contusion, sickness, fear; the rotten rum or gin they call blue ruin and the blue devils of its delirium; Russian cats and oysters, a withheld or imprisoned breath, the blue they say that diamonds have, deep holes in the ocean and the blazers which English athletes earn that gentlemen may wear; afflictions of the spirit—dumps, mopes, Mondays—all that's dismal—low-down gloomy music, Nova Scotians, cyanosis, hair rinse, bluing, bleach; the rare blue dahlia like that blue moon shrewd things happen only once in, or the call for trumps in whist (but who remembers whist or what the death of unplayed games is like?), and, correspondingly the flag, Blue Peter, which is our signal for getting under way; a swift pitch, Confederate money, the shaded slopes of clouds and mountains, and so the constantly increasing absentness of Heaven (*ins Blaue hinein*, the Germans say), consequently the color of everything that's empty: blue bottles, bank accounts, and compliments, for instance, or, when the sky's turned turtle, the blue-green bleat of ocean (both the same), and, when in Hell, its neatly landscaped rows of concrete huts and gas-blue flames; social registers, examination booklets, blue bloods, balls, and bonnets, beards, coats, collars, chips, and cheese . . .

Nothing in this impressive list broaches artistic uses, unless the reference to Hell suggests something like the work of Bosch. The painter takes one or some, or even nearly all of these, to the second degree, through framing, recombination, purification, and fiction.

6. Guillaume Apollinaire, *Les Peintres Cubistes* (1913; Paris: Hermann, 1965), 50.

7. Adrian Stokes, *Colour and Form* in *Critical Writings*, 24, 29.

8. C. A. S. Williams, *Outlines of Chinese Symbolism and Art Motives* (1941; New York: Dover, 1976). The codes invoked by Williams relate color to social class, mood, the four elements, and virtue (76–79).

Mai-Mai Sze, *The Way of Chinese Painting* (New York: Random House, 1959), 77, discusses the associations of the five traditional primary colors—blue-green, red, white, black, and yellow, with metals, animals, compass directions, the seasons, the planets and particular numbers. Thus green codes to wood, a dragon, the east, spring, Jupiter, and the number eight.

9. Ezra Pound, *The ABC of Reading* (1934; New York: New Directions, 1960), 22.

10. Both perceptions and codes are involved in a casual census like that of Julia Kristeva, "La Joie de Giotto," in *Polylogue* (Paris: Seuil, 1977), 393: "Color is to be deciphered each time according to 1) the scale of 'natural' colors 2) the psychology of color perception . . . and 3) the pictural system in force or in course of formation." This both offers a beginning and blurs the dialectic among attributes paradoxically by separating off their features. Nor are these three attributes either congruent or mutually exclusive. "Psychology" actually embraces at least the first two from the beginning, and the third the moment it happens; and of course one must distinguish for her third attribute between the cultural *langue* for color-coding and the sub-*langue* of the traditions used in a particular set of painting conventions, a traditional palette. Beyond all these but including them is the *parole* of an individual artist's act of painting. In Rubens's brown oil sketch *The Discovery of Purple* (Musée Bonnat), for example, the only other color than brown is the highlighted reddish purple flowing out of the mouth of the dog at the seashore. This work at once points at the general existence of a color, gives a mythic etiology for it, and includes it in the visual representation of an anecdotal moment. Presumably the dog has just eaten some murex, and the ancient source of "purpureus" is coded into a legend of accidental scientific discovery, a seventeenth-century sort of emphasis, as the reference of the color to antiquity still has a humanist tinge. The whole of this small sketch takes on a special severity of indicative pointing when it is set in the context of the general *oeuvre* of Rubens, a painter noteworthy for great Titianesque washes of multiple color rather than the single monochrome brown here, used to single out and point to another color connected to legend, the purple.

Eugene Clinton Elliott, "On the Understanding of Color in Painting," *Journal of Aesthetics and Art Criticism* 16(4) (June 1958): 453–70) has a slightly larger, somewhat random group of five functions for color in painting: the symbolic (with examples of Navajo and Buddhist codes), the realistic, the aesthetic, the expressive, and what he calls the "self-justifying" and others might call the "pure" use of color. Elliott goes on to give a good, detailed account of the interdependence of technique, perception, and signification in the Middle Ages, the Renaissance, and beyond. He indicates that discussions in the seventeenth-century French Academy had already singled out Titian as a colorist, as Vasari had much earlier.

11. Marcel Griaule, *Dieu d'eau* (Paris: Fayard, 1966), 74–76.

12. E. A. Wallis Budge, *The Gods of the Egyptians* (1904; New York: Dover, 1969), 2:26, citing "The Book of the Underworld." Other volume and page references to Budge are in parentheses in the text.

13. Eleanor Irwin, *Colour Terms in Greek Poetry* (Toronto: Hakkert, 1974). Irwin (112) discusses Egyptian color conventions in Greek practice, citing other

authorities, particularly with reference to the Egyptian convention of painting women's faces white and men's red, a practice persisting into some vase-painting styles.

14. Stokes, *Colour and Form*, 56. Stokes here offers striking subliminal impressions: "Red is the white form of blackness . . . there is a close affinity between red and black. The afterimage of black is not so much white as green, the afterimage of red."

15. A long chapter of Irwin's *Colour Terms*, 157–93, discusses dark and light contrasts through the whole range of classical poetry. For Homer, Irwin cites F. E. Wallace, *Colour in Homer and in Ancient Art* (Northampton: Smith College Classical Studies 9 [1927]: 29): "83 per cent of the color words in the Iliad are those words expressing value rather than hue, and 60 per cent in the Odyssey . . . So the use of black-and-white words is actually far greater than that of red-to-violet words."

16. See Albert Cook, "Visual Aspects of the Homeric Simile in Indo-European Context," *Quaderni Urbinati di Cultura Classica*, vol. 46, n.s. 17, no. 2 (1984): 39–59; reprinted with amplifications in Cook, *Figural Choice*, 203–24.

17. An elaborately structured decoding of these is offered by Austin Farrer, *A Rebirth of Images* (1949; Boston: Beacon, 1963), 216–28, 350.

18. J. André, *Étude sur les termes de couleur dans la langue latine* (Paris: Klincksieck, 1949).

19. E. Wunderlich, *Die Bedeutung der Roten Farbe im Kultus der Griechen und Römer* (Breslau and Tübingen, 1925).

20. Peter Dronke, "Tradition and Innovation in Medieval Western Colour-Imagery," *Eranos Yearbooks* (1972), 53–107. With his usual appositeness, discrimination, and sweep, Dronke provides rich examples from Paulus Silentiarius's description of colors in Hagia Sophia through Hildegard of Bingen to Richard of Saint Victor and Dante. There are all sorts of ephemeral personal codings of color, of course, not only in painters, but also in writer-painters like Blake, and in such general systems, which tend to draw on the codes as well as to extend them, as are found in works like Frédéric Portal, *Des Couleurs symboliques* (Paris: Treuttel et Würtz, 1857). Portal traces out allegorical dimensions for the colors of the spectrum, in which orange is divine love, violet ideas of death and immortality, and so forth. Under his three categories of divine, sacred, and profane, yellow is celestial light, faith, and love, respectively; red is celestial fire, Buddha-sacrifice, and combat; and green is creation, wisdom, and fertility. A survey that combines the anthropological and the artistic is the chapter entitled "The Whiteness of the Whale" in Melville's *Moby Dick*.

21. Benedetto Croce, as excerpted in *Discussions of the Divine Comedy*, ed. Irma Brandeis (Boston: Heath, 1961), 49–51.

22. Wie wir die Farben des Himmels und der Erde betrachten, die Veränderungen der Farben bei Affekten und Empfindungen an den Menschen, in der Wirkung, wie sie bei grossen Naturerscheinungen vorkommen, und in der Harmonie, selbst insoferne gewisse Farben symbolisch geworden sind, so geben wir jedem Gegenstande der Komposition, harmonisch mit der ersten tiefsten Empfindung und den Symbolen und Gegenständen für sich, jedem seine Farbe . . . Die Sehnsucht, die Liebe und der Wille, das ist Gelb, Rot und Weiss (Blau?). Philipp Otto Runge, *Die Begier nach der Möglichkeit neuer Bilder: Briefwechsel und Schriften zur bildenden Kunst* [Leipzig: Reklam, 1982], 95, 136).

23. See Ralph Matlaw, "Scriabin and Russian Symbolism," *Comparative Literature* 31(1) (Winter 1979): 1–23. "Scriabin saw colors for keys as well as indi-

vidual notes. He scored the second line of *Prometheus* for a light machine to produce a color for the root of the harmony indicated above it" (9–10).

24. "Pourtant, la couleur est liée au fugitif plus que beaucoup d'autres visibles. Mais ce fugitif est davantage celui de la chair du visible, difficilement mémorisable, que la ponctualité de la forme [et] du concept. Le rouge, la couleur est davantage du côté de la *participation* que de l'émergence solitaire du concept" (Luce Irigaray, *Éthique de la différence sexuelle* [Paris: Minuit, 1984], 149).

25. Ruskin, *Modern Painters,* vol. 5, chap. 9, note to para. 8. There are many aspects to the pathos of this statement, linking the art that was the domain of Ruskin's magnificent successes to the love in which he was twice, and differently, such a pronounced failure as to have lost his reason. The statement, so to speak, bursts well beyond Ruskin's confinement of it to a footnote and sets a measure to characterize his whole life.

26. A notably evocative expression of this idea is offered expansively in Bernard Berenson, *Italian Painters of the Renaissance* (1894; London: Phaidon, 1952), 3–35.

27. Oswald Spengler's animadversions on the symbolism of color are very suggestive here, though he would want to typify gold exclusively as a "Magian" color, and yellow as predominantly a Western one; Titian carries off the very fusions he would seem to disallow:

Yellow and red are the *popular* colors, the colors of the crowd, of children, of women, and of savages. Amongst the Venetians and the Spaniards high personages affected [*wählt der Vornehme*] a splendid black or blue, with an unconscious sense of the aloofness inherent in these colors . . . blue and green—the Faustian, monotheistic colors—are those of loneliness, of care . . . Gold is not a color [*überhaupt keine Farbe*]. As compared with simple yellow, it produces a complicated sense-impression, through the metallic, diffuse refulgence that is generated by its glowing surface. Colors— whether colored substance incorporated with the smoothed wall-face (fresco) or pigment applied with the brush—are natural. But the metallic gleam, which is practically never found in natural conditions, is unearthly [*übernatürlich*] . . . Everything that was taught in the circle of Plotinus or by the Gnostics . . . is implicit also in the symbolism of this mysterious hieratic background . . . But the individual brush-strokes—first met with as a complete new form-language in the later work of Titian—are accents of a personal temperament, characteristic in the orchestra-colors of Monteverde, melodically-flowing as a contemporary Venetian madrigal: streaks and dabs, immediately juxtaposed, cross over one another, cover one another, entangle one another, and bring unending movement into the plain element of color [*bringen eine unendliche Bewegtheit in das farbige Element*] (Spengler, *The Decline of the West* [New York: Knopf, 1926], 246–51; *Der Untergang des Abendlandes* [Munich: Beck, 1980], 318–26). Spengler goes on to interpret the brown of Rembrandt and others—a brown into which the yellows, and even the golds, of Titian sometimes shade. All his inferences can in fact be attributed to the colors of Titian, across the three cultures he is contrasting.

28. "Die Farben aber erfüllen als ein unendliches Vibrieren die Weite der Fläche" (Theodor Hetzer, *Tizian: Geschichte seiner Farbe* [Frankfurt: Klostermann, 1935], 172.

29. Ruth W. Kennedy, *Novelty and Tradition in Titian's Art* (Northampton: Smith College, 1963), 10.

30. Edgar Wind, *Pagan Mysteries in the Renaissance* (New York: Norton, 1964), 141–51, follows Panofsky in accepting the now conventional title, *Sacred and Profane Love,* assigned more than a century after the painting was done. He aligns many details around the clothed Profane Love: the courtly castle behind her, as opposed to the church behind the nude. He stresses the nobility

of the nude and makes deductions from the worldliness, albeit restrained, of the clothed figure; he makes much, too, of the "chastisement" of figures on the sarcophagus, as though we could deduce much from the mere presence of a live Cupid dipping into the waters their stone basin holds. The two rabbits in the foreground below the castle on the left are supposedly "sacred to Venus," though a hare is being hunted below the church on the right. Moreover, it is by no means clear that facing rabbits indicate Eros. If they do so in Carpaccio's *Presentation in the Temple,* it would be by contrast to the Virgin. And the prominent pair of rabbits who face each other in Giovanni Bellini's *St. Jerome Reading* can only be synecdochic representatives of the calm nature going on around him, like the squirrel munching on the ledge above him. In accord with all this peace is the lion shown couched under his arm, almost obscured in the grey-brown of the surrounding rocks.

Wind wants to read the women in Titian's painting, actually, not as Sacred and Profane Love, but as earthly love in contrast to celestial. The difference between these two pairs, indeed, is not great, even with the details about Ripa's prescription for showing "Felicità Eterna" and "Felicità Breve," on which Panofsky amplifies in "The Neoplatonic Movement in Florence and North Italy," in *Studies in Iconology,* 150–60, though Wind dissents. Panofsky correlates the painting with many categories in the discussion of the time, but his own statement about this work should give us pause: "'Sacred and Profane Love' seems to be the only composition in which Titian paid a conscious tribute to the Neoplatonic philosophy" (160). If Titian indeed did so, we might argue, why would he abruptly abandon so comprehensive a system? And why would the fact go unnoticed for more than a century? In the bibliographies provided by Wind and Panofsky, it is clear that the major identifications under the belatedly ascribed title were themselves uncertain: many writers made the clothed figure the celestial Venus, rather than the nude one. This, indeed, is just the way both Wind and Panofsky have read the clothed Venus of Botticelli's *Primavera.* And however noble a nudity may be, it is difficult to dissociate it from the splendors of carnal pleasure, which is what nudity seems to signify elsewhere in Titian.

Among the many divergent interpretations of this painting that would push its unity into univocality, G. F. Hartlaub, "Tizians 'Liebesorakel' und seine 'Kristallseherin,'" (*Zeitschrift für Kunst* (1950), 35–48), would re-entitle it *Love's Oracle.* For general and specific arguments against the univocal in such paintings, see Cook, *Changing the Signs.*

31. Erwin Panofsky, *Problems in Titian, Mostly Iconographic* (New York: Phaidon, 1969), 15.

32. "Farbe ist dem Tizian nicht ein Mittel, sondern der Urgrund der Malerei" (Hetzer, *Tizian,* 117). Hetzer also says, "In place of a real and given pigment, it may be said, there emerges an ideal and general color stuff concurrently with a chromatic world-material" (48) and "Depths of space and color are unified in a single movement" (54). Hetzer discerns six periods in Titian's use of color: (1) to 1516, the years of a balance not yet achieved (*"Unausgeglichenheit"*); (2) to 1530, the time of the desire for great, raw "ascent" (*"Aufstieg"*); (3) to 1540, a dangerous Mannerist near-tiredness; (4) to 1550, a brutal conflict with earthly powers; (5) to 1560, a "heroic and monumental struggle between heavenly and earthly," when Titian's color begins to show signs of aging; and (6) the struggle and conquest of the continuing full use of color. Of course these categories need the fleshing out that Hetzer in fact gives them, finding, for example, that hard contours tend to disappear in the second period.

Titian's color struck observers, though, from the very beginning. Vasari reports that Michelangelo admired the coloring in the *Danae* but said it would have been better "if . . . it had been exactly represented with craft and draftsmanship ("se . . . fusse punto imitato dall'arte e dal disegno"). Vasari claims that Titian "held it as axiomatic that one could paint just with colors, without other attention to draftsmanship on the surface" ("tenendo per fermo . . . che il dipegnere solo con i colori stessi, senz' altro studio di disegnare in carta").

33. Roberto Longhi, *Viatico per cinque secoli di pittura Veneziana* (Florence: Sansoni, 1946), 22: "shadow passes into 'tone' and transposes itself onto the ideal plane of color; that is, it inserts itself without a plastic leap, without chiaroscuro, without sfumato, into the contented felicity of a 'chromatic breadth.'"

34. So Augusto Gentile, *Da Tiziano a Tiziano* (Milan: Feltrinelli, 1980), 105, points out.

35. Claudette Kemper Columbus, "Painting Figures of Speech, Color as Language: J. M. W. Turner and Robert Browning" (unpublished manuscript). She says of the significance of color in Turner generally, "Color invites interpretation, but also provides its own contradiction . . . Turner uses blue in *The Ascent* to represent hope, triumph, heaven. But he uses the identical blue in the subsequent *The Descent* to represent despair, death, damnation. By virtue of the juxtaposition, that hue of blue through contradiction becomes a probe into the depths of color signifying, rather than a color pronouncement . . . A single shade of red suggest[s] an interestingly connected range from ecstasy to agony. The flux in the signifying properties of red is promoted to an impenetrable point . . . The space in the mirror, orange and all, is empty, dead. The orange of the drapes is as antithetically self-questioning as the proposed analogy between bed and mirror . . . orange as paradox."

36. Gage, *Colour in Turner,* especially "Turner and Goethe," 173–88, summarizes the likenesses and differences between Goethe and Turner, though he does not go as far as one might in discussing the significations in Turner's color, particularly in the watercolors.

37. The moment itself is blurred. According to Genesis (7.11–13), "the same day were all the fountains of the great deep broken up, and the windows of heaven were opened. And the rain was on the earth forty days and forty nights. In the selfsame day entered Noah (. . . and his family . . .) into the ark." Turner's "morning after" could refer to the first of the forty days of rain (if one assimilates the painting to *Rain, Steam and Speed*), especially since "the windows of heaven were opened." Yet there is also a possibility that he is referring to Noah's opening of a window in the ark after the forty days (Genesis 8.6).

38. Ruskin, *Works,* 3; *Modern Painters,* vol. 1, part 2, chap. 2, "Of Truth of Colour," para. 20, 298–301. In the chapter "Of Turnerian Light," *Modern Painters,* vol. 5, Ruskin goes to a great deal of preparatory trouble to convince his reader that Turner's handling of color and light is extraordinarily representational.

39. Stokes, *Colour and Form,* in *Critical Writings,* 3:18.

40. See note 32. One could easily apply Hetzer's remarks to Turner's preoccupation with "pure" paint—"the 'imagination' side of a polarity"—as stressed by Lawrence Gowing and the impressionists in their view of Turner before him. A different measure, however, is applied by Gage in *Colour in Turner: Poetry and Truth*—with a version of the inextricable terms of the polarity forming its subtitle.

41. Gauguin speculated on the possibility of detaching color wholly from perception or imitation: "Color, being itself enigmatic in the sensations which it gives us, can logically be employed only enigmatically. One does not use color to draw but always to give the musical sensations which flow from itself, from its own nature, from its mysterious and enigmatic interior force" (Paul Gauguin, *Diverses Choses* [1896–97], quoted in *Theories of Modern Art*, ed. Herschel B. Chipp [Berkeley: University of California Press, 1971], 66.

42. *Van Gogh: A Self-Portrait: Letters Revealing His Life as a Painter*, ed. W. H. Auden (New York: Dutton, 1963), 320. Henceforth I shall refer to page numbers of this work by parentheses in the text.

43. Martin Heidegger, "Der Ursprung des Kunstwerkes," in *Holzwege* (Frankfurt: Klostermann, 1950), 7–68, translated as "The Origin of the Work of Art," in *Poetry, Language, Thought*, ed. Albert Hofstadter (New York: Harper, 1971); Meyer Schapiro, "The Still Life as a Personal Object," in *The Reach of Mind: Essays in Memory of Kurt Goldstein*, ed. Marianne L. Simmell (New York: Springer, 1968), 203–9; Jacques Derrida, "Restitutions," in *La Vérité en peinture* (Paris: Flammarion, 1978), 291–436.

44. Meyer Schapiro, *Van Gogh* (New York: Doubleday, 1980), 130. Extensions of color into particular significations beyond such cultural codings as hope for green give an impression of both aptness and arbitrariness, like Sartre's attribution of "anguish" to the yellow sky of Tintoretto (Jean-Paul Sartre, *Situations II: Qu'est-ce que c'est la littérature* [Paris: Gallimard, 1948], 61).

45. See *Journal de Eugène Delacroix*, ed. André Joubin (Paris: Plon, 1932), and especially the entries for August 17, 1850, 1:413, and following. A note here refers to a book on Delacroix and color, René Piot, *Les Palettes de Delacroix* (Paris, 1931).

46. As quoted and discussed in Marc le Bot, *Figures de l'art contemporain* (Paris: Union générale, 1977), 12.

47. Guillaume Apollinaire, *Les Peintres Cubistes* (1913; Paris: Hermann, 1965), 88: "La dimension idéale, c'est la couleur . . . La couleur ne dépend plus des trois dimension connues, c'est elle qui les crée."

48. Rainer Maria Rilke, *Briefe über Cézanne* (Wiesbaden: Insel, 1952), 42.

49. Josef Albers, *The Interaction of Color* (1963; New Haven: Yale University Press, 1971).

50. Nelson Goodman, *The Languages of Art*, discusses many prior constraints on a "notational system" that he asserts must be considered before undertaking such discussions as this one. Independently of how fully he has proved his "requirement" of "the unambiguous," it can be remarked that pictures, like poems, do give at least an effect of ambiguity. This effect stops at the letter in a verbal notation: "g" cannot be "d" at any time. It does not stop at the perceptual, however, in a color. How much orange do we let into a red before it stops carrying the rich—and themselves ambiguous—significations of red?

Chapter 4. *The Wilderness of Mirrors*

1. Jean Paris, *L'Espace et le regard* (Paris: Seuil, 1965), makes much of such expansions. He says of the mirror, "Aesthetically it would augment the virtual space of the work with a space still more virtual, and for that reason supremely present." It is, perhaps, this uncanniness that leads Umberto Eco to question the signification in mirrors and what they reflect: "Are mirrors a semiosic phenomenon? Indeed, are the images signs that are reflected on the surfaces of mirrors? It could be that these questions are senseless, in the sense that good

sense would insist on replying that mirrors are mirrors" ("Sugli Specchi," in *Sugli Specchi* [Milan: Bompiani, 1985], 9).

2. For a further discussion of the symbology of windows, see Albert Cook, "The Windows of Apollinaire," in *Figural Choice*, 64–85.

3. M. L. West, *The Orphic Poems* (Oxford: Clarendon Press, 1983), 156–57. A complex coding is opened up when, as West says, "According to a Hellenistic text the cry *euoi* goes back to an exclamation made by the Titans in praise of the invention of the mirror." There is a reference to a continued Bacchic use of mirrors in the late *Dionysiaca* of Nonnos (6.170ff.).

4. Stuart Pigott, *Prehistoric India* (Harmondsworth: Penguin, 1950), 112.

5. James G. Frazer, *The New Golden Bough*, ed. Theodore Gaster (New York: Mentor, 1950), 203–4a: "When the Motumotu of New Guinea first saw their likeness in a lookingglass they thought they were seeing their souls. An Aztec mode of keeping sorcerers from the house was to leave a vessel of water with a knife in it behind the door . . . The Basutos say that a crocodile has the power of killing a man by dragging his reflection under water; while in Saddle Island, Melanesia, there is a pool 'into which if any one looks he dies.'" Assimilating reflections in water to those in mirrors, Frazer continues with illustrations from India, Greece, and modern times, interpreting in this light the modern superstition about a taboo on mirrors for the sick, lest their souls escape through the mirror.

6. The last three examples are drawn from G. F. Hartlaub, *Zauber des Spiegels* (Munich: Piper, 1951), 26–30.

7. This practice is noted in Paris, *L'Espace et le regard*, 247.

8. Michael Loewe, "TLV Mirrors and Their Significance," and "Classification and List of TLV Mirrors," in *Ways to Paradise: The Chinese Quest for Immortality* (London: George Allen & Unwin, 1979), 60–85; 158–91. "The earlier examples refer to the force of Yin and Yang and invoke the blessings that may be imparted by the symbols of the Five Phases; examples of the next distinct stage describe the habits of the immortal beings of another world, with some intermediate examples . . . The principal decorative features of the mirrors symbolize two views of the cosmos—one based on Five and one on Twelve—which are neatly reconciled together. The four animals, together with the central knob or boss, represent the cosmos of the theory of the Five Phases; the central square of the mirror, with its twelve divisions, represents the cosmos that is seen in parts of the *Huai-nan-tzu*, and also on the boards used by diviners to determine the position of an individual within the cosmos at a given moment of time" (60). "The four T's that stand around the square earth are four cardinal points . . . The four V's mark the four corners of the heavens . . . The four L's represent devices used by carpenters to set a straight line . . . They thus symbolize the ends of the two cosmic lines . . . as if they had been drawn with the help of an instrument" (74). Loewe links these mirrors to Han sundials and gnomon chronometer boards (74), and he deciphers from them a series of typical apotropaic mythological inscriptions (71). I owe this citation to David Lattimore.

9. The inscriptions are in Chinese or Arabic. These mirrors occur across a wide range of Siberia and Central Asia, and over a long time, from the fourth century B.C. to the sixteenth century. See E. E. Leischenko, *Prebozniye zerkala minusinskoi kotlovinoi* (Moscow: Vostochnaya Literatura, 1975).

10. Otto-Wilhelm von Vacano, *The Etruscans* (London: Arnold, 1960), 8–9; 98.

11. J. D. Beazley, "The World of the Etruscan Mirror," *Journal of Hellenic Studies* 69 (1949): 1–17. Beazley points out that "some legends are represented with more circumstance on Etruscan mirrors than on any extant Greek monument," a fact that could be variously interpreted. Though he says the earliest Etruscan mirrors are a hundred years earlier than the earliest Greek ones, a Greek mirror held by a Minoan goddess figurine on a seal ring is cited by Walter Burkert, *History of Greek Religion* (Cambridge: Harvard University Press, 1985), 41; H. G. Bucholz and V. Karageorghis, *Altägäis und Altkypros*, Tübingen, 1971, no. 1385. As for thematic developments, Beazley publishes a vase of 411 B.C., where a Myrine holds mirror and sash for a seated Lysistrata, a representation that suggests an advanced cultural development, though not in the direction of legend.

12. Yvette Huls, *Ivoires d'Étrurie* (Brussels and Rome: Palais des Académies, 1952).

13. In one from Marchena the Spotless Mirror is perched as though standing on a puff of golden cloud beside the Virgin; the one from the Arango Collection repeats this image, while that from Siguenca combines it with other symbols distributed in clearings of sky in the clouds behind the Virgin. All vary the one in the Prado.

14. The use of mirror writing as a cipher in Leonardo's notebooks, while an interesting correlation, is probably of only technical significance, though even if not psychoanalyzed, it can also be taken as an index of self-preoccupation.

15. Robert Baldwin, "Marriage as a Sacramental Reflection of the Passion: The Mirror in Jan van Eyck's *Arnolfini Wedding*," *Oud Holland* 98(2) (1984): 57–75. Erwin Panofsky, *Early Netherlandish Painting* (1953; New York: Harper and Row, 1971), 195–204.

16. Jon Manchip White, *Diego Velázquez* (Chicago: Rand McNally, 1965), 145.

17. Michel Foucault, "Les Suivantes," in *Les Mots et les choses* (Paris: Gallimard, 1966), 19–31; 30, 31.

18. John R. Searle, "*Las Meninas* and the Paradoxes of Pictorial Representation," *Critical Inquiry* 6(3) (Spring 1980): 477–88, concluded that there are two levels of paradox in *Las meninas*. The following three propositions describe the first level.

> 1. The picture is painted from the point of view of the subject, not the painter.
> 2. We the spectators are seeing ourselves in that mirror and hence we are Philip IV and Maria Ana, in the illusionist reading. [This is questionable.—AC] Neither of these propositions would need to bother us much if they were not underlaid by a third.
> 3. The artist, and indeed any artist, is precluded from occupying point A (the way the scene looked to the artist). [This is not much of a difficulty; it would obtain of all self-portraits, and *Las Meninas* is a kind of self-portrait.—AC] The second level comes from interpreting the painting in the picture as *Las Meninas;* then . . .
> 4. The painter, having lost his point of view, is painting the picture from another point of view inside the picture zone O. From that point of view he is painting O, but he can't be painting O from that point of view because the point of view which defines O is A: strictly speaking O only exists relative to A. He is painting the scene we see, but he can't be because he is in it (486).

Joel Snyder, in "'Las Meninas' and the Mirror of the Prince," *Critical Inquiry* 11(4) (June 1985): 539–72, argues that the term "paradox" cannot be applied to the perspective of this painting. He demonstrates how elaborate it is, citing and qualifying further articles of Svetlana Alpers and Leo Steinberg. He finds that the mirror can be reflecting not the king and queen but rather their portrait, but then he settles for a univocal reading of the work in the conventional vein of the medieval and Renaissance *Mirror for Princes*—a lesson hard to read here, given the centrality of the painter and the uncentered variety of the other figures represented. Much of Snyder's perspectival deduction was already presented by Bo Vahlne, "Velázquez's *Las Meninas:* Remarks on the Staging of a Royal Portrait," *Konsthistorisk Tidskrift* 51 (1982): 21–28. Vahlne discusses Justi's thesis (see note 20) and presents a case for the painting as mainly a portrait of the Infanta Margarita—who is, to be sure, the central figure. But too much else is going on in it for this conventional reading to give it an encompassing definition.

19. The actual tapestry is a modified copy of Titian's *Rape of Europa,* a painting that was in the Alcázar collection at the time; and so it may be taken to refer doubly to artistry—even to "mirror" that painting. This identification and location are given in Jonathan Brown, *Velázquez: Painter and Courtier* (New Haven: Yale University Press, 1986), 252–53.

20. Searle's article *"Las Meninas,"* 485, says, "The canvas he is painting on is much too large for any such portrait. The canvas on which he is painting is indeed about as big as the one we are looking at, about 10 feet high and 8 feet wide (the dimensions of *Las Meninas* are 3.19 meters by 2.67 meters). I think that the painter is painting the picture we are seeing." Here Searle is repeating the view of Carl Justi, *Diego Velázquez und sein Jahrhundert* (Bonn: 1888), 2:311, as cited in Madlyn Millner Kahr, *Velázquez: The Art of Painting* (New York: Harper and Row, 1976), 175–76, 185–202.

21. Typical of the genre, and including two mirrors in a much more casual way, is Watteau's *L'Enseigne de Gersaint*. In this work, which Watteau also engraved, a woman at the left in the crowd scene of a large gallery with many paintings looks at herself in a small mirror, of which only the back shows. Another person is holding it up for her. The paintings on the wall are of half-clothed or nude figures in erotic or mythological scenes, while the woman is dressed, like the shepherdesses in Watteau's more typical paintings. The group at the left gravitates around a packing box, complete with straw, into which a man is loading not still another large painting but rather a large mirror in which his arm and part of his body show clearly.

22. The qualities of this work that take it beyond simple erotic presentation or perspectival exercise are well evolved by Edward Snow, "Velázquez's *Rokeby Venus: The Body as Horizon,"* *Artspace* 9(2) (Summer 1985): 12–16:

> The long, languid spread of her body tends to make the first and most lasting impression. She unfolds before the eyes like some vast inner horizon. (The reflection in the mirror rests beyond her like a setting sun.) Her lines draw one out of and at the same time deep within oneself, to a sense of repletion; the gaze from the mirror stirs waves of well-being in the soul. An image of such physical assurance, of such unforced agreement of flesh and consciousness, is like an experience of grace, in both senses of the term—as if all those tensions within which Leonardo's *Vitruvian Man* so paradigmatically asserts and imprisons himself had suddenly relaxed . . . The face that gazes out from [the mirror] seems less an image reflected on a surface than an autonomous presence dwelling in a realm of its own, on the other side of the visible, where precise forms dissolve into an atmosphere of dream and reality.

23. These points were made by Malcolm Campbell in "Giorgio Vasari Paints Allessandro de' Medici: The Making of a Ducal Portrait," lecture at Brown University, March 12, 1983.

24. The original iconographic cues for this painting are provided by Lucian's description of the painting by Aetion of the marriage of Roxanne and Alex-

ander. The differences between this description and Sodoma's mural are detailed by Albert Jansen, *Leben und Werke des Malers Giovannantonio Bazzi* (Stuttgart: Ebner & Seubert, 1870), 104–5. Jansen's long description of Sodoma's mural (100–106), however, does not mention the central mirror. Nor does Lucian's text, as quoted and discussed in Andrée Hayum, *Giovanni Antonio Bazzi—"Il Sodoma"*—(New York: Garland, 1976), 166–70.

25. Pierre Schneider, *Matisse* (New York: Reynal & Co., 1985), 173–74, superimposes still another pattern on all these paradigms of representing three-dimensionality by pointing out that as a two-dimensional surface this canvas "imitates" a giant carpet, since the brown and violet pattern on floor and wallpaper, from top to bottom, completely covers that broken half of its surface which is not interrupted by the mirror, window, and objects:

> The question that *Interior with Eggplants* raises and tries to answer in the affirmative is this: can the Oriental carpet express the diversity of information that the Western system renders by distributing it along the lines of perspective? The solution lies in the rectangle of ocher cloth, stamped with white flowers, pinned to the screen. [This is still another square that I have not mentioned.—AC] . . . Each spatial plane, with the information it contains, is inscribed in a rectangle. Echoing the form of the fabric, it invites us to view it in its turn as a piece of material: even the window offers itself to the eye as a fabric. And the sum of these rectangles constitutes a sort of *patchwork:* the rectangle of the canvas itself.
>
> But there is something even stranger here. The five-petaled motif on the ocher fabric breaks away from the clearly delimited patch to which plausibility would have confined it, and, after undergoing an almost dreamlike transfiguration that expands it and makes it change into a blue periwinkle, invades the floor and walls of the room, except for those patches that are already occupied. The canvas as a whole admits to being a carpet, and as a result finds itself exposed to an endless expansion along the plane of the surface.

26. Jacques Lacan, *Le Séminaire* (Paris: Seuil, 1975), 1:138–44.

27. Examples of such mermaids in medieval illumination are discussed in Herbert Grabes, *The Mutable Glass* (Cambridge: Cambridge University Press, 1982). This book is an expanded and translated edition of *Speculum, Mirror and Looking-Glass* (Tübingen: Niemeyer, 1973).

28. For a discussion of the elaborate significations in this painting, see Albert Cook, "Change of Signification in Bosch's Garden of Earthly Delights," *Oud Holland* 98(2) (1984): 76–96. This article is expanded and amplified with relation to other works of Bosch in Cook, *Changing the Signs*.

29. Paris, *L'Espace et le Regard*, 10. He says there of the *Allegory* in the National Gallery at Washington, "Titian painted this . . . as a system of contrasts where the cause and the effect are two looks which, taken together, suppose and reject our own."

30. H. W. Janson, *Apes and Ape Lore in the Renaissance* (London: Warburg Institute, 1952), 262.

31. Lower to the right through a clearing of cliff and foliage a castellated town appears in a "window effect." A comparable scene shows dimly through a larger clearing on the right of the painting oddly matched to this, an allegory of Music in which a similar nude figure cons a music book while leaning on a viol with her right hand; a very fat, sleepy white cat faces us to the left.

32. Grabes in *The Mutable Glass* discusses a number of these mirrors. He points out (222–24) that Prudentia holds a mirror in the staple iconographic dictionary of Cesare Ripa's *Iconologia*.

33. J. A. Emmens, "Les Ménines de Velázquez: Miroir des Princes pour

Philippe IV," *Nederlands Kunsthistorisch Jaarboek* 12 (1961): 51–79, as cited in Kahr, *Velázquez*, 175.

34. Grabes has much material on the mirror's function of delineating reality, which he classifies as representations of things as they are (such encyclopedias as the *Speculum Mundi* of Honorius of Autun, the "Mariners Mirror," the *Miroir des Dames*, and others); of the way things should or should not be; and of things that may or will come to pass. He adds to these the category of things that do not exist, the fantastic of the "Mirror of Fancies," providing many subclassifications. The mirror of Saint Paul's "through a glass darkly" could be said to combine all of these.

35. Hartlaub, *Zauber des Spiegels*, 81.

36. Lacan, "Remarque sur le rapport de Daniel Lagache: 'Psychanalyse et structure de la personnalité,'" in *Écrits* (Paris: Seuil, 1966), 647–84. As Lacan's title indicates, he uses this arrangement as a metaphor for the particular relations among the imaginary, the symbolic, and the real in the psyche of a person through his interchanges with an Other. The fact that there is no difference between a real bouquet reflected and the reflection of a bouquet further reflected may be used, counter to Lacan, as an emblem of the virtuality, rather than the necessity, of the gap (*"béance"*) he finds in intersubjective relationships.

37. "Ce n'est là qu'élargissement de la coupure où on peut le dire résider dans la chaîne signifiante, pour autant que c'en est l'élément le plus radical dans sa séquence discontinue, et comme tel le lieu d'où le sujet assure sa subsistance de chaîne" (ibid., 666). Earlier he said that "the *fading* of the subject . . . is produced in the suspension of desire, by the fact that the subject is eclipsed in the signifier of the demand" ("le *fading* du sujet . . . se produit dans la suspension de désir, de ce que le sujet s'éclipse dans le signifiant de la demande" (ibid., 656).

38. Meyer Schapiro, *Modern Art* (New York: Braziller, 1978).

39. Quoted in Jacques Meuris, *7 Dialogues avec Paul Delvaux* (Paris: Le Soleil Noir, 1971), 18.

Chapter 5. Confrontations: The Agonies and Fusions of Goya

1. For a discussion of innovative possibilities toward the beginning of the Renaissance, see Cook, *Changing the Signs*.

2. For the particular schematisms of Blake in relation to each other and to his paintings, drawings, and engravings, see Albert Cook, *Thresholds* (Madison: University of Wisconsin Press, 1985), chap. 2. Ronald Paulson (*Representations of Revolution 1789–1820*, New Haven: Yale University Press, 1983, 286–387) also contrasts Goya's gloomy view of sexuality with Blake's. Paulson elaborately correlates Goya's career to Spanish politics through his time.

3. Michael Fried, *Absorption and Theatricality: Painting and Beholder in the Age of Diderot* (Berkeley: University of California Press, 1984).

4. "Goya paints 'apparitions' and, in this sense, fantasies" (José Ortega y Gasset, *Papeles sobre Velázquez y Goya* [Madrid: Revista de Occidente, 1950]).

5. This list, and the conjecture that Goya could have seen the paintings, at the Salon of 1824 is taken from F. D. Klingender, *Goya in the Democratic Tradition* (1948; New York: Schocken, 1968), 206.

6. Fred Licht, *Goya* (New York: Universe Books, 1979), 31. Licht goes on to say, "The very ground on which the figures in Goya's painting stand and kneel is so ambiguous that we don't have a solid footing. We cannot discover the peculiar accidents of terrain that separate the girl from her cavalier. Is she sitting

on the thin edge of a very sharp mountain ridge? And what of the cavalier?" Licht also compares the obscurity of the accident that has afflicted *The Wounded Mason* and his helplessness to a painting on the same sort of incident by Tiepolo, in which the mason is saved by angels.

7. Jutta Held, *Farbe und Licht in Goyas Malerei* (Berlin: de Gruyter, 1964), 19. She goes on to point out that Tiepolo, who was active at Madrid in Goya's youth, puts cool colors in the light and warm ones in the shadow (22–28). Goya's colors here, which loosely follow this pattern, are nevertheless much more modulated in value than Tiepolo's; and the warm greens here that stand in the light subvert this formula. Goya's colors are also more intensified individually, and more starkly contrasted, than the blander, paler colors of Tiepolo.

8. Goya returns to this theme in the *Disparate feminino,* the feminine "folly" in his series of "Disparates" (1819). In this etching expressions of wonder, joy, and contentment pass over the faces of the girls round the tarpaulin they are actively tossing, while two children ride topsy-turvy in air, their faces entirely obscured.

9. Held, *Farbe und Licht,* 46.

10. The disproportion suggested in the relative lack of connection to monumentality in the action depicted, here and elsewhere in Goya, may recall the range of emotions and conceptions evoked by Piranesi's preromantic transformed and unrelated ruins. For a discussion of this range, see Jürgen Klein, "Terror and Historicity in Giovanni Battista Piranesi as Forms of Romantic Subjectivity," *Notebooks in Cultural Analysis* 2 (1985): 90–111.

11. A small scene by Bayeu on this theme is much less ferocious and complex.

12. Licht, *Goya,* 88.

13. Held, *Farbe und Licht,* 37.

14. Ortega, *Papeles,* 276. Why does Goya leave his spectacles on in the self-portrait of the Musée Bonnat and leave them off in the more famous one of the Prado?

15. In Friedrich's *The Sailing Ship,* for example, the viewers are in a "concealed" posture, but the scene on which they look out makes it seem as though the world is all before them. In *The Garden Terrace* a statue faces our way, and the lady, in the midst of her open scene, has her back to us. Friedrich, like Goya, has revised his open-air pastorals, but in the service of what is, again, not a spiritual straining but rather a spiritual opening, an interpretation that Friedrich's own commentaries on his work endorse, whether or not one accepts the specific readings of theological symbolism that some critics attribute to his work. In the cliffs, open spaces, and moonlit seas of other Friedrich paintings, the melancholy evoked is an introspective counterpart to Goya's fiercely social agony. For Friedrich and melancholy see Tina Grütter, *Melancholie und Abgrund: Die Bedeutung des Gesteins bei Caspar David Friedrich* (Berlin: Reimer, 1986).

16. Goya, Prado Notebook No. 1. Baudelaire, "Caricaturistes Étrangers," in *Ecrits sur l'art,* ed. Yves Florenne (1846; Paris: Gallimaid, 1971), 363–65, seems to have the "Caprichos" strongly in mind in his comment on Goya: "In the works emanating from deep individualities there is something that resembles periodic or chronic dreams that regularly besiege our sleep . . . Goya's great merit consists in creating a verisimilitudinous monster. His monsters are born viable and harmonious."

17. "La fantasía abandonada de la razón, produce monstruos imposibles: unida con ella, es madre de las artes y origen de sus maravillas" (Goya, Prado Notebook No. 1).

18. Goya, Prado Notebook No. 1, mocks the central figure here: "Madame is hydroptique and they order her to go walking. God to grant her relief."

19. Goya, Prado Notebook No. 1, expands on the irony: "It appears that for feather-headed girls to settle down they cannot do better than to stand on their heads."

20. An iconographic parallel to this work, and to the one where witches look forward to sucking bones while carrying a basket of babies (*Mucho hai que chupar*, no. 45) is to be found in the motif of "Cupids for sale," works of Joseph-Marie Vien, Fuseli, and others, in which tiny Cupids are carried like chickens in a basket to be sold from one woman to another. These are discussed in Robert Rosenblum, *Transformations in Late Eighteenth-Century Art* (Princeton: Princeton University Press, 1967). In Goya's preparatory red wash drawing for *Ya van desplumados*, the direction is reversed and the women are inside a complicated edifice, complete with window grillwork that has disappeared in the concentration of the finished etching. Goya's comment, in Prado Notebook No. 1, emphasizes the results, "If they are already plucked, they let them leave— others will be along" ("Si se desplumaron ya, vayan fuera, que van a venir otros").

21. Goya, Prado Notebook No. 1.

22. In a Renaissance iconographic tradition the dovecote or the birdcatching devices can indicate erotic intrigue, as George Levitine demonstrates in "Some Emblematic Sources of Goya," *Journal of the Warburg and Courtauld Institutes* 22 (1959): (106–31). However, if the works he reproduces are indeed sources for Goya, Goya has transmuted them heavily by the cruel devastation of his central scene, for which these other works offer no parallel or clue.

23. In Goya's words (Prado Notebook No. 1), "Never will she escape what she desires to wait to catch" ("Nunca se escapa la que se quiere dejar coger").

24. André Malraux, *Saturne* (Paris: Gallimard, 1950), 66, says, "La Maja desnuda is inseparable for Goya from "la Vestida"; she is an unclothed woman who, without wholly looking at the spectator, is not unaware of him."

25. Edith Helman, *Trasmundo de Goya* (Madrid: Revista de Occidente, 1963), 178–86, gives the background for belief in witchcraft and the scepticism about it in Goya's time, as do other writers. She also traces *That Dust* (*Aquellos polvos*, no. 23) to a contemporary inquisitional trial over a figure who had claimed to make aphrodisiac dust from corpses (126–27).

26. Helman, *Goya*, 179, points out that *duende* (a synonym for *bruja* [witch]) was sometimes used in Goya's time in the sense of "priest."

27. What Goya says (Prado Notebook No. 1) comes at it from a different angle: "A big catch of infants did the previous night have; the banquet being prepared will be sumptuous; good provision."

28. Goya's comment in Prado Notebook No. 1 both orients this difficult work and further complicates it: "Fortune treats very badly whoever plays up to her. She repays in smoke the labor of mounting and one who has mounted she punishes by casting him down" ("La fortuna trata muy mal a quien la obsequia. Paga con humo la fatiga de subir y al que ha subido le castiga con precipitarle").

29. Goya's remark in Prado Notebook No. 1 generalizes the situation grimly, and well beyond sexuality or infanticide: "Those who arrive at 80 suck infants; those who become 18 suck adults. It appears that man is born and lives to be sucked" ("Las que llegan a 80 chupan chiquillos; las que no pasan de 18 chupan a los grandes. Parece que el hombre nace y vive para ser chupado").

30. Licht, *Goya*, 65, points out the unconventional placements in this work.

31. Helman, *Goya*, 32, relates *The Wounded Mason* to an edict of Charles III that mandates safe scaffolding. This historical situation would justify the choice of the work as a cartoon for inclusion on the walls of the royal palace, but it would not explain that choice among a wide range of other possibilities, especially since the work is fairly incongruous in comparison with the other cartoons. Licht, *Goya*, 62, says, in contrasting Goya to Tiepolo and Mengs, "Space that had always been conceived of as sacred space, and therefore free of terrestrial gravity, now became ordinary space." But Goya's "ordinary" space is constantly subjected to an intensified gravity, as to intensified values.

32. Titles to these paintings were assigned after Goya's death.

33. Goya's manuscript description, published in the first edition of *Desastres*, in 1863, long after his death.

34. Pierre Gassier and Juliet Wilson, *The Life and Complete Work of Francisco Goya* (New York: Reynal & Co., 1971), 164, 187.

35. Michel Foucault, *L'Histoire de la folie* (Paris: Plon, 1961).

36. I have compiled this list from the index to Gassier and Wilson, *Goya*, 392.

37. Ortega, *Papeles*, 279–306, emphasizes the popular stress on bullfighting and the vividness of the sport in Goya's time.

38. Gassier and Wilson read this caption as *Tontos*, ("Fools"), which would assimilate it to the representations of the mad.

39. Held, *Farbe und Licht*, 142: "Durch diese einander gleichberechtigten Farben gewinnen auch alle Dinge im Bild gleiche Bedeutung. Sie erscheinen stillebenhaft." Malraux, *Saturne*, 141, says, "Goya wants the world to admit it is only appearance—imposture, perhaps: he expresses this by a color that denies its color."

40. Gassier and Wilson, *Goya*, 244.

41. Nigel Glendenning, "Goya and Arriaga's *Profecia del Pirineo*," *Journal of the Warburg and Courtauld Institutes* 26 (1963): 363–66, points out the arresting parallel between *The Colossus* and a poem that describes, as the painting represents, "a Colossus on a height above a hollow, caught by the rays of the setting sun and with clouds encircling his waist." This colossus, however, clearly represents Spain rising against Napoleon; no cues within Goya's painting allow us to confine it to that signification. Goya's other representations of giants tend to pull his work away from such specificities. José Manuel B. Lopez Váquez, "Goya, Los Gigantes ye Los Emblemas," *Goya*, nos. 187–88 (July–October 1985: 102–12) modifies Glendenning and offers other parallels, via Ripa, relating the "no. 18" affixed to this work in the 1812 catalogue—somewhat unconvincingly— to the mountains in no. 18 of the *Emblemas Morales* of Sebastián de Covarrubias. He also has the work refer, on scant evidence, to particular points of political history.

PART TWO. MODERN INSTANCES

Chapter 6. Space, Time, and the Unconscious in the Collage Novels of Max Ernst

1. Ezra Pound, *The ABC of Reading* (1934; New York: New Directions, 1960), 76. I have referred to the following reprints: *Une Semaine de bonté* (New York: Dover, 1976), *The Hundred Headless Woman* (New York: Braziller, 1981), *A Little Girl Dreams of Taking the Veil* (New York: Braziller, 1982).

2. Ernst seems to have considered his original collages as sketches for the reproductions that appear in the original edition. In fact the original collages are so clearly and precisely done, to judge from the samples I have seen, that the lines of suture in them are nearly as imperceptible as in the reproductions.

3. The Dover reprint of *Une Semaine de bonté*, vi, says, "The art historian Werner Spies has identified three of the base-pictures (those for pages 20, 169, and 170) as illustrations from the 1883 novel *Les Damnées de Paris* by Jules Mary." This note (from the text whose numeration I follow throughout) goes on to mention Ernst's purchase of a Doré volume in Milan, some of which he may have used in the "Cour du dragon" sequence. And in the middle of the nineteenth century the very productive Grandville produced related fantasies, *La Vie Privée des animaux* and *Les Aventures d'un lion d'Afrique à Paris,* a work that features the activities of a humanized lion in a Parisian setting, very much like Ernst's lion-headed man.

Dozens of sources are presented by Werner Spies, *Max Ernst—Collagen: Inventar und Widerspruch* (Cologne: DuMont Schauberg, 1974), for the originals of collages in the three novels (his plates 210 and 458), as well as to other collages. But these just scratch the surface. And even if all were finally located, the elisions of Ernst's process and the erasures of his process effectually have decontextualized them in the very act of satirizing their context by the dreamframes both of his individual collages and the sequences into which their primary presentation has been ordered.

4. I am here drawing on the elaborate exposition of Margot Norris, *Beasts of the Modern Imagination* (Baltimore: Johns Hopkins University Press, 1985).

5. This violence arrests Ernst away from the "rhapsody" attributed to him by Éliane Formentelli, "Notes sur la pensée rhapsodique: Roussel, Ernst, Ponge," in *Collages* (Paris: Colloques de Cérisy, 1978), 60–79. She does notice the predominance of violence in the materials chosen: "The preexistence in the pre-text of disturbing drama and Max Ernst's initial choice of representations that are overwhelming and overwhelmed, agitated and explosive, [privilege] all the forms of rupture and disjunction: tempests, seas unleashed, winds, waterfalls and rapids; explosions of powder, of steam engines, torpedoes . . . violent death and catastrophe" (72). Renée Riese Hubert, "The Fabulous Fictions of Two Surrealist Artists: Giorgio de Chirico and Max Ernst," *New Literary History* 4(1) (Autumn 1972): 151–65, says that the work is "entirely composed of climactic moments." Hubert's compendious study, *Surrealism and the Book* (Berkeley: University of California Press, 1987), provides a large context for these works.

6. Werner Spies, *Max Ernst,* especially 11–28, discusses a number of modalities practiced, and evoked, in various forms of collage.

7. Max Ernst, *Écritures* (Paris: Gallimard, 1970), 253.

8. Spies, *Max Ernst,* plate 707, has located one, but only one, of the originals for this collage in part of a plate (a seated entrepreneur holds the hand of this half-kneeling danseuse) from a nineteenth-century work entitled *Les Mémoires de Monsieur Claude.*

9. Spies, *Max Ernst,* plate 661, has located the circle of skulls under an umbrella in a French popular account of Stanley's expedition to Africa. The interior jar—given a perspectival enlargement in its new context under the umbrella—is identified as coming from one of the plates in instructions to collectors of insects, *Aux Amateurs d'histoire naturelle,* a collocation that reads sadism on a small scale into coherence with sadism on a large scale, and then places it in the mind of a young girl who must be doubly unconscious because of her dream and her repressions.

10. Ernst, *Écritures*, 232.

11. Hubert, "The Fabulous Fictions," 162, finds in *Une Semaine de bonté* a possible ironic reference to the French "Be Good to Your Neighbor" Week.

12. Norris, *Beasts of the Modern Imagination*, 137. Norris is persuasive on the current of "biocentric" liberation that Darwin's implications accorded Nietzsche and Kafka, as well as Ernst, though she herself does not want to confine Ernst's work just to this revelatory angle. She says of *Oedipus Rex* (which she perhaps oversimply conflates with the sequential novels in signification), "Ernst's outsize fingers reaching blindly through the windows . . . lack any relative measure . . . the endless variability, inconsistency, and incoherence of Ernstian figures refute any neo-Platonic significance."

13. A collage of 1921, which forms an empty-headed mechanical woman as though decked out in armor-finery, is called *Perturbation Ma Soeur*.

14. Norris, *Beasts of the Modern Imagination*, 146, sees the paradoxical oxymoron-pun of the title as hinting at an implied pre-Derridean removal from classical thinking: "I cannot even think or describe what Ernst depicts without already contradicting in my words that which I wish to express. I cannot speak of a body without skin . . . without implying the original presence of skin . . . the pun *cent/sans* . . . expresses simultaneous presence and absence, like the zero suffix in linguistics."

15. For a discussion of the novel's presentation of a subject and its implications, see Albert Cook, *The Meaning of Fiction* (Detroit: Wayne University Press, 1960).

Chapter 7. The Sign in Klee

1. *Bewegung* appears often in Klee's writings, along with related notions like sparks ("*Funken*"), as discussed in Andeheinz Mösser, *Das Problem der Bewegung bei Paul Klee* (Heidelberg: Winter, 1976), 15–18. Mösser distinguishes three functions for *Bewegung* in Klee: (1) the "mediated motion formation" ("*mittelbare Bewegungsgestaltung*"), as in *Teppich der Erinnerung*, where a past is brought forward into paint, or paintings where traces of the process of painting are deliberately left visible; (2) the "unmediated motion formation ("*unmittelbare Bewegungsgestaltung*"), where the picture follows the dynamic principles of points, lines, and waves that Klee plots and discusses at length; and (3) "motion formation as growth" ("*Bewegungsgestaltung als 'Wachstum'*"), where a gradual buildup of constituents can arguably be discerned, as Mösser claims for *Full Moon (Der Vollmond)*.

2. Paul Klee, *Das Bildnerische Denken* (Basel: Schwabe, 1964). I indicate this as "BD" in the text.

3. Jean-François Lyotard, *Discours, Figure*.

4. *Das Bildnerische Denken*, 109.

5. Klee, who often blurs the dimensions in his paintings, organizes *Das Bildnerische Denken* from the beginning around questions of dimension. He says: "To summarize: the beholder of the work shall imagine that in the work he has his mirror image in front of him. Then can he suppose that in the work the dimensions above–below and left–right, as concerns the direction, correspond to his own dimensional feeling of direction, but that for the dimension behind–forward the direction of the work is opposed to his own direction: or that it so to speak comes against him with respect to direction. The work as a mirror image of the one who makes it . . ." ("Zusammengefasst: Der Betrachter des Werkes soll sich vorstellen, er habe im Werk sein Spiegelbild vor sich. Dann

kann er annehmen, dass im Werk die Dimensionen oben–unten und links–rechts, was die Richtung betrifft, mit seinem dimensionalen Richtungsgefühl übereinstimmen, dass aber für die Dimension hinten–vorn die Richtung im Werk seiner eigenen Richtung entgegengesetzt ist: oder ihm sozusagen richtungsgemäss entgegenkommt. Das Werk als Spiegelbild des Schaffenden . . ." (97). (Klee uses arrows where I have put dashes.) The first two dimensions, then, work in an opposite fashion from the third, and Klee devises various means to enlist this opposition in the painting.

6. In a letter to Émile Bernard, dated April 15, 1904, Paul Cézanne wrote: "Traiter la nature par le cylindre, la sphère, le cône, le tout mis en perspective, soit que chaque côté d'un objet, d'un plan, se dirige vers un point central. Les lignes parallèles à l'horizon donnent l'étendue, soit une section de la nature ou, si vous aimez mieux, du spectacle que le *Pater Omnipotens Aeterne Deus* étale devant nos yeux. Les lignes perpendiculaires à cet horizon donnent la profondeur. Or, la nature, pour nous hommes, est plus en profondeur qu'en surface, d'où la nécessité d'introduire dans nos vibrations de lumière, representées par les rouges et les jaunes, une somme suffisante de bleutés, pour faire sentir l'air" ("to treat nature through the cylinder, the sphere, the cone, the whole put in perspective, be it that each side of an object or diagram directs itself toward a central point. The parallel lines at the horizon give the extension, or else a section of nature, or, if you prefer, of the spectacle that the *Pater Omnipotens Aeterne [sic] Deus* spreads out before our eyes. The perpendicular lines on this horizon give the depth. Now nature, for us men, is more in depth than it is on the surface, from which the necessity of introducing into our vibrations of light, represented by reds and blacks, a sufficient sum of bluings that the air can be felt") in Paul Cézanne, *Correspondance*, ed. John Rewald (Paris: Grasset, 1935), 259.

7. James Bunn, *The Dimensionality of Signs, Tools, and Models* (Bloomington: University of Indiana Press, 1981).

8. "Cubism gives the viewer back his body." This notion, attributed to Hockney on the basis of his book *Cameraworks* (New York: Knopf, 1984) in a *New York Times* interview (October 7, 1984), presumably is based on the sort of constructive sense of the body-in-the-world discussed by Maurice Merleau-Ponty, especially in *La Phénoménologie de la Perception* (Paris: Gallimard, 1945). See also Jim M. Jordan, *Paul Klee and Cubism* (Princeton: Princeton University Press, 1984).

9. In *Tagebücher von Paul Klee 1898–1918*, ed. Felix Klee (Cologne: Dumont Schauberg, 1957), 347, Klee wrote: "When I say who Franz Marc is, I must recognize at the same time who I am, for much in which I take a share belongs also to him. In Marc the earthly thought precedes the universal thoughts . . . My ardor is more in the manner of the dead or the unborn . . . Art is like the Creation and is valid on the first day and the last" ("Wenn ich sage, wer Franz Marc ist, muss ich zugleich bekennen, wer ich bin, denn vieles, woran ich teilnehme, gehörte auch ihm . . . In Marc steht der Erdgedenke vor dem Weltgedanken . . . Meine Glut ist mehr von der Art der Toten oder der Ungeborenen . . . Kunst ist wie Schöpfung und gilt am ersten und am letzten Tag"). The importance of Klee's statement about himself here may be measured by the phrase that stands as an epitaph on his tombstone:

ON THIS SIDE I CANNOT BE GRASPED AT ALL
FOR I DWELL JUST AS WELL AS WITH THE DEAD
AS WITH THE UNBORN

SOMEWHAT CLOSER TO CREATION THAN USUAL
AND FOR A LONG TIME NOW NOT CLOSE ENOUGH.

(DIESSEITIG BIN ICH GAR NICH FASSBAR
DENN ICH WOHNE GRAD SO GUT BEI DEN TOTEN
WIE BEI DEN UNGEBORENEN
ETWAS NÄHER DER SCHÖPFUNG ALS ÜBLICH
UND NOCH LANGE NICHT NAHE GENUG.)

10. Will Grohmann, *Paul Klee* (New York: Abrams, n.d.), 284. Adapting Klee's notion of "divisionism," Grohmann sees the dots as collecting the force of the light and organizing the space of the picture.

11. Klee, *Unendliche Naturgeschichte*, ed. J. Spiller (Stuttgart, 1970). Also BD, 1–14, and passim. Richard Verdi, *Klee and Nature* (London: A. Zwemmer, 1984), abundantly documents Klee's early and persistent concern with the naturalist's observations of flora and fauna, and also his strong interest in theories from Goethe to his own contemporaries about natural biological forms.

12. Michel Foucault, *This Is Not a Pipe*, tr. James Harkness (Berkeley: University of California Press, 1983), 28, says, "It is there, on these few millimeters of white, the calm sand of the page, that are established all the relations of designation, nomination, description, classification." Foucault here oversimplifies Klee's work by attributing to it an equivalence between discourse and figure (32–37).

13. A painting of 1931, entitled *Chess* (*Schach*), shows a chessboard of normal squares, the black ones rendered in dots, the board intersected by eleven vertical lines of varied length. Klee, *Das Bildnerische Denken*, 223–31, has a long analysis of the two-dimensional implications of the chessboard as a representational problem.

14. Will Grohmann, in his compendious *Paul Klee*, 310, calls them enigmatic and lists them somewhat differently: "symbols, stars, a cross, little flags, two vases with star-shaped blossoms, a cut lemon. The arrow joins the fish with a flower that ends in a mask. What does it mean?" The lists suggests Bosch, but there is nothing pell-mell about Klee's picture. It wears a mask of soberness and fixedness that the matter-of-fact title seems to be reinforcing. Klee speaks of oppositions ("*Gegensätze*") in his writings, and early, in *Tagebücher*, 286.

15. There is an entire doctoral dissertation on Klee's arrows—Mark Lawrence Rosenthal, "Paul Klee and the Arrow," State University of Iowa, 1979.

16. "Wenn Örtlichkeiten zentral tendieren, hat dies seinen psychischen Grund. Das Rationale und das weniger Rationale sind gemischt. Der Sinn des Gesetzes ist der, dass ein natürlich-einfacher Schauplatz gegeben ist, dass bei diesem natürlichen Schauplatz etwas Besonderes betont ist. Die Zentrumsbelastung betont die Abweichung von der Norm." This remark is quoted under the rubric "Der Pfeil als aktive Handlung innerhalb der Bewegungsvielfalt des Gesamträumlichen," *Das Bildnerische Denken*, 56.

17. *Das Bildnerische Denken*, 403–20, deals effectually with the effect of arrows as represented motion. Some of this material is reproduced in *The Pedagogical Sketchbook*, tr. Sibyl Peech (New York: Nierendorf Galleries, 1944) (1925; reprinted Faber, 1969), 37. There Klee says, "The father of the arrow is the thought: How can I extend my range in that direction? . . . The contrast between man's ideal ability to penetrate at will the natural and the supernatural and his physical impotence is the origin of the human tragedy. Half winged, half-imprisoned— that is man. Thought as the medium between the earth and the cosmos . . . One must become movement and not merely be! . . . Never quite to reach the

point where movement is infinite! Consolation: a little further than usual!—than possible?" (I revise with Grohmann's English text version.) He makes much of the black arrow (40), distinguishing it from the red arrow, the hot arrow, and the cold arrow.

18. Jean Laude, "Paul Klee," in *Primitivism in Twentieth Century Art*, ed. William Rubin (New York: Museum of Modern Art, 1984), 487–502. The discussion in the catalogue of this show makes a number of interesting discriminations while obscuring this fundamental point. Laude points out that Klee early shared his contemporaries' enthusiasm for primitive arts and did incorporate such features from them as a striped mask for a face. Such features in his work are more vestigial as references than they are in Picasso's, and they only partially assist the visual orientation and schematism of the face in the mask form. Laude further says that, "a [borrowed] sign or form . . . itself functions as a sign, a sign of primitiveness, of primordiality." See also James Smith Pierce, *Paul Klee and Primitive Art* (New York and London, 1976).

19. Twenty-nine of these hieroglyphic pictures are listed and discussed in Tilman Osterwold, *Paul Klee: Die Ordnung der Dinge* (Stuttgart: Gerd Hatje, 1975), 171–82.

20. Osterwold, *Die Ordnung der Dinge*, 13.

21. "Unsere schöpferische Fähigkeit vermag uns indessen auch hier über die Mangelhaftigkeit der Erscheinung wenigstens zu einer Synthese der Vollkommenheit des jenseitigen Seins zu verhelfen" (*Das Bildnerische Denken*, 467).

22. "Diese geeinte Darstellung lässt die dreistimmige Bewegung wohl erkennen und leicht in ihrem Verlaufe verfolgen. Kanonartig setzen die Stimmen hintereinander ein. . . . Diese neue Figur könnte man den Kanon der Totalität nennen" (*Das Bildnerische Denken*, 489).

23. Grohmann, *Paul Klee*, 205.

24. *Tagebücher*, 292. He also spoke also of a "style-forming tension of the ego" ("Stilbildende Spannung des Ich") (*Das Bildnerische Denken*, 193).

25. Paul Klee, *Briefe an die Familie* (Cologne: Dumont, 1979), 2:1026.

26. Ann C. Colley, "Paul Klee and the Fantasy of Synthesis," *Kenyon Review* 9(3) (Summer 1987): 1–15, emphasizes the "drift towards the synthesis between words and images" in this painting, in which "once more the synthesis of word and image is suggested, but unrealized, for the difference between the distinctly colored and formed letters and the irregular patches drifting below work against fusion" (5–6). She says in her elaborate interpretation of *Child Consecrated to Suffering* (1935), "Here words and images neither displace nor benignly alternate with each other. Instead, they plunge into one another and, in their mixed form, construct sentences and shapes which simultaneously write, paint, and identify the face's text. The metaphoric title, which distinguishes a majority of Klee's works, is present within the framed picture" (8).

27. Grohmann, *Paul Klee*, 335.

28. Albert Cook, *Myth and Language* (Bloomington: Indiana University Press, 1980), chap. 9, "Parable." Klee himself assigned considerable force to the *Märchen:* "The corporeality of the *Märchen* is not only not yet to be grasped but it is far—very far and yet very clear" ("Die Leibhaftigkeit des Märchens, nur noch nicht greifbar, sondern fern, ziemlich fern und doch sehr klar") (*Tagebücher*, 291).

29. The various attempts to assign Klee's angels specific symbolic value seem to go as much against the grain of their openness as to deny them all reference to the other life "on the other side" ("*jenseits*") that he intermittently but ex-

plicitly mentions. The titles are almost all invented, and many have a nonce flavor: *Angel Handing over the Object of Desire* (1913), *Message of the Air-spirit (Botschaft des Luftgeistes,* 1920), *Angelus Militans* (1939), *Forgetful Angel (Vergesslicher Engel,* 1939); *Crisis of an Angel (Krisis eines Engels,* 1939), *High Guardian (Hoher Wächter,* 1940), *Archangel* (1938), *Angelus Dubiosus* (1939), *Poor Angel (Armer Engel,* 1939), *Watchful Angel (Wachsamer Engel,* 1938), *Angel in the Process of Becoming (Engel im Werden,* 1934), *Angel Still Female* (1939), *Angel Still Ugly* (1940). *Angel Applicant (Engel Anwärter,* 1939) shows decomposed hard features and typical rudimentary painted "wings," black and white on a grey-pink background with a half moon above. These works and their characteristic tone appear early. To be reckoned among the angel paintings is *Spirit Serves Continental Breakfast (Ein Genius serviert ein kleines Frühstück,* 1920). In this work the tray is prominent. A wing and a heart show through. There is also the angel series of fifty sheets on which Klee worked for twenty-five years (Grohmann, *Paul Klee,* 350).

30. Albert Cook, "Blake: The Exaltation of Fluidity," in *Thresholds,* 29–62.

31. To extend such notions into other possibilities of spatial organization, James Bunn says (private communication, 1987), "Klee was reworking Hokusai"s watercolor 'Flounders and Carnations' as the centerpiece for 'Um den Fisch.' Hokusai was probably referring to the *tai-chi-tu* via the structure of his composition. That led me to suspect that Klee's painting is about the organizing principles of 'around.' The mandala, the god's eye, the phases of the moon, all are about-and-around. Because Klee also has some decentered eyes, the painting is probably also about looking at 'around' from off-angled points, the perspective of jokes, wit and the grotesque, not to say metaphor."

32. "Doubtless painting is that which brings us as close as possible to transcendental activity [in Husserl's sense], if it is true that this activity is indeed forced to disjoin rather than to synthesize" (Lyotard, *Discours, Figure,* 28).

33. "The transcendence of the symbol is the figure, that is to say a spatial manifestation that the linguistic space cannot incorporate without being disrupted, an exteriority that it cannot interiorize into *signification.*" (Lyotard, *Discours, Figure,* 13). "Exterior" here plays fast and loose with the phenomenological facts of our perception and our consequent intellection. A text that is read is "exterior" in the same sense—a trivial sense—as a painting that is looked at.

34. Lyotard, *Discours, Figure,* 222.

35. The play of symmetry and asymmetry is notable specifically in the depictions of angels, often with lines that are sketchy and deliberately uncertain. See James Bunn, *The Dimensionality of Signs, Tools, and Models,* who writes, "If beauty is a response to human alienation, then nature is not beautiful, even though it may be appropriated by human act into landscape gardens of rare device . . . The wonderful phenomenon of nature is that randomness causes symmetry. For example, in the random distribution of flotsam on a seashore, groups of similar size and shape are assembled together in patterns. Then too, the formal cause of crowding induces the symmetry of gazelles and zebras, as they are distributed on the veldt. But good artists make symbols which allow us to return from alien asymmetry to grace" (178–79). Klee has, as it were, attained the grace by building in the asymmetry. Lyotard, *Discours, Figure,* 224, notes, however, that the dimensions in *Auserwählte Stätte* are close to the Golden Section.

36. A highly informed and discriminating correlation of Klee's statements

with such questions has been made by Hans-Martin Schweizer, "Die Immanenz des Transzendenten in der Kunsttheorie von Paul Klee," in *Festschrift für Georg Scheja*, ed. Albrecht Leuteritz et al. (Sigmaringen: Jan Thorbecke, 1975), 237–61. Schweizer says, "The principle character of the 'construction of the means of form-representation' is thus not wholly identical with the form-representation itself, even when the course of [artistic] movement which indicates the form-representation may scarcely be conceived without it, like a game which is based on no rules" (254). See also the more cursory treatment of such notions in Max Huggler, *Paul Klee: Die Malerei als Blick in den Kosmos* (Stuttgart: Huber, 1969).

Klee's works also lend themselves into classifications by representationality and signification, as Grohmann's three "circles" of outer, middle, and inner.

37. This combination of motion and rest was already expressed by Klee in the notion of "repose in motion" (*"Bewegte Ruhe"*) discussed in Mösser, *Problem der Bewegung*, 57–58.

Chapter 8. The "Meta-Irony" of Marcel Duchamp

1. Quoted in Robert Motherwell, *The Dada Painters and Poets* (New York: Wittenborn, 1951), 311.

2. Duchamp accompanied the bond with a supposed society, a list of "extracts from the statutes," and explanatory letters to Picabia and Jacques Doucet. Marcel Duchamp, *Duchamp du Signe: Écrits*, ed. Michel Sanouillet (Paris: Flammarion, 1975), 268–70.

3. Duchamp says that the title means "a widow aroused to the point of abandon" (*"délurée"*). Marcel Duchamp, *Ingénieur du temps perdu: Entretiens avec Pierre Cabanne* (Paris: Belfont, 1977), 113.

4. Duchamp's own remarks about the fourth dimension and the practices leading to questions of dimensionality in his major works have undergone considerable extension in the discussions of his commentators, notably Craig E. Adcock, *Marcel Duchamp's Notes for the Large Glass: An N-Dimensional Analysis* (Ann Arbor: UMI Research Press, 1983); Jean Clair, *Marcel Duchamp ou le grand fictif* (Paris: Galilee, 1975); and Jean-François Lyotard, *Les Transformateurs Duchamp* (Paris: Galilee, 1977). Adcock says, "The Oculist Witnesses are possibly meant to suggest a flattened version of a Riemannian spherical space or a hypersurface transformed through perspective projection" (109). Adcock is obliged to redefine and adjust in order to align Duchamp's intuitions with non-Euclidean geometry. The term *"tranformateur"* itself Lyotard borrows from Duchamp, who has a poem or list of that title whose items are as disparate as the constituents of the *Large Glass* (*Duchamp du Signe*, 272). A large survey of theories about the fourth dimension as these apply to cubism and other artistic enterprises in Europe and America, with a special chapter on Duchamp, is provided by Linda Dalrymple Henderson, *The Fourth Dimension and Non-Euclidean Geometry in Modern Art* (Princeton: Princeton University Press, 1983), especially 117–63.

5. This title is twice recorded in Duchamp's notebook of puns.

6. René Char, *Recherche de la Base au sommet* (Paris: Gallimard, 1971), 43.

7. Marcel Duchamp, *Rrose Sélavy* (Paris: Editions G.L.M., 1939; reprinted in Duchamp, *Duchamp du Signe*, 151–58).

8. Arturo Schwarz, *The Complete Works of Marcel Duchamp* (New York: Thames and Hudson, 1970), 29.

9. Duchamp goes well beyond the modern practice summarized by Michel

Butor, *Les Mots dans la peinture* (Geneva: Skira, 1969), 17: "The painter's work is presented as the association of an image on canvas, board, wall or paper, and of a name, be it void of association, pure enigma, reduced to a simple question mark."

10. I am here following the speculations of Gary Handwerk, *Irony and the Ethics of Narrative* (New Haven: Yale University Press, 1985). Handwerk brings the deductions of Grice, Schlegel, Kierkegaard, and Lacan, among others, to bear on the situational ramifications of an ironic stance.

11. Marcel Duchamp, quoted in Anne d'Harnoncourt and Walter Hopps, *Étant donnés: 1° la chute d'eau, 2° le gaz d'éclairage* (Philadelphia: Philadelphia Museum of Art, 1973), 13.

12. Anne d'Harnoncourt and Walter Hopps in ibid., 16.

13. Schwarz, *Complete Works*, 471.

14. Duchamp said, "You can put the verb you wish, provided it begins with a vowel" (*Ingénieur*, 102). Possibilities immediately suggest themselves—*Tu m'emmennes, m'accables, m'ouvres, m'arroses, m'ordonnes,* and so on. One may be reminded of the signature he scrawled onto Picabia's semicomposite *L'oeil cacodylate*, "*Pi qu'habilla Rrose*," where the name of the painter, the mathematical symbol *pi*, and Duchamp's alter ego are conjoined. Duchamp has put a suit on mathematics.

15. Inez Hedges, *The Languages of Revolt* (Durham: Duke University Press, 1983), discusses Duchamp and other surrealists in terms of the breaking of referential frames along the lines of Marvin Minsky and Erving Goffman. But again, Duchamp goes much farther than simply registering what such a procedure can account for.

16. Carol P. James, "Duchamp's Pharmacy," *Enclitic* (1) (Spring 1978): 65–70, offers many deductions for the red and green dots in *Pharmacy*.

17. Duchamp, *Duchamp du Signe*, 171. Careful attention to the spatial situation of this work can enlarge its significations. Robert Sowers, in a letter to the *New York Times Book Review*, March 15, 1987, says, "Before assuming that the artist did not invest this factory-made urinal with any perceptible esthetic qualities, they [Arthur Danto, the author of *The Philosophical Disenfranchisement of Art*, and Paul Guyer, who reviewed that book] ought at least to take note of what he manifestly did do: he rotated it a quarter-turn on its lateral axis—a rotation that the placement of the 'R. Mutt' signature serves to make clear and irrevocable. As a result, the flush connection, which normally would be at the top, is transformed into a rude mouthlike orifice at the bottom; the drain perforations, now above that orifice, become a Piccasoid constellation of eye-and-nostril elements; and given these, the overall concavity of the urinal begins to recall a similar concavity in the kind of African masks from which Picasso just 10 years earlier had been so profitably deriving his first truly radical visual vocabulary. In short, Duchamp's transformation of this ordinary object into a work of art is dependent upon an astute *visual* maneuver that enables us to read it representationally, stylistically and satirically in relation to an identifiable world outside the work itself."

18. Duchamp said that "America's unique contributions to art are hydraulic articles and bridges" ("The Case of Richard Mutt," in *The Blind Man*, no. 2 [May 1917], 5, quoted in Arturo Schwarz, *Almanacco Dada* [Milan: Feltrinelli, 1976], 73).

19. Duchamp refers to Seurat in *Infra-minces*, in Marcel Duchamp, *Notes*, ed. Pontus Hulten (Paris: Beaubourg, 1981), 1.

20. Therese Eiben, in an unpublished course paper on Duchamp's Ready-mades, Brown University, 1983.

21. Quoted in Anne D'Harnoncourt and Kynaston McShine, *Marcel Duchamp* (New York and Philadelphia: The Museum of Modern Art and Philadelphia Museum of Art, 1973), 295.

22. Duchamp, *Duchamp du Signe*, 182.

23. Ibid., 194. Duchamp says he got his start from Raymond Roussel, in whose *Impressions d'Afrique* a painting machine is to be found (173). He denies a connection of his own art with futurism, which he calls "an impressionism of the mechanical world. It was strictly a continuation of the Impressionist Movement" (171). He goes on to place Dada in a preliminary position: "Dada was very serviceable as a Purgative . . . I recall certain conversations with Picabia along these lines" (172).

24. Ibid., 195.

25. Octavio Paz, *Deux Transparents* (Paris: Gallimard, 1967), 16–17.

26. Gilles Deleuze and Felix Guattari, *L'Anti-Oedipe* (Paris: Minuit, 1972).

27. Duchamp, *Duchamp du Signe*, 62.

28. Ibid., 97.

29. Ibid., 77. The nine *stoppages étalons* are equated to the same malic molds in Duchamp's Note 120, in Hulten, *Notes*.

30. D'Harnoncourt and Hopps, *Étant Donnés*, 40.

31. Marcel Duchamp, quoted in Lawrence D. Stiefel, Jr., *The Position of Duchamp's Glass in the Development of His Art* (New York: Garland, 1977), 51.

32. Of *Tu m'* Duchamp said, "I have never liked it because it is too decorative; summarizing one's works in a painting is not a very attractive form of activity" (in Schwarz, *Complete Works*, 471).

33. Duchamp speaks of a *maladie de Messie* as a *machine à dire la messe* (Hulten, *Notes*, 209). Duchamp says that the weight consisting of the bottle of Benedictine is a "small naughtiness . . . an ironic concession to still lives" (97, 102). He also says, "This five-hearted machine will have to give birth to the headlight/lighthouse [*phare*]. This headlight will have to be the child-God, recalling sufficiently the Jesus of the primitives. It will be the divine expansion (*épanouissement*) of this machine-mother" (109).

34. André Breton, *les Vases communicants* (1933; Paris: Gallimard, 1959).

35. See Note 15.

36. The point is made by René Micha, "*Étant Donné* Étant Donnés," in *Marcel Duchamp* (Paris: Plon, 1979), 166. Micha also notes the classical theme of nymphs associated with forests and with springs.

37. Interestingly, a postcard from 1900 shows a nude holding in her left hand the Bec Auer, in the presence of an astonished man. It is printed in Jean Clair, *Duchamp et la photographie* (Paris: Chêne, 1977), 53.

38. David Burrell, *Analogy and Philosophical Language* (New Haven: Yale University Press, 1973), 10.

39. Lyotard, *Les Transformateurs*, 36.

40. Duchamp, quoted in ibid., 63.

41. Ibid., 87.

42. John B. Deregowski, "Pictorial Perception and Culture," in *Image, Object and Illusion: Readings from* Scientific American, ed. Richard Held (San Francisco: Freeman, 1974), 78–85.

43. Ibid., 99; Duchamp, *Duchamp du Signe*, 46.

44. Duchamp, *Duchamp du Signe*, 220.

45. "Hinge" ("*charnière*") recurs often in Duchamp's writings about the *Large Glass*, coming up also in his chess treatise; see Marcel Duchamp and V. Halberstadt, *Opposition and Sister Squares Reconciled* (Paris: L'Échiquier, 1932), especially 101–8. See also Lyotard, *Les Transformateurs*.

46. Wilhelm Köller, *Semiotik und Metapher* (Stuttgart: Metzler, 1975), 32.

47. Duchamp, *Duchamp du Signe*, 43.

48. Hulten, *Notes*, 180.

49. Duchamp's relation to photography is complex, going beyond just his friendship and association with Man Ray or his remarks to Edward Steichen, as Jean Clair shows in *Duchamp et la photographie*. Clair finds a similarity between the "virgin" look photography takes of the world and Duchamp's return to visual origins (7). Early silhouettes of 1903–4 already anticipate the Wilson-Lincoln effect projected for the *Large Glass*, the illusion of alternate originals for profiles. There are photogaphs of shadows of Readymades (13). Duchamp himself associates Marey, Muybridge, and the photographer Eakins to the *Nude Descending a Staircase* (25–30). Clair sees the aura around the *Portrait of Dr. Dumouchel* (1910) as the sort produced by the "Kirlian effect" in photography (14–20), though such auras are not absent from the tradition of painting, as in Rembrandt's *Turkish Gentleman*. *To Be Looked at with One Eye* employs a Kodak lens (55). Clair quotes the *Green Box*'s comparison of the "*éclaboussures*" ("*splashes*") in the *Large Glass* to an instantaneous photo. Duchamp did a three-dimensional film, or projected one, in 1925, and was interested toward the end of his life in "anaglyphs," a form of stereoscopic photography (83–86) (however, he may have been doing research for the stereoscopic effect between horizon and sky in *Étant donnés*). In the *Green Box*, Duchamp thrice underlines the word *photographie*.

50. Maurizio Calvesi, *Duchamp Invisibile* (Rome: Officina Edizioni, 1975), 59.

51. Quoted in Hubert Damisch, "La Défense Duchamp," in *Marcel Duchamp* (Paris: Plon, 1979), 65–117. Duchamp built chance into the *Large Glass* by letting air currents blow a gauze mesh three times against a screen imprinting rectangles that become its clouds; by incorporating into the work the *Network of Stoppages*, produced by dropping meter-length strings, and by shooting matches dipped in paint from a toy cannon to produce the "nine shots" (Harriet and Sidney Janis, *View*, March 1945).

52. Hulten, *Notes*, 188, 263.

53. *L'Homme qui a perdu son squelette*, *Plastique*, no. 4, 1939. This semi-erotic surrealist novel has the stamp of Max Ernst more than of any of the six other collaborators.

54. The text of *Transformateurs* is in Duchamp, *Duchamp du Signe*, 272; of *Infra-minces* in Hulten, *Notes*.

55. Adcock, *Marcel Duchamp's Notes*, 151.

56. Jean Suquet, *Miroir de la mariée* (Paris: Flammarion, 1974), 61, links this game to the *pendu* (woman) of the *Large Glass*. In this game the first and last letters are given and the missing ones are indicated by dots.

57. Hulten, *Notes*, 66, 164.

58. A similar puzzle is presented, both by the text and its relation to the physical ready-made, in the *Comb* of 1916. This object has lettered across the thin edge of its top: "3 OU 4 GOUTTES DE HAUTEUR N'ONT RIEN A FAIRE AVEC LA SAUVAGERIE." ("three or four drops of loftiness have nothing to do with savagery").

59. This phrase has been produced by the partial erasure of an identification

for Sapolin Enamel: "Manufactured by Gerstendorfer Brothers, New York, U.S.A." Thus Duchamp has brought about by "liberating" some letters and suppressing others—and by additions too—what happens gradually in place names like Aigues Mortes and La Rue Saint André des Arts. See George H. Bauer, "Enamouring a Barber Pole," *Dada and Surrealism,* no. 12 (Fall 1983): 20–36. Bauer correlates the fact that Duchamp's only addition to the advertisement is painting the girl's hair in the mirror with the double sense of the French word *"peigne,"* which can be attributed either to *peigner,* "to comb," or *peindre,* "to paint." He also remarks that *"epergne"* has different meanings in English and in French.

60. Pauline Yu, "The Poetics of Discontinuity: East-West Correspondences in Lyric Poetry, *PMLA* 94(2) (March 1979), 265.

61. Cabanne-Duchamp, *Entretiens,* 68.

62. Hulten, *Notes,* 66, 143, 69, 77.

63. Cabannes-Duchamp, *Entretiens,* 60.

64. Hulten, *Notes,* 250.

65. Mary Douglas, *Purity and Danger* (Harmondsworth: Penguin, 1966), 13, 78.

Chapter 9. Magritte: The Smoothing of the Mystery

1. The youthful Magritte wrote detective stories, and in his arch maturity he declared, "The world resembles Nick Carter" ("Le monde ressemble à Nick Carter") (René Magritte, *Écrits* [Paris: Flammarion, 1979], 40). Henceforth I shall make page citations to this work by simple number in the text.

2. Michel Foucault, *This Is Not a Pipe,* trans. and ed. James Harkness (Berkeley: University of California Press, 1982). Magritte's responsive but qualifying letters to Foucault, published here, are the more remarkable that the painter often showed himself to be surly in the presence of questioning interlocutors. See also the letters, with documentation, in Magritte, *Écrits,* 639–41. Magritte's own constant theorizing has given Rolf Schiebler, *Die Kunsttheorie Rene Magrittes* (Munich: Hanser, 1981), abundant material to systematize the sometimes elaborate notions expanded in the *Écrits.* Schiebler devotes a whole chapter to the conception of mystery (75–85). Petra von Morstein, "Magritte: Artistic and Conceptual Representation," *Journal of Aesthetics and Art Criticism* 41(4) (Summer 1983): 368–74, also bases general aesthetic deductions on the theory and practice of Magritte. She says of one of the pipe paintings that "the understanding of *The Use of Words I* . . . is not exclusive of alternatives . . . Magritte's works incorporate problems which systematically, and not just for the reason constituted by the nature of the artistic representation, elude rule-bound solutions. There is, for instance, no rule which enables us to decide what the demonstrative 'ceci' . . . refers to . . . nor indeed whether what looks like a sentence *is* a sentence" (372). And further, "there is nothing that I can see that allows us to *decide* whether the pipe detail is referentially or conceptually representational" (373).

3. "Parce que le trompe-l'oeil permet de donner à l'image peinte l'expression de profondeur propre au monde visible, et parce que ma peinture doit ressembler au monde pour pouvoir en évoquer le mystère" (537).

4. Magritte seems always to change the title from work to work of this group. Other titles are *L'Emploi des mots* ("Use of Words") and *L'Air et la Chanson* ("Tune and Song").

5. Foucault, *This Is Not a Pipe,* 16.

6. "The researches that led to these revelations, I am now aware, have been undertaken to find in objects a sense that is unilateral, not reversible. Actually, if the answers clarify the questions, the answers are not clarified by the questions. If the dagger is the answer to the rose, the rose is not the answer to the dagger; nor is water the answer to the boat, or the piano to the ring" ("Les recherches qui ont conduit à ces révélations ont été, je m'en rends compte à présent, entreprises pour trouver un sens unilatéral, non réversible, à des objets. En effet, si les réponses éclairent les questions, les réponses ne sont pas éclairées par les questions. Si le poignard est la réponse à la rose, la rose n'est pas la réponse au poignard; l'eau ne l'est pas non plus au bateau ni le piano à la bague") (326). In 1929 Magritte published "Les Mots et les images," an elaborate but elementary taxonomy of the relations between word and object, of eighteen categories, each accompanied by a small "improvised" drawing. In a 1938 version he expanded the categories to twenty under the title "La Ligne de vie" (a title he uses for two other discussions), finishing the series with "Ceci n'est pas un pipe" (Louis Scutenaire, *Avec Magritte* [Brussels: Lebeer-Hossman, 1977], 85–90).

7. "A nocturnal landscape and a sky such as we see in full daylight. The landscape evokes night and the sky evokes day" ("Un paysage nocturne et un ciel tel que nous le voyons en plein jour. Le paysage évoque la nuit et le ciel évoque le jour") (422). Magritte goes on, "This evocation of night and of day seems to me endowed with the power of surprising and enchanting us. I call this power: poetry" ("Cette évocation de la nuit et du jour me semble douée du pouvoir de nous surprendre et de nous enchanter. J'appelle ce pouvoir: la poésie"). A prospectus of 1924 gives a poem in the form of an invitation where only the last line clearly defamiliarizes the light, though the second line gives a cue by not naming the exact title of the country, replacing it by the generality of an implication any ambassador would want to make: "The ambassador/ of a beautiful country/ has the honor/ of inviting you/ to a grand dinner/ The salons will be lighted with candles." ("L'ambassadeur/ d'un beau pays/ a l'honneur/ de vous inviter/ à un grand dîner/ Les salons seront éclairés avec des bougies") (29).

8. Magritte earned his living for a while as a designer of wallpaper.

9. Foucault, *This Is Not a Pipe*, 20, 21.

10. "'Surrealism,' like 'Fantastic Art,' says something very vague and false, if it is given any other sense than the very limited one to which it exactly answers" ("'Surréalisme' comme 'Art fantastique,' dit quelque chose de très vague et de faux, si on lui donne un autre sens que celui très limité auquel il répond exactement") (446). Magritte declares himself to be bored by the plays of Ghelderode, the adaptation of folk forms to surrealist ends, and he evades the attribution of "the appearance of the invisible in the visible" to Ghelderode (684). He says, in a discourse before an academy, insisting on his freedom from "a so-called unconscious" ("un soi-disant inconscient"): "The art of painting, like many things, can give occasion to confusions that are easy or difficult. Notably the art that is called 'fantastic'" ("L'art de peindre, comme beaucoup de choses, peut donner lieu à des confusions faciles ou difficiles. Notamment l'art dit 'fantastique'") (441).

11. "Les passages qui me laissent *toujours* indifférent (et c'est curieux) ce sont ceux où des actes se passent sur le plan du rêve, de l'hallucination, ou de la rêverie" (452).

12. André Breton, *Surrealism and Painting* (1965; New York: Harper, 1972), 402.

13. "La lumière et l'ombre n'appartiennent plus à un monde systematisé, régi par des lois abstraites, elles sont unies dans un ordre qui évoque le mystère et qui interdit à la pensée de se satisfaire des interrogations que l'on pourrait poser et des réponses que l'on pourrait leur trouver" (549).

14. These remarks of Magritte, always occasional and fleeting, engage abstractions that are large enough, and full enough of connotation, occasionally to slant him toward contradiction. On the one hand, in a list of paintings, he takes the standard negative stance toward banality: "*Sentimental Colloquy.* Before an oblique window two wooden objects that have lost their banal signification speak of love and happiness" ("'*Le Colloque sentimentale.*' Devant une fenêtre oblique deux objets en bois qui ont perdu leur signification banale, parlent d'amour et de bonheur") (261). Yet in another connection he valorizes banality: "Banality common to all things, that is the mystery" ("La banalité commune à toutes les choses, c'est le mystère") (418). Then again, on a different tangent, he says that a new style can give only a familiar sense of mystery, as against the unfamiliar one to which he aspires and which he is here saying that Gaudi does not achieve (22).

15. Louis Scutenaire, *La Fidélité des images; René Magritte; La cinématographie et la photographie* (Brussels: Lebeer Hossmann, n.d.), 60. However, it is possible that Scutenaire had a hand in providing this title.

16. René Magritte, letter to Michel Foucault about *Les Mots et les choses,* May 23, 1966, quoted in Foucault, *This Is Not a Pipe,* 56. If we remember that what Nelson Goodman calls "resemblance" Magritte calls "*similitude,*" we may begin in this domain with the rigor of a skepticism that will not serve much further than to stimulate beginning. Goodman, *Languages of Art,* 231, says that "words are more conventional than pictures only if conventionality is construed in terms of differentiation rather than of artificiality. Nothing here depends upon the internal structure of a symbol; for what describes in some systems may depict in others. Resemblance disappears as a criterion of representation, and structural similarity as a requirement upon notational or any other languages. The often stressed distinction between iconic and other signs becomes transient and trivial."

17. "The art of painting—which truly deserves to be called 'The art of resemblance'—allows one to describe, by means of painting, a thought that is susceptible of appearing visibly. This thought comprises exclusively the visible figures that the world offers it: persons, stars, furniture, arms, mountains, solids, inscriptions, etc. This thought resembles when it unites the figure that it sees in the order that directly evokes the mystery. The description of thought, which resembles the world not separated from its mystery, does not tolerate either fantasy or originality" ("L'art de peindre—qui mérite vraiment de s'appeler 'L'art de la ressemblance'—permet de décrire, par la peinture, une pensée susceptible d'apparaître visiblement. Cette pensée comprend exclusivement les figures visibles que le monde lui offre: personnes, astres, meubles, armes, arbres, montagnes, solides, inscriptions, etc. Cette pensée ressemble lorsqu'elle unit les figures qu'elle voit, dans l'ordre [sic] qui évoque directement le mystère. La description de la pensée, qui ressemble au monde non séparé de son mystère, ne tolère pas de fantaisie ni d'originalité") ("L'art de la ressemblance," 655). Here, by effectually asserting mystery and forbidding fantasy, or by asserting the coexistence of the baldly visible and a mystery he elsewhere would connect to the invisible, Magritte at once evokes a full set of terms necessary to discuss these central questions and draws a veil over the possibility of any logical

solution, as does his inclusion of a general term like "solids" and a significative puzzle like "inscriptions" in his list here.

18. "Pour être plus parfaites en qualité d'images et représenter mieux un objet, elles doivent ne lui pas ressembler" (René Descartes, *Discours IV, Dioptrique*, as cited by Louis Marin, "Textes en représentation," *Critique*, no. 282 [November 1970], 920).

19. In a 1948 variant of *La Mémoire*, the head sits on a dark ground backed by a wooden fence of horizontal, grained planks.

20. "La 'femme surréaliste' a été une invention aussi stupide que la 'pin-up girl' qui la remplace à présent" (433). Yet Magritte exalts love and passion in his responses to a questionnaire about love (57–58). And in modification of these statements about surrealism, he especially praises de Chirico and Ernst (104). His cover for *Qu'est-ce que le Surréalisme* is a milder version of his painting *Rape* (*Le Viol*), a woman for whom the sexual parts of the body replace the features of the face.

21. Jacques Derrida emphasizes the fetishistic element in these two paintings, drawing them into play so as to make the valid but obvious point that shoes are sexually marked, while both Heidegger and Meyer Schapiro do not discuss that aspect in the shoes painted by van Gogh (Jacques Derrida, *La Vérité en peinture* [Paris: Flammarion], 1978, 291–436). Derrida quotes two London psychiatrists as testifying that "THE RED MODEL is a case of castration" (358), but such a psychic angling does not exhaust that particular painting. Fetishism, as Freud pointed out, exemplifies castration fear by displacing attention from the "castrated" mother onto the appurtenances of femininity. The *Red Model* has no displacement, only a discrepancy-fusion and a confrontation that is ambiguously assignable to the erotic.

22. The careful analysis of the newspaper I have drawn from A(braham) M(arie) Hammacher, *René Magritte* (New York: Abrams, [1973]), 112.

23. Scutenaire, *La Fidélité des images*, 47.

24. Xavière Gauthier, *Surréalisme et sexualité* (Paris: Gallimard, 1971), 117, says, "Woman is a festival all by herself" ("La femme est donc, à elle seule, un festin"). Still, it is impossible to confine Magritte to any of Gauthier's many categories. She draws on Magritte rarely for illustrative material, and when she does so, she tends to confine his significances.

25. Scutenaire, *La Fidelité des images*, 7. This photograph is closely similar to *Attempt at the Impossible* (*La Tentative de l'impossible*) (1928), except that in this painting the model is nude.

26. Magritte's mother, a suicide by drowning, was found with her head shrouded in one of her garments.

27. Foucault, *This Is Not a Pipe*, 56.

28. Again, Magritte repeats his titles. At least two other works have the same title. One work of 1930 has four "lexical" identifications: The word "*ciel*" is attached to a valise, "*l'oiseau*" to a jacknife, "*la table*" to a leaf, and "*l'éponge*" in the lower right corner to what looks like a sponge. This identity is a joker in the deck that Magritte does not include in the work I am mainly discussing, though in another work so titled of 1936 he does attach "*valise*" to a valise, as well as "*porte*" to a horse's head, "*vent*" to a clock, and "*oiseau*" to a pitcher. Many other works of Magritte include arbitrary, surrealized words in the middle of the painting. *La Clef de verre* shows a suspended rock in the mountains, and this performs oppositions of signification for the whole painting (between glass and rock, rough rock and smooth key, mountain and door, indoors and out-

doors, and so on). In *La Clef des champs* (1933) a broken window gives on a simple outdoor scene.

29. "Une fausse idée sur les oeuvres d'art attribue à la peinture le pouvoir d'exprimer des sentiments avec plus ou moins de précision et, même, d'énoncer des idées" (555).

30. A drawing of a year later, *Alphabet of Revelations,* has the same objects in a different order: bird, pipe, glass, and key. Here, too, the title indicates that they stand for letters, a beginning of a new system of quasi-Egyptian hieroglyphics, if closely identified, but referred to the "Revelations" if taken loosely. The distancing of the title allows either reading.

31. *La Fidélité des images,* 46. The date is 1937, the same as that of *Le Thérapeute.*

32. Il y a des titres de deux sortes:

1) "Mourir de ne pas mourir", par example, "dit" quelque chose, sans le livre.

2) "Divagations", ne dit pas quelque chose d'indifférent. Il fait penser au livre qui "dit" quelque chose.

Comme titre de la sorte no. 2, "Le Champ libre" est très honnête, sans plus: il faut lire les poèmes pour que ce titre indique ou rappelle quelque chose. en soi, seuls, "Le Champ libre", "Divagations", sont indifférents, ne disent rien.

Je préfère les titres no. 1, mais, à la reflexion, les titres de mes tableaux sont presque toujours des titres no. 2: La Tempête, L'Art de la Conversation, La Mémoire, etc. (La Fée ignorante est dans le monde des titres no. 1.)

Mais ces titres no. 2 deviennent "parlants:" en nommant des tableaux, à condition qu'ils soient exactement adéquats. Leur sens a de la force et de charme grâce aux tableaux et ceux-ci acquièrent plus de précision en étant bien nommés (487).

33. In *Praise for Dialectic* (*Éloge de la dialectique,* 1937), inside and outside generate a perspectival maze. The view is of an open window at the roof corner of a house, and inside the window a complete miniature house, with door, closed windows, and oeil de boeuf, fills the room.

34. Suzy Gablik, *Magritte* (New York: Thames and Hudson, 1985), 111.

35. In another version the carrot-bottle is on the left side and all three objects stand on a wooden dresser that opens on a bell-filled sky.

36. "Il y a des similitudes possibles et des différences possibles entre les choses séparées. Ces rapports sont décelés par la pensée qui examine, compare et évalue" (511).

37. This title is drawn from L. A. Cladel, *Ompdrailles, le tombeau des lutteurs* (1879), as Hammacher, *René Magritte,* 150, points out.

38. "L'arbre . . . se trouvait pour le spectateur à la fois à l'intérieur de la chambre sur le tableau et à l'extérieur dans le paysage réel. Cette existence à la fois dans deux espaces différents est semblable à l'existence à la fois dans le passé et le présent d'un moment identique comme cela se passe dans la 'fausse reconnaissance'" (111).

39. *L'ami du Tétanos, Remise des effets, Extraction légale, Les morceaux du Docteur, La boîte de l'amateur, Projet de confiture* (670).

40. James Thrall Soby, *Magritte* (New York: Museum of Modern Art, 1965), 19.

41. Scutenaire, *Avec Magritte,* 42.

42. Scutenaire, *Avec Magritte,* 123–24.

43. "Conçu sans préoccupation esthétique, dans l'unique but de RÉPONDRE à un sentiment mystérieux, à une angoisse 'sans raison,' une sorte de 'rappel à l'ordre'" (368).

44. Gablik, *Magritte,* 62, relates this painting iconographically to various

collages in Max Ernst's *Une Semaine de bonté*. (In that work, however, most frequently the man has the head of a lion, not wings. When wings are present, the lion is not.)

Chapter 10. The Modification of the Narrative in Art

1. Roy Schafer, *The Analytic Attitude* (New York: Basic Books, 1983); Cook, *The Meaning of Fiction*; Cook, *History/Writing* (Cambridge: Cambridge University Press, 1988).

2. For how these elements and their combinations in literature work, see "Thought, Image, and Story: The Slippery Procedures of Literature," in Cook, *Figural Choice*, 1–6.

3. Rudolf Arnheim, "The Unity of the Arts: Time, Space, and Distance," in *Yearbook of Comparative and General Literature* 25 (1976): 7–12.

4. For further discussion of such mechanisms in Arp's sculpture, see Cook, *Figural Choice*, 53–63.

5. See Louis Séchan, *La Tragédie grecque dans ses rapports avec la céramique* (Paris: P.U.F., 1947); Esther Jacobson, "The Structure of Narrative in Early Chinese Pictorial Vessels," *Representations* 8 (Fall 1984): 61–84; Margaret Webster Plass, *The Goldweights of the Ashanti* (London: Percy Lund, Humphries & Co., 1967), 32, 65–73; R. S. Rattray, *Religion and Art in Ashanti* (Oxford: Oxford University Press, 1923); E. A. Wallis Budge, *The Egyptian Book of the Dead* (New York: Dover, 1969); Claude Lévi-Strauss, *La Voie des masques* (Paris: Plon, 1979); Henri Frankfort, *The Art and Architecture of the Ancient Orient*, Pelican History of Art (Harmondsworth: Penguin, 1954), 154–89.

6. For a discussion that argues for the development of a radical modification of this tradition, see Cook, *Changing the Signs*.

7. "Pour Turner, le monde est un accord instable des fluides, la forme est lueur mouvante, tache incertaine dans un univers en fuite" (Henri Focillon, *La Vie des formes* [1943; Paris: P.U.F., 1984] 49).

8. Edward Snow, "Re-Thinking Brueghel" (unpublished book manuscript), says of this painting: "The more positive 'right-to-left' gesture of the curve . . . traces . . . virtually a Brueghel signature. It functions in his work as a kind of abstraction or archetype of the creative drive . . . connected with the impulse to transform the actual into something more primal and dynamic . . . it is present in *Landscape with the Fall of Icarus* as the shape of the furrows that signify man's cultivation of nature, and as a more transcendental form—a movement outward that ultimately folds back towards an immanent origin." All this can be read as interpreting the dominance of landscape in the painting.

9. Norman Bryson, *Word and Image* (Cambridge: Cambridge University Press, 1981). For qualifications of Bryson's application here of Roland Barthes's "effect of the real" to painting, see Cook, *Changing the Signs*, 13, 137.

10. For some amplified comment on this question see Cook, *Changing the Signs*, 132–33, as well as the whole discussion 1–13, 121–33.

11. For further elaboration of this specific question, see Lyotard, *Discours, Figure*, 239–70, who notes: "Le travail du rêve ne pense pas."

12. Sigmund Freud, *Jenseits des Lustprinzips* (*Beyond the Pleasure Principle*), in *Gesammelte Werke* (London: S. Fischer/Imago, 1955), 13:1–69; Erik Erikson, "The Dream Specimen of Psychoanalysis," in *Psychoanalytic Psychiatry and Psychology: Clinical and Theoretical Papers*, ed. Robert P. Knight and Cyrus R. Friedman (New York: Hallmark-Hubner Press, 1954), 131–70; James Hillman, *Dreams and the Underworld* (New York: Harper and Row, 1979).

INDEX